DANGEROUS EDGES OF (

Dangerous Edges of Graham Greene

Journeys with Saints and Sinners

EDITED BY

DERMOT GILVARY
AND
DARREN J. N. MIDDLETON

WITH A FOREWORD BY DAVID LODGE
AND AN AFTERWORD BY MONICA ALI

continuum

The Continuum International Publishing Group Inc
80 Maiden Lane, New York, NY 10038
The Tower Building, 11 York Road, London SE1 7NX

www.continuumbooks.com

Library of Congress Cataloging-in-Publication Data
Dangerous edges of Graham Greene : journeys with
saints and sinners / edited by Dermot Gilvary and Darren
J.N. Middleton ; with a foreword by David Lodge and an
afterword by Monica Ali.
     p. cm.
  Summary: "Informative, broad-ranging, and sheds new
light on the life and literary art of one of the last century's
most celebrated authors"– Provided by publisher.
  Includes bibliographical references and index.
  ISBN-13: 978-1-4411-5939-7 (hardcover : alk. paper)
  ISBN-10: 1-4411-5939-8 (hardcover : alk. paper)
  ISBN-13: 978-1-4411-6416-2 (pbk. : alk. paper)
  ISBN-10: 1-4411-6416-2 (pbk. : alk. paper) 1. Greene,
Graham, 1904-1991–Criticism and interpretation. I.
Gilvary, Dermot. II. Middleton, Darren J. N., 1966-
  PR6013.R44Z631895 2011
  823'.912–dc22
                                        2011012801

ISBN: 978-1-4411-5939-7 (hardcover)
ISBN: 978-1-4411-6416-2 (paperback)

Typeset by Pindar NZ, Auckland, New Zealand
Printed and bound in Great Britain

For
Caroline Bourget-Greene
and in memory of
Amanda Saunders

Our interest's on the dangerous edge of things.
The honest thief, the tender murderer,
The superstitious atheist, demireps
That love and save their souls in new French books—
We watch while these in equilibrium keep
The giddy line midway.

Robert Browning, 'Bishop Blougram's Apology'

Contents

Acknowledgements

For his courtesy, patience and scholarly devotion throughout the production of this volume, *Dermot Gilvary* would like to pay tribute to his co-editor, Dr Darren Middleton, who had the first idea for this book, and the writers who so kindly contributed their essays. For their generosity in granting him permission to accept the role of director of the Graham Greene International Festival, he would like to thank two headmasters of Oakham School (Rutland, UK), Dr Joe Spence and Nigel Lashbrook. For their hospitality, encouragement and tolerance, he would like to thank the chairman and treasurer of the Graham Greene Birthplace Trust (Berkhamsted, UK), (respectively) Giles Clark and Colin Garrett. He is particularly grateful to two more colleagues at Oakham: to Michael Stevens for his wisdom and guidance; to Rod Smith for sharing his genius and inspiration.

Darren J. N. Middleton would like to thank Dermot Gilvary, for his generous time, grace and hard work; our volume's contributors, who have helped us create something special; the Trustees and Friends of the Graham Greene Birthplace Trust, who are tirelessly attentive to the legacy of one of the last century's finest writers; Haaris Naqvi at Continuum International Publishing Group, for the astute work that lies behind this anthology; Jacqulyn Sisk, for her diligent assistance; Steve Roth, who saved Darren from at least one serious error; Rob Garnett, Brent Plate and Greer Richardson, for their loyal friendship; Betsy Flowers, who is one of the most purposeful readers he knows; and, Jonathan Middleton, because he is such a lovely son.

The editors, contributors and publishers would like to thank Nina Bevan and the Dacorum Heritage Trust (Berkhamsted, UK) for permission to reproduce the photograph of Graham Greene on the front outer cover; Dr Andrew Schoolmaster, Dean of the AddRan College of Liberal Arts at Texas Christian University (Fort Worth, Texas, USA), for his generous support; Marigold Atkey and the literary estate of Graham Greene, holders of copyrights, for their permission to cite Graham Greene's work in this volume; and, finally, Massimo

Moretti and Canal+ Image UK for permission to quote words from the screenplay of *The Third Man*.

EDITIONS QUOTED

When citing from Graham Greene's work, our volume's essayists use editions to hand, and each chapter provides comprehensive bibliographical information. For details regarding Greene's first editions, both British and American, see the section titled 'For Further Reading', which is located at the anthology's close.

Foreword

David Lodge

Most novelists have a short posthumous shelf life, and the reputations of even highly successful writers often decline sharply after their deaths. This process is inevitable: the collective mind has room for the work of a finite number of authors, so most of the dead ones must give way to new generations of living ones. Only a small select group continue to command widespread interest and attention after their demise. Of these today, Graham Greene is obviously one — but it was by no means a foregone conclusion.

Greene was a very important writer to me. In the 1940s and '50s he was probably the most famous and admired living English novelist. Only Evelyn Waugh seriously competed with him for this accolade, and it was encouraging to a young Catholic growing up in that period with ambitions to write, as I was, that both men were converts to the Roman Catholic Church. I read and reread their novels avidly. From Waugh I learned things about comedy that took some time to surface in my own fiction. The influence of Greene on my early novels was more immediate and obvious, and he also provided a focus for my interest as a critic, at that time, in something called 'the Catholic novel'.

I went on reading, rereading and sometime reviewing Greene's books till the end of his life, but over the years his views changed, mine changed, the Catholic Church changed, and the world changed. When he died in 1991, I wondered whether his reputation would hold up in the new conditions, and there were reasons to fear it might not. His best novels were informed by a Catholic theological metaphysic that he himself abandoned in later life, in which fewer and fewer educated Catholics believe literally any more, and which is starkly opposed to the prevailing ethos of secular society today. It was centred on the eternal destiny of the individual soul, and took very seriously such ideas as mortal sin, hell and damnation, the possibility of miracles, the intervention of God in human lives, and included some special Greeneian obsessions like 'mystical substitution', when an individual offers in prayer to take upon himself or herself the suffering of another. Would not the tortuous moral scruples of Scobie in *The Heart of the Matter* or Sarah's bargain with God in *The End of the Affair*, I speculated, seem increasingly foreign and even incomprehensible to future readers?

Greene's effort in one or two late novels to find some substitute in process theology for the lost certainties of the old orthodoxy are interestingly discussed in this volume by Darren J. N. Middleton, but its effect on his fiction was to substitute dialectic for drama. If I may quote myself, writing on Greene's later fiction in 1976: 'his growing scepticism concerning morals and metaphysics, however much to his credit as a human being, is to some extent at odds with the fictional form he has perfected . . . The epigraph to *The Honorary Consul*, from Thomas Hardy, expresses accurately enough his present view of the world: "All things merge into one another — good into evil, generosity into justice, religion into politics . . ." but his most successful work was based on the clash of antithetical ideas rather than this hazy, ambiguous flow of one idea into another'.[1]

I still stand by that judgement, but time has shown that the dogmatic underpinning of Greene's 'Catholic novels' has not prevented them from continuing to find appreciative new readers. Such is his mastery of narrative structure and style (he was one of the great English prose writers of the twentieth century) that he can make the spiritual crises and conflicts of his characters convincing and gripping to readers who do not share their assumptions. Greene's storytelling skills have enticed filmmakers to adapt nearly all his novels from *Stamboul Train* onwards for the screen — not always successfully, for the nuances of his prose are harder to transfer into visual imagery, and only Carol Reed, working in collaboration with Greene himself, really found a way to do it, in *The Third Man*. But film producers and directors persist in making the attempt, undeterred by the Catholic supernaturalism in which some of the novels are steeped. Recent remakes include *The End of the Affair*, while another of *Brighton Rock* is about to be released as I write this foreword.

There was, however, another reason to doubt whether Greene's novels would hold a place in the canon of English literature. Literary classics are established these days mainly by academic endorsement, and although Greene has attracted the attention of many fine academic critics, several of whom are represented in this volume, it is fair to say that during his lifetime as well as afterwards there has never been a critical consensus in this country that he is a great writer. During his most fertile period, English literary criticism was dominated by the school of F. R. Leavis, whose principles and values were hostile to those that drove Greene's imagination; and there was always an elitist suspicion, not exclusive to Leavisites, of a writer who was commercially successful, and who used popular forms like the thriller and the adventure story, and mass media like the cinema, to convey his vision. Later movements in academic criticism, from deconstruction to feminism, have been equally inhospitable to Greene's imagination. Neil Sinyard correctly points out in his contribution to this collection that 'Greene, though widely read, was rarely considered as being of sufficient stature to figure on the syllabus of a university English Department'. In France, however, as Professor François Gallix of the Sorbonne informs us, *The Power and the Glory* was recently a set text for the *agrégation*, the National Examination for aspiring university teachers, and he himself is one of many foreign scholars who have made significant contributions to the study of Greene. Greene may, paradoxically, have a more secure reputation in world literature than in English literature.

He is certainly a novelist whose work has a uniquely wide constituency, crossing boundaries of language, culture, and class. The success of the Graham Greene Festival, which has taken place annually at his birthplace Berkhamsted since 1998, celebrating and exploring his life and work, is itself striking evidence of this fact. It is, I think, a unique institution: not the gathering of a closed society of enthusiasts, of which there are many examples, keeping the flame of admiration for a particular writer burning in the face of general indifference, but, rather, a public event that attracts speakers and large audiences from all over the world and from many walks of life: academics, creative writers, journalists, filmmakers, and ordinary readers. All the essays gathered in this volume were originally lectures delivered at the Festival, and they give a good idea of the variety of Greene's most dedicated readers, and the diversity of their interest in him and his work.

I say 'him' advisedly, because there is no doubt that the fascination of the novels is intertwined with the fascination of the man who wrote them, generating an appetite for information and interpretation that has not been sated by a steady stream of publications over the last two decades: biographical studies both authorised and unauthorised, memoirs and interviews, collections of letters, and other works more or less tenuously connected with the writer, of which the most recent retraces the trek through Liberia that Greene undertook in 1935 and described in *Journey Without Maps*.[2] The paradoxes and enigmas of Greene's character are, it seems, inexhaustibly interesting: the shifts and contradictions in his religious faith and practice, his manic-depressive mood swings, his taste for mercenary casual sex combined with a capacity for love affairs of great emotional intensity, his conservative stance toward British political life combined with support for revolutionary movements abroad, his uncanny ability to sense what would be the world's next trouble-spot and position himself to write a novel about it . . . One could go on and on. There is certainly ample scope for more investigation and more festival sessions. Meanwhile aficionados will find plenty to interest them in this volume, and plenty of incitements, by way of quotation and appreciation, to send them back to the novels.

Introduction

Mark Bosco, SJ, and Dermot Gilvary

GRAHAM GREENE: A SORT OF LITERARY BIOGRAPHY

'If I had known it, the whole future must have lain all the time along those Berkhamsted streets'.[1] So begins *A Sort of Life*, Graham Greene's first memoir, written in 1971, when he was 67 years old. Much of this idiosyncratic autobiography of the first 28 years of his life begins with his recollections of growing up in Berkhamsted, Hertfordshire, a short distance from London. Greene remembers the broad High Street running through the centre of town, the Norman church rebuilt from medieval foundations, the first cinema, and, of course, Berkhamsted School, the place where he lived and was educated.

Throughout his long literary career, Greene continually returned to his childhood as inspiration for his writing, whether in the anxieties and betrayals among his schoolmates or in the excitement and escape afforded him in reading the adventure stories of Rider Haggard. It is significant that, while still an infant, Greene's earliest memory is of death: 'The first thing I remember is sitting in a pram at the top of a hill with a dead dog lying at my feet . . . the dog, as I know now, was a pug owned by my elder sister. It had been run over—by a horse carriage?—and killed and the nurse thought it convenient to bring the cadaver home this way'.[2] His mother, Greene tells us, revealed that his first spoken words months after the event, were 'poor dog'. His fascination with the precariousness of life and his sense of pity for the downtrodden were perhaps seared into his imagination at a very early age.

Henry Graham Greene was born in 1904 into a prominent English family, the son of Charles Henry Greene, a history and classics teacher and, later, the headmaster at Berkhamsted School. There, Greene lived at the school with his five siblings in a town populated by many well-to-do cousins, aunts, and uncles on his father's side of the family. His mother had some lineal distinction as well, as a first cousin of Robert Louis Stevenson, who was an important influence on Greene's desire to dedicate himself to the writing profession. In this relatively secure, middle-class environment, the young Greene struggled with divided loyalties between home and school, symbolised by the green baize door that separated his family quarters from the institution. As the headmaster's son, he felt alienated from the other boys: 'I had left civilisation behind and entered a savage country of strange customs and inexplicable cruelties: a country in which I was a foreigner and a suspect, quite literally a hunted creature'.[3]

His childhood paradise destroyed in starting school, Greene found it difficult to negotiate the balance of loyalties between his austere father and his classmates. He found various ways to remove himself from the psychological torment of his routine, often escaping for a few hours to read under the branches of a hawthorn hedge. But it was his experience with a class bully named Carter that helped form his awareness of evil and the consequences of betrayal. In the essay 'The Lost Childhood' (1951), Greene remarks: 'When—perhaps I was fourteen by that time—I took Miss Marjorie Bowen's *The Viper of Milan* from the library shelf, the future for better or for worse really struck'.[4] The novel's characters had a 'genius for evil' that matched Greene's dread of Carter's machinations in the school's dormitory. Greene gives Carter's bullying a theological gravity: 'Goodness has only once found a perfect incarnation in a human body and never will again, but evil can always find a home there. Human nature is not black and white but black and grey'.[5] The pressures of life in the dorm led to Greene's first crisis, when, at 16, he ran away from home and appeared to be heading for a nervous breakdown. After consultation, his parents sent him to live with the Jungian psychoanalyst Kenneth Richmond and his wife for six months of dream therapy. He returned from this brief respite more confident, though still in the throes of manic-depressive swings.

In 1922, he entered Balliol College (University of Oxford) to read history. There, Greene's youthful excesses exhibited themselves in a short-lived flirtation with the communist party and in his passionate devotion to his favourite authors and poets. He was taken with the poetry of Edith Sitwell and Edna St. Vincent Millay and filled his first volume of verse, *Babbling April* (1923), with the sensuous romanticism of his adolescent infatuations. Yet here, too, the young writer was beset with melancholy. In depressive moments he flirted with suicide by playing rounds of Russian roulette: five times, he reveals in his memoir, he placed a bullet in a revolver, spun the chamber, pointed it at the side of his head, and pulled the trigger. The adrenaline that surged through him, as he gambled momentarily with his life, rejuvenated him. This penchant for danger would later find expression in his peripatetic global voyages to areas fraught with physical hardships and political unrest.

Upon graduation, Greene embarked on a career as a journalist, landing a job with the *Nottingham Journal* in 1926. There, Greene's childhood experience of anxiety and dislocation, loyalty and betrayal, became fused with his formal engagement with religious faith. The first and best volume of Norman Sherry's biography uncovers the history of Greene's initial experiences of Roman Catholicism, centred on his infatuation with Vivien Dayrell-Browning, a recent convert. In order to marry her, he began taking instruction with a Father Trollope, a former actor on the West End stage, who also had been a convert. Trollope unwittingly brought home to Greene the risks that awaited him if he, too, converted to the faith: '[The priest] told his story, and it came like a warning hand placed on my shoulder. "See the danger of going too far," that was the menace his story contained. "Be very careful. Keep well within your depth. There are dangerous currents out at sea which could sweep you anywhere."'[6] Indeed, the currents of Catholic faith swept Greene into Vivien's arms, and they married a year later. Though Greene claimed that his initial promptings were merely an act to win his wife, it is also true that he intelligently embraced his new faith. What began as an intellectual conversion for personal reasons became, after his experience of the persecution of Catholics in Mexico, an emotional conversion, too. Though the author legally separated from his wife in 1948, they remained married throughout his life; he also remained, in faith, a Catholic, however tentative that affiliation became in later years.

The experience of Greene the schoolboy provided Greene the convert a reference point in understanding the black and the grey of modern life in the twentieth century. Greene often quoted from A. E. Russell's poem 'Germinal' in demonstrating the intersection of childhood betrayals and the religious imagination: 'In the lost boyhood of Judas/Christ was betrayed'.[7] This interweaving between the psychological and the religious became a creative thread in much of Greene's work. In a 1978 interview, he noted, 'The religious sense does emphasise the importance of the human act. It's not Catholicism, it's simply a faith in the possibility that we have eternal importance.

A religious sense makes the individual more important and therefore it helps to put the character on the page'.[8] Greene's Catholicism would give him a unique point of view throughout his literary career and would generate a consistency to his art; without Catholicism, he would not have developed the distinctive voice and style on which both his artistry and popularity flourished. From the beginning, Catholicism for Greene was a system of concepts that contained certain attitudes and a source of situations with which he could order and dramatise his intuitions about human experience.

The Man Within (1929) was Greene's first novel, which sold over 8,000 copies. The novel weds the genre of nineteenth-century romance with the action of a modern thriller. It is a skilfully plotted adventure about a smuggler named Andrews, on the run for betraying his gang. Andrews takes refuge and falls in love with the beautiful Elizabeth, only to betray her as well by giving himself to another woman. The novel ends with murder and suicide, as Andrews confronts his treachery and divided loyalties. Sherry's biography notes how influential Greene's wife, Vivien, was in his conception of this novel's heroine. Greene's penchant for creating female characters that, with few exceptions, are represented as idealised objects worthy of worship or maligned as egotistical temptresses for Greene's male characters became evident. This tendency to reify women into what might be called a 'Madonna/whore' dialectic was only reinforced by Greene's engagement with a Catholic faith that ritually venerated both Mary, the Virgin Mother of God, and Mary Magdalene, the reformed prostitute. Greene's female characters find a home in mythic descriptions and in the spiritualizing of the feminine that still lingers in the Catholic imagination today.

Greene's next two published novels — *The Name of Action* (1930) and *Rumour at Nightfall* (1931) — were not as successful. He later dismissed them as failures and withdrew them from consideration when his collected works were published. *Stamboul Train* (1932, released as *Orient Express* in the US) was written explicitly to satisfy publishers, with the hope that it could be transferred to film. The novel saved his writing career when it was honoured by a London book society, guaranteeing it 10,000 copies in sales, and then quickly turned into a successful film by 20th Century Fox. Greene himself admitted that it was not a good book, but he learned how to achieve a sustained excitement by placing his characters on a glamorous train ride en route through the socialist upheavals that marked the European continent at the time. All of the strands of Greene's major concerns — social, political, and religious — began to intertwine for the first time. The three novels that followed, *It's a Battlefield* (1934), *England Made Me* (1935) and *A Gun for Sale* (1936) were not as financially successful as *Stamboul Train*, but they are more ambitious works. One sees Greene honing his talent for novels stylistically fraught with dialectical tensions and melodramatic situations.

Greene's first travel outside Europe was to West Africa in the winter of 1934–35. Accompanied by his cousin Barbara, he ventured to write a travel book, but the result was much more than that. In *Journey Without Maps* (1936), Greene uses the African continent as topography to plot his own pursuit of the dangerous edge of life. His walk into the heart of darkness echoes the late colonial tropes of the period, but Greene adds psychological depth to his observations. He invites the reader into his own illusive quest for a lost world of innocence by traversing into areas untouched by what he considered the puritanical and antiseptic importations of European life. His attachment to Africa brought him back to Sierra Leone during the war years and, imaginatively, to the locale for two important novels, *The Heart of the Matter* (1948) and *A Burnt-Out Case* (1961).

With *Brighton Rock* (1938), Greene launched into his most prolific and successful era of writing, producing a series of novels that explored the boundaries and loyalties of religious faith, as understood in the dimensions of the Catholic consciousness of his characters. During this period critics began calling Greene a 'Catholic novelist', a label that inadvertently marked the restrictions of his talent. Reviewers of his earlier novels were amused by this supposed religious turn in a novelist who had shown such mastery for the psychological thriller. And yet, the themes in Greene's early novels, which are beset with criminals and conspirators, alienated protagonists and their betrayal of loyalties, actually found expression in all his great texts of this middle period: the Catholic Pinkie in *Brighton Rock*, who conspires to marry Rose in the fallout of a gang murder; the whisky priest in *The Power and the Glory* (1940), who betrays his celibate vows by fathering a child; the convert Scobie in *The Heart of the Matter*, whose double loyalties to wife and mistress precipitate his suicide; and in *The End of the Affair* (1951) the adultery of Sarah who plays a game of infidelity between her lover, her husband, and her God. In each instance, Greene's use of Catholicism extends the psychological and moral crises of characters beyond their own deception and treachery, and places it in confrontation with God. In fact, Greene illustrates that one's faith and belief in God is as treacherous a place as the worlds of politics and espionage.

Greene was busy writing *Brighton Rock* when he was asked to go to Mexico to report on the persecution of Catholics by its socialist government. He spent the winter of 1938 in the desperately poor regions of Tabasco and Chiapas and from this experience produced his second travel book, *The Lawless Roads* (1939). There, Greene's own emotional commitment to Catholicism solidified in light of his experience of faith under persecution. He wrote of churches being burned to the ground and of stories about officials hunting for priests celebrating Mass, a treasonable act punishable by death. A Catholic woman from Tabasco tells him that there was one priest 'eight leagues away over the border in Chiapas, but the people had told him to go — they couldn't protect him any longer'. Inquiring about this man, Greene is told, 'Oh he was just what we call a whiskey priest'.[9] Thus, Mexico provided not only the background for his next book, but also the inspiration for its main character.

Published in 1940, *The Power and the Glory* is considered Greene's finest achievement. It was awarded the prestigious Hawthornden Prize in 1941, and became a great success in France as a result of François Mauriac's strong endorsement. It received even more notice after it was turned into a successful film, *The Fugitive* (US, 1947), by the American director John Ford. The novel works well on two levels: the first is the fugitive priest's attempt to flee from the pursuing forces of the Mexican state; the second is the discovery that the priest is even more intensely pursued by the power of God, the hound of heaven. From the opening scene, when the nameless whisky priest arrives at the port from which he might have made an escape, to his death by firing squad, the narrative follows the cleric's journey in which his own purgation and self-knowledge grows in direct proportion to his ability to minister to those Catholics in need of the sacraments. At the novel's end, another nameless priest arrives at the door of a boy who, at the beginning of the novel, was bored by the clichéd piety of his Catholic upbringing but is now committed to the subversiveness of faith.

In 1941, to add his contribution to the war effort, Greene began work in the government's Ministry of Information. He was recruited into the Secret Service and sent for a year to Sierra Leone, where he decoded telegrams and wrote reports to superiors about movements in the port of Freetown. To occupy his time, Greene wrote *The Ministry of Fear* (1943), a convoluted thriller about a 'man acquitted of the murder of his wife by a jury (though he knows his own guilt), who finds himself pursued for a murder of which he is entirely innocent but which he believes he has committed'.[10] After a year, Greene returned to London and continued his covert work with the British Foreign Office, until the conclusion of the war. In 1946 he began *The Heart of the Matter*, set in Sierra Leone, as an investigation into 'the sinner at the heart of Christianity', a phrase from the Catholic writer Charles Péguy that Greene chose as the book's epigraph. A tragic drama about a good and sensitive policeman, Major Scobie, the novel charts his descent into psychological and spiritual affliction. Scobie is led to suicide as the only escape from the responsibilities he feels imposed on him by the divine. The book was a popular success, and Greene's reputation as a Catholic novelist became more and more a part of the conversation of his literary career.

Fresh from this success, Greene accepted Alexander Korda's invitation to write the screenplay for a film about the superpower occupation in postwar Vienna. *The Third Man* was released in 1949, and to this day rates as one of the great British films of the century. Directed by Carol Reed, with whom Greene had collaborated previously (*The Fallen Idol*, UK, 1948), the story follows an American writer, Holly Martins, in his pursuit to discover the truth about his friend Harry Lime, a hustler of black market penicillin. The labyrinth-like machinations that Lime orchestrates to fake his own death are mirrored in the final scenes of the police hunt that kills him in the maze-like sewers of Vienna. The film remains a masterpiece of film noir.

While working on *The Heart of the Matter*, Greene began an intense love affair with Catherine Walston, the American-born wife of a wealthy British landowner. Inspired by reading *The Power and the Glory*, Catherine converted to Catholicism and wrote to ask if Greene would be her godfather. He agreed, but was out of the country during the celebration, and so sent his wife Vivien to stand in his place. Sherry's second volume of the biography uncovers how important Catherine was to the final composition of *The Heart of the Matter* and how she became intimately involved with the entire process of his next 'Catholic' novel, *The End of the Affair*. Set in London during the blitz, the novel is striking in offering Greene's first well-developed female character, Sarah Miles, who is in no small part modelled on Catherine. Indeed, evidence from Greene's and Catherine's extensive correspondence, now housed at Georgetown University, shows that she played an integral part in helping Greene establish the proper 'voice' for Sarah's character.

Greene was 47 years old when *The End of the Affair* was published in 1951. He had felt the intense conflicts embodied in the book's religious themes, for his adulterous affair with Catherine paradoxically intensified Greene's identification with Catholicism as it fed his manic-depressive fluctuations. He claimed in one exchange with Catherine that 'I'm not even a Catholic properly away from you'.[11] As the ten-year affair began to wane, Greene's Catholic imagination became more muted in his work, though it did find expression in his dramas, written and successfully performed in the 1950s and 1960s. Three of his plays, *The Living Room* (1953), *The Potting Shed* (1958), and *Carving a Statue* (1964), consciously reworked the theological themes that had obsessed him while he penned the Catholic novels of the 1930s and 1940s.

Greene acknowledged in his second memoir, *Ways of Escape* (1980), that 'the fifties were for me a period of great unrest'.[12] He was often away from London on assignments for various newspapers and journals in many political hot spots around the world, both as a way to counter his melancholy and to give him material through which to map out his creative energies. He went to Malaya for an assignment with *Life* magazine, to Vietnam to report on French Indo-China for *The Sunday Times* and *Le Figaro*, to Kenya for an account of the Mau Mau rebellion, to the Belgian Congo to study life in a leper colony, and to the Caribbean to witness the oppressive regime of Haiti's François 'Papa Doc' Duvalier and to assess Cuba's political revolution just beginning under Fidel Castro. His extensive visits to such troubled places resulted in four novels, all quite different in tone, though not in style: *The Quiet American* in 1955, *Our Man in Havana* in 1958, *A Burnt-Out Case* in 1961, and *The Comedians* in 1966. Except for *A Burnt-Out Case*, in which the ambivalences of faith and belief are his central theme, these novels lacked the religious intensity of his earlier writing. In its place was a struggle to excavate the human factor in the affairs of globalisation, Cold War strategies, and state political repression. The loyalty and betrayal of characters became but a microcosm to the larger duplicitous relations and geopolitical movements in a postcolonial world.

The Quiet American takes place in Vietnam at the end of French colonial rule and explores the complex relationships between French colonialists, communist insurgents, and the growing American presence in the region. Alden Pyle, the naïve, 'quiet' American, serves as Greene's subject through which to investigate the shift between old world colonial rule and the new world order of US economic and diplomatic interests. Fowler, the English journalist whose first-person narrative offers a nominal Catholic consciousness, betrays the young American to the communist insurgents, thinking the betrayal will save innocent lives, as well as win back his Vietnamese lover, whom Pyle has promised to marry. The novel suggests that though Fowler betrays Pyle, it is the American's own naïveté about the reality of Vietnam that tragically kills him and that, presciently, will lead the US to war in the following decade. Greene's critical judgement of American foreign policy during this time focused on the inexperience of a new superpower meddling in unfamiliar territory. This critique of American involvement is less sinister and tempered with comedy in *Our Man in Havana*. Set in the final years before Castro's revolution, the novel finds Greene affecting a light touch, creating a satire about a vacuum cleaner salesman who inadvertently becomes wrapped up in the gamesmanship of Cold War espionage. Catholicism itself is satirised, more a cultural stereotype than a religious lens through which to focus reality. Indeed, the novel suggests that dream and fantasy are just as able as faith in grounding one's reality, as characters try to disentangle fact from fiction, reality from illusion. The novel's political resonance probes further the meaning of human loyalty in the confusion between personal and national identities, all under the shadow of a growing arms race that defined much of the century.

In *The Comedians*, his only novel written with the expressed political motive of bringing to light the tyranny of Haiti's dictator, Papa Doc, Greene uses gallows humour to expose the inadequacy of human agency to effect real change in the political order of that nation. Most of the novel's characters are outsiders to Haiti and would indeed be comedians, if not for the horror inflicted on Haitians by the abuse of political power. Except for long passages on a voodoo gathering, religious faith is practically absent from the novel or ceases to have much meaning in a world so dehumanised by oppression. Greene was denounced by Duvalier and deemed *persona non grata* in Haiti.

During the last three decades of his life, Greene continued to write and publish at a prolific pace. Critical reception of these late works often focused on an appreciation of the technical mastery of his texts, as he continued to return to old territories — the tension between loyalty and betrayal, innocence and corruption, and religious faith and political commitment — but with a perceptive sense of the changes that have occurred both in Catholicism and in global politics during the last part of the century. The 1960s continued to be a difficult time for him, not only because of his permanent move from England to France, but also because of his experience as a writer. The psychological intensity of writing *A Burnt-Out Case* and *The Comedians* left him in such a depressive state that he felt it would be the end of his fiction writing. So it was to Greene's own surprise that his response to his existential despair led him to write the comedy *Travels with my Aunt* in 1969. He notes that it is the first time that humour and comedy won out over his penchant for tragedy: 'I felt, above all, that I had broken for good or ill with the past'.[13] Part of that accomplishment was, perhaps, due to the fact that Catholicism had always been the most profound reference point for Greene's sense of the tragic, and in this novel, he felt there was no obvious Catholic fibre woven into the narrative. Readers and critics thought the novel a major literary achievement, and the effect of writing it renewed his creative energies.

In 1971, Greene published his first autobiography, *A Sort of Life*, in which he details his early years at Berkhamsted up through his publication of *Stamboul Train* in 1932. He ended there, apparently, to protect the privacy of his family and friends affected by his celebrity. In 1980, he published a second instalment, *Ways of Escape*, which related the rest of his literary career. It, too, is filled with insightful musings on what he considered the major influences on each of his works. Very little is actually revealed about Greene in these memoirs, except when they touch on the genesis of his writing. In fact, much of Greene's personal life escaped scrutiny until later in his career. Biographies of the author now abound, including the authorised three-volume version by Norman Sherry. The first volume (1989) came out before Greene's death, and he seemed to cooperate with Sherry, though he once noted that he would be content not to be around for the final volumes, which were not published until 1994 and 2004, respectively. Sherry's main contribution to understanding Greene was to provide other source material to reveal the complexity of his personal life and its effect on his creativity. Michael Sheldon, another biographer, wrote a rather disturbing psychological portrait quite cynical about the author, *Graham Greene: The Man Within*, in 1994. And W. J. West's *The Quest for Graham Greene* in 1997 filled in major gaps with archival research untouched by Sherry's unwieldy three-tome encomium.

Greene spent the last 20 years of his life travelling often to Central and South America and used his fame as a Catholic novelist as a privileged credential to investigate the postcolonial situation there. The articles and editorials from his travels highlight the central role that Catholicism was playing in these economically poor and oppressed nations. He was in Chile in 1971, during the short-lived government of Salvador Allende, and visited Panama five times in the late 1970s and early 1980s as the personal guest of Omar Torríjos Herrera, the charismatic general who had assumed power in 1968. Torríjos was the first leader of Panama who came from the *barrio*. He opened schools and instituted a range of reforms that redistributed agricultural land for the poor. Greene considered this man a great friend and published a memoir of their many conversations, called *Getting to the Know the General: The Story of an Involvement* (1984). Greene's extensive tours gave him an exceptional perspective on the situation in Nicaragua and El Salvador, where he met the political players and religious communities that worked there.

From his many experiences in Latin America came one of Greene's best novels, *The Honorary Consul* (1973). The title refers to the British honorary consul who mistakenly gets kidnapped by a group of Paraguayan rebels. Set on the border between Paraguay and Argentina, and populated with political and social exiles, the novel's plot could have been taken from the 1970s newspaper headlines of the region. Indeed, Greene's tale foreshadows real-life events, for in 1974, a year after the novel was published, the British ambassador to Argentina, Geoffrey Jackson, was kidnapped by guerrillas and held for several months before his release was obtained. The novel continues to explore the themes of pursuit and betrayal, played out in a drama that reflects the revolutionary turmoil of the region. But the novel is much more than that, for as one critic notes, the novel brilliantly parodies Greene's past fictions in a self-reflexive way, giving us 'a story about absent fathers, discussions of Jorge Luis Borges, the reading, writing and reflection on detective fiction, a gloss on the stories of Stevenson, Chesterton, and Conan Doyle, characters from old in new clothes— all speak to the themes of artistic influence and originality'.[14] Greene once remarked that he considered it one of his very best novels, both in its technical mastery and the complex way in which he interlaced the numerous themes that obsessed him throughout his literary career.

Five years after *The Honorary Consul*, Greene began work on *The Human Factor*, a spy novel that he had begun writing in 1967 but had stopped halfway through it because of his personal association with Kim Philby, a spy for the Soviet Union who had been Greene's superior in the British Secret Service during the war years. Philby's defection in 1963, and subsequent autobiography published in the West in 1968, convinced Greene to put the manuscript away for a while. Finally published in 1978, *The Human Factor* is set in greater London (including his childhood home of Berkhamsted) and explores the virtue of disloyalty when it comes to the state secret service apparatus. Greene continues to condemn the wasteland of modern espionage, especially as smaller nations get drawn into shady alliances between the super powers. Like *The Honorary Consul*, fiction and fact intersect in *The Human Factor* as well, for soon after Greene published the novel, a report was released in the media, citing stolen documents from the South African embassy in West Germany that had a striking resemblance to Greene's plot about arming South Africa with nuclear weapons to fight the Cold War.

In the final chapter of *Ways of Escape*, Greene ends by saying that 'a writer's imagination, like the body, fights against all reason against death', and so the 75-year-old writer notes that 'while at lunch on Christmas Day, 1978, in Switzerland with my daughter and my grandchildren, nine months after the publication of *The Human Factor*, a new book, *Doctor Fischer of Geneva*, came without any warning to my mind'.[15] The novel showed a surprising stylistic turn to fable-like composition: the stark realism of his narrative style was suffused with romantic idioms that heightened the symbolic weight of his characters. Greene manages to exploit a mixture of genres in this novel — allegory, fable, thriller, detective story — to propose various possible ways to read the text. The full title of the work, *Doctor Fischer of Geneva, or the Bomb Party*, suggests two possible approaches: the life-and-death story of the diabolical Dr Fischer or a tale of the macabre and grotesque 'bomb' party that he hosts. In a darkly parabolic tale about the corroding effects of greed and jealousy on human love, Greene displays the vacuous quality of late twentieth-century affluent culture.

This same stylistic technique of spare and allegorical writing is found in the rest of Greene's late novels. *The Tenth Man*, published in 1985, was initially written in the 1940s as a Hollywood script. It reads like a thrilling morality play, in which a group of men held prisoner by the Nazis are told to choose which three of them must die. One man trades his wealth for his life and lives to pay for his act in unexpected ways. So, too, in *The Captain and the Enemy* (1988), we find a dreamlike fairytale of misfits and adventurers who find their hope in the personal commitments to those they love. Characters roam the memory of the author's imagination, from its opening chapters at an English boarding school much like that of Greene's youth, to its climax in the political intrigue of Panama and Nicaragua that he observed toward the end of his life.

In *Monsignor Quixote*, published in 1982, we see the quixotic and mystical heart of Greene's religious imagination on full display. The novel was initially conceived as a short story to commemorate the deepening friendship between Greene and the Spanish priest, Leopoldo Durán. Much of its geographical description and theological conversation were taken from his many summer vacations in which he and Durán toured the Spanish countryside. Greene's overriding literary and religious concerns are brought together in a style that is as contemplative as it is comical. The traditional realism is undercut by the transparency of his character's search for a viable way to understand the timeless problems of human life. Filled with self-referential humour (the monsignor fears he is becoming 'a whisky priest'), the novel reduces the action to the barest picaresque form to create a culminating work that reverberates with metaphysical wonder.

Graham Greene died in Vevey, Switzerland, on April 3, 1991. A writer immersed in the political and religious events of the twentieth century, he came of age during the height of literary modernism. In this regard he stands in the company of T. S. Eliot, Edith Sitwell, Evelyn Waugh, and W. H. Auden, to name just a few artists who held fast to a Christian sensibility in their art. Like them, Greene demonstrated the personal apprehension and struggle to maintain faith and hope in a divine reality, amidst the travesties of modern life. And yet, Greene is unique because he continued to live and write well into the last half of the twentieth century. From his publication of poems in 1925, to his posthumously issued dream diary in 1992, Greene's 67 years of writing included over 25 novels, two collections of short stories, two travel books, seven plays, two literary memoirs, film scripts and criticism, and countless literary and journalistic essays. An artist who encountered the profound problems of modern alienation in faith, society, and politics, his writing offers us a lucid and profoundly moving perspective of the twentieth century.

THE BIRTHPLACE TRUST AND THE INTERNATIONAL FESTIVAL

The late Ken Sherwood (1935–2009), an accountant by profession, was prominent in civic matters in Berkhamsted. Inspired by Greene's immense literary accomplishments and aware of his importance to the town's heritage, he had the original thought to establish a Graham Greene Birthplace Trust. He floated the idea to David Pearce, the head of English at Berkhamsted School, and in 1995 the project was set in motion. Sherwood and Pearce realised that they would benefit from the knowledge of a lecturer Roger Watkins. For many years he had been a frequent supporter of the Cheltenham Literature Festival (Gloucestershire, UK) and the Hay Festival of Literature and the Arts (Hay-on-Wye, Herefordshire, UK), and his experience included an invitation to join a Home Office Voluntary Service Unit that advised on the work and organisation of charities. This triumvirate of Sherwood, Pearce, and Watkins epitomised vision, drive, and energy, and they immediately recognised the importance of involving Greene's family.

From its inception the Trust has enjoyed the active support of its patrons, all of whom are close relations of Greene. They were Caroline

Bourget (Greene's daughter), Louise Dennys, Nicholas Dennys and the late Amanda Saunders (children of Greene's younger sister, Elisabeth). After the death of her mother, Lucy Saunders succeeded Greene's niece Amanda (1945–2007), as patron. Otherwise, the patrons have remained unchanged.

At a public meeting in Berkhamsted on October 2, 1997, which was the ninety-third anniversary of the writer's birth in that town, the Trust was launched.[16] Pearce was the first chairman, and Sherwood the first secretary and treasurer. Other original trustees were Roger Watkins (the first festival director), Giles Clark, who is the current chairman, Jeff Edwards, Lindy Foster, and a lawyer, Michael Webster, who helped Sherwood with the legal establishment of the Trust. The charitable aim of the Trust remains to promote the appreciation and study of the works of Graham Greene. It was further agreed at the launch that its future business should include 'an annual lecture, conference or festival, including films and plays on or near the 2nd October each year'. At first Watkins was asked to arrange the annual lecture. However, as a film buff, he sensed the potential of the films of Greene's stories. So he suggested a weekend of lectures and films. His subsequent idea was to stage a four-day festival, so that the event was long enough to encourage visitors to travel from overseas. Sherwood and Pearce urged him to try this last idea in October 1998, and the Graham Greene Festival was born.

The difficulties facing the pioneers were considerable, as volunteers had to perform every task for the first time, and the living was hand-to-mouth. The brunt of the work was borne by relatively few people, performing chores as practical as sawing wood and making notice boards (which filled the owners' garages for most of the year), as technical as rigging sound systems, and as routine as licking stamps and envelopes. Sherwood promoted the Friends of the Trust, as he scoured lists of Old Boys of Berkhamsted School, *Who's Who*, telephone directories, universities and schools. Pearce was active in seeking out venues, such as the Town Hall, the Civic Centre, Berkhamsted School, and the King's Arms. By telephone and letter-writing, like the others, Watkins devoted himself to making contacts, while he also devised the first programmes. Though films proved to be a great attraction, in 1998 there was no cinema in Berkhamsted, and so the Festival had to move to a venue out of the town to the neighbouring Hemel Hempstead. Naturally, when Berkhamsted's beautiful 'art deco' Rex Cinema reopened in 2004, the Festival Director eagerly courted its owner.

While there was always a nucleus in the town of those favourably inclined, it was clear that support for the venture was neither unanimous, nor unequivocal. Some expressed views to the effect that Greene would have disapproved, though others believed that he would never have minded an opportunity to enjoy friendship. Although there was considerable cultural interest, some specialists in Greene were sceptical. Happily, nothing succeeds like success, and support was gradually forthcoming. After the difficult and unpredictable early years the Festival now enjoys widespread acceptance as a significant event in Berkhamsted's cultural and social calendar, and has earned an international reputation.[17] The Trustees were greatly encouraged by the loyal and steady support of enthusiasts from abroad — including Dr Ramón Porta, Dr Rudolf van Dalm (*Graham Greene at Random*),[18] and Dr Brigitte Timmermann.

Roger Watkins established the format of a four-day festival with talks, films, dramatised readings, socials, exhibitions, a book stall, and sales of memorabilia. He served as festival director for three years, and he was succeeded in turn by David Pearce (2001–2004), Mike Hill (a historian and teacher from Yorkshire, UK, 2005–2007), Dermot Gilvary (an English teacher at Oakham School, Rutland, UK, 2008–2010) and Yan Christensen (a trustee, 2011). Each has built upon the template that Watkins had established. The trustees never presented an incoming director with anything as banal as a 'job description', but instead bestowed the privilege of autonomy. Very importantly, each director has successfully attracted distinguished speakers from around the world.

The first directors were able to recruit eminent speakers who had known Greene personally, such as Sir John Mortimer, Michael Meyer, Bernard Diederich, the artist Paul Hogarth, and Greene's confessor Father Leopoldo Durán, or speakers who had worked with him, such as Roy Boulting (producer of *Brighton Rock*, UK, 1947) and Guy Hamilton (assistant director of *The Third Man*, UK, 1949). As time passes, sadly such people become harder to find in this world, but still many eminent public figures (such as Lord Roy Hattersley, Clement Freud, and Chris Mullin MP) have been pleased to talk about Greene, his life, work, and influence. In 2009 the BBC's former war correspondent, Kate Adie OBE, followed this tradition, as the England cricketer and psychoanalyst Michael Brearley did in 2010, along with the BBC's senior foreign correspondent Humphrey Hawksley.

In recent years the Festival has worked to develop stronger ties with schools and universities, to provide creative writing workshops in prose and screenplay writing, to offer awards in new creative writing competitions for writers of all ages, to widen the range of films, to enjoy music and after-dinner speeches and to build fresh audiences and contacts through internet sites such as Facebook,[19] Twitter[20] and the Director's Blog.[21] The Festival has benefited greatly from the loyal support of various highly respected academics, including Prof. Cedric Watts (University of Sussex, UK) and Prof. Neil Sinyard (University of Hull, UK).

With the establishment of an annual talk on 'New Research on Graham Greene', the Festival has also enhanced its status as a forum for the presentation of scholarly papers on the writer. The first such paper was delivered in 2009 by Dr Chris Hull (University of Nottingham, UK), whose talk is reproduced in this collection. In 2010 Tim Butcher, formerly a newspaper correspondent for *The Daily Telegraph* (London, UK) and author of *Blood River* (Vintage, 2008), presented his research on Greene's travels in West Africa.

In addition to the Festival, the Trust has five other main activities: the newsletter, the awards, the library, publications, and the archive.

For ten years Yan Christensen edited *A Sort of Newsletter* (ASON) aptly titled to echo Greene's autobiographical *A Sort of Life* (1971). ASON is published on a quarterly basis, and is sent to all Friends of the Trust. It has an informative, friendly style, and includes an eclectic mixture of festival and book reviews, news, anecdotes, quizzes, letters, promotions, obituaries, photographs, and other material.

The Trust offers awards between £250 or more each year to those who intend to pursue some scheme of travel or research that, in the opinion of the Awards' Panel, will further an understanding or aware-ness of Greene or that would have appealed to him, had he been alive. The awards are intended primarily to encourage young people. One such researcher was the young writer, Rebekah Lattin-Rawstrone, who founded the writers' group Tales of the Decongested, established her own publishing company and later joined the Festival as a leader of prose creative writing workshops, while the screenwriter William Ivory (*Made in Dagenham*, UK, 2010 and *Women in Love*, BBC TV, 2011) led screenwriting workshops. In this enterprise they have been joined by the children's novelist and academic Creina Mansfield. These workshops were launched at the Festival 2009 at the same time as the Trust's creative writing awards. The winners of the inaugural competitions in April 2010 were Cathy Hogan (best fiction), Susan Shemtob (best screenplay), Rebecca Barrow (best writer under the age of 21 years), Sid Sagar (best Berkhamstedian), and Anne Chinneck (best Old Berkhamstedian).

In Berkhamsted School there is a substantial library (collated by Sherwood) by or about Greene. In his former capacity as the school

Librarian, Pearce received from Greene signed copies of his books published by Bodley Head. In the collection there are also some of Greene's early novels, including *Babbling April* (1925), which the writer tried to suppress. The books are available for loan to Friends of the Trust. Rachael Guy is the current librarian.

The Trust publishes occasional papers given at the annual Festival, videos of most festivals, and some DVDs. Hazel Ward looks after the publications, of which a current list is available on the website. The Trust has a growing archive of Graham Greene memorabilia, newspaper cuttings, festival programmes, and so on, and it is held by the Dacorum Heritage Trust at the Museum Store in Berkhamsted.

The first volume to be authorised by the Trust, *Dangerous Edges of Graham Greene: Journeys with Saints and Sinners*, brings together writers, journalists and scholars to investigate as well as to assess Greene's life and literary art. Here the reader may explore everything from Greene's Vienna at the time of the filming of *The Third Man* to his often fraught relationship with Evelyn Waugh, from Greene's unconventional fictional treatment of women to his nonconformist approach to Christian theology.

CHAPTER 1

Stamboul Train:
The Timetable for 1932

David R. A. Pearce

The year is 1931. The place is Mud Lane, Chipping Campden. The music that can be heard is Honegger's Pacific 231. Graham Greene played the record on the wind-up gramophone in the little cottage he was renting with Vivien, in the early days of their marriage. The music conveys the beat of a steam train picking up speed. It evoked for Greene a world that was wide-ranging, and hard and bright with exciting possibilities; a world that was quite other from his rural retreat. For *that* was what Mud Lane was — a retreat, and a rather ignominious one. True that today the cottage looks a sweet little place, ideal for newly weds; an idyll of Cotswold Englishness. But, then, in 1931 it was the back-of-beyond, and Greene was not used to twee cramped living.

With the pulsing beat of that music it is possible to imagine Greene's life in terms of the antitheses of excitement and dullness. Here he was, a young man who knew that he wanted to do something special, extraordinary, but did not know what; who had cultivated expensive tastes, but had not the means to indulge them; who had had a model of conformity set before him in his upbringing, but revelled in the frisson of defying conventions — the 'frisson' when the revolver chamber has spun and the trigger is squeezed with a click. It was the story of his schooldays; it was the need for excitement.

His bride, beautiful Vivien, gave him the same electric charge in a head-over-heels commitment to love; a sexual excitement that was exhilarating and intriguing, and, the more so, because Vivien had held him at first at distance. With Vivien came also the adrenalin intellectual excitement of Roman Catholicism. That was a challenge remote from Greene's decorously Church of England education.

Catholicism, like the idea of Hell, as Greene wrote, 'gives something hard, non-sentimental and exciting'.[1] These words are a key to *Stamboul Train*, and to all Greene's future.

Charles Greene, Greene's traditionalist father, who had just retired, in 1927, from being headmaster of Berkhamsted School, must have sighed over his son's lack of sensible and conventional direction in life. With Charles Greene can be seen the other side of the equation: the dull, the humdrum, the perplexed with modern usages. Greene never had much patience for the predictable. His dear old father had become a schoolmaster by default, and he would not follow suit. No, for Graham Greene there would be excitement, danger, collision, the outré, shockingness — these were the life for a fellow not turned 30. But marriage had brought its responsibilities, and Greene had to make a living and support a family. Was it to be Gabbitas and Thring — the agency that appointed graduates from good universities to public schools; or the *Nottingham Journal* or *The Times* or the British-American Tea Company? In none of these was there appeal. Greene would be — a writer! The very uncertainty of that was exciting.

There were three books in quick succession, with two dedicated, in the flush of ardent love, to Vivien or Vivienne. *The Man Within* (1929) held out promise of success and Greene envisaged riches — houses in London, Somerset, even Rhodes. The world seemed all before him, but the next two novels — *The Name of Action* (1930) and *Rumour at Nightfall* (1931) both failed to catch either public imagination or critics' approval. Greene remarked ruefully that only 2,000 copies had been sold for them both. The irony is that one copy of *Rumour at Nightfall* would, now, pay off anyone's casual expenses. With these setbacks we find Greene in 1931 wrestling with debts, coping with disappointment, playing the gramophone, and trying to build a life with Vivien in unaccustomed and straitened circumstances. A baby's arrival was imminent. Greene knew what needed to be done. He had to make money and that quickly. He had gambled upon a hope in the youthful optimism of a living from real writing. There was no way back. There was nothing for it but 'retrenching' in Chipping Campden, with the Honegger record and a cottage rent of £1 a week. The prospect was not utterly without that frisson — the excitement — that he craved. Greene called it a 'dangerous cul de sac'[2] and remarked that Vivien never complained. 'Love in a hut with water and a crust,' John Keats would have said. But, however he might try to make the best of cosy rusticity, it was for Greene not a happy novelty. There were mice and woodlice; the paraffin lamps smoked and their clay mantles broke when he fumbled with them. He had asthma worse than ever, and summer hay fever. The growing of cos lettuces and cabbages gave him no sense of achievement.

Greene had known gardens, but they were idyllic places of green shade, of tennis and croquet. His father at School House had manicured lawns and greenhouses. In such a garden he could sit delightedly and read; he could even invite Walter de la Mare there. His father had had a gardener: his uncle at The Hall had an army of gardeners. Greene employed a gardener at Mud Lane, but the difference was that that garden did not conform to the needs of an aspiring gentleman writer. It was irksome and demanding. The Mud Lane garden was as unlike Greene's notions of horticulture as could possibly be. Vivien could cope and was happy. She had a maid, a dolls' house, and her little toy Pekinese that Greene had bought for her. It was cute and did tricks, but it was neurotic, 'suffered from hysteria', and had to be put down.[3] Greene was not that sort of dog-person. Vivien got on with the village folk, but it is doubtful whether Greene was a village-folk person either.

It was, perhaps, already clear that the marriage was not going to be a success. Greene's taste was for space and movement. Space — where his mind could escape and range; where nothing impinged. Here was only restriction and the cramping of his gangling frame under low ceilings. It was all so different from School House, from Balliol, from his London dwelling. He did not mind hardship and economy, but only when it was deliberately sought; not when it was forced upon him.

We should not then be surprised that there is nothing of Chipping Campden in his novels — although in *Stamboul Train* Greene does refer to Christmas gifts in the festive window of a country shop.[4] It was the nearest that he could come to acknowledging his contemporary surroundings. The situation weighed on him. His novels were not selling; his elder brother, Raymond, with whom he felt a silly competitiveness, had become annoyingly successful. Vivien described him as the 'darling of his time' at Oxford.[5] The praise irritated her husband. On top of all this, in March, 1932, Heinemann cut Greene's allowance down to £400 a year, with the threat that this would stop altogether in August.

Failure, then, is the theme. There are tax demands; the Greenes are down to their last £20. Greene warns younger brother Hugh who wants to visit: 'Frankly we are on the verge of bankruptcy. Come for two nights'. Hugh visits, and is sick out of the window. Graham Greene writes: 'The peke was being sick at about the same time as Hugh'.[6] One can feel the nightmare, and it is literally a nightmare, for Greene's dreams were full of disquiet, and of becoming 30! That lurking 30!

To escape from oppressive reality Greene takes himself off on long walks over the Cotswolds. He never minded being on his own. It was not, perhaps, that he wanted to be away from Vivien, but just that he could not bear to be in Mud Lane with the weight of failure — like those low cottage beams — on his shoulders. In his mind was gestating the idea for a popular book. If he called it an 'Entertainment', it would appeal. Perhaps — that was the hope — it might even be made into a film. That would solve the financial embarrassment. The novel was to centre on the Orient Express. The economy of the plot and the vehicle of this magnificent express train struck Greene with a wondrous force. It would be hard to imagine a subject with more appeal, or with more selling power in the 1930s. This train that travelled imperiously through a war-scarred Europe thrilled everyone; everyone longed to go on it, but few could afford it. It caught the imagination of a fast-fragmenting civilisation, and, indeed, had already attracted the filmmakers. Agatha Christie was at this very time weaving her thrills around the train journey. She had stayed in the Pera Palace Hotel in Istanbul, and was planning her *Murder on the Orient Express*. Complicated plots, the stuff of the detective thriller! Greene sensed the market; he knew he was on to a good thing. The idea appealed enormously.

Anyway, it was certainly time that he was off travelling. Travel, home — these were the ambivalent pressures. A train was free to cross frontiers, and in the concept of a journey was contained the paradox of travelling alone and yet in the company of strangers. Anonymity and the pleasure deriving from the passersby he could observe were to become creative poles of Greene's life.

By the spring of 1931, he already had the workable plan for a best-seller thriller. He just needed the background reality. He wrote to La Compagnie Internationale des Wagons-Lits asking for *free* passage on their wonderful train to Istanbul, and one can imagine their answer: 'Non, nous sommes désolés'. It was against company rules to issue free tickets he was informed. A German company — Greene lamented — would have been more accommodating. So what does he do? Instead of keeping his publisher happy by beavering away at the perfectly viable plan for a novel, he turns aside to write a 'sort of' biography on John Wilmot, the disgraceful seventeenth-century Earl of Rochester. This subject suddenly absorbs his thinking and completely overrides his plans for the Orient Express. What is happening?

In the first place the new venture was a way of escape from Chipping Campden; an excuse to head off to convivial Oxford, or to enticing London. In the second place, the unorthodoxy of Rochester had became a fascination, and, so, because Rochester had once lived at

Adderbury, not far from Chipping Campden, Greene's long walks headed in that direction. Now, the questions that come to mind are these, and the answers are obvious. Was Rochester a subject of general interest? Did Greene seek a reputation for scholarship and biography? Did people want to read about clever cynicism? Was Heinemann likely to publish the book? Was Vivien likely to approve? To all of these questions the answers must be an emphatic 'No'. The publishers, Heinemann, rejected the manuscript outright. The eventual biography, *Lord Rochester's Monkey*, was eventually published in the more sexually emancipated times of 1974.

So it was that the Stamboul Express of his mind grinds to a halt. The train was diverted at a life-stage frontier for Greene, and shunted into a siding. The wrong sort of snow. The thought-police had impounded it. For Greene it is a defining moment. It seems as if he is hijacked by some man within, whose face he saw vaguely in his own shaving mirror. It is as if he feels that the book on Rochester must be written to enable him to understand himself. There is to be no more pussyfooting with clumsy half-characters who were constantly explaining and exploring themselves. With the character of Rochester there was blood-reality, confidence, and direction — not a train-direction, but an intellectual one, immoral or amoral. And together with Rochester come wit, and sex, and the quirkiness of humanity: the whole razzmatazz of Restoration drama.

Lord Rochester had served as the model for Dorimant, the villain-hero of Sir George Etherege's *Man of Mode*. Of Rochester the playwright said: 'I know he is the Devil, but he has something of the Angel yet undefaced in him'.[7] Greene is drawn toward this figure. Not to a character who is good with the one single flaw that brings him crashing down; but to the character who has evil intentions and yet retains something of the angel. The whole emphasis is on the self-defining, the self-exploring, the doomed. It is a prurient and intellectual fascination.

The two men had so much in common. They were of a similar age. They were tall, suave, Oxford-educated. Both were scornful of conventional principles; they were ambitious, personally brave, funny, sexually driven. In Rochester's company, it is the *talented* sinner that fascinates Greene rather than the *repentant* sinner. It is almost as if he regrets repentance as a kind of compromise with evil. 'If God appeared at the end, it was the sudden secret appearance of a thief' writes Greene of Rochester's final reconciliation with the Church.[8] It is just the same game of blind man's buff that Greene plays with God in his novels.

Rochester was spectacularly unfaithful, but he retained a tender regard for his wife and his children. Infidelity was coupled with tenderness. It was as if education and the vocation of being a writer conferred license. Even now I can hear Vivien patiently explaining to my wife: 'You have to remember that he was a writer'. Rochester loved dressing up — or down — to play parts. As the mountebank, Alexander Bendo, he sold quack potions. He dressed as a tinker who knocked the bottoms out of pots and pans while pretending to mend them. Knowing this, we may recall how the undergraduate Greene hawked through Berkhamsted on market day — while his father was still headmaster — as an itinerant peddler with a barrel organ.

In these months of 1931 we can feel Greene latching on to Rochester and exploring down the circles of his Dantean *Inferno*. *Lord Rochester's Monkey* was not to be published for 43 years, but, for a true under-standing of Greene, it is important that we set it alongside *Stamboul Train*. Through 1931 the two enterprises were bedfellows in Greene's brain. The one was the catalyst for future novels: the other was to achieve a film contract, and Book Society acclaim.

From now on — from the time of *Stamboul Train* — there are to be no facile judgements that acknowledge *only* black or white. The excitement of realigning values becomes the click of the firing-pin. From now Greene enjoys teasing us with double-takes and questions. At what point does love merge into lust? Where does unbelief become itself a trust in faith? Where does mere goodness become a dull inertia, while evil is a striving quest? Where does heroic idealism become foolishness? Why is it that 'disillusionment, monotony, boredom — prey worst on the finest spirits'?[9] *Corruptio optimi* — it is the idea he was to explore in *Brighton Rock*.

From now on, no trite, comfortable delusions. Greene was going to write about heaven and hell, without any Miltonic belief in the ulti-mate victory of heaven. The creed is not fully developed in *Stamboul Train* but this gestating book has the new confidence of spirit, a new assurance of style, and a trust in the reader's willingness to explore with the writer. Chipping Campden was the dull rail siding. Yet Chipping Campden — because of its very inertia — helped produce *Stamboul Train*. If ever anything made Greene know what he wanted, it was this experience of what he did *not* want. Chipping Campden and Lord Rochester had defined our man.

It is relevant that Greene finishes *A Sort of Life* at the point of *Stamboul Train*; and that with *Stamboul Train* he begins *Ways of Escape*. It is as if he recognises that the lever has been thrown, that the signal has dropped, and that he is heading down a new stretch of main line. It is *the* defining moment. Yet it is strange that *Stamboul Train* is so little discussed.

Now, the signals are green for go. Our Greene has discovered his music. *Stamboul Train* is a compelling, and touching novel. The Heinemann manuscript reader found himself gripped by it. It is easy to understand why. A reader of this chapter will know the story, but it may be of help to clatter over the points.

For three days and nights, from Ostend to Istanbul, the Express is a microcosm, hurtling between European place names; lost in its own time, but subject to a fixed timetable. On board we meet a hotchpotch of characters. They can be grasped by simple handles.

First, there is Carleton Myatt, a rich young Jew who is going to Istanbul to prevent a financially undesirable merger for his company, which trades in raisins and currants. He is 'the Jew'; and is constantly referred to as 'the Jew', often disparagingly. Between him and Coral Musker there is a developing relationship. She is a poor, frightened dancer, who travels to join the dancing troupe of 'Dunn's Babies'. She can be defined as 'vulnerable virgin with a weak heart'. With them travels, rather ungraciously, Richard John, a schoolmaster of 56. He does not seem very English, and we come to learn that he is really a Slav and was once a medical doctor. His real name is Dr Czinner, and he had been involved in a socialist coup in Belgrade five years previously, and is now returning to lead another political uprising. On the train he tends Coral who has fainted from the effect of cold, hunger, and her heart condition. We may think of Czinner as 'the communist idealist'.

Other characters of less importance are introduced to us. We find the Reverend Opie (ridiculous clergyman) who wants to introduce cricket to Belgrade, and the ebullient Q. C. Savory (novelist, who drops his aitches). He has just published a successful but trivial book called *The Great Gay Whirl*. There is the ghastly Mr Peters and his wife, Amy. They are vulgar, and have rumbling stomachs. We can think of them as 'the worst sort of English tourists'. At Cologne, where the train stops for a while, we meet: Mabel Warren — Dizzy Mabel (rather scary lesbian journalist). She is with her partner, Janet Pardoe (good-looking Jewess), who is off to visit her uncle, Stein, in Istanbul. Mabel fears to let her go, for she may fall into the clutches of 'men'.

With these in place, the story, like the express, gathers speed. At Cologne, Mabel — doing a quick interview with Q. C. Savory — sees, on the platform, Dr Czinner, and recognises him as the wanted man of the Kamnetz trial in Belgrade five years before. She never forgets a face. She uses her journalist's pass to join the train in the hope of a newspaper scoop. The train stops at Würtzberg. Mabel — in pursuit of her story — has ransacked Czinner's case, stolen his Baedeker and deduced from certain diagrams in it that he is returning to lead a new revolution. Czinner, who has just bought a newspaper at the station, has discovered — shattering news! — that the revolution in Belgrade has already taken place without him, and that it has been ruthlessly suppressed. He resolves to go on to Belgrade and to inevitable death in the hope of making, from the scaffold, a glorious public statement of his ideals. He tries to throw Mabel off his track by saying that he is getting off at Vienna. She does not believe him. When the train stops at Vienna, she telephones her story to London. While doing this, she is robbed of her handbag and journalist's pass, by a new character, Josef Grünlich (nasty murderer) who is on the run and catches the Orient Express to take him to Istanbul where he has friends. Mabel with no pass and no money misses the train. By the time, the next day, that the train has reached Subotica in heavy snow, Myatt and Coral have made love in his first-class sleeper. They are touchingly sincere, and talk of marriage — well, of a relationship. Because of Mabel's telephoned newspaper scoop, the police border authorities now know that Czinner is on the train. At Subotica he is arrested. The now-ecstatically happy Coral just happens to be with Czinner at that moment of arrest, and he unintentionally implicates her by giving her an envelope that the police discover. She, too, is arrested and so fails to be on the train when it leaves. Grünlich is also arrested for carrying a revolver. The train leaves Subotica without the three of them, but breaks down in snow two hours later. (This always happens in Orient Express stories.) Myatt realises that something has happened and returns to Subotica — desperately, through the snow, through the night, and in a hired car.

In that lapse of time the travesty of a court martial has been convened by the jumpy police state authorities. At this, Czinner is sentenced by Colonel Hartep (dispassionate but not unreasonable chief of police) to be shot for treason. Grünlich will be imprisoned. Coral will be sent home. They are all put under guard. Grünlich picks the lock of the shed where they are imprisoned and they escape. Myatt has at that very moment arrived in his hired car to search for Coral. Grünlich forces his way into the car. There is no sign of Coral because she has selflessly given up her chance to escape in order to look after Czinner who has been wounded by rifle shots and is dying.

A little later, Dizzy Mabel arrives on the scene, and assumes responsibility for Coral, whom she intends as her new partner. Coral has a heart attack — a fact not made explicitly clear — and dies. The next day, in Istanbul, Myatt, who has rather too readily given up his quest for Coral, sorts out his trading affairs. He effects a takeover of the rival firm of Stein. Stein turns out to be the uncle of Janet Pardoe, and by offering Janet in marriage to Myatt Stein is enabled to compromise and retain a 'family' interest in the firm. Q. C. Savory, who has entertained the thought that he might have a chance with Janet, is given the brush off. Grünlich is smug because he has survived yet again.

These are the bones of the plot. They may not seem entirely convincing, but as with all good stories, when you are caught up in the action, you suspend disbelief. Greene is brilliant in forcing us to fidget at the characters — fingering them just as Grünlich fingers the sore place on his leg where his revolver snuggles — in order to determine whether we like them or not. From this résumé the ingredients for 'an entertainment' may be determined. Greene has an eye, and a feel, for what will work. Famously, he says that he is writing for popular appeal, but, as we have seen, this is not the whole truth for Greene in 1931 and 1932 was becoming remarkable. It is not hard to recognise the nature of the popular appeal of this 'entertainment'. The immediate appeal lies in the glossy brochure world of the Orient Express itself; in the sure-fire hit of the title. But what a curious fellow was Greene! Instead of exulting in this 'prince of trains', this 'magic carpet to the east', he makes the train no better than a nasty, trippery 'British Rail' affair. He drags on about third class, making us unpleasantly aware of shabby tourists sleeping upright or sprawled along the seats, of the sweaty-nightcap smells exuding from the short-haul riff-raff. A background guitar scrapes. It is all hideously, horribly, recognisable. Not elegance, not *Rome Express*, not even *From Russia with Love*. We lurch from the sublime to the sordid. 'Greeneland' has infiltrated Le Grand Express Européen.

The same is true of sex. The story might have been of gorgeous Mata Hari spies. Instead it deals with uncomfortable sex in a sleeping car. *Coitus interruptus* by a red danger light winking on the track. Lesbianism; the lascivious fondling of Coral's legs. Norman Sherry tells us of the woman who remarked that she once thought this the dirtiest book she had read![10] How sheltered were lives in the 1930s! Strangely, the physicality of lust is offset by the frequent romantic refrain 'Kisses, always kisses' that cuts through the snatches of conversation. Who says it? We do not know. It is Greene's commentary on how love *might* be. Sex is a seller, even if some readers tut-tut.

Humour is another popular ingredient. Do we sometimes rather overlook Greene's humour? Here, at moments, we are moved to laugh out loud. The Reverend Opie tries to interest Grünlich in his cricketing heroes Hobbs and Sutcliffe. 'Nobbs und Zudgliffe'

— Grünlich tries to master the names.[11] 'Have you been a runner yourself?' asks Opie of the man who has spent his life on the run. 'I vas a great runner. Nobody runned as well as I'.[12] It may be schoolboy humour but it delights Greene, and we chortle. Opie is the ludicrous Englishman with his gear and golf clubs. Czinner makes an appeal to him as a priest, and tries to make confession. Opie completely misunderstands; he deflects the request into a philosophical discussion. The farce is compounded by Savory. It is funny and desperately sad at the same time. The vulgarity and tummy rumblings of the Peters are sheer slapstick. You can tell that Greene is in his element. And he is sufficiently relaxed to turn the joke on himself. Stein does not want his niece, Janet, connected with Savory, the *writer*. 'He's well off . . . Yes, but a *writer*. I don't like it. They are chancy'.[13] Q. C. Savory is Greene's anti–J. B. Priestley joke: 'One 'opes, one 'opes . . . Bring back cheerfulness and 'ealth to modern fiction'.[14] He is making fun of the established older writer.

Greene is achieving mastery of characterisation. The characters fascinate as well as amuse. They both tug us and repel. It is a successful formula that Greene will hone for the future. Czinner, the revolutionary whose life is wasted in idealistic dreams, and Colonel Hartep, the focused chief of police who condemns Czinner, are to become the protagonists of *The Power and the Glory*. We have also the appeal of fast-moving events. These are the stuff of all good thriller stories. What is going to happen? What is the mystery of Czinner? Why does he keep consulting his watch? Will Myatt sort out the problems with Eckman? Will it end happily for poor, ill Coral? Greene is in his element. We have: murder, arrests, a trial, shootings, a Dick Barton–type rescue attempt. The book is full of nail-biting near-moments of tension. We are forced into reactions, and opinions, and emotional entanglements. It is terrific stuff. *The Third Man* is lurking in the years to come.

Any novelist knows full well that one of the ways of engaging a reader is to provide the envelope of reality — the context of place and scenery that the reader feels he recognises. Greene is a master of those touches of verisimilitude. The film-frame abruptness, economy, and speed. The medley of voices. It is all happening — here and now. Greene writes with assurance. But let me just whisper: 'Look closely'.

Greene is rather good on Ostend, and not bad to Bruges. Most commentators wax lyrical about the scene on the engine footplate: the regulator opened, the sparks flying, and those allotments that the train passes by! They say how accurate and cinematographic it is. Yes, but any schoolboy from those days could have told you as much — and aged steam-train buffs today, no doubt. Greene was proud of those allotments near Bruges: 'You may be sure the allotments . . . were just where I placed them,' he writes, as if to convince us that he is right about it *all*.[15]

But Greene is on a sticky wicket — as the Reverend Opie would say — because he has not managed to persuade La Compagnie Internationale to stump up that free ticket. Cologne was as far as he could afford. He travels third class, he tells his mother. 'Reluctantly, I . . . bought a third class ticket'.[16] However, he writes to Vivien that he is going second class but will come back third. And Vivien has made sandwiches for him to take.[17] He is obviously trying to impress with his economies. Do not believe it. There were no third-class 'through' carriages. If third-class coaches were added for some short hauls, the travellers in them had no access to the elegant Pullman-Nagelmacker coaches. We can believe in the sandwiches.

It is fun to scrutinise Greene's accuracy. Brilliantly, he makes the journey *seem* real enough: the acrid smoke, the rhythm of the wheels, the jerking stops and the gouts of steam. We hear all the traveller-talk of comfort and discomfort, of the views, of arrival and departure times. The characters look at their watches just to check; they take the opportunity for leg-stretching at the stations. Greene convinces us that he *knows*; that he is *there*; that it is *real*. He's got the map there in front of him as he writes: Nuremberg, Neumarkt, Passau, Vienna, Subotica. There is one detail, however, that must strike the observant reader as highly unlikely. A train door opens *inwards*. Mabel leaps onto the running-plate and falls against the door that opens *inwards*. Really! I checked this with the Orient Express archives and learnt that some doors did in fact open inwards. Greene was right.

But not on everything. The Ostend, Cologne, Vienna, Istanbul Express ran only *three* times a week, starting from Ostend on *Tuesdays*, not on *Wednesdays* as Greene claims. And we remember that there were no third-class *through* carriages. There is also a hiccup over the chronology. No one has noticed that Greene's calendar is wrong. He is writing in 1932. The journey takes place in 1932. He is writing about what is happening *at the time*. We know, because he very specifically dates the Kamnetz trial in Belgrade in 1927. Dr Czinner, heading the prosecution of Kamnetz, gave the chief of police the slip when the trial collapsed, and came to England. There he taught in a boys' school in Birchington for *five* years. That brings us to 1932. Exactly where we are with the novel. Greene introduces little tidbits of news from the actual weeks when he is writing — *contemporary* news-flashes such as that of the Ziegfeld chorus dancer who gets married to the cattle baronet. April, 1932, was a month of revolutions and brutal suppression in Yugoslavia and Russia. Greene was writing, as it were, a current news story. The reader must attune himself to 1932. Greene gives us apparent precision. We are told that Myatt will arrive in Istanbul on April 14. That is, in that very month of revolutions. Elsewhere we are told that Czinner — Myatt as well — started their journey on a Wednesday. So, there is our calendar. The train must set out from Ostend on Wednesday, April 11, and arrive in Istanbul three days later on the 14th. But it cannot. The dates don't work for 1932; they work for 1928. Greene creates an impression of exactitude. It's like the ash trees being in bud *seen* in the evening from a speeding carriage window; or, in the darkness, a couple embracing by the line. Can we really see them? Greene prided himself on his accuracy, and it is an entertaining game to be a little sceptical at times. Of course, little oversights are not material to his story. They may have had a bearing on *his* professed reservations about the book but they should not matter to us. Writers are always dissatisfied people. Greene was always self-critical, and so his pleasure in the Constantinople ending should be our pleasure too.

If ever you want real accuracy of detail about the journey and the disposition of the Orient Express carriages, go to Christie. She is bound to be right. But realise that Greene is seeking to direct you not to the passing scenery — here one moment, gone the next — but to the luggage that the characters carry around *within themselves*. This is the aspect of storytelling that was in 1932 assuming absolute importance for Greene. He is, here with this novel, introducing us to themes that are going to stay with him all his life. Of these themes, the main one is of the double-sidedness of everything. The book's Santayana epigram on the title page is one clue to where we are with Greene: 'Everything is lyrical in its ideal essence; tragic in its fate, and comic in its existence'. 'Everything,' says Santayana. '*Everything*,' echoes Greene. Moral dilemmas and people are all included in this multiplex of life. It is a question of how we see all that there is. The train pulls out of the station. Is the station moving, or is it the train? How would it look if it were different? Just the same. It throws us back to our perceptions of Lord Rochester. Villain or hero? What is our angle? Over and over in Greene we find this same duality. It is a matter of perception.

At least twice in the novel we are told that the scenery — 'the tethered boats', 'the trees' — *move backwards* away from the train.[18] The scenery moves; the train is still. Greene keeps hammering the same idea. It is how one perceives. From the windows of the train we look out into the darkness. We see blurred landscape and fiery spark; or, we can change our focal length and see own reflections in the glass. Consider the moment when the frail Coral collapses in the corridor. Dr Czinner is summoned to help. As Coral regains consciousness she has the distinct impression that *she* is bending over Czinner, and tending *him*. Who is the doctor and who the patient? Greene explores that moment twice to make the emphasis.[19] From what viewpoint do we observe? To observe dispassionately is the true strength of the writer, but the view, Greene knows, can always be seen differently. In the single observation is the inevitable obverse, the alternative. The fulcrum is the frontier. Both sides are relevant. It is impossible to have one without the other. Whatever we *desire* encapsulates our deepest *fears*. I think that for Greene the bravery is in the holding of both possibilities. That is also the vulnerability. We shall see that it is the characters who pursue absolutely what they desire, the narrow-focused ones who survive. Perhaps that is also a virtue. We should not discount it. Greene seems to tell us that we should not belittle *mere survival*.

There is nothing new in this you will say. And you will be right. Yet we tend to like our judgements and our solutions to be more definitive. Hero–villain, cowboys–Indians — you know where you are. But Greene, often to our perplexity, holds in hand both possibilities.

In Christie's *Murder on the Orient Express* it is very different. In the sharpness of focus is reassurance. The crooks are revealed. We know them, and we know why. With her there is a Christian and moral security. The evidence is all there, and can be sifted. Hercule Poirot's famous 'little grey cells' solve the mystery. The setting is the same, the thriller-tension is the same, but with Christie we can orientate ourselves by the secure landmarks.

Not only we, but the fictional travellers on Greene's *Stamboul Train* long to hold onto such security; hug the homely aspects of home — husband, wife, cricket, book, the English cup of tea. Like Myatt, we all finger the raisins in that box in our pocket. They are real and comforting. We know our raisins. Istanbul, when we get there, will be real. There Myatt can revert to type, 'unfurl again his peacock tail with a confidence' and expand in the air of home.[20] The book ends with the firm contract in his pocket. Home ground. Phew! What happens in the book is a three-days' dream of uncertain frontiers that we are forced to cross. Actual frontiers. And frontiers of the mind. Frontiers of uncertainty. They always are such.

The 1930s was a decade of frontiers. Europe was at the same time both more accessible and more uneasy. Patrols, passports, politics, police. Frontiers imply both engagement and escape. They are two-sided, like the famous green-baize door. For the loathsome Grünlich the frontier is simply another proof that he has, yet again, got away with it. For Czinner, the idealist, the frontier means death; he says: 'How old-fashioned you are with your frontiers and your patriotism. The aeroplane doesn't know a frontier; even your financiers don't recognise frontiers'.[21] The Orient Express is the visible sign of that high-minded ideal. Nagelmackers visualised his Stamboul Train transcending pettiness, riding the rails across Europe; his privileged clientele safeguarded from having to disembark, declare themselves, or change trains. Those who carry His Britannic Majesty's passport have an additional guarantee. I suspect that Greene loved the idea of the comfort, but he loved more the frontier frisson. He lived with the catch in the throat all his life, and had developed the mind-skills to deal with it. He was realist enough to know what frontiers signified — how the *included* implied the *excluded*, and how both will always exist in some form. The world is unforgiving whatever the idealist, and Nagelmackers, might wish. Greene knew. We learn it.

Subotica on the boundary of Hungary and Yugoslavia is our key border. It is the testing ground for Coral, Czinner, Myatt, and the Chief of Police. Frontiers emphasise opposing ideologies, and class and culture. All these impact on the characters. Fascism and conformity versus the communist vision of brotherhood and equality. Frontiers proclaim a polarisation. By 1932 the Nazi party controlled the Reichstag, and Germans were being taught to say, and think, aggressively, snarlingly. Hitler rants with his fist-clenched question: When did any benefit arise from inter-nationalism? For the fascist regime it is nationalism that enforces frontiers, and exclusion — most horribly, of the Jews. The year 1932, in many parts of Europe, was a time of tensions, pogroms, coups, uprisings of the people, condoned cruelties, and petty lawlessness. The frontiers give us nonconformists and outcasts. On the other side of whatever line we care to draw, are those who are *different*, the misfits: lesbian, Jew, poor dancing girl, political agitator with a price on his head, schoolmaster with the English name and the foreign accent. Even the minority snarl against a lesser minority. The lesbian says, 'I don't like Jews', and her partner, Janet, who is herself a Jew, concurs.[22] All this is at odds with the glamour and glitz of the train that bore the blue-gold livery of La Compagnie Internationale.

Greene is at home in these divided countries of mind and map. He travels like a sublime time-lord. He is the anonymous observer. In the opening pages he gives us an image of the Ostend crane driver detached from humanity, suspended in his cab 30 feet above the docks, parted by distance, 'mist and rain from purser, passengers, the long lit express'.[23] The purser, *stuck* with 'damned faces' felt an unaccustomed envy. Greene, like Myatt, welcomes anonymity for safety and observation. The crane driver is not just part of incidental scenery. We should never think that any image or symbol or diversion in Greene's writing is irrelevant, or accidental.

As a Jew, Myatt is the most obvious symbol of an unsettled Europe. Greene is the twentieth-century novelist whom we should most associate with restlessness and rejection; with the *unhomely* side of the frontier. He and the Jew recognise each other. Mutterings of 'Juif' may be heard from London to the Balkans. Everywhere the Jew has to establish for himself some little kingdom of possibility. Survival is his keynote. The wandering Israelite in the desert, at the oasis, is not a *hero*; but as a survivor he deserves our recognition. If he is transfigured with a moment of glory, then rejoice, but do not be surprised when he reverts to an habitual hard-nosed pragmatism. The Jew must adapt. Neither he, nor we, can take anything for granted. We are all homeless. That is why we are on a train. It is a matter of perception.

There are four Jews in the book, and, indeed, the characteristics are not always attractive. Greene has fingers wagged against him, but he was not the man to duck an issue. He is primarily concerned to see how Jews, among others, manage to hold on to what they are.

For Janet Pardoe, the Jewish lesbian partner, Jewishness can be worn or taken off at will — like a fur cape. Eckman, Myatt's Jew in Istanbul, is a Christian convert, and has a bible chained in the toilet. That is his camouflage. (A Catholic Jew called Andre Raffalovitch used to visit the Greenes at Chipping Camden.) Stein, the Jewish head of the rival raisin-trading firm acts parts. He is a pragmatist; the sentimentalist, and the manqué Englishman. His hair is dyed blond, his nose has been straightened. He wears tweeds, smokes a pipe, talks of golf, has a place in the country, denies an interest in money. Myatt cannot believe this last denial of identity. Stein achieves — by contract and the marriage of Janet — a proxy place on Myatt's board of directors. He is a survivor, even if he is a player of false parts. This adapting to circumstances may appear to be an attempt to bridge divides, but it does not seem so to Myatt nor, I suspect, to Greene. The submerging of one's personality is understandable, but it is still a denial. In his thick fur coat, padded to the cold and the world, Myatt is the wealthy Jew. He will not bow his head: 'I am not a Christian, Mr Stein. I don't believe that charity is the chief virtue'.[24] He has a point. What does Greene hold to be the 'chief virtue'? We wonder. Survival — possibly. Myatt can adopt and adapt in order to survive, but he does not abase himself. He can behave with warmth and sympathy, and can be amused at himself for doing so, for he is always aware of himself and Jewishness. But he does not compromise, though he tries to hide the giveaway mannerism of his spreading hands; and wishes to be invisible — a bit like Greene. Even during his desperate White-Knight journey in the snow back to Subotica, Myatt stops to send a *business* telegram to Eckman. Yet he can bestow princely largesse with consideration and generosity. In the blandness of an international hotel he moves with an obvious ease. Installed there, he gives his orders, trusts Kalebdijan, and conveys the serenity of a man with his hands on known ropes. Fidelity to his kind, to money, to the inevitable — make him a *survivor*.

Myatt is a key to the book and to Greene's thinking. Socially over-sensitive reviewers have pointed to Myatt as an example of Greene's anti-Semitism. 'Coarse and selfish' is Michael Shelden's verdict on Myatt, though he admits some readers may 'even finish the book thinking that Myatt is a good character'.[25] If we are going to be prissy about the world, then we must dislike Myatt, but Greene wishes to make us aware of his strengths. It is the mindless characters who are aggressively anti-Semitic. Those more perceptive see the type, but accept its differentness. Coral and Czinner are against oppression. 'I've always liked Jews', says Coral.[26] She can recognise Myatt at the end of a long train corridor for what he is, and she is not offended. All readers of Greene's writing should get one thing straight. We do not search his work for *good* characters. Let us be prepared to share a compartment — probably second class — with those who have enough human fortitude just *to press on*. Not even to press on to whatever is true and just and of good report, but simply to *survival*.

Greene turns on his heel and leaves us with the hard truths of this world. The business of living and believing is not made easy; we are not let off. Yes, that last sentence in *Stamboul Train* about the contract; and yes, that last awful sentence of *Brighton Rock*. This is not the world we would want it to be — if we are honest. But being honest we recognise it as truth.

Anti-Semitism is not Greene. It is society in 1932, and in an England not unduly malicious. The English could afford to view *Punch* stereotypes with some affection. Perhaps in the 1930s it seemed less reprehensible — and in the 1940s we had more serious battles to fight for both freedom and the Jews. Greene is exploring the conventional attitudes. It is the sort of reaction we might have now to beards and burkhas. It is not Greene saying 'Dirty Jew', but the customs officer at Ostend, the Bulgarian peasant, the Austrian guards. That is how novel-writing works. And if Greene is stressing it, he does so to make us consider our own position.

Three quick footnotes may be made on this matter of Jewishness.

The first is a comment made by Maria Couto, who interviewed Graham in the late 1980s on the subject of his alleged anti-Semitism. She wrote to me: 'You are quite right about Graham's attitude to Jews . . . Myatt is the underdog and the outsider, and a character treated with great sympathy. I interpret these novels as an attack on capitalism rather than against the Jewish race, or religion'.[27] Second, one does not have to know much about Greene's life to realise that in a number of ways he is, as it were, superimposed on Myatt. Here is an extract from *A Sort of Life*:

> It was . . . before I went to school, that I began regularly to steal currants and sultanas out of the big biscuit tin in the School House storeroom, and stuff my pockets with them, currants in the left, sultanas in the right, and feast on them secretly in the garden.[28]

Greene is Myatt and his raisins.

The third point relates to the *name*. Greene is precise, even fastidious, about names. Myatt's name is Carleton. It is not a common name. It was the name of Graham's grandfather on his mother's side — the Reverend. Carleton Greene. It is the baptismal name of Greene's favourite brother, Hugh. Hugh Carleton Greene. It does not seem likely that Greene would have given one of his characters that name, Carleton, lightly or wantonly. So what is the reason? It is because he wanted to give his lonely, outcast character in *Stamboul Train* a distinctive *personal* connection. He makes him, as it were, one of the family.

And, while we are on the matter of names, let me draw attention to Grünlich — quite the most repulsive character. He is a fat man with the sexual disgust of a Pinkie. He is a petty thief and an opportunist and a murderer. Yet he is a Roman Catholic, and he weeps to think of the cold match girls. What is more, 'Grünlich' means Greene-ish, and the word is deliberately spelt with three 'e's. At the very end Myatt reflects on the man: 'Someone he had known better a long time ago in a different country'.[29] It is as if Greene, too, is pondering an old relationship. Graham Greene — Grünlich. The two touch at the fingertips and we can sense Greene's amusement at a near-identification.

Grünlich takes pride in the neatness of his tools, in his efficiency. He has never been caught. He takes no avoidable risk. 'That's Josef. Five years now and never jugged'.[30] He has no remorse. It is this lack of sentiment that has raised him to 'the dangerous peak of his profession'; furthermore, he is 'precise in his methods, omitting nothing which was necessary, and adding nothing which was superfluous'.[31]

Does not that sound like Greene's pride in his writing? Grünlich may be repulsive but he is a survivor. He is a craftsman, and he operates effectively in his element. From Vienna to wherever — he 'is going the whole way'.[32]

Greene becomes his own outcast creations, not because they have an obvious worth, but because they have made a choice, and follow the prime command, which is to survive in a world of changing values. In this exactly, we find both Rochester and Pinkie.

So it is that we come to the concept of *home*. All the characters seek some *home*. Some notional haven of rest. Travel is an interesting diversion, and *home* is a comforting leap of imagination. Greene revaluates the concept. Myatt has romantic views about an oasis, but he has no real home; and so settling down with Coral would be impossible. Czinner seeks to come back home to Vienna — to the ghosts of his dead parents; but he, futile to the end, is shot in Subotica. Neither his ideals nor his body will find a home. Mrs Eckman has a home full of chairs but there is no one to sit in them. 'This isn't home,' she says. 'My husband's so modern . . . He may not want to come back for me'.[33]

Home is full of the fears of emptiness. Mabel orders curtains but the thought of her being domestic is a joke. It is a sad business, home. Greene recognised the unsatisfactoriness of it all. He was not happy in Mud Lane, however cosy Vivien tried to make it. *Home* is a dream; to achieve it is either to be lucky or to be an easily satisfied fool. How typical of Greene's restlessness — and honesty. He never lets us off the hook.

By travelling — just conceivably — one may find. That is the aim of the characters. 'Going all the way'. They keep saying it. It is what one says with pride and hope as one embarks on the Orient Express. Some go all the way; some don't. Going all the way depends, not upon goodness, but upon the capacity to survive. Together with 'going all the way' is the haunting refrain 'Remember me'.[34] It is another early-stated, almost biblical, theme. Why should Coral remember the purser? Why should he want to be remembered? He plays no part in the story. 'Remember me,' Mabel says bitterly to Janet, 'You'll have forgotten me in a week'.[35] Mabel is one of those 'who love and remember *always*'. Faithfulness and remembrance are intertwined threads of the book: 'Faithfulness was not the same as remembrance; one could forget and be faithful and one could remember, and be faithless'.[36] Greene joyously wriggles around the ideas. The book has this tightness of theme and structure. It has also an immense and striking vigour.

Stamboul Train is not just a thriller story or 'an entertainment'. The characters engage us; Greene's themes are being forged. He has become a novelist with something to say. With its aspirations, anxieties, unexpected delays, the journey is a paradigm of life. At the end, there is Istanbul. It *may* be home: but more likely a staging post. Greene, unlike Poirot, offers no certainties, no solutions, no moral or religious comforts. But ever haunting in the ear is the anguished: 'Remember me'. Why? Because says Greene in effect, 'I, too, am a traveller and have been there'.

This novel is the antecedent for all that is to come. Greene is on one of those journeys that excite him. The Stamboul Train will be held up, inevitably, by heavy snowfall, or by the jack-boot tramp of frontier police. In the same way in these early years of writing, Greene is held up — almost derailed — by the unexpected: by siren-songs, by the Earl of Rochester, by the discomforts of Chipping Camden. But Greene — like Myatt, Grünlich, and Savory — will hang on to the end. In the Pera Palace gardens the ghost of poor Coral shimmers above the gyrating Dunn's Babes. She was too good, too naïve to survive. But Greene — 'Remember me!' — is 'going all the way'. How gloriously he was to do that!

CHAPTER 2

'Ghost on the Rooftops': How Joseph Conrad Haunted Graham Greene

Cedric Watts

This discussion has three parts: 'Conrad as Career Model', 'Literary Debts and Connections' and 'Retrospective Influence'.

CONRAD AS CAREER MODEL

One of the major themes in the writings of Graham Greene is the appeal and the peril of hero-worship. The revered hero may be divine or mortal: God, Carlyon, Kite, Baines, Harry Lime or the Captain; but either way, the worshipper may encounter pains and perils and perhaps disillusion: idols may fall. From an early age, Greene repeatedly sought cultural heroes who might be emulated. One of those cultural heroes was Józef Teodor Konrad Nalecz Korzeniowski, alias Joseph Conrad, the Polish-born writer, who lived from 1857 to 1924. Four years after Conrad's death, Greene signed the contract for publication of his own first novel; and he signed it at the London office of William Heinemann, a firm that had also published Conrad. Greene says that as he sat in the office, 'the bearded ghost of Conrad rumbled on the rooftops with the rain';[1] yes, 'rumbled on the rooftops with the rain': even the rhythm and the onomatopoeic alliteration imply a tribute to the great author. They bring to mind passages like this, for instance, in *An Outcast of the Islands*: 'The voice of the thunder was heard, speaking in a sustained, emphatic, and vibrating roll, with violent louder bursts of crashing sound, like a wrathful and threatening discourse of an angry god'.[2]

Well, the bearded ghost of Conrad continued to haunt Greene

38

for many years. Both men wrote novels, tales, dramas, memoirs, reviews, and literary essays; Conrad wrote a series of prefaces for the Heinemann collected edition of Conrad's works, and 50 years later Greene wrote a series of prefaces for the Heinemann collected edition of Greene's works. And, when I say that Conrad haunted Greene, that is not just a melodramatic way of saying that he had some literary influence on Greene. Often, when reading about Greene or when reading his works, you may think 'I've been here before'. Well, you probably have: in the life and works of Conrad.

The most important influence that Conrad exerted upon Graham Greene was that of career model: he was a hero to be emulated. In his autobiographical writings, notably *A Personal Record* and *The Mirror of the Sea*, Conrad tells us that, as a boy, he enjoyed reading accounts, both fictional and nonfictional, of voyages and adventure on the high seas, and of explorations of the dark and dangerous places of the earth. Largely because of this reading, Conrad was fired with the ambition to go to sea; so, at the age of 16, he left Poland for Marseille and the Mediterranean coast. Later, in turn, he left France for England and the British merchant navy. He spent almost 20 years as a seaman, officer, and captain, visiting such exotic locations as the West Indies, the Gulf of Mexico, the Belgian Congo, Siam, Borneo, Sumatra, and Australia. He knew the perils of storm and tempest at sea, and was shipwrecked when the sailing ship *Palestine* exploded. From his letters it is evident that he did some gunrunning: almost certainly in the Mediterranean, and probably in the Gulf of Mexico.

His travels also nourished his political imagination. In 1857 he had been born into politics, because at that time Poland had vanished from the map of Europe, having been engorged by three great imperialist powers: Russia to the east, Prussia to the west, and Austria-Hungary to the south-west. Conrad's parents, loyal patriots, conspired against the Russian overlords, were arrested and found guilty, and were sent into exile in the remote Russian province of Vologda: the four-year-old Conrad accompanied them on that dreary journey. Largely as a result of the privations of exile, both Conrad's parents died early, so that he was an orphan at the age of 11. Human isolation would eventually become one of his great literary themes. During his maritime career, he served the British Empire on British ships, but he remembered his sufferings at the hands of Russian imperialists, and he observed at first hand the cruel treatment of the Africans in the Congo.

Consequently, when he embarked on his second career, that of a novelist writing in his *third* language, English, Conrad brought to fiction-writing an unusually rich and diverse experience of the world.

He wrote novels and tales that were exotic in location and romantically adventurous in their subject matter, but also reflectively critical and politically astute. He had received a Roman Catholic upbringing, but became predominantly sceptical, being capable of veering between agnosticism, atheism, and even antitheism.[3] (Incidentally, Greene claimed to have played Russian roulette; but the young Conrad's attempt at suicide was more drastic: the bullet from *his* pistol went in though his chest and out through his back, though it missed his heart.) In his writings, Conrad was ahead of his times in his love of philosophical paradox, in his great scepticism about imperialism, particularly economic imperialism, and in his world-weary sense that humans were, as political beings, in their infancy. He was pessimistic but humane, sceptical but magnanimous.

One of the lessons that Greene learnt from Conrad was the value to a writer of wide and risky travel. Like Conrad, Greene visited the Caribbean, the Gulf of Mexico, the Orient, and the Congo; indeed, when he travelled in a boat into the Congo, he held a copy of Conrad's *Heart of Darkness* in his hand. In 1890, Conrad trekked 200 miles through the jungles of the Congo; in 1935 Greene trekked 350 miles through the jungles of Liberia. Like Conrad, Greene resided for a while in the south of France; and, further away, he explored areas not reached by Conrad: Paraguay and Latvia, for example. Again like Conrad, Greene used a remarkable diversity of personally experienced locations in both his nonfictional and fictional works. As a mature novelist, Greene sought to combine the adventurous with the sceptically reflective and the shrewdly political, again seeking to emulate Conrad. Probably, none of Greene's novels rivals the audacity of *Heart of Darkness* or the epic scope of *Nostromo*; but in *The Power and the Glory* and *The Heart of the Matter*, you may feel, as when you read Conrad, that adventure fiction, with its raw vitality, is being fermented into philosophical fiction, thanks to the yeast of a painfully intense intelligence. But Mammon made both men compromise. Conrad was conscious of dividing his output between relatively intellectual works and relatively commercial works. He would struggle with *Nostromo* for part of the day, while for another part of the same day he was dictating *The Mirror of the Sea*. Of the latter he said: 'I've discovered I can dictate that sort of bosh without effort at the rate of 3,000 words in four hours. Fact! The only thing now is to sell it to a paper and then make a book of the rubbish'.[4] Greene, as we know, attempted to divide his works between 'entertainments', which would be relatively popular, and 'novels', which would be relatively demanding; but this created difficulties. *Brighton Rock* was subtitled 'A Novel' in its first

British edition and 'An Entertainment' in its first American edition. Eventually, Greene abrogated the division. One can still sense, in Greene's work as in Conrad's, that, partly as a result of financial pressures, some works are relatively rapid and slight, even though the author was at the same period capable of much more powerful writing. In 1939, for example, Greene dosed himself with Benzedrine in order to work rapidly on *The Confidential Agent* in the mornings; but he would work more carefully on *The Power and the Glory* in the afternoons.

Authors assuage their critical teething by biting the hands that feed them. Conrad described the movie as 'just a silly stunt for silly people',[5] but the burgeoning Hollywood film industry helped to transform his fortunes. For most of his literary career, Conrad was in debt; indeed, he accumulated massive debts, even though the British taxpayer subsidised him by means of a substantial civil list pension. Then, in the last decade of his life, 1914 to 1924, Conrad became wealthy; and that was largely because Hollywood, attracted by adventurous narratives set in exotic locations, was paying huge sums for the film rights of his works. Many of his novels were filmed, and one of them, *Victory*, was even filmed five times between 1919 and the end of 1930. In 1897 Conrad had famously declared: 'My task [. . .] is, before all, to make you *see*'.[6] He was always a strongly visual writer, and such works as 'An Outpost of Progress' (1897), *Heart of Darkness* (1899) and *Nostromo* (1904) were brilliantly cinematic at a time when movies were not, because movies were then in their technical infancy. Greene, long fascinated by the cinema, a brilliantly perceptive film critic, wrote his novels from the outset with one eye on the possibility that they might be filmed. So, film techniques influenced his descriptive techniques, and the potentiality for filming influenced the nature of his writings. Again, the financial rewards were huge. In 1931, 20th Century Fox paid him £1,738 for the right to film *Stamboul Train*; and, at that time, you could buy a new three-bedroom house in the south of England for £400. Sometimes, however, the filming of fiction seems to degrade the original work, perhaps by accentuating the dramatic or melodramatic elements of the text, and by reducing or eliminating the reflective observations of the fictional narrator. Thus the David Lean film of Conrad's *Lord Jim* has been regarded by various critics as reductive, and so has the John Ford film of Greene's *The Power and the Glory* (*The Fugitive*). As in Conrad's fiction, so in Greene's: much of the pleasure lies in the oscillation between the particular and the general, the concrete and the abstract, between vividly rendered particulars and a reflective commentary that is often bleakly sceptical and aphoristically intelligent.

I have cited analogies between the two men; but in case, like Greene, you resemble doubting Thomas, here is some specific evidence of connections. First: Greene's nonfictional writings make numerous references to Conrad. His admiration for Conrad was changeable and discriminating. He praised the Cambridge critic F. R. Leavis (whose lectures I used to attend in the 1950s) for emphasizing Conrad's moral intelligence and rescuing him 'from legend': that is, the legend of the yarn-spinning master mariner. Both Leavis and Greene saw that Conrad was no mere teller of maritime tales but a morally acute observer of life. Next: here's a connection that I noticed very recently. In the introduction, entitled 'A Familiar Preface', to the autobiographical work *A Personal Record*, Conrad famously remarked: 'Those who read me know my conviction that the world, the temporal world, rests on a few very simple ideas; so simple that they must be as old as the hills. It rests notably, among others, on the idea of Fidelity'.[7] Twenty-five years later, Greene, artfully echoing the phrasing, said this: 'The poetic cinema [. . .] can be built up on a few very simple ideas, as simple as the ideas behind the poetic fictions of Conrad: [for example,] a feeling for fidelity'.[8] A crafty adaptation, you may think. Again, Conrad's essay 'Geography and Some Explorers' (1924) famously denounces imperialism in Africa as 'the vilest scramble for loot that ever disfigured the history of human conscience', and says that the sordid reality that he found in Africa destroyed 'the idealised realities of a boy's daydreams'.[9] The counterpart essay among Greene's works is entitled 'The Explorers'. It cites the ruthlessness and hypocrisy of such explorers as Stanley, and bitterly remarks: 'The dream has vanished. The stores are landed, the trade posts established; civilisation is on the way [. . .]'.[10] Of course, Greene repeatedly reread *Heart of Darkness*. In 1933 he said that it made him despair of his own work but 'filled me with longing to write finely' and stirred ideas of '[a] dark pregnant kind'. On rereading it in 1959, Greene first found that what he termed Conrad's 'heavy hypnotic style' made him aware of 'the poverty' of his own style, but later he considered the language 'too inflated' and Kurtz unconvincing.[11] The fluctuations relate to Greene's own evolution in technical matters.

One of the finest brief critical appreciations of Conrad is Greene's essay 'Remembering Mr Jones', 1937. Here, Greene contrasts the adventurous Conrad with the urbane Henry James, and claims that two of the great English novels of the last 50 years are James's *The Spoils of Poynton* and Conrad's *Victory*. In this essay, predictably seeking to give Roman Catholicism credit for some merits of a predominantly sceptical writer, Greene finds in Conrad what he terms 'the rhetoric of an abandoned faith'. Greene continues:

> Conrad was born a Catholic and ended—formally—in consecrated ground, but all he retained of Catholicism was the ironic sense of an omniscience and of the final unimportance of human life under the watching eyes [. . .]. 'The mental degradation to which a man's intelligence is exposed on its way through life'; 'the passions of men short-sighted in good and evil': in scattered phrases like these you get the memories of a creed working like poetry through the agnostic prose.[12]

I think that's subtle criticism, for the time, 1937; and, curiously, that remark, 'the memories of a creed working like poetry through the agnostic prose' now seems to apply quite well to some of Greene's later works, notably A Burnt-Out Case, The Comedians and The Human Factor. Perhaps Greene should have acknowledged, too, that supernatural covert plotting can be found in Conrad's The Nigger of the 'Narcissus', Heart of Darkness, The Shadow-Line and Victory. (In these works, a supernatural covert plot runs alongside the secular overt plot.) Indeed, in Victory, Satan, disguised as Mr Jones, is almost as conspicuous a presence as is God in Greene's The End of the Affair.[13] Of course, Conrad often expressed vigorously anti-Christian opinions. He said: 'I always, from the age of fourteen, disliked the Christian religion [. . .]. Nobody—not a single Bishop of them—believes in it'; 'Faith is a myth and beliefs shift like mists on the shore'. But it was Greene who said: 'I have never believed in hell'; 'If God exists—I am not convinced he does'; and 'With age [. . .] doubt seems to gain the upper hand'.[14]

If we compare the politics of Conrad and Greene, we see that though Conrad is sometimes deemed a conservative, his closest literary friendship was with R. B. Cunninghame Graham, the militant pioneering socialist who was jailed for his violent part in the Bloody Sunday demonstration of November 13, 1887. Conrad and Cunninghame Graham were both outspoken critics of imperialism and capitalism; indeed, by the standards of his times, Conrad was sometimes startlingly anti-imperialistic, and Nostromo incorporates, albeit critically, a view of economic determinism that brings a Marxist view to mind. In the essay 'Autocracy and War', 1905, Conrad predicts the Great War and the Russian Revolution, but remarks that in Russia a long time will elapse after the revolution before the people succeed in gaining freedom. So the large paradox of Conrad's politics was that while he endorsed many left-wing criticisms of capitalism, he took the apparently cynical (but actually astute) view that revolutionary politicians who promised liberty, equality, and fraternity would probably become dictators and exploiters in turn when they gained power. Greene veered politically; he was a strikebreaker when working for *The Times*, and in 1984 he said he would certainly have voted for Mrs Thatcher; but hostility to imperialism is a marked feature of numerous works including *Journey Without Maps*, and a well-known paradox of many of his writings is the implication that there could be a constructive compromise between the Catholic church and atheistic communism. The 'Liberation Theology' of the period 1960–80 made this paradox seems plausible. Curiously, both Conrad and Greene often expressed anti-US views. Conrad was indignant when, in 1903, the US government fomented a revolution in Panama so that it seceded from Colombia, thus bringing the Panama Canal, which was then being constructed, under US control. Seventy-four years later, there was some political redress when the Panama treaty of 1977 was ratified in Washington by President Carter of the US and General Torríjos of Panama. (This treaty gave Panama a share in controlling the canal, and some of its revenue.) On that historic occasion, one member of the Panamanian delegation was Greene, whose view of the historic secession was the same as Conrad's. Incidentally, that secession of Panama was one of the sources of Conrad's novel *Nostromo*; and, of course, Greene's involvement with Panama found expression not only in the novel *The Captain and the Enemy* but also in the memoir, *Getting to Know the General*. Thus, sympathy with the political underdog is an important impulse in the writings of both men. Both Conrad and Greene declined knighthoods (perhaps because they did not wish to become 'Commanders' of the 'Order of an Empire'). By that criterion, both writers stand on the political left of such celebrities as Sir Harold Wilson, Sir James Callaghan and Sir Michael Jagger.

LITERARY DEBTS AND CONNECTIONS

Greene's first three novels, *The Man Within*, *The Name of Action*, and *Rumour at Nightfall*, appeared in 1929, 1930, and 1931 respectively. The author later acknowledged that they were all, alas, influenced by some of Conrad's inferior work. In 1903 Conrad and his collaborator, Ford Madox Hueffer, had published the novel *Romance*. In *The Man Within*, as in *Romance*, the hero is involved with smugglers, moves on a borderline between the guilty and the innocent, falls dangerously in love, and is the central figure in a trial. Frankly, the Conrad/Hueffer novel is embarrassingly bad, managing to be both melodramatic and prolix; and the same could be said of the Greene novel, which the author himself described as 'very young and very sentimental'; but at least it sold 8,000 copies initially, confirming Greene in his literary career.[15] He had climbed toward fame from the shoulders of Conrad and Hueffer.

The Name of Action and Rumour at Nightfall were both eventually suppressed by Greene: he forbade re-publication, so that they are now valuable collectors' items. Both are disappointing in quality, and The Name of Action seems extensively anti-Semitic. Greene said that here his debt was to Conrad's late romantic novel The Arrow of Gold, which he later called 'Conrad's worst novel'.[16] In The Arrow of Gold, the English hero becomes disenchanted with a political conspiracy, has a love affair with the Spanish mistress of a rich man, and fights a duel over her, though finally he and she separate. In The Name of Action, the English hero becomes disenchanted with a political conspiracy, has a love affair with the wife of foreign ruler, and fights a duel over her, though finally he and she separate. In the case of Rumour at Nightfall, Conrad's Arrow of Gold provided the political background-matter, the Carlist Legitimist rebellion in nineteenth-century Spain, and Conrad's Doña Rita was the model for Greene's heroine. Conrad's novel also encouraged Greene to offer some over-elaborate simile-laden prose. After the failure of The Name of Action and Rumour at Nightfall, Greene tried to break away from an influence that he now described as 'too great and too disastrous': 'Never again, I swore, would I read a novel of Conrad's— a vow I kept for more than a quarter of a century'.[17]

So, in this initial stage of Greene's career, Conrad's influence was unfortunate, because Greene was choosing the worst Conrad to be influenced by. But matters soon become more interesting.

As is often noted, Greene experienced what he termed 'the deep appeal of the seedy':[18] he sometimes regarded the 'seedy' as a fascinating intermediate region between the primitive and the civilised. In 1972, Volume I of the Supplement to the Oxford English Dictionary defined 'Greeneland' as 'the world of depressed seediness reputedly typical of the setting[s] and characters of the novels of Graham Greene'. Of course, the author repudiated this term, but it stuck. Greeneland has many sources, one being Greene's own depressive tendencies, and a second being a work by another depressive author: Conrad's novel The Secret Agent (1907). This is a murky urban novel of political crime and espionage, featuring sordid, seedy locations and drab lives. The central location is a shop in Soho where, we are told, the sun never shines (though the shop lies at the heart of the empire on which the sun never sets), and where Adolf Verloc sells latex contraceptives and pornographic items. Greene's debt to *The Secret Agent* is almost embarrassingly evident in *It's a Battlefield*, 1934. He had reread *The Secret Agent* just three weeks before starting this new work. The debt is not simply a matter of seedy London locations and dingy lives. In Greene's political novel, the assistant commissioner of police is clearly a twin of Conrad's assistant commissioner in *The Secret Agent*. Both men have served in the tropics before returning to London; both like to leave their desks to explore the streets of the city to investigate crime personally; and both deal with a parliamentary private secretary who is devoted to a busy minister. Greene's Caroline Bury is partly based on Lady Ottoline Morrell, who met both authors; but she is also, obviously, the counterpart to Conrad's aristocratic Lady Patroness: each character is liberal in outlook and ready to give help to a convict with revolutionary sympathies. In these two novels, Conrad and Greene offer pessimistic vistas of struggling selves lost in the urban crowd, of fallible authority, of hypocritical idealists and rather naïve patronesses. In both works, a vulnerable individual is killed while making a futile political gesture. The pessimistic irony that political action may prove counterproductive, self-destructive or absurdly unavailing is common to both writers. Characteristically, Greene included an allusive acknowledgement of his source. The hero's name is 'Conrad Drover', and his Christian name, we are told, was inspired by that of 'a seaman, a merchant officer', who had once lodged in his parents' home. Thus, the real Conrad is provided with accommodation in the fictional Greeneland he had helped to create: appropriate literary hospitality.

When Greene travelled to central Africa, he was consciously emulating Conrad. In 1890, the latter had kept a 'Congo diary'; in 1959, Greene kept a 'Congo journal'. In the essay 'Analysis of a Journey' and in the book *Journey Without Maps*, Greene actually quotes his predecessor's diary when showing that he, like Conrad, associated the so-called darkness of the interior of Africa with the darkness of the unconscious mind of a European. Greene said that his own exploration of Africa could be called a quest for the 'heart of darkness' and that he associated the land with the unexplained brutality illustrated when Conrad's 'Congo Diary' records the finding of the stinking corpse of a slain African (who had probably been shot by a Belgian officer).[19] Conrad's *Heart of Darkness*, of course, repeatedly formed a reference point for Greene: it is cited in *Journey Without Maps*, the 'Congo Journal' and *A Burnt-Out Case*. Both writers espouse a form of primitivism (here meaning 'nostalgia for the primitive'), for both suggest that the Africans are best left to themselves and are corrupted by the incursion of Western trade and exploitation. On his journey down the African coast, Marlow, Conrad's narrator in *Heart of Darkness*, had observed a township that he calls 'Gran' Bassam': in actuality, this was the Grand Bassa that would be the terminus of Greene's purgatorial progress in *Journey Without Maps*. Incidentally, Greene found that the dictator of Grand Bassa, Colonel Davis, seemed to resemble a soldier of fortune, J. F. K. Blunt, the proud and courageous American who is described both in Conrad's autobiographical work *The Mirror of the Sea* and in his novel *The Arrow of Gold*. Of course, *Journey Without Maps* resembles *Heart of Darkness* in that both authors were seeking to evaluate civilisation and human nature. Comparing Europe and Africa, Greene says this:

> The 'heart of darkness' was common to us both. Freud has made us conscious as we have never been before of those ancestral threads which still exist in our unconscious minds to lead us back. The need, of course, has always been felt, to go back and begin again. Mungo Park, Livingstone, Stanley, Rimbaud, Conrad[,] represented only another method to Freud's, a more costly, less easy method, calling for physical as well as mental strength. The writers, Rimbaud and Conrad, were conscious of this purpose, but one is not certain how far the explorers knew the nature of the fascination which worked on them in the dirt, the disease, the barbarity and the familiarity of Africa.[20]

In that passage, Greene's very phrasing echoes *Heart of Darkness*, which spoke of 'a fascination [. . .] that goes to work upon him [i.e., upon the explorer of a wilderness]. The fascination of the abomination'.[21] Like Conrad, Greene saw central Africa and the Africans partly as ominous, indicating a sensual savagery from which civilised people have emerged, and partly as benign, representing a primitive innocence that civilisation tends to corrupt and destroy.

Another connection between Greene and Conrad is that Querry in *A Burnt-Out Case* has intermittent resemblances to the Marlow of *Heart of Darkness*. Marlow looks compassionately on the suffering Africans and finds that his role is misinterpreted by fellow Europeans, who think that he is an idealistic member of Kurtz's 'gang of virtue': Querry is similarly compassionate to the suffering lepers and is infuriated by the attempts of Rycker, Parkinson and some of the priests to stereotype him as an intrepid idealist. In this case, however, Conrad is more politically militant than Greene: Conrad indicts imperialism in Africa, which inflicts muddle, waste, cruelty, and rapacity;

but Greene's emphasis falls rather on the selfless work undertaken by European Catholics to help the African sufferers in the leper colony.

Conrad's *Heart of Darkness* has also left its mark on *The Third Man*: that brilliant film, directed by Carol Reed, for which Greene provided the story and the script. Holly Martins is a descendant of Conrad's Charlie Marlow; Harry Lime is a powerful descendant of Kurtz, that eloquent figure of charismatic corruption; and Anna shares the mournful fidelity of Kurtz's Intended: each woman remains trapped in love for the man who betrayed her and has died. Perhaps Conrad's long 'river of darkness' is transmogrified as the vast dark sewer beneath the city. If you doubt such connections, notice that, once again, Greene has incorporated sly homage to a source: one of Lime's loyal henchmen is known as 'Mr Kurtz': he becomes 'Baron Kurtz' in the film. A large thematic connection can be seen, too. One of the characteristics of the Romantic movement was a preoccupation with the paradoxical theme of 'the virtue of evil'. Famously, Blake and Shelley saw Satan as the true hero of Milton's *Paradise Lost*, and Romantic literature repeatedly offers us the charismatic hero-villain: the person who is morally bad but ontologically intense and therefore fascinating. Examples include Montoni in Ann Radcliffe's *The Mysteries of Udolpho* and Heathcliff in Emily Brontë's *Wuthering Heights*. Conrad's Mr Kurtz in *Heart of Darkness* belongs to this romantic tradition, for he is corrupt but potently charismatic; and so does Greene's Harry Lime, who is wicked but witty, urbane, powerful, and sexually attractive. There is also a 'Gothic' feature that links both characters. Marlow, on meeting Kurtz, refers to him as though he is a vampire arisen from death: he speaks of 'the disinterred body of Mr Kurtz' and describes him as 'an initiated wraith' and 'a shade'. When Martins first sees Lime in Vienna, he describes the sight as an encounter with a ghost, for Lime's funeral has taken place previously. 'Do you believe in ghosts?' he asks. 'I do now'.[22]

Partly because of his early bitter experiences in Poland, one of Conrad's preoccupations is with human isolation and failures of communication; another is with the paradoxical theme that loyalty may entail treachery: loyalty to one person or cause may entail treachery to another. Both these preoccupations can obviously be found in Greene, too. Conrad's novel *Victory* emphasises the isolation of the protagonist, Heyst, the failure of communication between that protagonist and his partner, Lena, and the irony that if Heyst is loyal to his father's philosophical doctrines, he must be disloyal to other people. (His father had advocated strict detachment from a treacherous world.) Heyst says: 'I only know that he who forms a tie is lost. The germ of corruption has entered into his soul'.[23] Greene chose these words as the apt epigraph of his novel *The Human Factor*. You can see how the epigraph fits Castle, the novel's protagonist. Being grateful to communists, who helped his black wife and her son escape from South Africa, Castle has been betraying his employers, the British Secret Service, by passing secrets to Moscow. But when he escapes to Moscow, he finds that he has been used as a pawn by the communists, and it seems that his wife and child will never be able to join him. As in *Victory*, the hero's recognition of the truth comes tragically late. As in Conrad's *Under Western Eyes*, the double agent discovers the ruthlessness and duplicity not only of the organisation he is betraying but also of the organisation that he is serving.

If we turn from thematic connections to matters of style, we encounter the following question asked by Greene in the volume *In Search of a Character*. 'And how often,' says Greene, Conrad 'compares something concrete to something abstract. Is this a trick that I have caught?';[24] to which the answer is, 'Yes, even if Conrad was not the only source'. In *Heart of Darkness* we find, for instance, the following comparisons: 'the silent wilderness [. . .] struck me as something great and invincible, like evil or truth'; and 'his words—the gift of expression, [. . .] the pulsating stream of light, or the deceitful flow from the heart of an impenetrable darkness'. In Greene we find those related linkages of concrete and abstract that he called 'leopards'; for instance: 'The small pricked-out plants irritated him like ignorance', or 'The sun shot into the sky the stains of agonies and endurances'. More frequently, however, the abstract precedes the concrete, as in 'She carried her responsibilities carefully like crockery across the hot yard', or 'His sympathy could be peeled off his eyes like an auction ticket'.[25] Greene has also cited what he calls 'a piece of pomposity which I had learned from Conrad at his worst: "A clock relinquished its load of hours"'.[26] To be fair, however, we should notice that stylistic pomposity, whether of journalists or politicians, was actually one of Conrad's satiric targets. (Such satiric mockery can be seen in 'An Outpost of Progress' and *Heart of Darkness*.) Certainly, both Greene and Conrad soon developed parody-inviting styles. Conrad was brilliantly parodied by Max Beerbohm in *A Christmas Garland*, while Greene was parodied by himself (under a false name) to win a prize in a *New Statesman* competition. Then, as Greene and Conrad aged, both attained styles that were relatively lucid and transparent.

Of course, they both liked to play games with names. In *Heart of*

Darkness Mr Kurtz has a surname that means 'short', but we are told that 'he looked at least seven feet long', so his lying name establishes a paradox that is true to his divided nature as an enlightened genius and a monster of depravity.[27] The narrator sardonically remarks that his name was as true as everything else about him. In *The Shadow-Line*, a steward called 'Ransome' is the self-sacrificing centre of goodness aboard ship, and we may recall that the New Testament calls Christ a 'ransom' for sinners (Mk 10.45; 1 Tim. 2.6) Again, the narrator jokes about the homophone, saying that the steward 'was a priceless man altogether'.[28] Greene's names were sometimes jocularly self-referential: thus the brutal Austrian murderer in *Stamboul Train* has the name Grünlich, meaning 'Green(e)-like'. Some of the fictional surnames look suspiciously ordinary — Jones, Brown, Smith — and may, in the case of Jones and Brown in *The Comedians*, be taken for the pseudonyms of rogues: Greene recalled the duplicitous 'Mr Jones' of Conrad's *Victory* and the scheming 'Gentleman Brown' in *Lord Jim*. In *The Comedians*, however, Jones, the confidence trickster, eventually becomes the hero he had pretended to be, while Brown, who once sold forged paintings, is in the closing pages poised to commit himself to a left-wing cause.

As I mentioned just now, Conrad displays a technical interest in covert plotting. Covert plotting occurs when a plot sequence is presented so reticently or obliquely that we are unlikely to see it as a whole until we make a second or subsequent reading of the work. Examples are the covert murder plot in *Heart of Darkness* and the covert supernatural plot in *The Shadow Line*.[29] In Greene's *Brighton Rock*, there is a minor covert plot concerning the mode of Hale's murder — what exactly happened? And in *The Power and the Glory* there is a small and a large covert plot. The small covert plot concerns the exact fate of Coral Fellows, and the large covert plot concerns the extent to which the whisky priest (who deems himself a failure) has bestowed grace and the possibility of redemption on those he encounters, ranging from Tench the dentist, to Coral, to the boy Luís, and even to the Marxist Lieutenant. Another Conradian technique was the use of transtextual narratives. The story of Tom Lingard unfolds in three texts, the story of Hamilton in two, and the story of Marlow in four. Greene used this technique when depicting Kite, the gangster. In *A Gun for Sale*, we are told of the circumstances of his murder by rival gangsters at a London station. In *Brighton Rock*, that previous murder of Kite proves to be the premise of the plot, for Pinkie is concerned to avenge his death. Thus the story of Kite extends across two different works. Again, I am not suggesting that Conrad was the sole model for these techniques;

but I am suggesting that Conrad's example would have strengthened Greene's interest in them.

RETROSPECTIVE INFLUENCE

Influence works backward. The present can change the past. As Greene repeatedly suggested, the future may change the present. A novel, tale, or poem that you write this year and that looks like a failure may be granted cultural immortality by some genius who, in a century to come, alludes to it in one of his or her artifacts. Some literary works are good but sterile: they have produced no offspring. Other literary works are good and fertile: they have produced offspring, and thereby gain the prestige of parentage. Thanks to Greeneland and particularly to *It's a Battlefield*, Conrad's *The Secret Agent* is now a better novel. As we read that Conradian book published in 1907, we sense that its sleazy terrain extends through time, so the original terrain becomes more important and more plausible; and, as we follow the first assistant commissioner through the Soho streets, we know that he is engendering a later assistant commissioner who will also help to resolve a criminal matter, so the earlier one is accompanied by a ghostly counterpart or literary son who increases his significance. Conrad's *Heart of Darkness* would wield immense parental prestige even without Greene, because the tale *Heart of Darkness* has generated not only George Steiner's novel *The Portage to San Cristóbal of A. H.* but also several stage productions and the films *Heart of Darkness, Apocalypse Now,* and *Hearts of Darkness.* In addition, thanks to Greene, *Heart of Darkness* may bring to mind, as we read it, *Journey Without Maps, A Burnt-Out Case,* the tale 'The Third Man', and the film *The Third Man.* Conrad's Kurtz is made more powerful not only by his two namesakes in Greene's works but also by our memory of his virtual reincarnation in the imposing form of Orson Welles. All this is not just a matter of associative connections; it is also a matter of recognition of cultural continuities, of continuing cultural problems and paradoxes. Conrad and Greene remind us that, repeatedly and dangerously, in political matters and elsewhere, people are inclined to admire not the morally *good* person so much as the ontologically *strong* person: meaning someone who is seductively vital or engagingly intense: thus virtue is defeated by charisma, or fidelity vanquished by hedonism.

Furthermore, to compare is to contrast: to see likeness entails perceiving difference. Greene never achieved the epic scale and scope of *Nostromo*, nor did he achieve the almost inexhaustible richness of

Heart of Darkness. On the other hand, Greene surpassed Conrad in the depiction of sexual jealousy and also in narratives of pursuit, so that *The Power and the Glory* has a distinctively gripping intensity and deft economy of implication. Both men wrote psychopolitical novels, in which the psychological and political are interwoven. Both were brilliantly adept at setting isolated individuals within a vividly rendered location. Both were capable of taking not only a worm's-eye view but also a mountaintop view of humanity, so that characters veer between intense significance and mere ephemerality. Together, both writers provide a brilliant panoramic survey of global ideological forces in the late nineteenth century and in most of the twentieth century. What an American critic, Albert Guerard, said of Conrad's *Nostromo* often applies to Greene's work. Guerard remarked: '[T]he novel's own view of history is sceptical and disillusioned, which for us today must mean true'.[30] Nevertheless, the authors of *The Rover* and *Monsignor Quixote* both found, late in their lives, a place for the genial affirmation of human goodness; an affirmation that, nowadays, is needed more than ever.

CHAPTER 3

The Making of the Outsider in the Short Stories of the 1930s

Rod Mengham

This chapter focuses on Graham Greene's stories of the 1930s to bring out the extent to which his work reflects the common concerns of his generation. Tropes of spying, betrayal, class-consciousness, and failed domesticity are uppermost in many of the early stories, as they are in the writings of Greene's contemporaries, but a close examination of patterns of imagery, specific items of vocabulary and linguistic habits suggests that Greene is unusual for his subtle distinctions between shared culture and received ideas, between authentic forms of community and mechanical forms of social connection. The chapter provides a survey of the organizing principles of Greene's entire short story output during the 1930s, but will give particular attention to 'I Spy' (1930), 'A Day Saved' (1935), 'Brother' (1936), 'The Basement Room' (1936), 'Jubilee' (1936), 'A Chance for Mr Lever' (1936), 'The Innocent' (1937) and 'A Drive in the Country' (1937); all are governed by issues of loyalty and betrayal, attachment and loss, belonging and abandonment that are revolved with a complexity unusual among contemporaneous treatments of these and related themes.

Greene's first published story from the 1930s is 'I Spy'. It adopts the point of view of a child, characteristically anxious, furtive, incapable of grasping the derivation of his fear and guilt while also revolving in his mind the delicate questions of loyalty and betrayal, the dilemma so vividly apparent in the work of many writers of the 1930s and 1940s, although nowhere more damagingly than in the stories of Greene — the dilemma presented to the mind by its own conviction that loyalty to one person or idea necessarily involves betrayal of another. The child tries to measure his love for both mother and father, consciously preferring the mother, but identifying closely with the father who is guilty of an unspecified crime, and who is secretive like his son, and possibly even treacherous. The only clue to the nature of his wrong-doing is in the title's reference to spying. The story is set during the First World War, in a climate of hysterical animosity against Germans, and the prevailing atmosphere of suspicion and recrimination helps to deepen the boy's feelings of guilt and apprehension when he is disturbed in the act of attempting to steal from his father's stock of cigarettes. Smoking is taboo for underage children, and can only be accomplished by subterfuge, one forbidden activity compounding the effect of another. The boy creeps downstairs to his father's shop when the door to the street opens, admitting the father in the company of two policemen. The boy remains hidden although the room is suddenly flooded with light — 'A torch flashed and the electric globe burst into blue light'[1] — in a sudden illumination that corresponds to the probing, exposing glare of the searchlights, combing the dark sky for enemy airships. Although the boy escapes discovery, his evasiveness is not only incriminating in its own right but also suggestive of a moral proximity to enemy activity. The father has been allowed to return home briefly before being taken to the police station, but does not take the opportunity to tell his wife about the situation, preferring to take his coat and pocket a few cigarettes, in a duplication of his son's act of appropriation. His exit from the story — in all probability his exit from the boy's life — is a betrayal of family echoing the betrayal of national interest implied as the reason for his arrest. The most disturbing element in the story is the casual deceptiveness of the language used by both father and son to temper their sense of alienation, their awareness of flouting convention, of hiding behind appearances; they both deploy cliché in order to neutralise their transgressions, to domesticate their distinctly unhomely ideas. The boy repeats to himself the phrases 'May as well be hung for a sheep' and 'Cowardy, cowardy custard,' while the father 'fortifies' himself with adaptations of proverbial sayings: 'A stitch in time,' 'Never do today what you can put off till tomorrow,' 'While there's life . . .,' disguising egotistical behaviour with the everyday language of the group, of a shared outlook that can be taken for granted. Their use of language is symptomatic of a dissimulation of common interests that is simultaneously their betrayal.

The 1935 story, 'A Day Saved,' one of Greene's most unconventional experiments, begins with a cliché. Or rather, it begins with a cliché that it distances itself from almost immediately: 'I had stuck closely to him, as people say like a shadow. But that's absurd. I'm no shadow'.[2] This slightly phantasmagoric narrative is a first-person account by a character whose behaviour recalls that of Edgar Allan Poe's protagonist in the short story, 'The Man of the Crowd'. Poe's narrator tells of his own obsessive behaviour in following an anonymous passerby in search of information about his identity, his history, his relationships. It is a futile quest that is abandoned at the end of the story. Greene's narrator is similarly dogged, with the difference that his pursuit of the object of his enquiry is more threatening, more unstable, more unpredictable; and his own psychological health seems to be placed under serious threat: 'Of course I never believed that talk would be enough. I should learn a great deal about him, but I believed that I should have to kill him before I knew all'.[3]

If 'I Spy' is concerned with the shadowing of the father by the son, with the duplication of ways of acting and speaking, 'A Day Saved' is concerned with emulation, rivalry and mimicry in a much more conscious and bizarre fashion. Although the narrator feels that he will never accomplish his aims, never uncover the secret of his quarry, to the reader it becomes increasingly clear that what is maintaining and even increasing the distance between the subject and object of this quest is the object's ordinariness, his familiarity, everything in his behaviour that is recognisable despite his anonymity. Whether he is called Jones or Douglas, Wales, Canby, or Fotheringay, makes no difference; his conduct, which the narrator calls 'stupid and good-natured,'[4] is quite simply generic, typical, unexceptional; he represents everything that the narrator feels he is not; he embodies a capacity for empathy with others, for participation in a feeling of 'unity and companionship' that the narrator is excluded from.[5] The pathos of this story is embedded in the perverse dismissal by the narrator of everything that he is drawn toward instinctually; it culminates with the narrator's holding back from entering a house where his counterpart is expected: 'I stepped back and he went in and almost immediately the room was full of people. I could see his welcome in their eyes and in their gestures'.[6] The description of hospitality that follows entails a dual response that both registers the value of this sociability while expressing a conscious rejection of it: 'I could not bear the sight for long'.[7] The inability to bear the sight of others' happiness is attributable to pain and envy as well as to exasperation and contempt. The story ends with the narrator willing onto the object of his quest his own ghostly condition: 'when he has the most desperate need, when he is following another as I followed him, closely as people say like a shadow, so that he has to stop, as I have had to stop, to reassure himself: you can smell me, you can touch, you can hear me, I am not a shadow: I am Fotheringay, Wales, Canby, I am Robinson'.[8] The real poignancy of this final statement is that it sees embodied experience as being in conflict with individual identity; the reality of touch is clearly preferred to the unreliability of the imagination; the senses offer a kind of certainty while language produces confusion; and the proclamation of identity at the end is immediately cancelled out by being multiplied. All that the narrator has to hold onto is a sense of difference, but this is acquired at the expense of friendship, community, psychological security. Each of the narrators of these two stories is set at a distance from shared culture; and it is only in a form of hostility or betrayal that they can convert a passive into an active condition, the outcome of an imposition into one of apparent choice.

The year 1936 was an especially productive year in terms of Greene's short story output: 'Jubilee', 'Brother', 'A Chance for Mr Lever', 'The Basement Room', and the unfinished novel, 'The Other Side of the Border', published eventually in the *Complete Short Stories*, all date from this year. I am going to concentrate especially on 'Brother' and 'The Basement Room', because they deepen the themes of confused identity and betrayal that are so powerfully explored in the earlier texts.

'Brother' has a Paris setting and an atmosphere of urgent topicality, dealing as it does with armed insurrection by communists against the police and against the bourgeois values of the protagonist, the proprietor of a bar in the 'Combat' district. As with 'I Spy', the ruling tension of the story derives from the threat of misappropriation and the undermining of identity through the invasion of the space or spaces associated with the self that is constructed by habit, convention and received ideas. The bar becomes the temporary bolt-hole for a group of communists on the run; their exchanges with the proprietor emphasise their belief in the practice of sharing everything, whether this be cognac or knowledge: 'the Red [. . .] made a gesture with open palm as if to say: You see, we share and share alike. We have no secrets'.[9] The proprietor's identity is constructed on the basis not only of private property but of hidden knowledge, his sense of self is defined by its practice of dissimulation, of saying one thing while thinking another: 'One of the men at the door came up to the bar and told him to pour out four glasses of cognac. "Yes, yes," the proprietor said, fumbling with the cork, praying secretly to the Virgin to send an angel, to send the police, to send the Gardes Mobiles, now, immediately, before the cork came out, "will be twelve francs."'[10] The motivation for this secret train of thought is a selfish materialism that corrupts precisely those values the bourgeois pay lip service to, giving angels the same value as the police, recruiting prayer in the service of commerce. But although the

proprietor seems entrenched in his meshing of establishment values
with an underlying acquisitiveness — 'every slow casual step he took
was a blow for France, for his café, for his savings'[11] — he is thrown
off balance for reasons that are not immediately apparent but that
are connected with the couple he mistakes for lovers, but who are in
fact brother and sister. His mistaking one kind of love for another is
telling in itself but symptomatic of a disturbance to his understanding
of certain key words and concepts. The crucial moment occurs when
his unconscious throws up an image at once inexplicable to him but
revealing to the reader:

> Perhaps they were to be pitied, cut off from the camaraderie round the
> counter: perhaps they were to be envied for their deeper comradeship. The
> proprietor thought for no reason at all of the bare grey trees of the Tuileries
> like a series of exclamation marks drawn against the winter sky. Puzzled,
> disintegrated, with all his bearings lost, he stared out the door towards the
> Faubourg.[12]

Contemplating the difference between superficial camaraderie and a
more profound sense of connection, profound enough to have brought
these two Germans to the capital of a traditional enemy in order to
risk their lives for an ideal of comradeship, the 'proprietor' (and this is
all he is ever called) loses his self-possession and is almost literally dis-
orientated ('with all his bearings lost'), looking toward the Faubourg,
while seeing in his imagination a scene in the Tuileries, a scene of bare
grey trees, stripped of cover, naked, exposed, incapable of shading or
concealing anything, in the immediate proximity of the royal palace
and everything it represents. This image of something that has been
stripped away, of explicitness ('like a series of exclamation marks')
marks an unconscious turning point, the beginning of a turning away
from dissimulation, from the division between public and private
selves, from a deceptive use of language and from self-deception.
The story ends with the proprietor giving resonant meaning to the
only two words of German that return to him from the past, *Kamerad*
and *Bruder*, as he utters them without thinking over the body of the
dead German communist, killed in the police raid that smashes up
his café. Unlike the communists, the police pay for their drinks and
for the damage, but the experience has produced a *volte-face* in the
proprietor's attitudes. It is now the forces of law and order who are
regarded as intruders, whose abuse of private property is sanctioned
only by financial reparation. On the one hand, comradeship and open
dealing; on the other, superior force and the ability to pay. Greene's

story is a surprisingly partisan challenge to received values with clear implications of the desirability of separating the concepts of community and solidarity from traditional forms of society in favour of experimenting with more radical political solutions.

'The Basement Room', on the other hand, returns to the setting of the family home for its powerful examination of the child's confusion over the rights and wrongs of loyalty and betrayal. Although the child Philip's parents are absent, the dynamics of the family romance are reproduced and even magnified in the conflicting impulses of affection and dislike that Philip feels toward his carers, Mr and Mrs Baines, the family butler and his wife. In fact, Philip feels that he only really begins to live when his parents leave and he can spend his time in the basement with the servants, which suggests that the basement of the title allows for the acting out of desires and possibilities that remain unrealised and even unthought-of above stairs. The upper floors have forbidden areas, with the furniture and ornaments symbolically all covered up, 'muffled and secret'[13] in the absence of the parents, while downstairs Philip can go where he pleases and listen whenever he likes to Baines's reminiscences about colonial Africa, of a time and a place where affection could be expressed openly, and even physically:

> I loved some of those damned niggers. I couldn't help loving them. There they'd be laughing, holding hands; they liked to touch each other; it made them feel fine to know the other fellow was around. It didn't mean anything we could understand; two of them would go about all day without loosing hold, grown men; but it wasn't love; it didn't mean anything we could understand.[14]

Philip's deepest attachment is to Baines, and his conscious loyalty to the butler is little short of fervent. There is never any suggestion of a sexual dimension to this passion, but at the same time it is equally clear that the strength of his sympathy for Baines and of his antipathy toward Mrs Baines arises from nothing he can identify, nothing he can understand. When he discovers that the Butler is having an affair with the young woman he has misleadingly referred to as his niece, it is precisely the realisation that Baines is sexually active that means an adjustment in his feelings of loyalty toward the butler and his unconscious betrayal of him.

There are two occasions in the story when Philip is seen outside the house, the first when he disobeys Mrs Baines and wanders the streets in order to escape the spectacle of Baines defeated by his marriage — 'the sad hopeless hate of something behind bars'[15] — and the second after Mrs Baines's spectacular and fatal fall down the stairs. On the first occasion, when Philip stands at the window of the café where Baines is meeting his lover, he is deeply impressed by their interactions without understanding why; the narrator informs us that 'He would never escape that scene. In a week he had forgotten it, but it conditioned his career, the long austerity of his life'.[16] The tableau is more important than anything he has ever seen, and in the same proportion it is more deeply repressed than anything else. It involves a protracted negotiation between the lovers culminating in mutual understanding, a *rapprochement* that is no sooner established than it is shattered by Philip's extraordinary intervention, which takes the form of an accurate mimicry of the voice of Mrs Baines summoning her husband.

Philip, who has partnered himself imaginatively with Baines, sabotages his rival's attempt to get closer than he himself has managed, by a momentary identification with the ultimate figure of censorship, the detested marriage partner herself. In order to supplant the threat to his own liaison with Baines, he must turn himself into the very object that has absorbed his own hate, an object of primal fear: 'she was darkness when the night-light went out in a draught; she was the frozen blocks of earth he had seen one winter in a graveyard when someone said, "They need an electric drill"; she was the flowers gone bad and smelling in the little closet room at Penstanley'.[17] These evocations of dread at the idea of extinction, at the threat of one's own mortality, are simultaneously intimations of a desire to see Mrs Baines dead herself, a desire that will be realised by the train of events leading to her fall, events in which Philip will play a pivotal role. The spontaneous identification with Mrs Baines's power of veto has the desired effect, at least temporarily, when the startled lover vanishes almost immediately, leaving Baines and Philip in the café. But in some degree, the identification is irreversible, and this is made apparent on the return to the house, where Mrs Baines is seen watching at the window, in a duplication of Philip's own stance at the café window. In the brief interlude, the moment of respite in which Philip can sustain for a short while the illusion that he has restored the *status quo* in his relationship with Baines, a note of reassurance but also of fatuity is struck when Baines attempts to return to normality with an unconvincing use of cliché: 'May as well have another cup,' Baines said. 'The cup that cheers'.[18]

Paradoxically, Baines's adultery is not understood as inimical to domesticity, but is in fact part of a fantasy about a longed-for homeliness, a scenario in which his girlfriend will redeem the sterility of his married life: '"If it was you, Emmy,"' he says, '"this'd be like a home."'[19] And the fantasy about everyday life in Britain cultivated during his colonial exile is a miscellany of clichés which all have to do with background details, with the setting for a story, not with the story itself that might unfold against that setting: 'for years he had waited [. . .] in the hope of this long day, that cat sniffing round the area, a bit of mist, the mats beaten at 63'.[20] That Philip's wishful thinking is more subversive than the butler's is evident from the recurrence of his phobia about the letter flap and the threat of violence that it poses: 'some letters rustled down and someone knocked. "Open in the name of the Republic." The tumbrels rolled, the head bobbed in the bloody basket. Knock, knock, and the postman's footsteps going away. Philip gathered the letters. The slit in the door was like the grating in a jeweller's window'.[21] The historical shock of the French Revolution, with its undermining of rank and privilege, is the implicit outcome of a developing intimacy between master and servant. And it is notice-able that in moments of panic and fear, Philip regains some degree of balance by resorting to cliché and habit, routine ways of speaking and acting. During the frightening episode, when Mrs Baines searches the house for the two lovers, 'carefully from habit [Philip] put on his bedroom slippers and tiptoed to the door'.[22] But routine is confined to the family home, and it is in his second exit from the house that Philip discovers the severe limitations of convention and habit, revealed as a barrier against sociability and gregariousness, shutting him out of a world of easy-going camaraderie: 'The air was full of voices, but he was cut off, these people were strangers and would always now be strangers; they were marked by Mrs Baines and he shied away from them into a deep class-consciousness'.[23] What is shutting Philip out is not just a lack of familiarity with the ordinary and the everyday, but an active investment in conspiracy, confidentiality, secret knowledge. He is held in the double bind of trying to keep the secrets of two people at cross purposes with one another. In the final scene, when Philip interprets the facial expressions of Baines as further attempts to enjoin him to silence in order to avoid accidentally incriminating the Butler, Philip hears in imagination the Butler employing a succession of familiar phrases, once comforting, now wholly inadequate. The effect is one of failed espionage: 'But the wires were cut, the messages just faded out into the vacancy of the scrubbed room in which there had never been a place where a man could hide his secrets'.[24]

'The wires were cut' is a phrase that seems to come straight from a poem by W. H. Auden, echoing 'They ignored his wires', in the 1928 poem later given the title 'The Secret Agent', which is replete with the language of conspiracy and betrayal, and ends with a translation of the final line of the Anglo-Saxon poem 'Wulf and Eadwacer', which is concerned with the parting of two lovers.[25] This affective, and even erotic, dimension is never made explicit in Auden's poem, yet underlies and controls it. The same, unadmitted yet undeniable, connection is what motivates the behaviour of the protagonist and the direction of Greene's writing in 'The Basement Room'.

'Jubilee' (1936) is a story that refracts the sexual tension conditioned by youthful ignorance into a different kind of tension, the tension produced by too much knowledge of sex, by the compulsive use of sexual attraction to stave off financial disaster. The resulting nervous strain is a symptom of moral defeat and of a finite capacity for endurance in the aging gigolo, Mr Chalfont. The story ends with Chalfont and the comfortably-off ex-prostitute Amy who has seen through his façade walking arm in arm 'into the decorated desolate street'.[26] This phrase compresses the division between public bravado and private vulnerability whose psychological outcome is one of desolation. Chalfont's existence remains bearable only as long as his 'decoration' — his camouflage of 'Good Taste'[27] — remains successful, but Amy pierces through his defences immediately, and only deepens his sense of desolation by attempting to console him for it. The street is decorated for the 1935 Silver Jubilee of George V, and therefore represents a superficial and mechanical form of social unity, one from which Chalfont is excluded by his impecuniousness: 'Too many people whom he had once known (so he explained it) were coming up from the country; they might want to look him up, and a fellow just couldn't ask them back to a room like this'.[28] Chalfont's explanations are for no one but himself, and the fact that they are quarantined inside a parenthetical aside suggests the extent to which he is trying to convince, and even to deceive, himself.

There is an interesting colonial dimension to the Jubilee celebrations, which seem to elicit a more enthusiastic and more concerted response from the visiting expatriate community than from the London locals. Patriotism is clearly more effective at a distance, rendering somewhat abstract the sense of belonging to a shared culture that the Jubilee project might expect to draw on. 'A Chance for Mr Lever', also dating from 1936, explores the expatriate experience in an African setting. Mr Lever, a casualty of unemployment in the Depression, tries to reverse his fortunes by acting as agent for a company apparently engaged in mining for gold but actually engaged in selling shares in an operation that does not exist. Whether in the London suburbs or in the

African wilderness, Lever is preoccupied by a deficit of 'companionship' and 'fellowship': in the suburbs, he can sustain the illusion of
companionship, but only in a reverie prompted by alcohol, while in
the wilderness, there is only stark disillusionment, so that the chimera
of 'good fellowship' disappears altogether. The sense of isolation is
made geographically diverse but remarkably cohesive. London and
Africa are bound together by the economics of imperialism, which
instrumentalises both those who gain work within its system and those
who lose it. The caustic irony of Greene's story inheres in the fiscal
'faith' invested in venture capitalism by those who are its victims,
and that transforms faith itself into an investment opportunity; an
opportunity that does not repay the investment, but whose articles of
faith are consistently actuarial: 'He thought: Prayer. I'll pray tonight,
that's the kind of thing a fellow gives up, but it pays, there's something
in it'[29]; 'He wouldn't believe what he had been told; it wouldn't pay
him to believe'.[30]

   The company that has hired Mr Lever is based in Brussels and has
given him the task of tracking down another of its agents who has
gone missing in an especially inhospitable tract of jungle. The parallel
with Joseph Conrad's *Heart of Darkness* is a calculated one. Norman
Sherry's biography of Greene makes clear how protracted was his negotiation with Conrad's influence on his work, particularly with reference
to the relationship between *The Secret Agent* and *It's a Battlefield*.[31] In
1936, it was a reading of *Heart of Darkness* that determined the plot,
cast of characters and settings, of both 'A Chance for Mr Lever' and the
first two parts of the abandoned novel 'The Other Side of the Border'.
This latter text begins with the protagonist Morrow, contemplating a
map of Africa in the office of the New Syndicate, exactly as Marlow
studies the map in the office of the steamship company in Brussels.
But the most significant difference between Greene's and Conrad's
treatments of their maverick agents, is that Marlow feels an obscure
kinship with Kurtz — and both are regarded by other colonists as
members of the same 'gang of virtue' — while Morrow wishes to dis-
sociate himself from Hands and to expose his dishonesty in a report
that the New Syndicate does not actually wish to receive, since it suits
them to turn a blind eye to the nature of Hands' activities. Conrad's
text counterpoints the destruction of social relations under colonialism
with an impulse toward companionship, however tenuous, and toward
loyalty, however naïve. It is the paradoxical mixture of resolute honesty
and quixotic idealism in Marlow that Morrow (even their names are
close) is unable to convert into a basis for action in 1930s England. On
his return from Africa, he is sure that he owes no loyalty to Hands, and

yet the map, which is referred to at the end as well as the beginning of the first section, seems to him not to stand for a simplification of a complex situation, but to stand for its opposite, representing 'a whole obscure state of mind, a mystery'[32]; 'Morrow in the waiting room allowed himself to be drawn, with a feeling of obscure distress, towards the map'.[33] The transposing of 'obscurity' from substantive to adjective paradoxically makes clear the extent to which the map of relationships, indicated by terms such as loyalty, fellowship, companionship, has become confused and perversely disorientating.

By contrast, the immoral Hands is presented in terms that suggest how a resolute dishonesty will clear a path with such a degree of success that no map could ever hold any mysteries for him: 'and as he started on the long fake tale he felt happy and ready for anything because no one here knew of the last jobs and the borrowed money and the accumulated failures. The whole world was at his feet . . '.[34] Interestingly, this geographically inflected self-confidence is not only the consequence of successful lying, it is also the pretext for an association with photography:

> The whole world was at his feet while the photographer leant on the plaster pillar and under the reading-lamp in the inner room the woman raised her compliant and patient face, the kind of face you feel has known too much unimportant pain, the sprained ankle, the disappointment at the local hop, the varicose veins, a series of small humiliations uncomplainingly borne.[35]

This raises the issue of how much the camera can 'read' of the face under the 'reading lamp', of its ability to reveal the kinds of details that are elicited by the writer's empathy. The face certainly seems to be 'compliant' in response to interpretation, but what method of interpretation is it complying with? It is true that the writing is calibrated precisely in a way that resembles the careful focussing of a camera lens — the 'pain' is 'unimportant' but nevertheless excessive, 'too much' — but there is also an emphasis on how 'you' are expected to 'feel' the signs of pain rather than actually see them. The photographer himself is carefully posed — 'the photographer leant on the plaster pillar' — and this reference to his studio prop is a reminder of how all photography relies to some extent on framing, contrivance, manipulation.

On arrival in Africa, Hands makes straight for the premises of a second photographer, Billings, whose name echoes that of the first, Millet. Billings is a figure whose psychology and behaviour are much more comprehensively linked to various forms of deception. His ambition is to become minister of the local mission church, but his motivation is the opportunity this will give him to siphon off a percentage of the collection money. His shop is in some degree a front for less respectable transactions: 'He could develop films but few people came to Billings for that purpose'.[36] Hands has come for the purpose of acquiring alcohol. Billings interposes photography between the aspirations of the spirit and the needs of the body, between altruism and selfishness, rendering the relations between all these things confused and obscure. The world of Greene's photographers is a world in which appearances cannot be believed, in which belief neither pays nor means what it should.

With the two stories dating from 1937, 'The Innocent' and 'A Drive in the Country', Greene achieves two very powerful articulations of a dissociated sensibility, the first in connection with the estrangements of memory, the second in response to the catastrophic effects of economic depression on social, domestic, and intimate relationships. 'The Innocent' is built around the narrator's visit to the town of his childhood, in the company of a girl he is paying for sex. The story explores the roots of his tendency in adulthood to opt for relationships that are friendly and easy-going, but that pose no threat of significant attachment. The exploration of the narrator's psychology is guided by his perception of physical changes to the environment he remembers, and his attempts to project in the imagination both what is missing and his associations with what is missing. At its heart, the text reverts to the trope of the map to reflect the significance of memory's omissions, the significance of its dynamic relationship with forgetting that is revealed as a process driven by the experience of rejection, a rejection that turns out, poignantly, to have been largely imagined: 'It was like a map which had got wet in the pocket and pieces had stuck together; when you opened it there were whole patches hidden'.[37] It is precisely a hidden scrap of paper, rediscovered at the end of the narrator's itinerary, that holds the clue to his emotional retraction.

The exploratory movement of the text gradually discloses a pattern of syncopations, a series of recollections of sensory impressions that were themselves sharpened by yearning, by the youthful anticipation of what would happen in the future. The narrator's yearning for a love never realised emerges as the basis for an adult life in which relationships have never been more than provisional and perfunctory. His chronic lack of commitment is reflected in an occasional use of the parenthetical aside that shows him to be more trusting, more confidential, and more intimate with the reader than with his companion of the moment. (Communicating with the reader is even more short-lived and inconsequential than transacting business with a prostitute.) It is only when he is in the vicinity of the house where he attended dancing lessons as a seven-year-old child that he remembers consciously his passionate longing for an unattainable girl of eight. He appears to stumble on the house by chance, but there is nothing in his itinerary that is not determined in some degree by his childhood sense of loss. His memories are varying illustrations of a theme of defeat, such as his sudden recall of a suicide attempt: 'We came over the little humpbacked bridge and passed the alms-houses. When I was five I saw a middle-aged man run into one to commit suicide; he carried a knife and all the neighbours pursued him up the stairs'.[38] The totality of the neighbours' response, involving *all* of them, not just some of them, seems like a gesture of compensation for the ultimate solitude of the suicide attempt; the text carefully says nothing about the outcome of the attempt, about the success or failure of this eleventh-hour neighbourliness.

The story ends with an epiphany of the unfinished business that has cast its shadow over the narrator's emotional development. He never received a response to the message of love that he left in a crack in the wooden gate of the dancing establishment. What his return to the town has enabled is the revelation that the message never reached its addressee, because it is still secreted in its original hiding place. And there is a further twist, because the 'message', which the reader imagines to have been a relatively unambiguous textual message, turns out to have been a drawing that would admit of different interpretations:

> Then I struck a match, a tiny glow of heat in the mist and dark. It was a shock to see by its diminutive flame a picture of crude obscenity. There could be no mistake; there were my initials below the childishly inaccurate sketch of a man and woman. But it woke fewer memories than the fume of breath, the linen bags, a damp leaf, or the pile of sand. I didn't recognize it; it might have been drawn by a dirty-minded stranger on a lavatory wall.[39]

What the story's denouement allows is the realisation that the narrator's lifelong inability to relate to others cannot be attributed simply to the experience of rejection, because his own sense of self is based on a projection back into the past that does not correspond to the material evidence that has survived from that time. His earlier self is now nothing less than a 'stranger' to him, which means that his alienation is more comprehensive than even he had imagined, perhaps no less complete than that of the would-be suicide whose desperate action had made such a deep impression on him.

But a suicide in an almshouse suggests the importance of other factors, pressures other than those of loneliness, unrequited love, and a sense of betrayal; they might include impoverishment, social stigma, a crushing loss of self-respect. These stresses either run through the lives of certain of the characters in 'A Drive in the Country', or circumscribe the lives of others who spend an inordinate amount of energy in resisting the threat they pose. The sequence of events covered by the narration revolves around an unsuccessful elopement, involving the unnamed daughter of a head clerk and an unemployed youth named Fred, who proposes a double suicide rather than marriage, but who ends up killing himself under a hedge. What is chiefly remarkable in this story is the extent to which the vocabulary of economic crisis pervades the customary actions, thoughts and feelings of all the characters. The anonymous heroine is first seen in the house of her father, who is described as 'presenting accounts' both in his clerical work and at church in his attitude to worship, and who is dedicated to 'improving' his property at the same time as he is paying for it, over a period of 15 years, after which things will be 'much easier'.[40] The father's prudential habits have their roots in a profound anxiety, reflected most vividly in the obsessiveness with which he secures his property every evening. According to the Latin etymology, to be obsessed is to be besieged, and it is the literal parallel between these two conditions that oppresses the daughter and fosters her desire to escape. Part of Fred's attractiveness is that his unpredictable and wayward behaviour is predicated on risk rather than security. While the father is absorbed continually in the task of balancing accounts, Fred has an 'air of unbalanced exultation'[41] and grins at her 'with unbalanced amusement'.[42] While the father's master plan for his family is predicated on saving and investment, the improvidence of his daughter's relationship with Fred is centred in physical forms of expenditure: 'For a long time she expended on his lips all she had patiently had to keep in reserve . . . She expended herself against dry unresponsive lips as the car leapt ahead and his foot trod down on the accelerator'.[43] The unresponsiveness of Fred's lips is an early sign of the lack of mutuality in his repudiation of the conventional virtues of thrift and caution in favour of risk and chance. But it is his attitude toward suicide as a 'gamble'[44] and his determination to go through with it that makes her realise that Fred is no less fixated than her father, subject to an equal and opposite form of siege mentality.

After Fred shoots himself, in a muddy field on a rainy evening, the daughter finds her way home and intends to conceal the fact that she has ever left it. The pathos in her situation is that there is no third way, only a choice of opposing forms of imprisonment, opposing attitudes between which there can only ever be hostility. The two dominant registers in the narration are economic and military; hoarding and spending are opposed to one another like enemies on a battlefield: 'she was like a recruit in the first months of a war. The choice made she could surrender her will to the strange, the exhilarating, the gigantic event'[45]; 'She could hear the clink of coins in fruit machines, the hiss of soda; she listened to these sounds like an enemy, planning her escape'.[46] In the first of these two quotations, the daughter is intending to gamble on life with Fred, even though it involves a surrender of the will; in the second quotation, Fred has already killed himself, and it is now gambling itself, indicated by the fruit machines, that has become the threat. Neither alternative offers genuine freedom of choice, and there is no exemption from being at war: if you are not for us, you are against us. It is primarily an economic war, one in which it becomes impossible for the characters to think of their lives in anything but economic terms. The unnaturalness of this situation is conveyed movingly by the complete inability of the eloping couple to find names for the trees and plants they encounter in their 'drive in the country'. The title's ironic suggestion of a casual excursion also places an emphasis on the importance of the rural setting for this fictional study of the poverty of the British social imagination:

> They belonged to the city; they hadn't a name for anything round them; the tiny buds breaking in the bushes were nameless. He nodded at a group of dark trees at the hedge ends. 'Oaks?'
> 'Elms?' she asked, and their mouths went together in a mutual ignorance.[47]

Again:

> She said, 'My father calls you crazy. I like you crazy. What's all this stuff?' kicking at the ground.
> 'Clover,' he said, 'isn't it? I don't know'. It was like being in a foreign city where you can't understand the names on shops, the traffic signs: nothing to catch hold of, to hold you down to this and that, adrift together in a dark vacuum . . . At the hedge end they came to the trees. He pulled a twig down and felt the sticky buds. 'What is it? Beech?'
> 'I don't know'.[48]

The sustained attention paid here to an entire missing lexicon is symptomatic of the attention paid in all Greene's stories of the 1930s to a missing dimension in the lives of his characters; by analogy, this dimension is precisely one that allows for growth and development, for interdependence and renewal; a social dimension in which attachment and belonging are able to thrive. In story after story, this dimension remains out of sight, and the obverse is given over to representations of a society adrift, of economic warfare, of domestic failure, and of an entire spectrum of betrayals.

CHAPTER 4

The Riddles of Graham Greene: *Brighton Rock* Revisited

François Gallix

INTRODUCTION

The origins of the manuscript for Graham Greene's *Brighton Rock* remain a mystery. We do know that it is not kept at the Harry Ransom Humanities Center (HRC), which is part of the University of Texas at Austin (US), and, as Richard Greene suggests, it may have been destroyed during the Blitz.[1] Still, the HRC houses the collected editions of Greene's works, including *Brighton Rock,* together with the corrections he made and the introductions he wrote. There is also the screenplay for *Brighton Rock,* co-written with Terence Rattigan, which includes Greene's precise commentary; his remarks are as meaningful for the book as they are for the film. For example, one typescript details one of the film's last sequences:

> 'A Convent Parlour'. This set must be done with complete realism and free-dom of sentimentality: pitchpine furniture, a clock with a chime, a hideous holy picture above the mantelpiece, a table and two uncomfortable chairs. Rose sits on one with an old suitcase and the portable gramophone at her feet, and the mother Superior sits opposite her.[2]

The burden of this chapter involves using the HRC's materials — like this one — to engage in literary sleuthing, to think through and comment upon some of the many riddles associated with *Brighton Rock.*

REVEAL AND CONCEAL

In order to protect his privacy, Greene wore many masks and left us several puzzling mysteries; he concealed *as well as* revealed his multi-layered life, as the titles and contents of his autobiographical texts illustrate. Some critics even suggest that Greene often covered the truth of his life with clouds of smoke. He once told Father Leopoldo Durán: 'The writer should be a somewhat mysterious figure, he owes it to his readers. It is what he writes that matters, not the personality of the writer'.[3] And in *Ways of Escape*, Greene declared: 'this book has not been a self-portrait. I leave such a portrait to my friends and enemies'.[4] Such portraits eventually appeared, as we know, though not without some controversy.

In 1974, Greene chose Norman Sherry to be his authorised biographer, mainly on the strength of the way he had written about Joseph Conrad, one of Greene's mentors. Sherry followed Greene's tracks all over the world for 20 years and produced three volumes of a biography that became, in spite of what he had several times promised Greene, more and more personal, the biographer digging into his private life. Then there was the unauthorised biography, *The Man Within*, which Michael Shelden published in 1994 — an extremely rare case of a biographer hating his biographee.[5] *The Man Within* provoked the anger of many Greeneans and there were several heated debates, including one at a London bookstore, with Sherry calling Shelden a 'literary terrorist'.[6] A further paradox is that those highly polemical, often-quoted biographies, added to others, have finally become useful tools for understanding Greene's works, if one proceeds out from them cautiously.

What puzzled biographers and reviewers — but how could it be otherwise — concerns Greene belonging on and off to the British Secret Intelligence Service (MI6) from the 1930s to the 1980s. There is now a 45-page file from the Central Intelligence Agency at the HRC filled with rather comical, often totally inaccurate observations, 16 of which are crossed out in heavy ink.[7] Then there was his constant friendship with Kim Philby, the British intelligence officer who spied for Russia and defected to the Soviet Union in 1963. Philby was Greene's chief at MI5 in 1943–44 and he remained his friend until the end of his life. Greene wrote a laudatory introduction to Philby's autobiography, *My Silent War*, which Philby published in 1968. On January 1, 1990, he wrote to Marie-Françoise Allain: 'I never believed in the importance of loyalty to one's country. Loyalty to individuals seems to me more important',[8] almost echoing E. M. Forster's famous remark that if he had to choose between betraying his country and betraying a friend, he hoped 'he would have the guts to betray his country'.[9] In the proofs for the collected edition of *The Confidential Agent*, housed at the HRC, Greene added in red ink: 'I was glad when more than twenty years later Kim Philby quoted this novel when explaining his attitude to Stalinism. It seemed to indicate that I had not been far wrong, although at that period I wrote I knew nothing of intelligence work'.[10]

The fact that, almost like Thomas Pynchon, Greene never liked being filmed and interviewed only added to the mystery surrounding his personality. In 1968, he agreed to be filmed and interviewed on a train as long as only his hand could be visible. This request is comparable to the French author Louis Aragon who only agreed to appear on television, near the end of his life, wearing a Venetian mask. In 1989, Greene agreed to collaborate with Nigel Finch for a TV film called *The Other Graham Greene* and, as Greene read selections from *Ways of Escape*, Finch illustrated the author's voice with written documents and other visuals — Elisabeth Dennys, Greene's sister and secretary, appeared, as did Sherry, and several actors playing various people who had been fooled by this mysterious man.

About the many riddles that Greene carefully scattered throughout his works, what James Joyce ironically wrote to one of his translators could apply to most of Greene's novels, especially *Brighton Rock*: 'I've put in so many enigmas and puzzles that will keep the professors busy for centuries arguing over what I meant, and that's the only way of ensuring one's immortality'.[11]

A SENSE OF TITLES

It all starts with Greene's amazing talent for choosing titles that stick in people's minds from one generation to the next, the best example being *The Third Man*, which seems to reappear again and again in the most unexpected situations. Thus, in 1955, MPs in the House of Commons, during the Burgess-Maclean spying affair raised the question: Who is the third man? *Brighton Rock* is another thought-provoking title, one that immediately needs to be decoded and that fits in so well with all the ambiguities of the novel.

Why Brighton? Greene's connections with the seaside resort were biographical, emotional and long-lasting. He told David Lodge that the town played a large part in his life. It was his refuge whenever he had to recover following health problems, as early as the age of six after a bout of jaundice and, for instance, one September night in 1926, after an appendix operation when he talked to a strange man in one of the shelters on the Promenade.[12] This 1926 incident might have prompted him 12 years later to use a similar shelter to which Pinkie's gang brought Hale's body and where Cubitt would also sit, when running away from Pinkie.[13] One of the consequences of this pleasure of staying in Brighton was that it was there he would go whenever he had a writer's block, getting his inspiration from watching the crowds of people from various social status there. There is no doubt that Greene was partly in *terra incognita* when writing about the racing gangs in Brighton and that he had to get information about a milieu he did not know from personal experience, even if he once told Lodge — with a laugh — that he had made contact with a man who had himself been slashed and belonged to one of those gangs.

It seems that the young Greene, in order to build up the seedy world that would later be called 'Greeneland' — a term he utterly disliked — had to experiment with a background (the slums to the East of Brighton) totally different from his own, as he would do with Soho in London and Pigalle in Paris when he was there. When the film was shown in Britain (with an A Certificate), a disclaimer was needed, explaining that 'this other Brighton of dark alleyways and festering slums [from which] the poison of crime and violence and gang warfare began to spread [. . . is] happily no more'.

If one wants to get at the germ of the story, as Henry James put it, one possible entry seems to be a very ingrained biographical track, so deeply rooted that one needs to read between the lines. What Greene wrote in his essay 'The Young Dickens' in *The Lost Childhood*, might justify what follows: 'the creative writer perceives his world once and for all in childhood and adolescence, and his whole career is an effort to illustrate his private world in terms of the great public world we all share'.[14] Several times in the private world of his autobiographical texts, Greene mentions that, strangely enough, his very first memory was when he was a baby, seeing the body of a dead dog that had been put into his pram.[15] Greene also evoked this episode in an unpublished poem ('Toll no Bells'), housed at the HRC. Written in pencil and blue ink on paper with Greene's address in Paris and dated April 7, 1961, it includes the following lines:

> A dead dog I remember in my pram;
> It had a vulpine air even in death.
> I cried out to the squint-eyed nurse, but words
> Were still a miracle I had not learned [. . .][16]

Very revealingly, the poem ends in such a way that it may be one of the germs of *Brighton Rock*, secretly hidden in Greene's private world:

I lay and watched that vulpine grin of death
Until the squint-eyed nurse to comfort me
Delved in her tomb-like bag and found interred,
Long [illegible adjective] and pink, a stick of Brighton rock.[17]

There is no rock in Brighton and the dramatic white cliffs of Beachy Head and the Seven Sisters (a wonderful décor for a Hitchcock film), are 7 miles away from Brighton. A British reader has no difficulty in recognizing the child's favourite hard stick of candy on which the spiralling word 'Brighton', usually in red lettering, remains wherever it is broken. Indeed, Ida, one of the characters in the book, confirms this and gives the sweet an added metaphorical meaning: 'I've never changed. It's like these sticks of rock'.[18] In a letter to John Boulting, Greene explained that he had meant the title to have two meanings: the place where Hale was killed in one of the small booths where Brighton rock is sold, and the fact that Pinkie knows no place except Brighton 'wherever you bite it, it leaves the name of the place showing'.[19] This said, there are more than two meanings implied in the title; let me explain.

In the Penguin centennial edition of the novel, there is a note for the American reader. It states: 'Brighton Rock is a form of sticky candy as characteristic of English seaside resort as saltwater taffy is of the American. The word "Brighton" appears on the ends of the stick at no matter what point it is broken off'. As for those who read the book in translation, and the novel has appeared in about 50 different languages, they had to be helped. Thus the French publishers this information on the flyleaf: 'A Brighton rock is a kind of very popular stick of barley sugar that could be compared to some of the sweets one gets in our seaside resorts in Dieppe or Le Tréport. The word 'Brighton' remains visible on the stick of candy wherever one breaks it'. (Le Rocher de Brighton est une sorte de sucre d'orge très populaire qu'on peut comparer aux spécialités de certaines de nos plages: 'cailloux' ou 'galets' de Dieppe ou du Tréport. Le nom de Brighton apparaît au bout du bâton de sucre, quel que soit l'endroit où on le casse.) In fact, the translation into French as '(Le) Rocher de Brighton' was not very far from the mark and almost evoked the two meanings of 'rock', the same word, 'rocher' suggesting a mountainous rock and a well-known chocolate piece of confectionery, but, contrary to the British rock, the French sweet is desperately soft and could never threaten anyone except perhaps in a Monty Python film or in a novel by Roald Dahl.

When the film version of the novel appeared in 1947, several translated titles had to modify the original version due to the impossibility of rendering the polysemy based on the play on words. The French film was called *Le Gang des tueurs* (The Killers' Gang). In Spanish it was translated as *Brighton Rock Parque de Attractiones* (Brighton, the funfair); in Polish, *W. Brighton* (In Brighton); in German, *Abgrund des Leben* (Abyss of Life); in Austria, *Finstere Gassi* (Dark Alley); and, in Brazil, *Rincao de Tormentas* (The Rock of Torments). The American distributor renamed the film *Young Scarface*, probably in the hope of evoking the 1932 film by Howard Hawks, with Boris Karloff and Paul Muni. (More recently, by Brian de Palma, with Al Pacino.) Still, the most surprising translation was in Afrikaans, *Die eendstert*, by the South African novelist, André Brink. When I asked what it meant in English, he replied: '*Ducktail*, which was the closest I could come in Afrikaans in the sixties to suggest the world of the Beatniks'.[20] It seems that the characteristic hairstyle of the British Teddy boys in the 1950s (ducktail or duck butt) could evoke the underworld of Pinkie and his gang to Afrikaner readers, at the cost of an anachronism.

Greene's title also perhaps reminded the British in the 1930s, of a popular comic song with cheeky innuendoes that was recorded on a 78 r.p.m. gramaphone record in January 1937 entitled 'With my little stick of Blackpool rock'. Greene even unknowingly anticipated free advertising as holidaymakers at the time could read on the posters placed on the front of the local sweetshops: 'Buy Brighton rock!' In the same way, the title of the book was so successful that it spread to what would later be considered by-products and, in 1939, a new line of women's undergarments, called 'Brighton Rock', appeared in the shop windows of Peter Jones. As all good titles, 'Brighton Rock' never died, and it was even reborn in the 1950s, with the arrival of rock 'n' roll. Later, in 1973, Brian May wrote a song entitled *Brighton Rock* for Freddie Mercury, Queen's flamboyant singer.

THE ART OF WRITING *BRIGHTON ROCK*

When rereading *A Gun for Sale* for the collected editions of his novels, which appeared in the early 1970s, Greene realised how the character of Raven seemed to be a first draft of what Pinkie would have turned out to be, had he not died when the police tried to capture him. More than that, *Brighton Rock*'s plot seems to spring from the story of *A Gun for Sale,* except that Brighton is never mentioned in *A Gun for Sale.* Readers of *Brighton Rock* will recall that Raven knifes Kite — Pinkie's boss and protector — at St. Pancras train station; intriguingly, Raven reveals the crime's circumstances in *A Gun for Sale.*[21] It is to be noted that, to help the spectators, the film starts with an added shot: a close-up on the front page of a newspaper covering the face of a man lying on the beach. The spectators can read very clearly the headlines and the beginning of the article, which is about the discovery of William Kite's mutilated body. The name of Fred Hale is also clearly mentioned, so that this article may best be seen as a very short synopsis of *A Gun for Sale.*

Employing a transtextual narrative, a device that Greene borrowed from Conrad, is not an usual or infrequent literary strategy.[22] Here, though, it is totally reversed, since Greene first built up what Pinkie might have been if he had not died because of police intervention. Greene realised that he had given his character a Peter Pan syndrome; Raven is a Pinkie who has aged but not grown. This reversal's effect is striking — Pinkie is condemned to be killed from the start, one might even say that Greene has killed his character twice.

Other parallels can be drawn between the two novels — they both exploit the theme of revenge, for example, and they are both based on current events of the time. The background of *A Gun for Sale* is the private sale of arms and the looming war. *Brighton Rock* evokes the 1936 racecourse gangs, the reports from the Lewes's Assizes, and perhaps the tone of several press articles about two horrifying murders that were committed in the Brighton of 1934.

Finally, another consequence of those twin novels is that what Greene explained about one character may also apply to the other. On the manuscript of *A Gun for Sale,* which is housed at the HRC, and on the first chapter's first page, Greene offers an explanation for why Raven 'never had a girl', an explanation that he eventually crosses out, and it is a revealing statement, one that could well apply to both Raven and Pinkie: 'He [Raven] had sublimated his sexual emotion as effectively as a writer, but his method was different'.[23] This remark may help the reader of *Brighton Rock* to understand why the narrator insists on the fact that Pinkie hates sex, the sublimation being his vicious sadistic cruelty toward Rose.

IS *BRIGHTON ROCK* A DETECTIVE STORY?

One of the great pleasures of reading Greene is that it transforms every reader into a detective looking for clues and trying not to be fooled by the plot's red herrings, as in the best detective stories and crime thrillers. Of course, there are several definitions of 'detective story'. Ronald Knox once insisted that a detective novel must have a detective who detects, who is the story's protagonist, and who triumphs over the criminal.[24] In *Brighton Rock*, though, this scenario is not the case. If Ida plays an amateur detective because she has realised that the police did not get at the truth about Hale's death, and if she succeeds in preventing Pinkie from having Rose kill herself, she cannot be considered the story's protagonist. For W. H. Auden, in a detective story, 'a murder occurs; many are suspected; all but one suspect, who is the murderer, are eliminated; the murderer is arrested or dies'.[25] Again, this definition does not apply here. A list of suspects is totally useless as the reader knows from the very beginning that Pinkie ('the Boy') is responsible for the murder of Hale. What is lacking, however, is the usual last chapter in which, in a novel of detection, the detective rewinds the whole story from the start, recapitulates all the clues, destroys the lures, and confounds the culprit. Finally, according to Dorothy Sayers, detective novels are 'stories of crime and detection in which the interest lies in the setting of a problem and its solution by logical means'.[26] Sayers's definition could apply to *Brighton Rock*, up to a point, the problem being limited to *how* was Hale killed?

In *Brighton Rock*, the plot is overflowing with information from the very beginning. By putting together the various pieces in the puzzle, the reader can also discern *where* Hale was killed. Hale's body was discovered in a shelter a mile away by the West Pier where he was expected to be according to his itinerary published in the Press. He was murdered next to a small underground shop selling Brighton rock near the Palace Pier and his body was later moved. As for the time when the crime was committed, Bernard Bergonzi has successfully worked out the schedule — sometime between 1.30 p.m. and 1.45 p.m.[27] At 1.30 p.m. Ida hears a clock striking when she leaves the ladies toilet and, at 1.45 p.m., Pinkie is at a shooting booth trying to secure an alibi. Following David G. Wright, Bergonzi also notes that Hale dies from a heart attack brought on when a stick of rock is shoved down his throat.[28] As for Ida, the amateur detective, she has her own theory: 'They took Fred down under the parade, into one of those little shops and strangled him — least they would have strangled him, but his heart gave out first . . . They strangled a dead man'.[29]

It is something of a paradox to reveal the crime weapon as early as the title of the book, on the front cover, but is this unique? When asked, the British crime story author, Peter Lovesey cited *The Poisoned Chocolates Case* by Anthony Berkeley and *Sparkling Cyanide,* by Agatha Christie, as texts with an implied double meaning, but, Lovesey added, 'not so neat, without Greene's clever twist'.[30]

One rule of the detective fiction genre is that there should be a minimum of fair play between the author and reader. It is taken for granted that no vital clue should be concealed and that there should be enough clues to allow a complete elucidation by the novel's end. Greene appears as a teaser from the very beginning, playing cat and mouse with his reader: the sticks of Brighton rock for the holiday-makers are mentioned at the very beginning of the novel,[31] the cheap shops selling Brighton rock appear halfway,[32] and the whole truth is made quite plain toward the end,[33] if the reader can fill in a few suspension points when Cubitt, one member of Pinkie's gang, uses 'Brighton rock' and 'carving' in the same sentence.[34] Similar references also tease the reader.[35]

The reader has to reach almost 200 pages before grasping how Hale was killed; to me, this fact casts a doubt on Greene's commentary in *Ways of Escape*:

> *Brighton Rock* I began in 1937 as a detective story and continued. I am sometimes tempted to think, as an error of judgement [. . .] The first fifty pages of *Brighton Rock* are all that remains of the detective story; they would irritate me, if I dared to look at them now, for I know I ought to have had the strength of mind to remove them and to start the story again.[36]

This statement is not entirely convincing. For one thing, the detective story continues in the second part of the novel, which is not totally divided into two separate parts. In his interview with Lodge, Greene explained that his book had not developed as he had originally planned it, his first intention having been to write a detective story, but the char-acter of Pinkie had 'taken over' and that Greene finally ended up with a totally different novel — an interesting modern case of a character dictating to his (or her) author what to do.[37] To question Greene on that point, one could say that, precisely the introduction of Pinkie and the fact that 'he took over' needed the structure of the detective novel into which he had been integrated, to come out fully.

Pinkie's arrival also meant the inclusion of the religious dimen-sion, albeit in non-traditional ways. By making his murderer a Roman Catholic whose peculiar credo invokes Satan, Greene's task was certainly much harder than it was with *The Power and the Glory*, where the protagonist is a fairly traditional priest.[38] Throughout *Brighton Rock*, Greene also elects to pit 'right and wrong' versus 'good and evil', a decision that inclined Greene to praise Charles Péguy, when the priest at the novel's end turns to Rose and announces: 'There was a man, a Frenchman, you wouldn't know about him, my child, who had the same idea as you. He was a good man, a holy man, and he lived in sin all through his life, because he couldn't bear the idea that any soul could suffer damnation'.[39] With the religious dimension, then, *Brighton Rock* resembles a novel of ideas, written with a thesis to develop, yet this admission does not imply that the detective plot was secondary. Far from being erased at the end of the novel, it left marks, and this trace is probably one of the reasons why the novel has not aged and has been read with the pleasure one gets out of a thriller from one generation to the next.

What Greene first wrote by hand on the proof pages of the 1969 German collected edition of *Brighton Rock*, currently housed at the HRC, that he reproduced in *Ways of Escape* might help us conclude this little spot of literary sleuthing: '*Brighton Rock* was a very poor substitute for *Kravonia*, like all my books, and yet perhaps it is the best I ever wrote'.[40] In the 1969 edition, he added after a dash: 'a sad thought after more than thirty years' — a remark that *Ways of Escape* omits. This remark constitutes an arresting allusion to Greene's first visit to Brighton when, aged six, he had been sent there to convalesce after a bout of jaundice. He had then seen his very first film, *Sophy of Kravonia*, Anthony Hope's story of a kitchen maid becoming a queen. This first film (in black and white) seems to have left such a deep impression on the child and later on the adult, that he tried to represent similar scenes in his books in order to escape life's sad reality, but had failed every time. This interpretation, which might seem rather excessive, would then link *Kravonia* with the 'rosebud' of Orson Welles's *Citizen Kane* and account for Greene's imperious need of writing, always looking for an untraceable text — a search triggered off by *Brighton Rock*.

CHAPTER 5

Innocence and Experience: The Condition of Childhood in Graham Greene's Fiction

Peter Hollindale

When Henry James's novel *The Turn of the Screw* was adapted for stage and film, it was re-titled *The Innocents*. This title is inescapably both literal and ironic as a summary of the story, encapsulating an enigma that remains perpetually unresolved. At the heart of the story are two children, Miles, aged ten, and Flora, aged eight. Merely by the fact of their ages they are by definition 'innocent': inexperienced in the ways of the world and at the mercy of the adults who care for, nurture and 'possess' them, and whose responsibility it is to offer them conditions for beneficent growth. In the eyes of the young Governess who inherits custody of the children, this normative 'innocence' is compromised by evidence that they are preyed upon and potentially corrupted by the ghosts of a dead former governess and a dead male servant, Miss Jessel and Peter Quint, and a struggle develops between the living Governess, ostensibly a force for good, and her dead predecessors, ostensibly a force for evil, for possession of the children. One child, Flora, is manifestly damaged by this struggle. The housekeeper, Mrs Grose, observes that 'It has made her, every inch of her, quite old'.[1] The boy's fate is still worse: he dies.

Criticism has long debated whether the governess, as protagonist and narrator, is a reliable guardian and witness, or whether the children are the victims of neurotic hallucinatory projection on the governess's part, ignited by her own subconscious fears and desires. The story is famously enigmatic. What is clear, however, is that on any reading 'innocence' is a contested term, shifting not only because of

79

adult influences but because the children, and perhaps all children, are unreadable. The fluidity of innocence in turn creates contested understandings of 'child' and 'childhood'. In *The Turn of the Screw*, one consequence is that despite the minor difference in their ages Miles cannot be considered either 'child' or 'innocent' in quite the sense that Flora can.

James's novel *What Maisie Knew* raises comparable questions and uncertainties. Maisie also as a small child is the object of a struggle between adult forces, though of a more domestic kind. Following her parents' divorce, custody of Maisie is divided equally between her father and mother, who use her as a missile through whom they can exchange their mutual vindictive hatred, so that 'the only link binding her to either parent was this lamentable fact of her being a ready vessel for bitterness'.[2] Neither parent, when the legal arrangement was made, 'figured in the least as a happy example to youth and innocence'.[3] One kindly relative tries and fails to mitigate this cruel arrangement. '"Poor little monkey!" she at last exclaimed; and the words were an epitaph for the tomb of Maisie's childhood'.[4] Thereafter the novel becomes a profound enquiry into the exact residual nature of Maisie's childhood and innocence, bound up with the question of what and how much she understands, with what effect on her, so that childhood and innocence — words to which at a simple level a high positive value is attached — again become ambivalent and uncertain concepts.

Graham Greene's devotion to James is generally acknowledged. Peter Mudford, for example, refers to 'his memorable essays on Henry James, whose religious sense of good and evil he admired and imitated'.[5] Although Greene had no need of literary precedents for his own presentation of childhood and children, it is striking how many variants there are in Greene of the preoccupations so ambivalently explored in *The Turn of the Screw* and *What Maisie Knew*. In Greene also a positive value is consistently accorded to childhood and innocence as necessary stages in human development. Along with this goes a moral consciousness of the harm that does or may occur when this development is violated, denied, or repressed. Greene is much less impeded than is James by any sense of the inscrutability or unknowability of childhood: he is a more confident and familiar observer, more accustomed than is James to using his own memory as a passport for excursions across the frontier to the lost childhood of the self and hence of others, but it is still the adult standpoint that essentially prevails.

The key antitheses observable in the two James novels are also prominent in Greene, and provide a thematic core for his many variations on innocence and childhood. Innocence is balanced against experience, especially premature experience, as it variously is in Miles, Flora and Maisie; it is balanced against guilt, as it arguably is in Miles; and it is balanced against knowledge and understanding, especially premature understanding, as in Maisie. In Greene, moreover, failure to experience timely innocence and childhood is equalled in danger, to the self and others, by failure to outgrow them. The antitheses are not mutually exclusive; they can perilously coexist, as they normatively and riskily do in adolescence. And they can persist into adult life, where they may take the form of a naïve irresponsibility, perhaps most memorably expressed concerning Pyle in *The Quiet American*:

> Innocence always calls mutely for protection when we would be so much wiser to guard ourselves against it; innocence is like a dumb leper who has lost his bell, wandering the world, meaning no harm.[6]

As in James, therefore, so in Greene we must allow for the fluidity of key terms, and especially of the word 'innocence'. It is an absolutely fundamental and recurrent term in Greene's fictional vocabulary, but slippery and elusive, ranging from the admiring to the pejorative, from a sacred quality to a dangerous vice. Set against its central antitheses, it changes meaning: innocence the opposite of experience is very different from innocence the opposite of guilt.

Greene is not in his full-length fictions much concerned except in passing with actual children. Apart from the late minor novel *The Captain and the Enemy*, there is no novel in which a child is a major character. Children are more frequent and significant presences in the short stories. But both 'innocence' and 'childhood' must be stretched beyond actual children to cover their significance in Greene, and they dominate two novels in particular. *The Ministry of Fear* is a major novel of childhood and innocence, though it includes only one self-remembered child. And the most important text of all concerns a boy-man, an adolescent, a poisoned mixture of developmental stages, Pinkie in *Brighton Rock*. He is the figure against whom all Greene's other innocents and children must be set.

BRIGHTON ROCK: INNOCENCE AND SIN

Although the usual antitheses of innocence in Greene, like those in James, are experience, knowledge, understanding, corruption, and guilt, the spiritual dimension of the word is never wholly absent in the

Roman Catholic novelist. Greene's usages of 'innocence' are chiefly secular, but the major exception is his presentation of 17-year-old Pinkie Brown in *Brighton Rock*. Pinkie (like his 'wife' and victim, 16-year-old Rose) is a Catholic, and he imports the terms of his faith to corrupted presence in his short career of immature evil. *Brighton Rock* is Greene's most comprehensive and inclusive study of innocence, its meaning and deformities, and also of childhood, in that Pinkie (always 'the Boy') is a psychologically rigorous and astutely imagined amalgam of child, boy, adolescent, and man, both prematurely adult and never other than a child.

In Pinkie's case the fundamental theological terms are necessary. We must think of original sin, and distinguish it from the sinful actions that Pinkie repeatedly commits. Original sin is the universal condition in which human beings enter the world, as a result of humanity's disobedience: religious understanding of the term derives from Genesis 3. The doctrine of original sin decrees that human beings arrive in the world with a nature that is prone to sinfulness. Therefore, the child at birth is not 'innocent' in an absolute sense, but is innocent of sinful actions. Pinkie, who throughout his evil career is much preoccupied (abusively) with innocence, in one key episode tries to trace its origins, and fails to find them anywhere in life, because for him the life of sinful actions is as absolute as the condition of original sin. The psychological causes of his spiritual plight lie buried in the very beginnings of his own life experience, which in Catholic terms has been deprived of the protective aid of parents and godparent, whose care allows the grace of Baptism — the sacrament that erases original sin and turns the child back toward God — to develop and unfold.

In Catholic terms again, before the first disobedience, which is the 'origin' of original sin, humanity existed in a state of original innocence (or original holiness). It is possible to use 'original innocence' in a modified spiritual sense to denote the period after birth (however brief) before the infant has committed sinful acts or has knowledge and experience of them. This reflects Pinkie's own attitude, in the passage I shall shortly consider. We can also think of 'original innocence' in a comparable but purely secular way, to cover the time of life preceding, in legal terms, the age of criminal responsibility, the ability to distinguish right from wrong. The word 'innocence' can be generally used to cover this infant phase, but the term 'original innocence' is best reserved for strictly theological application, not least because to do so illuminates the moral atrocity of Pinkie's offence against Rose.

Pinkie the boy-man gang leader marries Rose because potentially she is a dangerous prosecution witness in the murder of the journalist Hale that inaugurates the story. Legally, a wife cannot be obliged to testify against her husband, so for Pinkie marriage means safety. But it is a union he views with revulsion, because he is revolted by sex. Rose at 16 is innocent of sexual experience, but she is not innocent of insight into the connection between the act of sex and loving commitment to another person. Pinkie, who is himself pervertedly 'innocent' of sexual knowledge, uses the word against her, contemptuously, at the very beginning of his evil courtship. Asked by Pinkie whether she has been in love, Rose says she has:

> The Boy retorted with sudden venom, 'You would have been. You're green. You don't know what people do'. The music came to an end and in the silence he laughed aloud. 'You're innocent'.[7]

To place Pinkie's actions against Rose in their full Catholic context we can cite a formulation of 'original innocence' given by Pope John Paul II in 1980:

> Original Innocence belongs to the mystery of Man's beginning, from which historical man was then separated by committing original sin. This does not mean, however, that he is not able to approach that mystery by means of his theological knowledge. Historical man . . . tries to understand original innocence as an essential characteristic for the theology of the body, starting from the experience of shame. Original innocence, therefore, is what 'radically', that is, at its roots, excludes shame of the body in the man-woman relationship. It eliminates its necessity in Man, in his heart.[8]

It seems, then, that the nearest we can get as fallen humanity to glimpsing original innocence lies in the shame-free act of physical love within the sacramental union of marriage. The nature of Pinkie's marital transaction with Rose is a comprehensive violation of this. The union, as Rose herself is aware, is not a true marriage, because it is confirmed only by a civil contract and not by a religious sacrament. It is not even legally watertight, because Pinkie's actual age is fortuitously concealed. The notion of parental 'giving away' of the bride is perverted because Rose is in practice bought by Pinkie. Worse, however, far from being a ceremony of mutual love it is contracted on Pinkie's part in hate, made cruelly explicit in the sadistic recording that in the event is Pinkie's legacy to Rose. Pinkie's strategy involves luring Rose by the fraudulent pretence of a suicide pact into committing mortal sin, from which she narrowly saves herself. Worst of all, Pinkie is indeed governed in the physical relationship by 'shame of the body': he loathes the act of love, and yet their one feared consummation brings him as close as anything does to redemption. He is briefly freed of hate, both for Rose and for the act, instead finding 'a kind of pleasure, a kind of pride, a kind of—something else'.[9] Something strange, like love (Rose's, God's, the body's) confronts him, and is spurned. Therefore his relationship with Rose remains a comprehensive violation of everything redemptive in marriage and sexual love. He experiences a nameless intuition of original innocence, and rejects it.

The background to Greene's thinking here is necessary to appreciate the true enormity of Pinkie's offence against innocence. The vitriol that finally destroys Pinkie (perhaps Greene recalled the very similar destruction of the evil Huish in Robert Louis Stevenson's *The Ebb-Tibe*) is not so much divine retribution as symbolic of his evil's repeated tendency to recoil upon itself.

Pinkie hates and despises innocence. Shortly before his marriage, he inwardly complains: 'To be beaten by experience was bad enough, but to be beaten by greenness and innocence . . . by a little bitch of sixteen years . . '.[10] And yet at another level he also values innocence. His prolonged self-violation is only understandable if traced back to his own deformed childhood. In this key passage he is returning to the Brighton slums of his childhood to buy off Rose's parents:

> The children were scouting among the rubble with pistols from Woolworth's; a group of girls surlily watched. A child with its leg in an iron brace limped blindly into him; he pushed it off; someone said in a high treble, 'Stick 'em up'. They took his mind back and he hated them for it; it was like the dreadful appeal of innocence, but *there* was not innocence; innocence was a slobbering mouth, a toothless gum pulling at the teats; perhaps not even that; innocence was the ugly cry of birth.[11]

Pinkie is exact. He tracks innocence back through childhood, and finds it nowhere later than the moment of birth. Lack of innocence later is tied for him to the sexual mystification and disgust aroused by witnessing the Saturday night copulations of his parents. We can locate in the child Pinkie the toxic confusion of one innocence with another. Privy to this adult intimacy and yet alien from it, he is not innocent of premature experience but innocent of understanding. He is present yet excluded, and as an adolescent gangster this one exclusion undermines all his other precocious efforts to usurp adult criminal leadership. Hence his union with Rose is symptomatic of his spiritual chaos. "'It's mortal sin," he said, getting what savour there was out of innocence . . .'.[12] Cheated of true childhood innocence — a childhood undeformed by premature experience — he gladly spits on 'innocence' as a delusion. When he finds that Rose has known more than he supposed about the Kolly Kibber execution, 'he laughed softly with infinite contempt and superiority at a world which used words like "innocence."'[13]

We can see Pinkie, then, as psychologically explicable: the deformed product of a deforming childhood. The hints Greene gives us of Pinkie's later boyhood are consistent with Pinkie the boy-man: the bully who never shakes off the humiliating roles of outsider, underling and victim. He has put boyhood behind him very fast, becoming the boy-man gang leader at 17. Yet in other ways he has never grown up at all, never ceased to be a boy. Explicit proof of this comes in the final climactic episode of his life, his attempt to seduce Rose into suicide. (Seduction is how it is perceived by Rose herself, as she alternately consents to and resists his deathly blandishments as if they were an act and test of love.) Over and over in the closing pages Pinkie reverts to the child he has never escaped being. 'He looked with loathing into the past — a cracked bell ringing, a child weeping under the cane'.[14] And again, 'he was like a boy playing on an ash-heap'.[15] And again, 'Pinkie called out suddenly in a breaking childish voice'.[16] And again, 'his face . . . was like a child's, badgered, confused, betrayed—he was whisked back towards the unhappy playground'.[17] As he doubles up under the agony of the vitriol, 'He looked half his size', as if physically shrinking back into the dimensions of childhood, and finally, he 'shrank into a schoolboy flying in panic and pain'.[18] The boy stands fully revealed at last as, indeed, a boy.

In Pinkie the boy, then, we see Greene the Catholic and Greene the psychologist. Also present is Greene the post-Romantic. All writers — and all readers — in Western societies are heirs of the writers and artists of the Romantic period in our attitudes to childhood. Like it or not, we are William Wordsworth's children, whether or not we consciously share his ideology of childhood. He is part of our consciousness. Greene knew his Immortality Ode, and the resonance of the lines: 'Not in entire forgetfulness / And not in utter nakedness / But trailing clouds of glory do we come / From God, who is our home: / Heaven lies about us in our infancy!'[19] For Greene, in his own condition of post-Romantic disenchantment, these lines were open to revision. In the Prologue to *The Lawless Roads*, where he is recalling his own childhood, he remembers the teacher and the school bully met when he was 13 at Berkhamsted, and he wrote that 'one met for the first time characters, adult and adolescent, who bore about them the genuine quality of evil . . . Hell lay about them in their infancy'.[20] Teacher and bully not only made life hell for the young Greene. Since neither adult nor adolescent is any longer an infant, hell has in some sense *inhabited* them. It seems to be at once their heredity and their environment, as heaven was for Wordsworth. Similarly, we find Pinkie, full of aggressive teenage bravado after his interview with the police, proud of having killed his man: 'He trailed the clouds of his own glory after him: hell lay about him in his infancy. He was ready for more deaths'.[21]

The question then is raised, equally by Pinkie and the real-life terrorists of Berkhamsted: in what condition did they enter the world? Did they arrive not only in the condition of original sin, like all humanity, but with particular tendencies to evil already implanted before birth? Did Pinkie arrive trailing clouds not of glory but of evil, and is he therefore wrong to equate the loss of innocence with birth itself? Or is he in adolescence the product of the hell of his own infancy and childhood, the early experience of pain, humiliation, and sexual disgust that he hates to remember? The hell that lies about these real and fictional people in their infancy may or may not be a hell of their own making, and Greene's twice-told Wordsworthian inversion does not precisely resolve the ambiguity any more than Wordsworth's own positive vision does. In all these cases the creation of hell for other people may be an act of predetermined nature or an act of revenge against childhood experience.

This, of course, is the classic argument between nature and nurture. Greene's rewriting of Wordsworth in these two passages seems to leave his options open, but the bias in this and other stories appears to be toward nurture. The blame seems to lie with the damage caused by lack of love, by deforming experience, by mental and physical abuse, above all by the denial of childhood and the brief grace of provisional innocence. Pinkie is often regarded as a figure of pure evil, but in fact his early life accounts for him.

THE CHILD WITHIN

Even Pinkie, a mere adolescent, revisits his childhood for some atavistic knowledge of his older self. Elsewhere in Greene his treatment of childhood and innocence is made up of adults who do the same. Much the most extensive of these revisitings is that of Arthur Rowe in *The Ministry of Fear*. In most respects *The Ministry of Fear* is a Buchanesque thriller, very like *The Thirty-Nine Steps* in putting the hero in a series of seemingly ordinary but actually surreal and threatening events and situations. On this familiar level it is excellent, but two things make it quite exceptional. One is its humane and psychologically subtle approach to mercy killing, and the effects of it on the killer: an exemplary study that is far ahead of its time. The other (in its first phase one by-product of the killer's guilt) is Rowe's nostalgia for childhood.

One afternoon during the London Blitz, Rowe is accidentally drawn to a charity fête. Now free after serving the short sentence in a mental institution that a lenient judge has imposed for his 'crimes', Rowe has been refused useful war work and is eking out a dingy and guilt-ridden life as an outcast. Happier times are evoked by the seemingly innocuous event he comes across. 'The fete called him like innocence: it was entangled in childhood, with vicarage gardens and girls in white summer frocks'.[22] He approaches hesitantly, like 'an exile who has returned home after many years', and, when he pays his shilling and goes in, 'Arthur Rowe stepped joyfully back into adolescence, into childhood'.[23] In adolescence, he remembers, he went to the local fete in hope of meeting some ideal girl, but 'because these dreams had never come true there remained the sense of innocence'.[24] Now, 'His heart beat and the band played, and inside the lean experienced skull lay childhood'.[25]

These insistent evocations of remembered happiness all come in the first few pages, and the contrast with Pinkie is marked, reminding us that while Greene is consistently emphatic on the lasting importance of appropriate innocent happiness (or its denial) at the start of life, his gallery of fictional childhoods is remarkably diverse and free of stereotypes. Rowe was lucky in his beginnings. The little cluster of key words is reiterated like a musical theme: Rowe's childhood and adolescence are both linked with innocence and offset against experience, and their recall here comes to a man who, as we shortly learn, is an adult steeped in guilt. What Rowe finds in his first ingenuous encounter with the charity fête is a miniature replay of his long-lost fortunate early encounter with life itself. And again like life itself, it is not a state he can hope to maintain for long.

The change occurs with sinister absurdity when Rowe, prompted by a fortune-teller's hint, correctly guesses the weight of a cake and therefore wins it. The cake contains a file of secret documents, in process of transfer to enemy agents, and by sheer chance Rowe has uttered to the fortune-teller the words that wrongly identify him as the courier. He duly claims the cake, but the error is quickly realised by the quisling conspirators at the fête, and the mood changes. 'It was as if the experience of childhood renewed had taken a strange turn, away from innocence'.[26]

Thereafter, it is Rowe's persistence, first in carrying off his prize in defiance of efforts to stop him, and then in following up his curiosity about the mysterious events that follow, which leads him into danger and opens up the novel as a wartime spy thriller. His curiosity is nearly fatal: he is blown up in an assassination attempt, which fails to kill him but causes him to lose his memory. Before this happens, as the culmination of a nightmarish pursuit, he is trapped into believing himself the innocent chief suspect in another killing, and while needlessly on the run and sleeping rough he has a dream about his dead mother:

> 'My dear, my dear, my dear. I'm glad you are dead. Only do you know about it? do you know?' He was filled with horror at the thought of what a child becomes, and what the dead must feel watching the change from innocence to guilt and powerless to stop it.[27]

This first phase of the novel, then, until Rowe's loss of memory, begins with the brief nostalgic recovery of childhood innocence and then replays the process of experience. In this new adulthood Rowe's mind is tormented, as his dream reveals, between innocence of a killing of which he thinks the world considers him guilty, and guilt for a killing (a mercy killing) of which the law has deemed him morally innocent.

In the novel's second phase, after the memory loss, Rowe finds himself confined again in a mental institution, but this time one run by the enemy. To all appearances a private rural clinic, it is actually an outpost of the German spy network. Rowe as a patient with loss of memory is less embarrassing to the enemy than Rowe dead, so he finds himself immured there with a new name, Digby. He remembers his childhood and adolescence, though not his name, but nothing beyond. So the second half of the novel is a more deep-rooted rerun of the first. Again Rowe begins as a remembered child, but now with nothing later than childhood to distress him. He is well treated and innocently happy. In the first phase he and Anna, an Austrian refugee who is one of the enemy network, have fallen in love. Now, as her own loyalties are compromised by her love for him, she is still trusted by the enemy and allowed to visit him to assess the state of his memory. Naturally he does not recognise her:

> She stood there as he seemed to remember her from very far back, small, tense, on guard, and yet she was part of a whole world of experience of which he was innocent.[28]

This innocence too is naturally fated not to last. Sometimes Greene and Rowe are barely distinguishable. Rowe's first phase of regression includes affectionate recall of the High Street and King's Arms in (unnamed) Berkhamsted, and now, as Rowe's, or Digby's, re-entry into experience brings suspicions with it, he explores a part of the clinic closed off from his comfortable memory-free quarters:

> Ahead of him was the green baize door he had never seen opened, and beyond that door lay the sick bay. He was back in his own childhood, break-ing out of dormitory, daring more than he really wanted to dare, proving himself.[29]

Clearly we are back in Greene's own childhood, too, and Rowe's dou-ble reenactment of progression from innocence to experience makes him in part a surrogate for Greene. In the final phase of the novel, as these two progressions merge, the process of maturity is played out: 'Rowe was growing up; every hour was bringing him nearer to hailing distance of his real age'.[30]

The end brings Rowe and Anna together, in love and permanence, but a permanence flawed by a benign deception. Rowe's memory has largely returned, but Anna is desperate to protect him from the guilty knowledge of his first wife's death, the mercy killing that ruined his earlier life. Rowe, however, has discovered the truth, unknown to Anna, and in turn is desperate to prevent her from realizing that her effort to protect him is in vain. So even here, where Greene does not explicitly use the words 'innocence', 'experience', and 'knowledge', these concepts are still actively in play. Anna might well say, without the moral duplicity of the original, Macbeth's lines, 'Be innocent of the knowledge, dearest chuck / Till thou applaud the deed'.[31] But Rowe can never now be innocent of the knowledge, can never be innocent at all, can never in his own eyes atone for, still less applaud, his deed of mercy. In consequence, the very expression of love involves permanent mutual deception, in which pretended innocence of knowledge cov-ers a pretended innocence of guilt. And thus the primary innocence of childhood, experienced by Rowe three times in all, is carried into adult life as forged contraband essential to survival. *The Ministry of Fear* is a key text in our understanding of Greene's search into these themes, a profound and compassionate novel that makes nonsense of the reductive term, 'entertainment'.

Elsewhere in Greene there are other adult re-entries into child-hood. Perhaps the finest of these is the long short story, 'Under the Garden'. If Rowe is (as indeed he is) at least partially healed of adult damage by regressive memory of childhood, the hero of 'Under the Garden' is more evidently so. William Wilditch, a middle-aged man, has been diagnosed with what may be terminal cancer. An operation could save him, but he is disposed to accept his fate and, having lived his life abroad, intends to leave the country again. But first he is drawn to revisit Winton Hall, the country house where he spent summer holidays as a boy, and which is now owned by his brother. He is curious about an adventure he had there when he was seven. He remembers a lake, with a little island, in a hidden part of the garden. At seven, casting himself as an explorer (just as Rowe did as a boy) he crossed the lake, surveyed the island, and found a gap at the foot of a tree, like the opening to a cave. Bravely the boy crawled into it, and far below the garden came across mysterious living quarters underground, inhabited by an ancient man called Javitt and his partner, Maria, an inarticulate crone. (Greene himself notes the echo here of Beatrix Potter's *The Tale of Tom Kitten*, and hence the influence of his own childhood reading memories.) Here the boy, as William remembers it, was half-willingly imprisoned for several days, listening to Javitt's stories of his treasure and his observations on life in general, before escaping with one treasure, a golden po, back to the world above.

This could not really have happened. (Could it?) It must have been a dream. (Must it not?) On his return, William naturally finds that dimensions have shrunk; the lake is actually a small shallow pond, and the island barely worth the name. His later life has been one of materialist rationality and imaginative contraction. In the house he finds another earlier William, his 13-year-old self, who has written a story for the school magazine — obviously based on this adventure, but drained of much of its mystery and turned into a kind of *Treasure Island* pastiche. Even so, it had brought loud complaints from William's mother, who strongly disapproved of any mystery or fantasy. William's long-dead mother never appears, but casts a long shadow. She was a rationalist, a dealer in facts and statistics, a leftish political figure, militantly secular in outlook. She has insisted that the boys' schooling excludes contamination by religion. So even William's modest little fantasy at 13, a mere hackneyed sketch of the seven-year-old's adventure, roused her anger. And William's nomadic later life has obediently featured jobs purged of all fantasy.

Yet now that death is approaching, William in middle age is curious about this remembered adventure. However diminished the child explorer's world now seems, his memories of Javitt and Maria are remarkably circumstantial and detailed, including matters far beyond the knowledge or understanding of a seven-year-old. Back at the house, he starts to write down what he remembers about his underground adventure, and compare it with what his brother George recalls about his short disappearance. The two are not a good match:

> And here I am, already checking my story as though it were something which had really happened, for what possible relevance has George's memory to the events of a dream?
> I dreamed that I crossed the lake, I dreamed . . . that is the only certain fact and I must cling to it, the fact that I dreamed. How my poor mother would grieve if she could know that, even for a moment, I had begun to think of these events as true.[32]

'Under the Garden' is largely the story of William revisiting his childhood self, who is someone else, an ancestor. He *calls* the 13-year-old who wrote the school story his 'ancestor', and the boy of seven is the ancestor even of the 13-year-old. Wordsworth-like, the child is father to the man. The child we were both is and is not ourselves in later life. As he writes his memoir, the grown-up William seeks help from words that cut the adventure to rational size. He calls it story, imagination, game, legend, and above all 'dream'.

And he fails, or appears to. On the little island he finds an old tin chamber pot. 'He turned the pot over and over; it was certainly not a golden po, but that proved nothing either way; a child might have mistaken it for one when it was newly painted . . . There was no certainty'.[33]

This seems to be not just William's verdict, but Greene's. The options are kept open, certainly not omitting rational explanations, but not conceding them authority, either. Perhaps it is indeed the case that children have access to mysteries and truths that are erased by the rationalism of adulthood. Even if young William dreamed, what exactly is the power and truth of dream (a question that preoccupied Greene constantly)? We think again of Wordsworth: 'where is it now, the glory and the dream?' And of John Keats: 'Was it a vision, or a waking dream? / Fled is that music—Do I wake or sleep?'[34]

For William, at any rate, the revival of the child and his adventure is redemptive. 'He had a sense that there was a decision he had to make all over again. Curiosity was growing inside him like the cancer'.[35] He will not after all settle for death. The reawakened buried child can be an agent of self-renewal.

Greene's thinking is perhaps exemplified most clearly by the excellent short story, 'The Innocent'. A man of 30 arranges at modest cost to spend a night with Lola, a girl he has picked up casually, and takes her to a hotel in the country town where he grew up. The autumn evening of their arrival stirs memories of childhood. He breathes the smell of autumn dusk, and writes, 'I thought I knew what it was that held me. It was the smell of innocence'.[36] Tempted by this to retread the past, he recalls his first love affair, with a little girl in his dancing class when he was seven and she nearly eight. Remembering its intensity, he claims never to have made the mistake of laughing at children's love. Considering the intervening years, he says, 'It seemed a long journey to have taken to find only Lola at the end of it. There *is* something about innocence one is never quite resigned to lose'.[37] The little boy he once was, he remembers, wrote a passionate note to the little girl and left it in a wooden hole in a gate. Sure enough, after all these years it is still there. But he is shocked to find that it contains 'a picture of crude obscenity', a childish sketch of a man and a woman.[38]

At first he feels betrayed. Eager to trace his lost innocence, he finds what seems to him proof at first that the child was no more innocent than he is now, that childhood innocence is a myth and a self-deception. Only later, in bed with Lola, does he realise he was wrong. 'I began to realize the deep innocence of that drawing. I had believed I was drawing something with a meaning and beautiful; it was only now after thirty years of life that the picture seemed obscene'.[39] This story is another testament to Greene's belief in the brief existence (and vulnerability) of a secular 'original innocence' in children. What has taken it away in this instance is no form of corruptive molestation from the adult world, but the obduracy of mere time, experience, and adulthood itself.

THE CHILDREN

Childhood recalled by adults is generally a more benign and positive experience in Greene than is his representation of childhood in the act of being lived. Retrospects are often productive: there is even the cheering example, in the curious story 'The Hint of an Explanation', of a strange case of attempted spiritual child abuse that has the opposite effect to that sought by the abuser. Direct experience is usually much darker. Two contrasting but equally bleak instances occur in *The Power and the Glory*, in the persons of the whisky priest's seven-year-old daughter, Brigitta, and 13-year-old Coral Fellows, both in their different ways the victims of premature maturity.

When Brigitta's father, the fugitive priest, sees her after an interval, he does not at first recognise her. She was 'one who had been sharpened by hunger into an appearance of devilry and malice beyond her age. A young woman stared out of the child's eyes'.[40] Later, when he sees her for the last time, 'He was appalled again by her maturity'.[41] As with Flora in *The Turn of the Screw*, assaults against early innocence cause body as well as mind to age prematurely. Brigitta is a girl already corrupted by the world she lives in, by knowing too much too soon. 'The world was in her heart already, like the small spot of decay in a fruit'.[42]

Coral Fellows at 13 is the victim of another kind of deforming experience. Her parents are inept beyond belief, and make her another girl-woman, the victim of child-adult role reversal, forced by their failure to be more mature than they are and to manage their affairs because they cannot. Greene is clear about the consequences. As she checks off the bananas because her father has forgotten to, 'She felt no resentment at all at being there, looking after things: the word "play" had no meaning to her at all—the whole of life was adult'.[43] And then, when the pains of menstruation start, 'You couldn't call it childhood draining out of her: of childhood she had never really been conscious'.[44] And yet, stranded as she is between states of growth, she still is in part a child: 'The child stood in her woman's pain'.[45] Moreover, she questions the whisky priest 'with the cold curiosity of a child',[46] much as Victor Baxter in *The Captain and the Enemy*, another victim of enforced developmental incongruities caused by adults, remembers in himself at 12 'the cold curiosity of my age'.[47]

Coral's mistreatment is obviously very different from Brigitta's, but just as damaging. The harm to both lies in being old-young, and suffering an inversion of norms between adult and child. It may, as here, cancel childhood and hence cause a distorted version of maturity. On the other hand, it may as in the case of Victor lead to failure ever to grow up at all. Victor is not loved by anyone; he is merely used by adults as an instrument of their own frustrated or imperative needs, with the consequence that he never learns to love, has no models of feeling by which he can learn to feel. So he remains dangerously innocent, an innocence coterminous in his case with ignorance. Never growing up, he is destroyed in the end by a final regressive childlike impulse, sentenced by early life to be always an outsider. (Victor is in some respects a tragic infantile version of the fortunate Henry Pulling in *Travels with my Aunt*.)

Greene's most famous treatment of a breach of early innocence causing permanent emotional arrest comes in the short story 'The Basement Room', which became the film *The Fallen Idol*. Here in very different circumstances from those of Baxter is another child abused by adults, so undergoing premature and, in this case, actively unwanted exposure to the adult world.

The heart of the story lies in several references to Philip Lane dying, 60 years after the story's events. At seven he is a well-off boy, between nurses, left by his parents in the care of the married butler and housekeeper, Baines and Mrs Baines. This terrible hate-filled mockery of a marriage is not Philip's business. Baines is conducting an affair behind Mrs Baines's back, but not alas without her knowledge. This is not Philip's business, either. Nor does he wish it to be. He is a perfectly normal little boy, until Baines and Mrs Baines have finished with him. He wants grown-ups to keep their distance. 'Let grown-up people keep to their world and he would keep to his'.[48] He does not like it when Baines behaves childishly. 'For if a grown-up could behave so childishly, you were liable to find yourself in their world'.[49] Naturally, he does not understand their world, and 'the things he didn't understand terrified him'.[50] Instead of keeping their distance, the adults entrust him with secrets he does not want, and involve him as a hapless conspirator in affairs he does not comprehend. Again we see the terrible damage caused by an inversion of roles.

One of the story's ironies is that Philip is innocent, but the word is not used about him. It is used only about Baines, whose previous life on service in Africa has left him an extremely inept adulterer. Greene insistently applies the word to Baines: 'he kept on reverting to the Coast as if to excuse himself for his innocence. He wouldn't have been so innocent if he'd lived in London, so innocent when it came to tenderness'.[51] Adult innocence is dangerous. It savages Philip's innocence, exposing him to scenes he can never outgrow. The result is a life of 'long austerity'[52] and loneliness, in which he 'never built anything, never created anything, died the old dilettante, sixty years later with nothing to show . . .'.[53] 'Life fell on him with savagery, and you couldn't blame him if he never faced it again in sixty years'.[54] This great story's psychology of boyhood is exactly the same as L. P. Hartley's in *The Go-Between*, nearly 20 years after Greene's was first published.

Creativity is killed in Philip's case. In that of 14-year-old Trevor in 'The Destructors', creativity is perverted. This is the story of a gang of teenagers, led by Trevor, who systematically destroy a house — a Christopher Wren house — in the owner's absence over a bank holiday weekend. This famous story is a controversial class reader in the American 2001 film, *Donnie Darko*, a psychological fantasy. When the lead character in the film is asked in class why the destructors do the destructing, he says: 'Destruction is creative. They just want to see what happens when they tear the world apart. They want to change things'. The remark is perceptive, but it applies strictly to Trevor himself, who shows disturbingly the power of psychotic leadership to recruit and control the young. Greene's key line in the story is 'destruction after all is a form of creation. A kind of imagination had seen this [dismantled] house as it had now become'.[55] But *what* kind of imagination? Trevor stands for the exact reverse of creativity. His father is an architect who has come down in the world, and Trevor is the complete anti-architect. A feature of his artwork of destruction is that he meticulously unmakes the house and its contents in the exact reverse order of that in which they came together. And he does it without profit: bank notes are systematically torn up, not stolen. And he is virtually free of personal malice. His gang partner Blackie assumes that he must hate 'Old Misery', the owner. "'Of course I don't hate him," Trevor said. "There'd be no fun if I hated him. All this hate and love, it's soft, it's hooey. There's only things, Blackie."'[56] Trevor wishes to change things, not people. W. H. Auden observed that 'there is something slightly sinister about every practical joker, for they betray him as someone who likes to play God behind the scenes'.[57] The destruction of the house is a kind of practical joke, yet Trevor escapes all Auden's definitions of the practical joker, because his target is things, not people, and is pursued with utter joylessness.

Trevor is the most disturbed and alarming of all Greene's children, but his perverted artistry is shown to be rooted like the disorder of so many others in the ruinous condition of not having been a child. When Old Misery threatens the work's completion by returning early, Trevor protests against the unfairness of it, 'with the fury of the child he had never been'.[58]

CONCLUSION

In Greene's depiction of children across the novels and stories we find again and again a note of compunction and remorse concerning the effect of the adult world on children, the effect of experience on innocence. Sometimes it is voiced by an adult character, sometimes implied by the narrator. It is there very early, in the so-called entertainments, and is still there in *The Captain and the Enemy*. Some of the most interesting voices are heard in the early novels, like that of D in *The Confidential Agent*. D inadvertently causes the death — the murder, in fact — of the 14-year-old hotel chambermaid, Else, who has helped him. As he gets to know her in the hotel he is horrified by the evidence of her innocence, coupled as it is with ingenuous premature streetwise knowledge, her encounter with the world that will steal her innocence away. In D's remarks about Else there are clear signs of that compunction I have mentioned, the sorrow that a child has been exposed to premature contamination. 'She had all the innocence,' he says, 'of a life passed since birth with the guilty'.[59] Again, 'Her innocence and her worldly knowledge filled him with horror'.[60] And again, 'Fourteen was a dreadfully early age at which to know so much and be so powerless'.[61] Else is a minor character, but Greene's treatment of her plight is typically reiterated and insistent: a kind of indignation habitually underlies his presentation of this theme, so powerfully felt that here as elsewhere the voices of author, narrator and character become all but indistinguishable.

In *The Quiet American* Pyle is told by Thomas that there is no such thing as an uncomplicated child.[62] Every child and recollected childhood considered in this chapter is indeed complicated, and the complication lies in that hazardous transaction in child and adolescent between innocence and experience as the mysteries of adulthood impinge. Like his character in 'The Innocent', Greene sees innocence as something he is not quite resigned to lose, so in his writing we find a clear alignment with the child, coupled with a troubled knowledge of the frailty of innocence and the necessity of its loss. This vision of childhood is remarkably consistent across his career.

There is a curious expression in English: 'injured innocence'. It is often used of children, and describes a look on the face of a guilty person, claiming to be hurt and wounded by unjust accusations. If we strip that usage away, and take the phrase in its serious, literal meaning, it stands for something we repeatedly find in Greene. 'Injured innocence' exactly describes the typical condition of his children, as the scar tissue of adult humankind begins to form.

CHAPTER 6

Janiform Greene: The Paradoxes and Pleasures of *The Power and the Glory*

Cedric Watts

This chapter has four parts, entitled respectively 'Preamble', 'Paradoxes', 'Pleasures of the Text' and 'Comedy'.[1] The argument of the whole is that Graham Greene's novel *The Power and the Glory* is, on large and small scales, more paradoxical in content and therefore more durable than might once have been thought. We may fruitfully regard it as janiform, its tutelary deity being Janus, the two-faced god who looks in opposite directions at the same time. One emerging paradox of its reception is that, these days, this reputedly Roman Catholic novel may appeal to the sceptic as much, or almost as much, as to the Christian.

PREAMBLE

Recently, having agreed to lecture on *The Power and the Glory* at the annual Graham Greene Festival at Berkhamsted, I reread the novel in some trepidation. David Lodge once stated that it 'stands up to re-reading less well than some of the later works'.[2] I had long regarded it as Greene's most brilliant novel; and numerous critics treat it as the best of Greene's fictional works. *The Power and the Glory* was first published in 1940, and won the Hawthornden Prize. When I started to reread it, the reason for my trepidation was obvious. I thought: 'Surely, by now, it will seem dated. The prose will seem old-fashioned. Its dilemmas will belong to the past. The Roman Catholic Church today is not the Church that Greene knew in the 1930s: its doctrines and rituals have variously been modified. Many of today's British students regard as natural and proper a secular materialistic outlook. The conflict of Marxism with Catholicism, which greatly preoccupied Greene, has dwindled. Today, it is not Marxism that looms large on the political horizon. It is Islamism'.

Hence my trepidation when rereading *The Power and the Glory*; but, to my relief, it seemed better than ever. It revealed subtleties that I had missed at previous readings. This novel is concise, vivid, elegantly structured, sharply intelligent, thematically rich, philosophically and theologically searching, and emotionally moving. It is a 'chase novel', a suspense thriller, and a thought-provoking study of persecution. The prose is still fresh, clear, surprising, distinctive, and engaging, with no fat or vapidity. The intelligence is often heterodox, seeking to challenge conventional attitudes. Ironies interlace the narrative. And its paradoxes, large, medium, and small, operate through the mind and the senses.

PARADOXES

A paradox is an apparent contradiction that yields a truth or part truth; it resembles a discord resolvable as harmony. Here follows a small (but expanding) paradox. The main character is called 'the whisky priest'. He calls himself that; others call him that; and it's what the academic commentators call him. 'The whisky priest'. And now, your attention having been thus solicited, you may already have noticed what is odd about that term. Throughout the novel, that priest never touches a drop of whisky. Oh yes, he drinks brandy, wine and beer, and more brandy. But not whisky. There is a mismatch. It seems deliberate. If so, why? Probably because it provides a little clue to what happens extensively in this novel. Repeatedly, there is a mismatch between seeming and being, between label and reality. For instance: the jacket of a romantic novel conceals the priest's Latin breviary. But the romantic novel is called *La Eterna Mártir* (The Eternal Martyr), so the mismatch indicates a truth: martyrdom continues. The novel's ending, in which the protagonist is executed but is replaced by a newcomer, is here adroitly anticipated. Again: the priest drunkenly baptises a boy with a girl's name, Brigitta – a farcical mismatch; but a man comments, 'It's a good saint's name'.[3] It still does a Christian job. But why 'Brigitta'? Much later, we learn that it's because the priest was thinking of his daughter, and that is *her* name. (When making the nomenclatural choice, he may aptly have invoked Saint Brigitta of Ireland, for she was generous to the poor.)

Of course, a *big* paradox in this series is that while the central character, that anonymous priest, increasingly regards himself as a great mismatch (a religious failure), we increasingly realise that he is a saint in the making.

His grounds for seeing himself as a failure are obvious. He is a semi-alcoholic; he has known despair; he has fathered an illegitimate child, and he finds that his love for that child prevents him from being properly penitent for his sexual sin. He recalls that once, when he led a comfortable life, he was proud and complacent. But he now covertly remains in a dangerous region of Mexico (a Mexican state in which religion is forbidden and priests may be shot), so that he can minister to the ordinary people. Surely that entails moral courage? The priest himself denies it. Near the end, he says this: 'It would have been much better, I think, if I had gone [. . .]'. (By 'gone', he means 'fled from the region'.) He continues:

> Because pride was at work all the time. Not love of God [. . .]. Pride's the worst thing of all. I thought I was a fine fellow to have stayed when the others had gone. And then I thought I was so grand I could make my own rules. I gave up fasting, daily Mass. I neglected my prayers—and one day because I was drunk and lonely—well, you know how it was, I got a child. It was all pride. Just pride because I'd stayed [. . .]. I'd got so that I didn't have a hundred communicants a month. If I'd gone I'd have given God to twelve times that number.[4]

And, when the Marxist lieutenant says, 'Well, you're going to be a martyr,' the priest replies, 'Oh no. Martyrs are not like me. They don't think all the time—if I had drunk more brandy I shouldn't be so afraid'.[5] So our priest is apparently condemned out of his own mouth. On the morning of his execution he feels 'only an immense disappointment because he had to go to God empty-handed, with nothing done at all'.[6] He had expected, and still expects, damnation for himself. Indeed, like such later Greenian protagonists as Scobie in *The Heart of the Matter*, Sarah in *The End of the Affair*, and Father Callifer in *The Potting Shed*, he tries to make a substitutive bargain with God. (A whole book could be written on this preoccupation of Greene's.) The priest's bargain involves his illegitimate child, who is depicted as having fallen from innocence into tainting experience. He says: 'O God, help her. Damn me, I deserve it, but let her live for ever'.[7] Nevertheless, as he prepares for death, he reflects that he has been so useless that perhaps he is not even 'Hell-worthy'. Greene was potently influenced by T. S. Eliot's notorious essay on Charles

Baudelaire, which declares: 'The worst that can be said of most of our malefactors, from statesmen to thieves, is that they are not men enough to be damned. Baudelaire was man enough for damnation'.[8] So *one* half of the paradox of the whisky priest is that he is a disgrace to the church, a semi-alcoholic with an illegitimate child; a man who, if he is to be believed, has been motivated largely by pride and is a complete failure. He doesn't even look like a hero: he is small, with sloping shoulders and yellow decaying teeth. He leaves a trail of death: four hostages have been slain because they would not betray him.

The *other* half of the paradox is that he is clearly a saint in the making. The more he rebukes himself for pride, the more we are aware of his humility. He constantly criticises himself and endeavours to see the best in others. By remaining, at the risk of his life, he has not only administered the Mass to the faithful, he has set an influential and salutary example. He thinks he is useless; but we see that numerous people have had their lives touched by his life. After his execution, a pious mother speculates that he may become a saint, and she mentions that, already, precious relics, perhaps pieces of a bloodstained handkerchief, are being sold. The theme of the priest's influence is extensive; indeed, *The Power and the Glory* has an extensive covert plot on this theme.

A useful technical term coined by Ian Watt is 'delayed decoding'.[9] Delayed decoding occurs when a writer gives first an *effect* and second, but only after a marked delay, the *cause* of that effect. *The Power and the Glory* abounds in delayed decoding. For instance, the novel's second paragraph tells us that Mr Tench passes 'the Treasury, which had once been a church': pages elapse before we understand why a Treasury has replaced a church; and we may then recognise the irony that an atheistic régime (reversing the actions of Jesus as reported in Mt. 21.12, 13, and Mk 11.15-17) has put the money-changers back into the temple, perhaps creating a new 'den of thieves'. Another example, given just now, was the delay before we learn why the priest uttered the name 'Brigitta'. When delayed decoding is used on a large scale, it may become covert plotting. A covert plot is one that, at a first reading of a literary work, is not seen by the reader as a coherent sequence. The reader sees elements of it, but not the entirety. Only at a second or subsequent reading is the plot-sequence likely to emerge as a clear, coordinated entity.[10] A second reading of *The Power and the Glory* reveals that numerous seemingly disparate elements of the plot are coordinated by the changes for the better that have been effected by the priest's presence. Mr Tench, the boy Luis, Coral Fellows, some of the villagers, the hostile woman in the jail, and even the Marxist lieutenant: all have apparently been touched by grace.

Tench, the dentist, after meeting the priest, is moved to write to his wife in England to try to re-establish their relationship. He may not succeed (for she has fallen into bad ideological company), but at least he has made the effort. The novel's treatment of the boy Luis is more extensive. The realism of Greene's narrative concerning the whisky priest is made the more persuasive by its lengthy contrastive quotations from a supposed work of Catholic propaganda and hagiography. A Catholic mother reads to her children the story of a recent martyr, Father Juan, who defied the atheistic law by ministering to the people but was arrested and shot. The story stresses ad nauseam the supposed virtues, the sweet saintly nature, of this priest. Understandably, the boy Luis shows signs of rebellion against such indoctrination: he expresses boredom and scepticism. For him, a more convincing hero is the local Marxist lieutenant: he is delighted to be allowed to touch the officer's revolver, and the lieutenant feels proud that he is winning young followers for the atheistic cause. But Luis, after hearing of the execution of the whisky priest, turns in resentment against the officer and spits on his revolver butt. In contrast, as the novel ends, the boy kisses the hand of a new priest who clandestinely arrives to take the place of the martyr. We do not hear the new priest's name; it is the continuity of the sacred office that counts. Just before the knock at the door from the newcomer, Luis had dreamt that the dead whisky priest 'winked at him — an unmistakable flicker of the eyelid, just like that', so that we may detect a sign of complicity, a hint of resurrection, a glint of victory for the faith.[11] Greene was strongly influenced by J. W. Dunne, who had accumulated evidence to demonstrate that dreams could be truly premonitory: a theory related to the orthodox Christian belief that all time is simultaneously present in the mind of God or, as Dunne called Him, the 'Master-mind'. (Greene's most modernistic tale, *The Bear Fell Free*, is exuberantly Dunnian, chronologically layered like an onion.)[12]

The whisky priest returns from safety to danger, knowingly entering an ambush, in order to administer the last rites to James Calver, the dying gangster.[13] Calver is aware that he is being used as bait, and in his dying moments he tries to help the priest by offering him a knife. The priest prays for him, saying, 'O merciful God, after all he was thinking of me'; and though the prayer is 'without conviction', a kind of altruism was indeed there in the gangster's action.[14] One cruel irony of the situation is that Calver's victims, we gradually realise, include Coral Fellows, who had previously sheltered the priest.

So, in addition to the large-scale covert plot concerning the priest's transformative power, there is a briefer covert plot concerning Coral's death. That death is never directly described. Once again, we experience markedly delayed decoding that becomes a short sequence of covert plotting. When the fugitive priest had revisited the Fellows' homestead, he had found it deserted except for a broken-backed starving dog: some disaster had befallen the place. Near the end of the novel, we find that Coral's parents are returning to England. They try not to talk about her death, but the topic obtrudes; and random references combining with the couple's mutual recriminations enable us eventually (probably at a second reading) to infer what has happened. The references include the phrases 'that scoundrel', 'running away and leaving her', and 'If you'd been at home'.[15] Slowly, we work out that what happened was this: When Captain Fellows was away from the homestead, Calver had arrived there. Mrs Fellows, a depressive hypochondriac, always fearful of death, fled from the intruder. Coral, always brave and responsible, tried to drive Calver away. We know that long previously, she had warded off the lieutenant, threatening to set the dog on him; but on this occasion, it appears, the intruder maimed the dog and shot Coral. It may seem strange that such dramatic material is not presented directly by Greene but is left to be inferred by us. One explanation is that Greene admired Joseph Conrad, who liked oblique techniques. For instance: in Conrad's novel *The Secret Agent*, the violent death of the innocent boy, Stevie, is not presented directly, but gradually has to be inferred by us. Conrad once remarked: 'One writes only half the book; the other half is with the reader'.[16] But there is a better explanation. By leaving plot gaps, which we subsequently fill by inference, Greene attunes us to the notion of a God who (in William Cowper's words) 'moves in a mysterious way / His wonders to perform'.[17] The Christian God is a covert plotter, too. Furthermore, Greene employs the paradox that Eliot exploited in *The Waste Land*: an apparent absence of God may simply be a test of our ability to recognise His presence, by intelligence or faith. Covert plotting and theological 'hide and seek' are parts of the Christian tradition.

In *The Power and the Glory*, Coral's parents appear to have no religious belief; and Coral herself had said that she lost her faith 'at the age of ten'.[18] She, however, had met both the lieutenant and the priest, and had sided with the priest, taking him food and drink, and resenting his persecution. She teaches him part of the Morse code, as a means of communication, and actually chooses two longs and a short: the Morse for G: perhaps it stands for God. Her parents later remark that 'she went on afterwards—as if he'd told her things'.[19] One implication is that the priest may have restored Coral's faith. The confirmation of this, in Greenian terms, is provided in the following way. After her death, and on the eve of his execution, the priest has a strange dream. In a cathedral, he feels detached from the Mass until Coral appears and fills his glass with wine. She says, 'I got it from my father's room'.[20] The cleric and congregation then tap a sign in Morse code: three longs and a short. To us and to *Webster's Dictionary* it may be merely a coded exclamation mark;[21] but Coral decodes it as the word 'News'. And it's evidently good news: the priest wakes with, we are told, 'a huge feeling of hope'.[22] Well, a sceptic may say, 'It's only a dream'; but it hints that Coral, after death, has become an intermediary who can offer the priest a glimpse of his salvation to come. Perhaps, like Beatrice with Dante, she may guide the pilgrim heavenwards.

One of Greene's later tales is called 'The Last Word'. It describes a future era in which atheistic totalitarianism has prevailed and the last Pope is kept alive only as a figure of scorn. Eventually, he is taken before the arch dictator, a general, and shot. Yet, even as the trigger is pulled, the general reflects, 'Is it possible that what this man believed may be true?', and the implication is that the message of faith has, after all, been transmitted to posterity.[23] In *The Power and the Glory*, Greene has established an elegant contrast and contest between the whisky priest and the atheistic lieutenant. Both are idealists; both work hard for their ideals; and both are concerned about the poor and the children. And both are ideologically opposed. The lieutenant is in some ways priest-like. We are told this:

> There was something of a priest in his intent observant walk—a theologian going back over the errors of the past to destroy them again.
>
> He reached his own lodging [. . .]. In the light of a candle it looked as comfortless as a prison or a monastic cell [. . .].
>
> He was a mystic, too, and what he had experienced was vacancy — a complete certainty in the existence of a dying, cooling world, of human beings who had evolved from animals for no purpose at all. He knew.[24]

During the meetings between the lieutenant and the priest, some fellow feeling is established. Eventually, experiencing sympathy with and respect for the priest, the lieutenant seeks (illegally and unavailingly) to fetch a confessor for him. Here the cowardice of Padre José, the married ex-priest, contrasts tellingly with the courage of the whisky priest. (Repeated use of such mutually illuminating contrasts helps to generate the book's vividness.) Next, the lieutenant brings our priest, again illegally, a bottle of brandy. 'You're a good man,' the priest had told him earlier. 'You aren't a bad fellow,' the lieutenant tells him now.[25] After the execution, the officer finds that (in Greene's acerbically paradoxical phrasing) 'the dynamic love which used to move his trigger-finger felt flat and dead'. Perhaps that atheistic commitment will return; but perhaps, like the general in 'The Last Word', the lieutenant has been inflected toward religious belief.[26]

And numerous other people, whom the priest has met or helped, have possibly been strengthened in their faith or nudged toward the faith because of him: notably the fellow sufferers in the stinking jail, and the people of his home village. A proud woman in the prison rebukes him for bringing the Church into disrepute, but, later, in a charitable lie, intervenes to save him from being recognised by the lieutenant. Again, his sly daughter, termed a 'little devil', temporarily, if unintentionally, saves him. She identifies him to the lieutenant as her father; and the lieutenant (familiar with the rule of celibacy) is thereby persuaded that the fellow must really be a peasant and not a priest. Furthermore, even the treacherous Judas figure grudgingly observes, 'You may be a saint for all I know,' and seeks the whisky priest's blessing.[27] The priest's execution takes place not in the customary public location, a cemetery, but in a private yard. The reason given is that otherwise '[t]here might have been a demonstration', a popular protest against the authorities.[28]

Thus, the narrative in which a representative of the Church is apparently defeated is one of covert victory for the faith. Abandonment has not, after all, been total. When in Mexico, in Orizaba, Greene felt that 'it was like Galilee between the Crucifixion and the Resurrection'. He says this in the travel book *The Lawless Roads*.[29] According to the New Testament, after Christ's crucifixion the disciples felt abandoned on the journey to Emmaus, but Christ was present and accompanied them unrecognised. At the outset of *The Power and the Glory*, abandonment is repeatedly stressed: there is a symphonic orchestration of the theme. Tench experiences 'the huge abandonment'. The priest feels that 'he was abandoned'. The church has been abolished by the state; and Luis's father says, 'We have been abandoned here'.[30] Greene, in his travels through those regions of Mexico where the Catholic Church had been prohibited, had not only experienced a sense of nightmarish vacancy but had also recalled Cardinal Newman's sombre words about the 'aboriginal calamity' of a human race 'discarded' from God's presence.[31] As *The Power and the Glory* unfolds, however, and as irony dovetails with irony, plot detail with plot detail, so the overt and covert plotting of the narrative imply a covert plot in the world: that the apparent defeat of faith is merely a test for the faithful and the ground of new victories for divine grace. To put it another way: in the novel *The Power and the Glory*, the emerging paradox of the title phrase from the Lord's Prayer is this: the *power* of God is manifested in apparent weakness and defeat, while the *glory* of God is manifested through the base, mundane and sordid. Like the immediate author, the ultimate author is a covert plotter who loves paradox.

But those last few sentences are not quite right, because they make the novel sound too much like Christian propaganda. The novel succeeds because it entertains.

PLEASURES OF THE TEXT

The large sales of *The Power and the Glory*, the high critical praise accorded it, and (in the experience of teachers) the responses of students from a variety of religious and irreligious backgrounds, show that the novel has a remarkably wide appeal. It seems to be enjoyed almost as much by sceptics as by believers.

One reason for this is that Greene boldly preempts the sceptic. He lets the lieutenant and other characters voice familiar hostile arguments. One such argument is that priests line their own pockets while promising 'pie in the sky' to the poor. The lieutenant uses that one. The priest is sheltered by Mr Lehr, who criticises his Church from a Lutheran standpoint: Roman Catholic churches value luxury, Lehr says, while the people starve. Some Catholics (Luis's mother, and that proud woman in jail, and Maria) criticise the priest for being a disgrace to the faith. He himself is his own severest critic, noting his own pride, lust and cowardice. He also comments bitterly on the prosperous, complacent levels of the Church's hierarchy: he has known them at first hand. So the readers' scepticism is preempted and incorporated. Furthermore, the priest attracts left-wing sympathy. He moves among the poorest of the poor, sharing their squalor and wretchedness. Stinking, confused and weary, he makes a credibly flawed and sympathetic victim.

Numerous atheistic readers can suspend disbelief in religious premises when reading and enjoying religious poetry by, for example, John Donne or John Milton, or Gerard Manley Hopkins. Similarly, such readers may suspend disbelief when reading *The Power and the Glory*. They may choose temporarily to imagine that among the characterisations, God is as real as is the priest. Even if they cannot, the novel may still be powerfully effective. It may seem to describe eloquently the folly of human beings who are seduced into intolerance or suffering by inflexible ideologies that sacrifice the pulsing present on the altar of an illusory future.

But that, again, may make it sound too moralistic. The value of a good literary work lies less in any paraphrasable message than in the richness of the imaginative experience that the work offers. To engage us with that experience, suspense is necessary. A student, after reading *The Power and the Glory*, said to me: 'This novel is a good page-turner, isn't it?' Obviously, he meant that it gripped him and made him read on rapidly to discover the outcome. One secret of 'a good page-turner' is this. Early in the reading, we formulate some big question that engages our mind and emotions and that seems to have at least two opposed answers. As we proceed through the work, we inspect the accumulating evidence to see which of the answers may prevail. The more evenly balanced the evidence, for and against, the greater is our suspense. The authorial trick is to keep the scales in motion but not clattering down on one side or the other. In the case of *The Power and the Glory*, we are soon engaged by this question: Will the priest elude pursuit, or will he be caught and killed? Evidence to *support* the notion that he will escape is ample. He is intelligent, kind, and resourceful, and we like him. But the evidence *against* his escape is also ample. He is absentminded, he is isolated; and his pursuers are numerous and are driven by the lieutenant, who himself is intelligent and resourceful. What's more, the terrain is often hostile, and the priest's sense of duty imperils him. So there is *one* big suspense principle. But Greene loves paradoxes. Therefore he gives another, and conflicting, suspense principle. Now the big question is this: Will the priest evade his religious destiny or fulfil it? Evidence that he will evade it includes, again, the fact that he is so resourceful: he could indeed manage to cross the border into safety; and he does so. In contrast, evidence that he will fulfil it includes the fact that he repeatedly jeopardises his own safety by trying to minister to those who request or need him. At the beginning, he *literally* misses the boat to safety because a woman requests his priestly ministration. At the end, he *metaphorically* misses the boat to safety because, although he has crossed the border, he responds to the request to attend the dying gangster. So Greene has mastered a *double* suspense principle in which the theological plays against the secular. Our secular imagination wants the priest to escape. Our theological imagination, in contrast, wants the priest to fulfil his destiny, which is not to escape but to be a martyr and eventually a saint. A janiform structure thus emerges. I suspect that many an atheistic or agnostic reader has been seduced not only into imagining that the most important character in this novel is, after all, God rather than the priest, but also into estimating how God's intentions are being fulfilled as the events unfold. In this novel, covert characterisation accompanies covert plotting.

Another reason for the appeal of *The Power and the Glory* is that, although the territory traversed is a familiar Greeneland, it is now a Greeneland within which there is scope for sympathy, compassion, and even joy. Since his hero must express the Christian virtues of love, charity, and compassion, Greene is obliged to mitigate his own former sombre harshness. In such previous novels as *Stamboul Train* and *Brighton Rock*, and even in the nonfictional *The Lawless Roads*, that harshness came all too easily to Greene's depressive imagination. In *The Power and the Glory*, Greene moves toward a more humane balance. If the priest's daughter seems tainted, young Coral exudes hope. 'Hate was just a failure of imagination,' reflects the priest.[32] This novel works hard to encourage an extension of the sympathetic imagination. The wretchedness of the villagers in the forest; the squalor of the prisoners in the jail; the mourning of the Indian woman with her slain child; even animals such as the burdened donkey and the maimed dog: all these are evoked by an eye that does not glare with fascinated disgust, but rather seeks to observe, discriminate, and understand. As it does so, it craftily plays a gamut of theological and political feelings in the reader. Right-wing, liberal, and left-wing feelings are mingled: the traditional Catholic faith is made to seem relevant to the present, and is linked to the sympathetic observation of the poor and the oppressed. There Greene anticipates 'liberation theology' by about 30 years.

Another feature of the novel that may be underestimated is the nature of its realism. *The Power and the Glory* is richly evocative, and the descriptions of people and places have strange vividness. In a novel, realistic descriptions can be tedious if they report what we already know or assume to be the case. On the other hand, realistic descriptions can be persuasive and engaging if they offer information that is cogent but new to us, or if they surprise us into fresh awareness of a situation, or if they seem to be looking at the situation from an unexpected angle. Repeatedly in *The Power and the Glory*, Greene provides this oblique and surprising quality. Here are just three examples. On his journey, the priest reflects: 'One of the oddest things about the world these days was that there were no clocks — you could go a year without hearing one strike'.[33] And we learn that that's because the clocks were on the churches, which have been demolished. Second example: when the *jefe*, the Chief of Police, is playing billiards, the score is recorded not on a board but by means of rings strung on a cord across the room; and when the Chief's game is briefly interrupted by the lieutenant, we are told that 'somebody raised a cue and surreptitiously pushed back one of the *jefe*'s rings'.[34] The little detail of cheating gives utter plausibility to that unexpected method of keeping score, and in turn to the locality and its denizens. Third example: this is how the novel describes the priest's entry into the yard where he is to be shot:

> A small man came out of a side door: he was held up by two policemen, but you could tell that he was doing his best—it was only that his legs were not fully under his control. They paddled him across to the opposite wall [. . .].[35]

The reflective priest whom we have known so intimately is suddenly seen in a coolly objectifying perspective as 'A small man'. You can tell he's 'doing his best', we are told: presumably because he holds his head up and looks determined; but of course his legs are not fully under his control: when we are in a state of terror, our knees go wobbly. And that word 'paddled' in 'They paddled him across' is unexpected but precise. If you paddle a canoe, there is an alternating pressure on first one side and then the other, and a slightly zigzagging course; so, that word 'paddled' fits surprisingly well the motion of someone who, with legs disabled by fear, is being swung along between two other people.

Another open secret of the book's descriptive vividness is the abundance of 'leopards'. In the autobiographical volume *A Sort of Life*, Greene says that he used to be all too fond of 'leopards', his term for similes that are so unusual they seem to leap out at you.[36] Like the 'conceits' of English metaphysical poetry, some may be remarkable for their oddity rather than for their aptness. They often have a quality of paradox because they link the abstract with the concrete, or vice versa. Two quite famous examples are: 'He drank the brandy down like damnation', and 'She carried her responsibilities carefully like crockery across the hot yard'.[37] The former may seem rather melodramatic and parody-inviting, but its context is the priest's reflections on how easy it is to relapse into complacency, and the intensity is appropriate to someone who feels (as Christopher Marlowe's Mephistopheles asserted) that hell lies within him. The latter simile is fine: carrying responsibilities 'like crockery' evokes succinctly young Coral's earnest concern to discharge her duties well; we think of someone carrying a heavy load of fragile china. But there are hundreds of original similes in the novel; and some are very striking. For instance, when Mrs Fellows gives her husband a rapid frightened smile, we are told, 'It was like a trick you do with a blackboard. Draw a dog in one line without lifting the chalk—and the answer, of course, is a sausage'.[38] The simile, recalling that 'dog' (as in 'hot dog') is a colloquial term for 'sausage', is an ingenious way of suggesting a response that is rapid and proficient, but deceptive and disappointing. Then, we are told this of the priest: 'His conscience began automatically to work: it was like a slot machine into which any coin could be fitted, even a cheater's blank disk'.[39] So, even a fraudulent appeal evokes the priest's habitual charity; even virtue may seem mechanical. Another strikingly complex example is this one: 'an oil-gusher [. . .] was like the religious sense in man, cracking suddenly upwards, a black pillar of fumes and impurity, running to waste'.[40] That one seems peculiarly negative, but it is prompted by the priest's encounter with the Judas-figure, who feverishly seeks to confess his sins: he gushes.

Greene said that he became embarrassed by his leopards, and sought to eliminate them from his later prose. Indeed, his prose did, in later years, become more transparent and less stylised. Frankly, I think that's a pity. These striking similes of his repeatedly surprise us into fresh linkages and reflections. Furthermore, in *The Power and the Glory*, they connect well with another engaging feature, which is this: the priest's reflections are often intelligently paradoxical too. You could derive an anthology of Greene's subversive 'wit and wisdom' from this novel alone. Consider these three instances. 'Man was so limited: he hadn't even the ingenuity to invent a new vice'. 'It was too easy to die for what was good or beautiful [. . .]; it needed a God to die for the half-hearted and the corrupt'. 'God might forgive cowardice and passion, but was it possible to forgive the habit of piety?'[41] In each case, a radical thesis is compressed into an aphorism that aspires to the condition of paradox. At one point in the novel, the priest reflects that if the Judas figure betrays him for 700 pesos, this, far from damning the Judas figure, might actually save him:

> [A] year without anxiety might save this man's soul. You only had to turn up the underside of any situation and out came scuttling these small absurd contradictory situations. He had given way to despair—and out of that had emerged a human soul and love—not the best love, but love all the same.[42]

Fiercely intelligent reflections, infused with the paradoxical and perhaps even with the saintly. The lack of anxiety might save the Judas figure from vice and damnation; and the priest links that man's situation to his own, for he had found that the sin of despair led to the sin of fornication, and thereby engendered new life (his daughter's life), and thus engendered love. And a typical bold linkage of abstract and concrete lurks in that metaphorical phrasing: 'You only had to turn up the underside of any situation and out came scuttling these small absurd contradictory situations' — the metaphor links paradoxical reflections with the familiar experience of turning over a stone in the garden and finding earwigs or woodlice hurrying out. Eliot once remarked that to John Donne, the metaphysical poet, 'a thought [. . .] was an experience; it modified his sensibility'.[43] In *The Power and the Glory*, the descriptions of localities are, of course, richly sensuous: you may recall the 'sour green smell [. . .] from the river', the snake that 'hissed away into the grass like a match-flame', and the stench from the 'full and very heavy pail' in the prison cell.[44] But Eliot's point about Donne seems to apply particularly well to Greene: because you find that in *The Power and the Glory*, original thinking is repeatedly given a sensuous familiarity, while familiar thinking is given originality by the vividness of expression. For instance: 'Why should anyone listen to prayers? [. . .] He could feel his prayers weigh him down like undigested food'.[45] In those three words, 'like undigested food', you find shock tactics, paradox, a familiar notion, and unexpected precision. Sometimes, when reading such prose, you may recall Virginia Woolf's suggestion that the meaning of life is a matter not of 'the great revelation' but of local illuminations: just 'matches struck unexpectedly in the dark'.[46] Greene's novel about mismatches revealing matches is itself an open matchbox.

COMEDY

One of the features that gives a paradoxical quality to *The Power and the Glory* is this. Although the main plot obviously has grim, sombre, painful, and tragic aspects, the narrative invokes various comic modes. The work as a whole is richly ironic, and sometimes the ironies yield a dry or dark form of comedy.

When the priest, utterly weary, arrives one night at a village, he simply wishes to sleep, but an old man infuriatingly insists that the villagers are eager to confess their sins to him now. The priest reluctantly agrees to hear them, but weeps in exhaustion and anger. The old man then wakes up the sleeping villagers, and, though they wail that they are weary and only wish to sleep, he insists that they must now confess to the priest — who is clearly 'very holy', for he is 'weeping for our sins'.[47] Mordant comedy: the exhausted people reluctantly confess to an exhausted reluctant confessor.

A large instance of darkly ironic comedy is the priest's attempt to buy wine for Holy Mass. Beer is permitted by the state, but other alcoholic drinks are not, and in any case the priest is a fugitive, so his position is doubly risky. He negotiates with a beggar, who in turn negotiates with the Governor's cousin. Eventually, after tough haggling, the cousin sells the priest a bottle of brandy and a bottle of wine. The priest courteously offers the vendor a glass of brandy; but of course the cousin takes a glass of wine, while the priest and the beggar drink brandy. Then the cousin decides to have a second and a third glass, while the priest watches in dismay. Next, the Chief of Police arrives, and has a glass of wine, takes the bottle, and proceeds to reminisce. And what does he reminisce about? Of all things, his first communion, and the thrill his soul experienced at the time, and the fact that later he was dutifully obliged to shoot the priest who had officiated. Then our priest begs to be allowed to take the remaining wine away; but the Chief of Police empties the bottle, and is then puzzled to see the priest weeping. It's a scene of drunken comedy given a bitter edge as we see the wine intended for the Mass gratifying the priest-killer, the Chief of Police. The novel also, however, provides a running joke about the Chief's toothache, and that has its culmination when our whisky priest dies. The Chief, in the dentist's chair, is left moaning in pain, because Tench the dentist is distracted from dealing with his tooth; and he is distracted by his reflections about the priest who has just been shot. It's a kind of revenge against the Chief of Police. Numerous scenes in the novel have this black-comic or mordantly ironic edge.

Then we find that a more important mode of comedy emerges. Long ago, in the fourth century BCE, Plato's *Symposium* had described a banquet at which Socrates was engaged in debate. At its close, Socrates claims that a skilful writer could be a creator of both tragedy and comedy. But the hearers fall into drunken sleep, so Socrates leaves them, and we never learn his full argument.[48] The proof of his claim is provided, however, by Greene's *The Power and the Glory*. In a profound sense, this novel is both tragic and comic. The whisky priest dies young: a good man is destroyed early. Readers may experience that eloquently depicted waste that is a characteristic of great literary tragedies. Nevertheless, the priest has died for a continuing cause. Readers may imagine him as a martyr and potential saint; one whose sufferings gain heavenly reward. If you are a believer, you may think that Greene has created the following big paradox: *The Power and the Glory* reconciles human tragedy with what Dante originally termed simply *La commedia* — the Divine Comedy. If, however, you are a sceptic, you may find another big paradox: *The Power and the*

Glory depicts the human readiness to live, kill, and die for ideological illusions: a perennial tragicomedy. As Conrad pointed out, even the person who says 'I have no illusions' has retained at least that illusion.[49] And, as Greene reminds us, while the living close the eyes of the dead, the dead open the eyes of the living — as his words still do. While the dead priest may be commemorated by the holy relic of a bloodstained handkerchief, Greene continues to live in the vivid pages of *The Power and the Glory*. And we, the faithful and faithless alike, can experience that easy paradox as a mundane but sustaining miracle.

CHAPTER 7

Sigmund Freud and Graham Greene in Vienna

Brigitte Timmermann

I never knew the old Vienna before the war, with its Strauss music, its glamour and easy charm, Constantinople suited me better. I really got to know it in the classic period of the Black Market . . .[1]

Strauss music, glamour, and charm are popularly associated with Vienna, Austria's capital city. Sigmund Freud and Graham Greene's film classic *The Third Man* are also, albeit in very different ways, landmark names in the image the world has of Vienna: Freud as an intellectual icon of a glamorous, sophisticated, cosmopolitan Vienna in its heyday, which produced a plethora of intellectuals and pioneers in all fields of the arts and sciences, and *The Third Man* as a mirror image of Vienna in its lowest hour, a city on its knees, an intellectual and moral wasteland in the aftermath of Nazi occupation, war, and terror.

Vienna was at the very centre of Freud's life. There he received his classical education, read medicine with the most prominent professors of the city's renowned medical school, practised as a neurologist, wrote his seminal works on the unconscious, and started the psychoanalytic movement. Vienna was his post, and he could never leave it, as he told his friends who had rushed to Vienna for his rescue in 1938. Vienna was also at the very centre of *The Third Man*. When Greene came to Vienna in 1948, ten years after Freud had left, it was an occupied city, marred by ghastly ruins, a playground of Cold War politics, and a hub of international espionage. Far removed from its erstwhile glamorous image, it provided the perfect setting for his gripping story of black market racketeer Harry Lime and his school-time chum, Holly Martins. Sinister and full of menace and duplicity, it had turned into *Greeneland*, the realm were fact and fiction melted into one another.

Film producer Alexander Korda had asked him to write the screen-play for a thriller set against the dramatic background of a bombed-out European city. Greene delivered a 132-page story, a simple thriller at first sight, but at closer look a multilayered psychological study of humanity's conflicted existence. With great sensitivity and feeling for the locale he also captured the very spirit and essence of the city — he may have developed this special gift when, as a boarding school teen-ager with a suicidal tendency, he had a few months' psychoanalytic treatment in London — adding to *The Third Man* the additional dimension of a culture study, an elegy lamenting the loss of humanity and civilisation in general and the destruction of the city's former glory in particular.

The impact of the elegiac character can only be fully appreciated against the background of Vienna's once rich and colourful intel-lectual and political history. Putting *The Third Man* into its historic context adds a new and largely neglected dimension to it. One has to dig deeper, just as Major Calloway had to dig deeper than a grave to discover the true identity of the person buried in Harry Lime's place.

Until the end of World War I, Vienna was the jewel of the Habsburg crown, the undisputed political, economic, and social centre of the vast Austro-Hungarian Empire. It was the second largest country in Europe, had a population of almost 60 million and stretched from what today are Italy, Slovakia, Croatia, and Bosnia-Herzegovina in the south, across today's Czech Republic, Slovakia, and Hungary as far as Romania and the Ukraine in the northeast. From the mid-nineteenth century people from all parts of the Empire, from all walks of life, from any of the many nationalities living under Habsburg rule, poured into the Empire's capital city. Its population rose to well over 2 million, making Vienna Europe's greatest ethnic and cultural melting pot, until in 1938 its unique ethnic and intellectual amalgamation, one of Austria's hallmarks, received its death blow through the incorporation of Austria into the Third Reich. It was 'Vienna's golden autumn' — a term coined by Austro-British writer and social critic Hilde Spiel.[2]

During the second half of the nineteenth century the city rapidly expanded beyond its boundaries, grand boulevards were laid out and magnificent buildings erected reflecting the growing prosperity and self-consciousness of the bourgeoisie. It became, if not for everybody, a 'city of splendour', a myth comparable to the 'golden West', and came to be associated with economic opportunity and advancement but also good life, gaiety, glamour, and easy charm. Vienna was attractive

for Jews. For tens of thousands of 'His Emperor's Israelite subjects'
it became the 'New Jerusalem' — Freud's family was among them
— opening up the opportunity of escape from the confinement of
Bohemian small towns and the poverty and hardships of the Galician
'*shtetl*'.[3] By 1900 roughly 10 percent of the city's population were
Jewish. By 1910 Vienna was the third largest city in the world, a city of
great wealth and unlimited creativity, comparable in many ways only
to Paris. At the same time it was a city of decadence, ripe for something
new. Far-reaching political, social, and intellectual changes, the rise
of mass parties and militant nationalism had started challenging the
old order, and proved the perfect breeding ground for a plethora of
scholars, thinkers, and pioneers in the arts and the sciences, many of
whom helped to shape the twentieth century worldwide.

One of the most widely known representatives of this seminal period
was the painter Gustav Klimt. With the Secessionist break-away from
the academic establishment he spearheaded a cultural revolution
in search for a new artistic identity. Inscribed above the entrance of
the Secessionists' exhibition hall in Vienna, 'To Every Age its Art, to
Every Art its Freedom' became their motto. One generation his junior,
Egon Schiele set out to explore not only the human form, but also
sexuality in a most disturbing fashion, paving the way for international
expressionism. Even more provocative was Oskar Kokoschka. His
intense expressionistic portraits and landscape paintings were deemed
degenerate art by the Nazis, and prompted the rebel artist to immigrate
to England and adopt British citizenship. The Secessionist movement
also triggered a break from tradition in architecture and design. Otto
Wagner and Adolf Loos pioneered modern architecture, paving the
way for the internationalist style of architecture. Trying to unify the
fine arts, decorative arts, and architectural arts, in 1903 Josef Hoffmann
founded the Wiener Werkstätte, a groundbreaking production co-
operative of visual artists and craftsmen, and made Vienna a centre of
internationally acclaimed design. Their trendsetting creations were
characterised by minimal decoration and geometric patterning.

Turn-of-the-century Vienna was also known as the undisputed
'capital of music'. The city that hitherto had been mainly associated
with Haydn, Mozart, Beethoven, Brahms, or the Strauss dynasty of
kings of waltz, now produced Gustav Mahler, one of the most important late romantic composers and the leading orchestral and operatic
conductor of his day. Under his directorship the Imperial Court Opera
became one of Europe's leading musical stages. Arnold Schoenberg,
Anton von Webern, and Alban Berg revolutionised music with new
composition methods. Renouncing the traditional concept of tonality,

they spearheaded the musical avant-garde of the twentieth century. In 1933 Schoenberg was forced to immigrate to the United States, where the twelve-tone technique was readily adopted. Canadian-born pianist Glen Gould was particularly drawn to it and recorded all his idol's works.

At the same time Franz Lehár became the uncontested star of a more light-hearted musical tradition with which Vienna is associated all over the world. The *Count of Luxembourg, Gipsy Love, The Land of Smiles, The Czarevitch,* and most of all *The Merry Widow* are remembered and performed in music theatres throughout the world to this day. Together with fellow Hungarian Emerich Kálmán, he triumphed by fusing Viennese sentimentality with the colourful rhythms of their native Hungary. Equally opulent and operetta-like were the music scores that Viennese composers Max Steiner, Erich Wolfgang Korngold, and Ralph Benatzky wrote for Hollywood classics such as *Gone With the Wind, Casablanca, The Adventures of Robin Hood,* and *The White Horse Inn.*

Like music, literature and theatre featured highly in Vienna before 1938: Hugo von Hofmannsthal is best known for his libretti for Richard Strauss' *Electra* or *The Rosenkavalier.* In 1920 with Strauss he co-founded the renowned Salzburg Festival. He also closely collaborated with Max Reinhardt, the doyen of the German-language theatre. By employing powerful staging techniques and harmonizing stage design, language, music, and choreography, and transforming the role of the modern theatre director from general manager to the key figure in theatrical production, Reinhardt made history. He collaborated with the leading actors, playwrights, designers, and composers of his time, and was mentor of the Austrian-born American film director Otto Preminger. For several years Reinhardt was also managing director of the Josefstadt Theatre, one of Vienna's most celebrated stages. In *The Third Man* it served as setting for the rococo play featuring Harry Lime's lover Anna Schmidt. In 1957 Greene's *The Potting Shed* was premiered there in German. After Hitler's rise to power Reinhardt left the country, first for England, then the US. There he made himself a name by staging *A Midsummer Night's Dream* at the Hollywood Bowl and by directing the Warner Brothers' film version starring James Cagney, Mickey Rooney, and Olivia de Havilland. This film was banned by the Nazis because of the Jewish ancestry of Reinhardt and Felix Mendelssohn, whose music (arranged by Erich W. Korngold) was used throughout the film. Leopoldskron Castle, his Salzburg residence, which was the movie home of the von Trapp Family in *The Sound of Music,* and his remaining property in Austria were seized during the *Anschluss* of 1938. His passing in 1943 was commemorated with a memorial concert by the New York Philharmonic.

Arthur Schnitzler was one of the most illustrious exponents of Austrian literature of the day. Like Freud he was one of the many bourgeois Viennese doctors of Jewish background. He abandoned a splendid medical career in favour of his literary pursuits, and became the foremost writer to diagnose the moral hypocrisy of early twentieth-century Viennese society. Many of his plays, novels, and novellas caused public furore for their sexual explicitness. Freud regarded him as his *Doppelgaenger*, his alter ego, and wrote in a letter to him: 'I have formed the impression that you know through intuition . . . everything that I have had to unearth by laborious work on other persons'.[4] Stanley Kubrick's final film, *Eyes Wide Shut*, is based on Schnitzler's *Dream Story*.

Novelist Stefan Zweig was both writer and pacifist, and a restless spokesman for a cosmopolitan Europe without boundaries. His epoch-making autobiographical novel *The World of Yesterday*, a paean to European culture, made him one of the early twentieth century's great chroniclers. At the zenith of his career he was forced to emigrate, first to England, then the US, from where he left for Brazil. Despairing at the political and cultural future of Europe and isolated, with his wife Lotte he committed suicide near Rio de Janeiro in 1942.

Franz Werfel, Austria's foremost expressionistic writer, also died far from home in his Los Angeles exile. He is best known for *The Song of Bernadette* and *The Forty Days of Musa Dagh*, the latter an epic set against the background of the Armenian genocide by Turkish forces during World War I. A passionate warning against the dangers of racism, this important novel from the early 1930s remains the only significant treatment, in fiction or nonfiction, of the first genocide in the twentieth century's long series of inhumanities.

Much more light-hearted was *Bambi*, the story of a male roe written by Felix Salten, another popular Viennese author of Hungarian background. Published in 1923, it became an instant blockbuster, but it was not until it was translated into English that it attracted the attention of Walt Disney. He bought the rights and launched a hit with his animated version in 1942. A member of the literary circle *Young Vienna (Jung Wien)*, Salten was one of the most productive writers in town, publishing plays, novels, and essay collections as well as film scripts and even operettas. In 1927 he became president of the Austrian PEN club. Only a few years later his books were banned by Hitler, and Salten forced to emigrate.

Theodor Herzl, the 'Father of Zionism', was also originally from

Hungary, but came to Vienna to study law. He took a degree, but decided to devote himself to journalism and literature. He worked as correspondent and later as literary editor of one of the leading liberal Austrian newspapers, and wrote for Viennese stages. After he was sent to Paris to report on the ominous 'Dreyfus Affair', which was accompanied by massive outbursts of anti-Semitism, he abandoned his dreams of Jewish emancipation and assimilation in Europe. He became obsessed with the question of how to solve what he termed the 'Jewish problem', and became convinced that the only solution was a mass exodus of Jews to a territory of their own. The idea of a state of the Jews was born, and Vienna was its birthplace. Hertzl voiced his ideas in his seminal paper of 1895, *Der Judenstaat* (*The State of the Jews*), and consequently became the leading spokesman for Zionism. He travelled extensively, engaged in numerous diplomatic initiatives, and organised the First Zionist Congress in Basel, Switzerland. On several occasions he was received by the German emperor, was granted an audience by the Ottoman leader in Jerusalem and negotiated with the Egyptian government through Joseph Chamberlain, the British secretary of state, for a charter for the settlement of Jews on the Sinai Peninsula. His efforts took their toll: a heart failure ended Herzl's life long before its time. He was only 44, when he was laid to rest at one of Vienna's most prestigious burial grounds. Yet, in accordance with his will, his remains were moved in 1949 to the newly founded state of Israel, for which he had so fervently fought.

Vienna was also a hotbed of philosophy and the place of origin of modern empirical philosophy. Names such as Ludwig Wittgenstein, Ernst Mach, or Karl Popper, to name just a few, are commonly associated with Vienna. Wittgenstein's father was one of the wealthiest men in Europe and a foremost patron of art in Vienna. Brahms, Mahler, and the Viennese intelligentsia walked in and out of the family home. His sister Margaret Stonborough-Wittgenstein was immortalised in a portrait by Klimt. Maurice Ravel composed the *Piano Concerto for the Left Hand* for his brother Paul, who had lost an arm in combat. With his seminal work, the *Tractatus Logico-Philosphicus*, Wittgenstein hoped to solve all problems of philosophy. It was prefaced by Bertrand Russell, with whom Wittgenstein had studied at Trinity College, Cambridge, before the outbreak of World War I, and who once described him as the most perfect example of a genius he had ever known. Despite extensive travelling and frequently commuting between England, Austria, and the US, Wittgenstein remained attached to Cambridge throughout his life. For eight years until 1947 he held the chair in philosophy, and lies buried in the city's Parish of the Ascension cemetery. A most unusually talented but equally eccentric personality, Wittgenstein also gained fame by designing an extravagant modernist family home for his sister Margaret, a project in which he was joined by Viennese architect Paul Engelmann in 1926. Strikingly austere and coldly beautiful, it still stands today attracting architecture buffs from all over the world.

Pre-1938 Vienna was also one of the undisputed centres of the medical and legal professions producing numerous pioneers and Nobel Prize laureates such as Robert Bárány, Karl Landsteiner, and Otto Loewi. The latter was awarded the coveted prize for the discovery of the chemical transmission of nerve impulses. He was also an honorary member of the Physiological Society of London and held numerous honorary degrees, among them one from Yale University. Prague-born and Vienna-educated Hans Kelsen is considered one of the preeminent jurists of the twentieth century, recognised as the founder of legal positivism and pioneer of international and constitutional law. He worked on drafting not only the constitution of the First Austrian Republic in 1920 but also the constitution of the United Nations, and he held chairs at the most renowned law schools in Europe and the US.

Freud's Vienna also produced remarkable female intellectuals, whose haute-bourgeois salons were the city's prime stages for intellectual encounter. Baroness Berta von Suttner, Alfred Nobel's one-time secretary, went down in history as one of the foremost pacifist leaders on the Continent. In her anti-war novel *Die Waffen nieder* (*Lay Down Your Arms*) her heroine suffers all the horrors of the war. The implied indictment of militarism and her call for disarmament were so telling that the impact made on the reading public was tremendous. The book became an immediate best seller, and was translated into a number of languages. Suttner also received generous praise by luminaries including Russian novelist Leo Tolstoy, who compared the work's influence on the peace movement to the impact of American author Harriet Beecher Stowe's *Uncle Tom's Cabin* on the anti-slavery movement. From this time on, she became an active leader in the peace movement, devoting a great part of her time, her energy, and her writing to her cause — attending peace meetings and international congresses, helping to establish peace groups, recruiting members, lecturing, corresponding with people all over the world to promote peace projects and to fight against the rising nationalism and arms race of her day. No woman of her time was in direct communication with so many proponents of the intellectual life of the day. In 1905 she was awarded the Nobel Peace Prize. In the years to follow she played a prominent part in the Anglo-German Friendship

Committee to further Anglo-German conciliation. She spoke at the 1908 Peace Congress in London; she repeated again and again that Europe was one and that uniting it was the only way to prevent the world catastrophe that seemed to be coming. It came, two weeks after this charismatic peace activist's ashes had been laid to rest in Gotha, Germany, and it certainly changed the world.

Another prominent Viennese peace activist was Bertha Zuckerkandl. Her father was a brilliant liberal media tycoon and close friend and advisor of the doomed heir to the throne, Rudolph. Her husband was an eminent surgeon and anatomist. Through him she met Vienna's leading academics. Her salon also hosted celebrities such as Klimt, Mahler, Max Reinhardt, and Schnitzler. Freud also moved in her circles. Benjamin Disraeli had taken a fancy to the dashing young intellectual, and Paul Clemenceau, the brother of the future French Prime Minister, Georges Clemenceau, married her sister, giving the salon connections to the highest Parisian circles. When the old emperor died in the midst of World War I, his successor Karl harboured hopes of a separate peace with the Entente powers. Bertha had similar aspirations, and hoped that through her sister she would be able to have some influence on French politics, but sadly to no avail.

'Vienna's golden autumn' would not be complete without a mention of Alma Mahler-Werfel, composer, pianist, writer, and notorious femme fatale. Alma was married to Mahler, Bauhaus architect Walter Gropius, and Franz Werfel. She also had a most tumultuous affair with Oskar Kokoschka, who created many works inspired by his relationship with her, including, most famously, his painting *Bride of the Wind*. Eccentric Madame d'Ora pioneered celebrity photography and Emilie Flöge set the trend in modern fashion. She is best known to the world from Klimt's most iconic painting, *The Kiss*, an uncredited homage to the great love of his life.

The Vienna-born physicist Lise Meitner was a very different kind of woman. She was the second woman to receive a doctoral degree in physics from the University of Vienna, and made history with her discoveries in the field of nuclear fission and in the recognition of the possibility for a chain reaction of enormous explosive potential. Following a letter written by Albert Einstein to President F. D. Roosevelt, she was invited to work on the development of nuclear weapons in Los Alamos, but refused. After the war she became a Swedish citizen, but moved to England in 1960, where she died a few years later. She was several times suggested for the Nobel Prize, but her name lives on in the chemical element 109, named 'meitnerium' in her honour.

19, Berggasse, Vienna's ninth district: there is nothing striking about the late-nineteenth-century apartment building, if it were not for two memorial tablets affixed to its walls next to the entrance and a 5-foot sign with Freud's name at the front. And yet, as the cradle of psychoanalysis, it is one of the town's most popular addresses. Here one of the great intellectual pioneers of the twentieth century lived, practised as neurologist and researched the subconscious mind. Here Freud wrote *The Interpretation of Dreams*; here his followers paved the way for the dissemination of psychoanalysis around the globe; here he broke with his most dedicated disciples. Fascinated by Freud's groundbreaking theories in the beginning, they eventually developed their own schools: Alfred Adler became the father of individual psychology, Carl Gustav Jung of analytic psychology, and by carrying Freud's concept of the domination of the sexual drive to extremes Wilhelm Reich became notoriously known as the 'father of the sexual revolution'.[5]

Jung's emphasis was on the importance of balance, harmony, and spirituality far beyond sexuality. To him, humanity's main task was to fulfil one's innate potential. It was the psychoanalyst's task to take his or her patient on a journey to meet his or her self. In 1921 young Greene was taken on this journey. His psychoanalyst was Kenneth Richmond of London, a self-proclaimed Jungian.

Greene was a lonely child, deeply uncertain about himself and a boarder at Berkhamsted School where his father, Charles Greene, was headmaster. It was a situation that permanently divided Graham's loyalties between his family and his schoolmates. Other pupils preyed on the shy boy, tormenting him physically and manipulating his craving for affection. When one of his few friends conspired with his worst foe, a boy named Carter, to betray his friendship, Greene had a breakdown that even made him consider suicide. His alarmed family decided to send him to London for psychoanalytic treatment. It became a seminal experience in Greene's life. They chose Richmond, who had gained a reputation at Oxford for his treatment of disturbed schoolboys: 'a choice for which I have never ceased to be grateful, for at his house at Lancaster Gate began what were perhaps the happiest six months of my life,' Greene remembered.[6] Richmond never received any formal training or qualification and 'had more the appearance of an eccentric musician than anyone you might suppose concerned with curing the human spirit'.[7] Yet he seemed to be qualified in his own way to cure Greene. He introduced the adolescent to the intellectual and literary circles in which he himself moved, and encouraged him to indulge his passion for the cinema and the theatre. He opened up to him to a more relaxed, uninhibited and intellectual world that was so very different from the world of his headmaster father. 'My life with him did me a world of good, but how much was due to the analysis and how much to the breakfasts in bed, the quiet of Kensington Gardens, the sudden independence of my life I would not like to say, nor whether the analysis went deep enough. In any case, as Freud wrote, "much is won if we succeed in transforming hysterical misery into common unhappiness.""[8]

Richmond gave Greene the freedom to express his opposition to things in which he did not believe, and the courage to question authorities and loyalties that eventually turned him into the rebel in religion and politics he came to be in later life. Not surprisingly, Greene also developed a curiosity for, and fascination with, the darker sides of human life.

> It was a life transformed . . . I returned [to my classes] with the proud sense of having been a voyager in very distant seas . . . I gained a knowledge of human nature that it would take many years for my companions to equal . . . I had left for London a timid boy, anti-social, *farouche*: when I came back I must have seemed vain and knowing. Who among my fellows in 1921 knew anything of Freud or Jung?[9]

Treatment not only had a positive effect on Greene's mental equilibrium. He now found it easy to make friends and would no longer allow his schoolmates to bully him. He started writing poetry and in his dreams he saw himself as an established writer who was making enough money to support himself. It helped to sharpen his eye for the world beyond the limited scope of his traditional Berkhamsted public school education. Throughout his life, Greene remained a voyager in very distant seas. His travels took him to Africa, Haiti, Cuba, Vietnam, and, in 1948, to Vienna.

Europe, 1933. Dark clouds began to descend over the continent. With Hitler and the Nazi party rising to power, an unprecedented intellectual and cultural upheaval set in. Many of central Europe's leading minds came from a Jewish background. Their books were now piled up high in Berlin and burnt, Freud's among them. Fascist regimes took hold of much of the continent. Austria was also transformed into an authoritarian corporate state modelled on Mussolini's Italy in 1933. In the civil war that broke out in February the following year, a young left-wing Cambridge graduate was sent to Vienna as a courier for the *Comintern*, and helped socialist fighters escape through the sewers of Vienna. During the war he was Greene's supervisor at the Secret Intelligence Service and undoubtedly one of his prime inspirations for Harry Lime.

The fighting — aptly described by Stephen Spender in his poem 'Vienna' — left the city shell-shocked. All of Red Vienna's dreams of a more humane world were crushed. The city of dreams started becoming more and more of a myth used as a marketing tool of the film industry. Over centuries the Austrians had identified themselves through the Habsburgs, the House of Austria. The newly created republic of 1918 left people with little specifically Austrian except the memories of a more glorious past, which seemed to be full of music, wine, women, and song. Like the Hollywood westerns, schmaltzy Viennese films became a genre in their own right, permeating the myth during the Nazi period and particularly the years following the war. Austrians still love to identify themselves through Mozart, the *Lippizaner* horses, and the *Sachertorte* flair of days gone by. Needless to say, Hollywood and the British film industry also jumped on the bandwagon. Erich von Stroheim's *Wedding March*, a Paramount production, conjured the spirit of Vienna's one-time imperial grandeur as much as did the British Gaumont picture *Waltzes from Vienna* directed by Alfred Hitchcock in 1932.

And what did the Viennese say when the *The Third Man*, a film so unlike the tradition to which they were accustomed hit their local cinemas in 1950? They loved it for its brilliant photography and their local stars, but on the whole they raved as little about their city's sinister image as did the people of Brighton rave over *Brighton Rock*. Where had all the operetta music gone? If Greene and Carol Reed had only listened to David O. Selznick's well-meant advice, then they would have got a glamorous Hollywood soap opera entitled *A Night in Vienna*.

In March 1938 the *Führer* arrived in Vienna. What is known as the *Anschluss* is Austria's integration into the Third Reich as Ostmark. Austria was wiped off the map of Europe. There were cheering crowds and youths in smart uniforms waving swastika flags, dreaming of a great future. For many Austrians the 're-unification' with the proclaimed successor state of the Holy Roman Empire and Kaiser Wilhelm's Reich seemed to be the logical revenge for the humiliating Parisian peace treaties of 1919. For too many being part of the Third Reich sounded like a most promising option, but not so for Chancellor Schuschnigg who desperately fought for Austria's independence, nor for the many Austrian patriots and intellectuals who were arrested by the Gestapo and deported to Dachau concentration camp a mere fortnight after the annexation. And matters got worse. Viennese Jews were rounded up into street-cleaning gangs, and the burning of synagogues became the order of the day. The intellectual elite left in haste and so did whoever could afford to leave or was lucky enough to do so. Tens of thousands of Viennese Jews were deported to annihilation camps. It was the end of Vienna's golden autumn, the greatest exodus that had ever hit the country, the end of the world of which men like Freud were symbolic.

On June 4, 1938, an 83-year-old professor and his family boarded a train for London. Even if Freud had variously professed his dislike of Vienna as a notoriously anti-Semitic city, he was more than reluctant to leave. It was only through diplomatic intervention by President Roosevelt in Berlin that exit permits were provided. Four of his sisters were less lucky. Deported to Theresienstadt concentration camp in the Bohemian Protectorate in 1942, none of them survived.

Hitler had promised the Viennese that Vienna was a pearl and that he would give her the setting. However, a city in ruins was what Greene found when arriving in Vienna in February 1948, far removed from its glamorous old-world image of waltz music and the achievements of the city's elite before the *Anschluss* and the outbreak of the Great War. St. Stephen's Cathedral, Austria's most holy national shrine, was a burnt-out carcass, the Vienna State Opera, the city's great pride, was a hollow shell. The Ferris wheel of the Prater amusement park revolved slowly 'over the foundations of merry-go-rounds like abandoned millstones and the rusting iron of smashed tanks which nobody had cleared away'.[10] The once fashionable Innere Stadt (Inner City) was now policed by an International Patrol: 'four military police, one from each power, communicating with each other, if they communicated at all, in the common language of their enemy'.[11] There was a flourishing racket going on in diluted penicillin and there were kidnappings: 'such senseless kidnappings they sometimes seemed to us — a Ukrainian girl without a passport, an old man beyond the age of usefulness, sometimes of course, the technician or the traitor'.[12] The city was full of displaced persons carrying forged passports, and men in overcoats sipping ersatz coffee. And there was Crabbin, Wilfred Hyde-White's cameo cultural officer: 'I represent the C.R.S. of the G.H.Q. Cultural Re-education Section. Propaganda, very important in a place like this'.[13] Too many books had been burnt. Too many had been blacklisted as degenerate art. The city's bookshelves now had to be replenished by the cultural institutions of the liberators.

Korda's lifelong Vienna connections and Greene's wartime contacts with the SIS were of great help. They opened doors to a knowledge of the city that would certainly have been closed to others. Greene was put up at the Sacher Hotel, the one-time social hub of Vienna now requisitioned by the British military, and was introduced to the highest-ranking Allied officials and the crème-de-la-crème of Vienna. He spent nights drinking in the seediest bars of town, attended a talk at the British Council and descended into the city's sewers. *The Times*' correspondent Peter Smolka, coincidentally a former friend of Kim Philby from Austrian Civil War days, provided him with ample material on the penicillin racket in the city. Greene listened. He observed. He took notes. Nothing escaped his attention. And he wrote a story that, in the summer of 1948, when he returned to Vienna, he rewrote into a screenplay closely collaborating with director Reed. It was one of the finest collaborations between an author and his film director.

Reed's direction gave Greene's thriller story its final shape. With his unfailing feel for atmosphere he wonderfully succeeded in translating Greene's Vienna onto celluloid. If *The Third Man* was just one of Greene's light entertainments, Reed made sure that it became a classic one, giving to the cinema one of its greatest moments. It became his masterpiece. His direction and Robert Krasker's expressionistic cinematography gave Vienna stardom status making it into one of the most impressive locations in the history of film. Reed loved the city's faded charm and grand architecture, even if it was badly battered. Never before or ever again has Vienna been more impressively photographed. Countless are the intrinsic pictures in which the squalor and plight of the city filters through, whether it is a burnt-out car wreck dumped on a mound of ruins, a warming quilt wrapped around an old woman's shoulder, or a homeless man searching a dustbin for food. His spectacular night photography with eerie shadows moving along historic façades and rain-glistening streets, tilted camera angles and bizarre special compositions conjure an inimitably dense atmosphere of darkness and gloom, and add to the city's nightmarish quality.

Simultaneously, Greene never forgot to conjure the spirit of Vienna's better days. The film abounds with glimpses of impressive squares and grand buildings, which had at least partly survived destruction. There are musicians' memorials and Greek statues, baroque fountains and marbled corridors of palatial dimensions. Yet one of Reed's most powerful elegiac metaphors is a romantic old-world carriage drawn by a white horse past one of the ghastliest bomb sites of town, the Café Marc Aurel location where Holly Martins had agreed to play Major Calloways's decoy duck.

Ironically, many of those working on, or appearing in, the reputedly best British film of the century, either on location in Vienna or in the London Shepperton studios, were Austrian emigrants who had fled their native country, either because they were Jews or political opponents. The numbers of Austrian surnames in the unpublished credits speak for themselves. Some had left their home country for England and stayed. Oswald Hafenrichter was one. He was the most prominent expatriate in Reed's crew, earning an Oscar nomination for Best Film Editing. Others were given odd jobs by Korda as bit players, extras, or light doubles to help them to earn some bonus money and to survive a little more comfortably in exile. One of the actresses in the rococo play at the Josefstadt Theatre was one of them. The actor who played Hansl's father was another, and so were most of the audience of Holly Martins' talk on modern literature, 'James Joyce, now, where would you put him?'[14] On location in Vienna, most of the American cultural officers who smoothed the way for Reed's British film crew came from emigrant backgrounds. They procured shooting permits for the various occupational zones, established contacts between local and Allied authorities or saved Joseph Cotten from being arrested by the Russians. One of them, Ernst Haeussermann, was no less than the future director of the National Burg Theatre. For character actor Ernst Deutsch the part of the artful Baron Kurtz was his first engagement after his return to Vienna from exile in the USA before the war. He had been one of the stars of the German-language theatre, and his Shylock was legendary.[15]

The Third Man was the first British film production to be shot almost entirely on location. A sensational six weeks of location shooting made sure Vienna was breathtakingly real, as authenticity was pursued to the minutest detail. Yet, the city's seediness, poverty, and squalor only served Greene and Reed one single purpose: to use Vienna as a metaphor for the world's evil, evil personified by (never explicitly named) political leaders such as Hitler, Stalin, and Mussolini — and of course, Harry Lime, Greene's symbol of evil incarnate.

Greene and Reed claimed that all they wanted was to entertain, to give no message, and to offer just a fast-paced thriller in the fashion of the popular film noir of the day. Yet, as one might have expected from such a team of excellence, *The Third Man* became a lot more than just what meets the eye: it is a psychological study of divided loyalties, guilt and redemption, of the destructive force of evil, and, as far as Vienna is concerned, a most intriguing time capsule: 'Victims? Don't be melodramatic. Would you really feel any pity if one of those dots stopped moving—for ever? If I said you can have twenty thousand pounds for every dot that stops, would you really, old man, tell me to keep my money? Or would you calculate how many dots you could afford to spare? Free of income tax, old man, free of income tax?'[16]

What would Freud have been without Vienna? He would certainly have missed the professors of Vienna's famous medical school who shaped him, the affluent bourgeois patients whom he would treat on his famous couch (now in his last home at 20 Maresfield Gardens, Hampstead), the cafés and salons where he would socialise with the élite, the little antique shops that would sell him the Egyptian gods and goddesses he loved so much to collect, and, most of all, his shelf-packed study where he would write all the books that triggered off a revolution of the perception of the mind.

What would *The Third Man* have been without Vienna? There would have been Greene's multilayered, suspense-laden, dead-man-walking story turned into an exciting thriller by Reed. There would have been the stars, surely at their best. But just about everything else would have been missing: the uniqueness of the metaphoric wheel and the spectacular architecture of Vienna's sewers, the elegant Sacher Hotel, the Josefstadt Theatre and Anna's baroque street, the night-time cityscape with its hosed down cobbled streets captured at odd angles. There would have been no cameo characters such as Baron Kurtz, Dr Winkel, Popescu, Harry's porter, or little round-faced Hansl, and definitely no zither score. Would *The Third Man* still be among the 100 best films of all time?[17]

CHAPTER 8

Going Especially Careful: Language Reference in Graham Greene

David Crystal

If Graham Greene's leading characters had had the opportunity to read Graham Greene, they would never have got themselves into such awful scrapes. It is all a matter of spotting the danger signals. And with Greene, the danger signals are often to do with language. I do not mean the way Greene *uses* language; I am not talking about his style. I mean the way in which he talks *about* language — about accent, dialect, words, and grammar — and the way in which he refers to individual languages and dialects at points where we are introduced to a character, a situation or a development in a plot. Without exception, whenever Greene makes explicit reference to language or languages, there is trouble brewing.

An immediate clue is if someone has a linguistic idiosyncrasy. You can guarantee that he is going to be a bad guy. Take the moment Rowe meets Hilfe for the first time, in *The Ministry of Fear*. Rowe thinks Hilfe and his sister are going to be helpful. His sister will be. But Hilfe himself? Rowe should have paid attention to Greene's linguistic signal:

> The young man spoke excellent English; only a certain caution and precision marked him as a foreigner. It was as if he had come from an old-fashioned family among whom it was important to speak clearly and use the correct words; his care had an effect of charm, not of pedantry.[1]

Out-of-date language? That is not good. And Hilfe turns out to be the bad guy, despite the charm.

Often the clue is on the very opening page. Here is Brown describing Jones at the beginning of *The Comedians*. This is one of the first things we learn about him: 'His slang, I was to find, was always a little out of date as though he had studied it in a dictionary of popular usage, but not in the latest edition'.[2] Out-of-date slang. And Jones turns out to be a con man who causes all kinds of trouble for Brown. Then, on the opening page of *The Confidential Agent*, the man known as D enters the third-class bar, where a rugby team is drinking:

> D couldn't always understand what they were shouting: perhaps it was slang or dialect. It would take a little time for his memory of English completely to return; he had known it very well once, but now his memories were rather literary.[3]

Slang again. D, we can be sure, is not going to have a pleasant experience. And his language soon gets him into trouble. A chauffeur threatens him in a lavatory: "'Saucing me again." "I did not intend that." His pedantic English seemed to infuriate the other. He said, "Talk English or I'll smash your bloody lip." "I am a foreigner."'[4] A distinctive use of slang is always a sign that there is trouble ahead, and even more so when someone does not use it consistently, such as Anthony in *England Made Me*:

> His slang began the evening bright and hollow with the immediate post-war years, but soon it dripped with the mud of trenches, culled from the tongues of ex-officers gossiping under the punkas of zero hour and the Victoria Palace, of the leave-trains and the Bing Boys.[5]

People who speak like this are not going to have a happy end. On the opening page of *It's a Battlefield*, we are introduced to the assistant commissioner of police. It is a rare instance of Greene adding an adjective to reinforce the message that talking about language is an ominous sign: 'As usual before a sentence was finished he became lost in the difficulties of expression. Slowly, with a fateful accumulation of hesitant sounds, he hacked his way forward'.[6] Fateful.

Let us explore another novel in a little more detail. On the opening page of *Stamboul Train*, a traveller, Coral Musket, leaves a ship to catch the train. The purser asks her if she wants a porter to carry her bag. "'I'd rather not," she said. "I can't understand what they say. It's not heavy"'.[7] Cannot understand what people are saying? That is a very bad sign. We are all familiar with the horror film where the girl approaches a closed door, and the spooky music makes us want to shout 'Don't Go In There!' It is like that here. If Greene points to a problem of communication, he is offering his characters a warning.

Don't get on the train, Coral! Then the ship's purser spots a 'tired grey man in the macintosh', and has a bet with the chief steward about his nationality. '[Purser] "I win the bet. He was English." [Steward] "Go on. You could cut his accent with a knife." [Purser] "I see his passport. Richard John, Schoolteacher."'[8] So now we have an accent that is not what it seems to be. Nor, of course, is Richard John who he seems to be.

Once Coral is on the train, there are other linguistic signs that all is not going to be well. A man in the same compartment asks her to get a sandwich for his wife: '"Would you, miss? I don't know the lingo." And why, she would have liked to cry at him, do you suppose I do? I've never been out of England'.[9] And when Myatt talks to her for the first time, he gets her wrong:

> 'Mine's Myatt'.
> 'Mine's Coral — Coral Musket'.
> 'Dancing?'
> 'Sure'.
> 'American?'
> 'No. Why did you think so?'
> 'Something you said. You've got a bit of an accent'.[10]

A little later she faints, and the grey stranger, who turns out to be a doctor not a schoolteacher, looks after her. But is he safe? As she comes round, she hears him talk: 'she became aware for the first time of his accent'.[11] And indeed, another person from her compartment has noticed the same thing: '"What intrigues me," the stranger said, "is his accent. You'd say he was a foreigner, but he gave an English name"'.[12] Beware this stranger, Coral! But he is not the only ambiguous character on the train who has an accent. The author Q. C. Savory drops his aitches. And Mr Opie's French leaves something to be desired: 'His French seemed to the other full of little copybook phrases, used with gusto and inaccurately'.[13] Coral should trust none of them. Then, at the very end of part one, the mysterious teacher/doctor John falls asleep, and in his sleep speaks once — in German. Definitely: get off the train, Coral. But whatever you do, do not get off at Subotica! As the train waits there she opts to do so, but wonders whether she is making the right decision: 'Strangers might come in and take his seat, and she would be unable to make them understand. She would not know what the customs men said to her'.[14] She should pay attention to these linguistic misgivings. As we know, from the trouble this causes, getting off the train at Subotica was not the right decision.

These are not chance comments by Greene. Explicit reference to language is a major (albeit neglected) element in Greene's narrative artistry, invariably conveying danger signals. Here is Jones, in *Doctor Fischer of Geneva*: 'I remember every detail of that uneasy day. The toast at breakfast was burnt — it was my fault; I arrived at the office five minutes late'[15] For some writers that would be enough. The bad signs might have stopped there. But not for Greene, who goes on: '. . . two letters in Portuguese were sent me to translate, although I knew no Portuguese'[16] That clinches it. It is definitely going to be a bad day. And, as Jones waits in a cafe for Anna-Luise to return from her skiing, a waiter arrives like a linguistic death's-head: 'He was a surly man with a foreign accent'.[17] In *The Honorary Consul*, Dr Plarr arrives at the kidnappers' place for the first time and sees one of the group, an Indian: 'He couldn't understand the words — they were not Spanish. "What is he saying, Leon?"'[18] It is not a good omen, as Plarr will discover at the cost of his life. In *England Made Me*, Anthony is on his way to Krogh's factory: 'The umbrellas passed like black and dripping seals; a foreign language he could not understand fretted his nerves. If he wanted to ask for a match, to ask the way, he would not be able to make himself understood'.[19] The encounter with Krogh will not save Anthony either. In *Travels with my Aunt*, Aunt Augusta asks her manservant Wordsworth if there has been a telephone message: 'Oh, poor old Wordsworth not understand one bloody word. Ar say to them you no talk English. They go away double quick'.[20] And a lack of comprehension underscores the uncertain relationship between Henry and Wordsworth. They meet in Paris, where Wordsworth talks to some call girls:

> He began to talk to them again in a kind of French which I couldn't follow at all, though they seemed to understand him well enough.
> 'What are you talking, Wordsworth?'
> 'French'.
> 'I don't understand a word'.
> 'Good Coast French . . '.[21]

In *The Quiet American*, Fowler arrives at a house guarded by a military policeman: 'He was a young Foreign Legion corporal. He stopped cleaning his revolver and jutted his thumb towards the doorway beyond, making a joke in German. I couldn't understand it'.[22] In *The Comedians*, Brown, driving in the city at night, encounters an old man. 'I couldn't make out the meaning of his *patois* and I drove on'.[23] A warning signal. In the short story 'The Hint of an Explanation', the narrator remembers from his childhood a strange baker who he would meet on country walks: 'He would have a stick in his hand and stab at the hedges, and if his mood was very black he would call out after you strange abrupt words that were like a foreign tongue'.[24] Another warning signal. The baker, we learn, hated the little boy. In the short story 'The Lottery Ticket', Thriplow goes to a bank to discuss his lottery win with the manager: 'all the English words he knew had Latin roots — the result was rather like a tongue-tied Dr Johnson'.[25] If Thriplow had read Greene, he would know that this was another bad sign. And indeed, after his disastrous experience, the story ends with a final linguistic put-down. As he walks away weeping: 'A passer-by, mistaking him for a fellow-countryman, addressed him in Spanish'.[26] That is rubbing linguistic salt into his wound.

Two examples from *Our Man in Havana*. A visitor arrives in Wormold's shop. Wormold greets him in Spanish: '"Don't speak the lingo, I'm afraid," the stranger answered. The slang word was a blemish on his suit, like an egg-stain after breakfast'.[27] Slang again? We soon learn that he is a secret agent. And then, later in the novel, Hasselbacher has a visitor, and Wormold asks about him: '"What nationality was this man?" "He spoke English like I do, with an accent. Nowadays, all the world over, people speak with accents."'[28] Hasselbacher is right to be suspicious, for he will soon be killed by this man or his associates. In Greene novels, if people are said to speak with an accent, they are up to no good or not who they claim to be. They *might* turn out to be innocent, but the point is we do not know this in advance, and Greene subtly signals the ambiguity with a linguistic clue. Take Mr Hickslaughter in 'Cheap in August'. When Mary Watson finally agrees to eat with him, her comments on the food results in this exchange: '"Tomatoes even with the trout!" "Tomatoes? Oh, you mean tomatoes," he said, correcting the accent'.[29] A couple of pages later she reflects: 'Was it possible that the old man could be dangerous?'[30] American versus British accent differences turn up quite often, and usually prompt us to be suspicious. In *The Captain and the Enemy*, Baxter meets Quigly:

> I noticed not for the first time that he spoke certain words ('American' was one) with something of a Yankee ring. 'You are English?' I asked.
>
> 'You can see my passport,' he said. 'Born in Brighton. You can't be more English than that'.
>
> 'It's only,' I apologized, for after all wasn't he trying to help me? 'that sometimes your accent . . .'.
>
> 'An Atlantic accent,' he admitted.[31]

'Admitted'? That is a negative word. And was he trying to help? A couple of pages earlier, the Captain had told Baxter: 'I wouldn't trust him far'.[32]

In *The Quiet American*, Granger attacks Fowler: '"I don't like you, Fowler, but you talk English. A kind of English . . ." He made a feeble attempt to mock my accent. "You all talk like poufs."'[33] In *The Human Factor*, Sir John Hargreaves's wife, Mary, is singled out: '"I don't like those apartheid buggers." Common English obscenities always sounded strange in her American accent'.[34] And was there ever a more ambiguous character than Aunt Augusta? Henry describes her thus, in *Travels with my Aunt*:

> She formed her sentences carefully like a slow writer who foresees ahead of him the next sentence and guides his pen towards it. Not for her the broken phrase, the lapse of continuity. There was something classically precise, or perhaps it would be more accurate to say old-world, in her diction. The bizarre phrase, and occasionally, it must be agreed, a shocking one, gleamed all the more brightly from the old setting.[35]

Perhaps David Bishop runs second to Aunt Augusta for ambiguity. In 'The News in English', all we know about Bishop is that he has replaced Lord Haw-Haw as the voice of propaganda news broadcasts from wartime Germany: 'Tonight Lord Haw-Haw of Zeesen was off the air. All over England the new voice was noticed; precise and rather lifeless, it was the voice of a typical English don'.[36] We have to wait a while before we learn whether he is what this negative linguistic clue suggests he is.

In *The Quiet American*, a man cannot get his Vietnamese driver to understand what he is saying, and Fowler has to explain. 'He said, "But that's just what I told him, but he always pretends not to understand French." "It may be a matter of accent."'[37] There we have a reference to French. People are in risky or dangerous situations when the names of languages are mentioned, and especially when they know they do not speak a language well or at all. In 'The Lottery Ticket', Thriplow arrives in a Mexican port: 'Thriplow could speak very little Spanish: he had a phrase book for his vital needs: and he had little hope that in this blistered and comfortless town there would be anyone at all who spoke English'.[38] It is not going to be a good visit. In 'Across the Bridge', the narrator is introduced to Calloway, in a Mexican border town, sitting in the square with Spanish blaring out of the radios in the shops: 'I could tell he didn't understand a word from the way he read his newspaper — as I did myself picking out the words which were like English ones'.[39] We soon learn that the authorities are after him. He's a crook. And he dies.

This sense of isolation has a biographical origin. In *The Lawless Roads*, Greene arrives in Salto, Mexico, and feels isolated because of his language inability:

> I had a sense of being marooned . . . he said something I couldn't catch and disappeared . . . Why the hell was I here?
> For the first time I was hopelessly at a loss because of my poverty of Spanish; always before there had been *someone* who spoke English . . . Now I felt a mistake might land me anywhere.[40]

So many of Greene's characters feel isolated or unable to do what they have to do because of their lack of language skills. In 'An Appointment with the General', the journalist arrives for her interview with the general. It is only the second paragraph of the story, but things are already not looking good:

> She said, 'I don't speak Spanish', as Columbus might have said, 'I don't speak Indian'. She then tried them with French — that was no good — and after that with English, which had been her mother's tongue, but that was no good either.[41]

In 'The Lottery Ticket', Thriplow talks to the proprietor of the hotel, but once again things are not looking good: 'After a while the proprietor found a few words of English, a few words of French: a doubtful communication of ideas was set up between him and Thriplow'.[42] In *A Burnt-Out Case*, on the opening page, the ship captain, killing tsetse flies with his fly swatter, talks to his passenger, Querry: 'whenever he made a kill he held up the tiny corpse for the passenger's inspection, saying "tsetse" — it was nearly the limit of their communication, for neither spoke the other's language with ease or accuracy'.[43] In the evenings, Querry listens to the singing of the cooks, 'but he couldn't understand the words'; and when they talked, it was 'in garbled French or garbled Flemish'.[44] Querry will find that this linguistically problematic world is fatal.

In *Travels with my Aunt*, Henry talks to a train conductor, hoping for breakfast:

> 'No, monsieur. I leave the train at Milan. There is another conductor'.
> 'Italian?'
> 'Yugoslav, monsieur'.

'Does he speak English or French?'
'It is not likely'. I felt hopelessly abroad.[45]

A little later in the book, as he travels by boat to Asunción, an old
man wants to read Henry's hand: 'He asked me a question in Spanish
which I couldn't answer . . . He was making some demand on me, but
I could not guess what'. Somebody translates: 'He sees a death'.[46] And
Henry is about to land himself in trouble. In *It's a Battlefield*, a French
prostitute talks to Jules Briton: 'Jules answered in good careful uneasy
French; so long as his mother was alive he had been allowed to speak
nothing but English, for she had borne a grudge against her husband
. . .'.[47] And later, when he attends a French Mass, French words in
the sermon seem to haunt him: 'the word *péché, péché, péché*, held
down his sermon like so many brass tacks driven into a wood coffin'.[48]
Careful . . . uneasy . . . grudge . . . coffin . . . these are the words that
form the sense associations for language in Greene. People have to go
careful, especially when language is the subject matter.

It does not have to be a real language, to introduce an ominous
note. In *The Confidential Agent*, the man we know simply as D
receives a letter at his digs from the Entrenationo Language Centre,
where he is to find his contact. He meets his friend Rose: 'I think
we're being followed'.[49] Then he tells her: 'It's only a man who teaches
Entrenationo'.[50] Only?! I cannot think of anything more ominous than
a man who teaches a language, in a Greene novel — and an artificial
language, at that! Greene actually has a dismissive view of artificial
languages. In *England Made Me*, he describes Krogh's attempt at
dancing: 'he was like a man without a passport, without a nationality;
like a man who could only speak Esperanto'.[51] Artificial languages are
definitely trouble zones. And indeed, in order to meet his contact, K,
D has to pretend to take a class in this supposed language, in order to
discuss their plans.

Actually, I *can* think of something more ominous than an artificial
language, and that is a speech impediment. In the short story 'Proof
Positive', we are given a description of Weaver, when he began to
speak: 'He seemed at first to be in a hurry. It was only later that the
terrible impediments were placed in the way of his speech. He had
a high voice, which sometimes broke into a squeal . . .'.[52] No wonder
Weaver has a speech impediment. He is dead. And what on earth is
the child encountering below ground, in 'Under the Garden', when
he meets an old woman, who squawks at him: 'I learned later that she
had no roof to her mouth and was probably saying, "Who are you?"
but then I thought it was some foreign tongue she spoke — perhaps

aboriginee . . '.[53] Later, she turns out to be the real threat to the child's means of escape.

If you tell lies about language, that surely is the ultimate sin. It is a sign that Wormold, in *Our Man in Havana*, is in really desperate straits when he deliberately gives a wrong translation. Beatrice, his unwanted Home Office visitor, wants to meet his supposed contact Teresa. Wormold takes her randomly to a building, and calls her name. 'A thin woman comes forward, saying in Spanish "I'm Teresa: *Soy* Teresa." Beatrice is puzzled, and Wormold has to do some quick thinking. Beatrice said, "Is that Teresa? You said she was fat — like that one with the mask." "No, no," Wormold said. "That's not Teresa. She's Teresa's sister. *Soy* means sister."'[54]

Even if people talk the same language there can be an isolating effect. Here is the young boy in *The Captain and the Enemy*: 'when I read the Captain's letters I found myself entering a foreign land where the language was totally strange to me, and even when a word was identical to one in my own tongue, it seemed to have a quite different meaning'.[55] The Captain is an ambiguous character. He does not treat language with respect. He makes up words — a very bad sign. Not that the child is totally innocent. He has made up words too: 'There are certain words which I do remember, but I invent far more of them, in order to fill in the gaps between their words'.[56] This is language as mystery. Language, for Greene, is a bit like a mysterious maze, which has an entrance but not necessarily an exit, and in which one might get lost forever. Indeed, he uses this metaphor in 'The Blessing', when Weld meets an old man in the crowd while the blessing is taking place: 'Weld said to the old man, speaking very simply because his command of the language was weak, "I do not understand."'[57] The man tries to explain, but Weld's confusion remains: 'Weld could not follow. It was as though he had found himself in a very simple landscape, yet one where every path led into a maze from which there was no visible exit'.[58] But the clearest example of mystery is in *A Burnt-Out Case*, when the curiously named Deo Gratias disappears in the jungle and Querry goes looking for him. When he finds him, he hears him repeat the mysterious word 'Pendélé' — a word that no one knows.[59] Querry cannot get it out of his head. And its meaning is never really resolved.

Whenever Greene talks about language, it is to draw attention to a lack of communication or to make people feel isolated. In *A Burnt-Out Case*, Marie Rycker could not talk to a man she sees outside. 'They had no means of communication: she couldn't even curse him, as her father or husband could have done, in words that he understood'.[60]

Lack of language is loneliness for her. In *Stamboul Train*, Dr Czinner, finally identified, feels alone as he notices the language around him: 'The station began to float away from him; names slipped by in a language which his father had never taught him'.[61] In *The Human Factor*, Castle, after leaving the country, feels alone: 'It seemed to him that all his life after he joined the service in his twenties he had been unable to speak. Like a Trappist he had chosen the profession of silence, and now he recognised too late that it had been a mistaken vocation'.[62] In 'The Last Word', a former Pope feels alone. He dreams of talking to an audience, but he has a problem: 'He couldn't remember what he had been saying, for the words were in a language — or several languages — which he didn't know or couldn't remember'.[63] Even body language is affected. In *The Honorary Consul*, we are told that Dr Plarr's behaviour differed from the way local men talked and touched each other: 'In public, Doctor Plarr touched nobody, only his book. It was a sign, like his English passport, that he would always remain a stranger; he would never be properly assimilated'.[64]

These are cases where people feel out of their depth, not knowing how to deal with a situation, and inadequate language is always at the heart of the matter. The secret service man Daintry feels out of his depth in *The Human Factor*: 'Daintry, with a feeling of being lost among strangers, drank the first [martini] down. He said, like a man picking a sentence from a phrase book in a language he doesn't know, "I was at a wedding too . . ."'[65] In *Monsignor Quixote*, the Mayor is nonplussed when he encounters a couple who 'seem friendly'. He asks them for some food. So what are we to expect, given this initial description? 'The man said in an American accent, "I am afraid I don't understand much Spanish."'[66] An American accent plus lack of understanding? Double ominousness. They try to communicate with the help of a dictionary, in a rare passage of Greene humour. But it is black comedy, because after a while, the couple debate the meaning of *amigo*: 'Oh goodness . . . do you think it could be that corpse we saw them carrying . . .?' And the Mayor, confused after this non-conversation, thinks: 'Has the Guardia tracked them down?'[67] When K is defeated in *The Confidential Agent*, he completely loses his linguistic ability: 'In his fear he lost his English altogether — he began to beseech them all to wait and listen in a language only D could understand. He looked ill, beaten . . . he sought in Entrenationo to express something, anything'.[68] And he fails.

Anyone who has difficulty with language, or gives the impression of having difficulty, is going to pose problems. In 'An Appointment with the General', a female journalist is invited to lunch by an editor she does not know, who is going to suggest an unusual assignment: 'his vocabulary seemed limited, perhaps by the rules of journalistic protocol'.[69] Don't go on with this assignment! In 'The Over-Night Bag', we observe the man on the plane with a bag he is very concerned to protect. Nothing should be placed on top of it. 'When they were safely airborne he relaxed and began to read a *Nice-Matin* — he spent a good deal of time on each story as though his French were not very good'.[70] That does not seem right. And then we learn he has a dead baby in his bag. In 'The Moment of Truth', the Hogminsters ask for Arthur Burton's help in the restaurant: '"We don't know all these French words in the menu." "But it's put in English, sir." "I guess we don't understand that sort of English either."[71] Soon after, just as Arthur warms to them, and they to him, the Hogminsters fail to appear'.

The characters queue up to complain about not understanding. The Mayor, in *Monsignor Quixote*: 'I don't like anything that I cannot understand'.[72] Brown arguing again with Martha about Jones in *The Comedians*: 'Two different languages cause misunderstanding'.[73] Understanding is the critical thing, especially for secret agents. In 'A Branch of the Service', the narrator reflects on his childhood:

> What I learnt were languages — never very well but a smattering of many. I could understand better than I spoke. The man who later recruited me understood that. I remember him saying, 'To understand is the only important thing. We don't want you to talk'.[74]

This qualification is ideal for a secret agent posing as a restaurant inspector. Parkinson, the manipulative journalist in *A Burnt-Out Case*, is fed up with failing to understand: 'Father Thomas was talking excitedly, as Colin entered, in what even the doctor recognised to be very odd English'. Colin then talks to him. '"What's he saying?" Parkinson asked Father Thomas. "I'm tired of not understanding. What was the good of the Norman Conquest if we don't speak the same language now?"'[75] A rare language joke, hiding a deadly situation. We do not get language jokes in Greeneland. Language is no laughing matter.

Sometimes, the mention of language points to a situation that is not deadly, merely uncomfortable or awkward. Nonetheless, the backdrop is dangerous. In *The Human Factor*, the agents Castle and Daintry have difficulty communicating, giving Greene an opportunity to use two of his best similes: 'Silence fell like an old-fashioned smog, separating them from each other . . . Silence dropped again like the heavy safety curtain in a theatre'.[76] In *The Honorary Consul*, Dr Plarr has an uncomfortable conversation with his mother at a hotel tea table:

All around him in the Richmond he heard the chatter of women's voices. He could hardly distinguish a single phrase. He might have been in an aviary, listening to a babel of birds from many different regions. There were those who twittered in English, others in German, he even heard a French phrase which his mother would appreciate, 'Georges est très coupable'.[77]

This overhearing of phrases is not always innocent. In 'A Branch of the Service', it turns out to be an important part of the training of an agent. The narrator's mentor tells him:

> There are phrases in conversation that you hear in a restaurant which are worth attention. Pas de problème is less interesting in France where it is in such common use, but if one of your neighbours in a small unfashionable restaurant in Manchester (a restaurant which hasn't got even one star) says, 'There's no problem' it's worth paying attention.[78]

He takes it all in, and later observes a woman meeting a friend: 'I write "friend", but the greeting which he gave her struck me as very odd — "Pleased to meet you", that very antiquated English phrase, was spoken in a distinctly foreign accent'.[79] Danger signals, again.

In 'May We Borrow Your Husband?' the narrator observes the newly married couple who have come to stay in his hotel: 'Something was not going well; that was sadly obvious'.[80] Why? '. . . they never seemed to be in conversation when they returned from their walk, and at table I caught only the kind of phrases people use who are dining together for the sake of politeness'.[81] In 'Two Gentle People', we observe a man and a woman sitting together on a park bench, not communicating. Then some youths harm a bird and the man talks. But are we to trust him? '"Infernal young scoundrels," he exclaimed, and the phrase sounded more Edwardian because of the faint American intonation'.[82] Probably not. He kills the wounded bird, and they start to talk to each other. She has a linguistic character too: '"I could not myself have done it," the woman said, carefully grammatical in a foreign tongue'.[83] Are we to trust her? Again, probably not. But then we read: 'He admired the way in which she spoke English and apologised for his own lack of French, but she reassured him . . .'.[84] Maybe all will be well after all. When people praise each other's language, things are going to go well. And they have a nice dinner together.

In the whole of Greene, I have found only one clear case of unqualified praise. That is in The Comedians, where Mrs Smith is praised by her husband: 'Mrs Smith is a wonderful linguist. Give her a few hours with a grammar and she'll know everything except the pronunciation'.[85]

He is right. She uses her linguistic skills to great effect when she gets rid of Captain Concasseur.[86] If you are good at languages, you must be a good guy. The only problem is: there are not many of them around. The only other case really does not count — the man in a railway compartment in 'Awful When You Think of It', who comments happily: 'We spoke the same language'.[87] This sounds promising, but the man is talking to a baby, while its mother is absent, and the communication takes the form of bubbly saliva. The baby blows a bubble at him: 'I blew a bubble in my turn — we spoke the same language'.[88]

Unqualified language praise is very rare in Greene. Normally, a piece of praise is immediately followed by some sort of qualification, as when, in *The Confidential Agent*, Rose advises the agent D, as he tries to escape: '"You've got a chance. Your English is good — but it's terribly literary. Your accent's sometimes queer — but it's the books you've read which really give you away. Try to forget you were ever a lecturer in the Romance languages."'[89] Even when someone plans a nice chat, the purpose is not what it seems. In 'A Day Saved', the narrator plans to meet his mark in the train:

> Because I knew nothing about him, I should begin in the usual way by asking whether he minded the window being raised a little or a little lowered. That would show him that we spoke the same language and he would probably be only too ready to talk, feeling himself in a foreign country; he would be grateful for any help I might be able to give him, translating this or that word.[90]

How nice. But he adds laconically, two lines later: 'I should learn a great deal about him, but I believed that I should have to kill him before I knew all'.[91]

When opportunities arise for someone to use language to improve a situation, they turn out to be unsuccessful. In *The Human Factor*, Castle, working through a crisis, approaches the confessional: 'To talk was a therapeutic act'.[92] But his effort fails. In *The Honorary Consul*, Humphries says to Plarr: 'I would have thought the Governor might have invited you [to dinner] . . . he must need someone who speaks English for his dinner tonight'.[93] But no such invitation ever arrives. In *The Quiet American*, Fowler offers his services as a translator between his girl Phuong and Pyle. He does the job, but at what cost? Pyle is the man who is going to come between them, and who will eventually be killed.[94]

An attempt to understand what is going on might even be forestalled by someone else's language, as in 'The Invisible Japanese Gentlemen', when the writer in a restaurant notices a girl and her fiancé arriving at a nearby table. Why does he notice her? The accent, of course: 'she had a harsh way of speaking — perhaps the accent of the school, Roedean or Cheltenham Ladies' College . . '.[95] He tries to hear what she is saying to her fiancé, but another language gets in the way: 'I missed some of the conversation then, because the eldest Japanese gentleman leant across the table with a smile and a little bow, and uttered a whole paragraph like the mutter from an aviary . . '.[96]

Sometimes people use a language as a way of maintaining a distance between themselves and someone else. In 'The Blessing', a group of journalists talking in a bar try to use a language in this way: 'They spoke in English in a hazy hope that the barman might not understand'.[97] In 'Cheap in August', it is an accent that keeps the distance. Mary Watson is approached by an American lady who invites her to join their party: 'Mary exaggerated her English accent to repel her better'.[98]

Quite often it is simply a person's name that causes a problem. Names have great power in Greene's stories. In 'Under the Garden', Javitt tells the boy who is exploring his underground kingdom all about names, especially secret names, in a long paragraph: 'Up where you come from they've begun to forget the power of the name'.[99] Greene has not forgotten. His names are regularly sources for comment. Take the three characters at the beginning of *The Comedians*: 'Smith, Jones, and Brown — the situation was improbable. I had a half-right to my drab name, but had he?'[100] Monsignor Quixote finds lodging near the Church of Saint Martin, and reflects on his dislike of the 'sentimental nickname' given to St Theresa, the Little Flower. He gives her a different name: 'the Church of Saint Martin — that name again — the name by which he always thought of her . . . He would even sometimes address her in his prayers as Señorita Martin as though the family name might catch her ear'.[101] And it is always a negative comment. I have found no cases in Greene of someone saying unequivocally 'I love my name' or 'I love your name'. On the contrary. In *Doctor Fischer of Geneva*, the narrator comments on his name:

Unfortunately for me my father had combined diplomacy with the study of Anglo-Saxon history and, of course with my mother's consent, he gave me the name of Alfred, one of his heroes (I believe she had boggled at Aelfred). This Christian name, for some inexplicable reason, had become corrupted in the eyes of our middle-class world: it belonged exclusively to the working class and was usually abbreviated to Alf. Perhaps that was why Doctor Fischer, the inventor of Dentophil Bouquet, never called me anything but Jones, even after I married his daughter.[102]

In *It's a Battlefield*, Conrad does not like his name: 'His parents had no business calling him by such a name, the name of a seaman, a merchant officer who once lodged in their house'.[103] In 'May We Borrow Your Husband?' the opening paragraph is entirely taken up with a diatribe about poor Poopy: 'I resented the name'.[104] In *England Made Me*, Kate and Tony have an argument over names: '"I suppose this is Loo's doing. What a bloody silly name it is." "I don't see anything wrong in it. Names are just sounds, anyway. Kate, Loo — one's no sillier than the other."'[105] In *The End of the Affair*, Bendrix reflects gloomily: 'For some reason I am a man known by his surname — I might never have been christened for all the use my friends make of the rather affected Maurice my literary parents gave me'.[106] In *Our Man in Havana*, Wormold is talking to Lopez, wanting to get him to be an agent: '"You called me, Señor Vormell." For some reason the name Wormold was quite beyond Lopez' power of pronunciation, but as he seemed unable to settle on a satisfactory substitute, it was seldom that Wormold went by the same name twice'.[107]

Is there any kind of language in Greene where people can feel safe? Yes, two, but both are safely removed from the present day. In *The Honorary Consul*, Plarr says to Fortnum:

> 'I like to know the meaning which people put on the words they use. So much is a question of semantics. That's why in medicine we often prefer to use a dead language. There's no room for misunderstanding with a dead language'.[108]

The other safe haven is an older state of the language, if we can judge from the letter he writes to Eva Kearney, about the new language of the post-Vatican II liturgy:

> Words have a certain holiness; they should be able to represent truthfully a certain emotion as well as a certain belief and I do think the language of the 17th century succeeded in this better than the language of the 20th century which is apt to date from one year to another.[109]

Interestingly, this is the only comment on language in the whole of Richard Greene's recent selection of Graham Greene's letters. You can also be safe as a child, for the horrid adult world is then a long way away. In *The Power and the Glory*, a village child watches Mr Tench talking to the priest: 'The child watched them as if he didn't care. The argument in a foreign language going on in there was something abstract: he wasn't concerned'.[110]

I have now quoted from all the novels, novellas and short stories where I have been able to find language references. If we plot Greene's writing on a language explicitness scale going from least to most, we find very few texts where overt language reference plays no part — some of the short stories, and several of the early novels: *The Man Within*, *Brighton Rock*, and *A Gun for Sale*. Perhaps their immaturity accounts for their lack of language references. *The Man Within*, after all, is a novel about which Greene said: 'It is like the book of a complete stranger'.[111] But, at the other end of the scale, we have *The Third Man*, far and away the most linguistically aware of all Greene's works. I have so far made over a hundred quotes from 36 texts. The one with the most quotes is *Stamboul Train*, with nine examples. Over half the texts have just one or two references to language. *The Third Man* has over 40. Its language variety is unparalleled in any of Greene's other works. Language is a leitmotif in this film. So let us look at its language references in the light of what we have found in Greene's other works.[112]

The theme of unintelligibility is introduced in the film's opening monologue, when the narrator describes the international patrol: 'What a hope they had, all strangers to the place and none of them could speak the same language, except for a sort of smattering of German'. We have seen how a lack of understanding is an ominous sign. The point is amplified in the novella when Calloway describes the way the International Patrol arrest Anna:

> The Russian policeman pulled a fast one on his colleagues and directed the car to the street where Anna Schmidt lived. The British military police-man that night was new to his job: he didn't realize, till his colleagues told him, that they had entered a British zone. He spoke a little German and no French, and the Frenchman, a cynical hard-bitten Parisian, gave up the attempt to explain to him. The America took on the job. 'It's all right by me,' he said, 'but is it all right by you?' The British M.P. tapped the Russian's shoulder, who turned his Mongol face and launched a flood of incompre-hensible Slav at him. The car drove on.[113]

Calloway comments: 'try and explain your own point of view on any subject in a language you don't know well — it's not as easy as ordering a meal'.[114] Indeed it is not, as in the film Holly Martins quickly learns when he meets the Porter: '"Speak English?" [Porter] "English? Little, little. Sie kommen zehn minuten zu spat. Ten minutes too late."' At the cemetery, Martins' lack of understanding is compounded: the prayers during the burial service are in German. Martins then goes to see Anna's play. That too is in German, and he doesn't understand any of it. When he meets Anna he compliments her: "'I enjoyed the play very much . . . You were awfully good." [Anna] "Do you understand German?" [Martins] "No, no . . . But I could follow it fine.'" That is a language lie, as we see later when Martins tries to help Anna with her lines, and gets everything wrong.

Kurtz and Martins visit the Porter again. This time, translation is available, but it is used to keep Martins away from the truth: [Martins] "'Well, who used to visit Mr Lime?" [Porter] "Visit? Was will er wissen?'" Kurtz explains. The Porter replies that he is not sure. "'You . . . Popescu . . . and I don't know everybody" [Martins] "What does he say?" [Kurtz] "He says he doesn't know everybody.'" No mention of Kurtz and Popescu.

'What does he say?' That becomes almost a Martins catchphrase. We hear it when he visits the Porter with Anna: 'What's he saying?' We hear it twice when Anna's landlady tells her about the police searching her room, in a long German monologue: 'What is it? . . . What's she talking about?' Martins visits Dr Winkel, but when the maid answers the door in German he has to say: 'Dr Winkel — I'm sorry I don't speak German'. Martins visits Anna late at night. He knocks on the door, and Anna responds with "'Wer ist da?" [Martins] "That mean come in?'" Anna and Martins decide to visit the Porter again. They agree Anna should do the talking: 'His English is very bad'. (Actually, it is bad only in the film. In the novella it is excellent.) There is a crowd outside the Porter's apartment. Martins goes to ask what has happened, and someone tells him in German that the Porter has been killed. Martins is in trouble again: 'I don't understand' When little Hansl recognises Martins, and tells his father, they talk to each other in German. The father asks Martins if he has had a row with the porter. Again Martins is stuck: 'I don't understand'. His lack of understanding is getting him into deeper water. He gets back to his hotel, and finds a car waiting for him. He thinks he is going to Calloway's office, but it shoots off in a different direction: "'Hold on! Hold on! I haven't even told you where to take me yet." The driver says in German "I don't speak English.'"[115] Poor Martins. His language inability is at the root of his problems. It even affects his hopes for a love life, as we read in the novella. He looks at Anna, as he realises he is falling in love with her, but he cannot quite make her out: 'I felt as though I'd come into a new country where I couldn't speak the language'.[116]

Linguistic idiosyncrasy, especially in an accent, we have seen in the novels and stories, means trouble. And one of the first things we notice about the film of *The Third Man* is that everyone has an accent. Imagine, in the light of my earlier comments, how Greene would be describing these people in a novella of the book written *after* the film. We have heard his views on the ominous ring of foreign accents. Calloway never knew the old Vienna before *The Third Man*, with its Strauss music, its glamour and easy charm; in this Vienna, everyone is foreign. As a man says to Martins, outside the Porter's flat: '"He [Hansl] thinks you did it just because you are a foreigner. As though there weren't more foreigners here these days than Viennese."'[117] This is not an impression we get from the novella as a whole, where people speak standard English pretty well throughout. The Porter speaks excellent English. So does Cooler (Popescu in the film). The novella is not nearly so menacing, as a consequence. In the film, this is what we get:

- The American accent of the soldier when Martins arrives at the station.
- Martins' own American accent.
- The bad English of the Porter.
- Calloway's British English, which leads to a British–American confrontation. When Calloway asks Martins about his books, Martins mocks his accent: '*Death at the Double X Ranch* — Ra-a-nch'.
- Paine's London accent.
- Crabbin's very elegant Received Pronunciation.
- Kurtz's Austrian accent, and his distinctive, correct way of speaking: 'I may call you Rollo, mayn't I?' And Greene comments in the screenplay: 'His English accent is really too good. A man ought not to speak a foreign language so well'.[118]
- Anna's elegant Austrian accent.
- Anna's German landlady with her very idiosyncratic speech style.
- The accents of the International Patrol (not that they speak much).
- Dr Winkel, who has such a careful style of speech. In the novella we are told: 'His statements were so limited that you could not for a moment doubt their veracity'.[119]
- Popescu's clipped tones and non-native grammar (this was an American voice, Cooler, in the novella, who has no linguistically interesting features mentioned at all, and none in his speech): 'That's a nice girl that, but she ought to go careful in Vienna. Everybody ought to go careful in a city like this'. The replacement of *be* by *go* in the film adds greatly to the authenticity of this piece of dialogue.
- The citizens outside the Porter's flat, all with marked accents.

- Little Hansl saying 'papa' which gets a comment in the novella: 'the lips forming round those syllables like the refrain of a grim ballad'.[120]
- The Austrian driver of the taxi, with his gruff tones.
- All the people attending the British Council lecture, each with an accent: 'Where would you put James Joyce' in what category?'
- Brodsky's Russian accent.
- The balloon seller, another distinctive voice.
- The echoing shouts of the sewer police.
- And finally, Harry himself, who hides himself away, and who is the only one to have nothing linguistically distinctive about him at all.

If noticing an accent (especially a foreign accent or a British versus American one) is an ominous sign, then we get them nonstop in the film version of *The Third Man*.

All the other signs are there too. Noticing someone's slang, jargon, or awkward style are all signals of a tense situation, as we have seen. In the film, Anna picks on a term used by the British member of the international patrol: [Soldier] '"I'm sorry, Miss, it's orders. We can't go against Protocol." [Anna] "I don't even know what Protocol means." [Soldier] "Neither do I, Miss."' Even someone as innocent as Crabbin speaks in an odd way: '"Oh, Mr Martins, my name is Crabbin. I represent the C.R.S. of G.H.Q." [Martins] "You do!" [Crabbin] "Yes, Cultural re-education Section Propaganda."' And a little later: [Martins] '"I was going to stay with him, but he died Thursday." [Crabbin] "Goodness, that's awkward." [Martins] "Is that what you say to people after death? Goodness that's awkward . . ."' Then, when Calloway tries to persuade him to get out of Vienna, Martins ripostes: 'Didn't you hear Mr Crabbin offer me the hospitality of the H.Q.B.M.T.?' It is a linguistic joke. For this relief, much thanks. But we must not expect another one. Crabbin's use of 'awkward' stays with Martins. In the screenplay, after learning of the true story behind Harry Lime, Martins reacts to Calloway's sympathy: '"I'm sorry, Martins." [Martins] "Awkward. Sorry. What a vocabulary you English have got."'[121]

The other source of tension in a Greene story, as we have seen, is the way people treat names. And names are a special source of confrontation in the film version of *The Third Man*: [Martins] '"Listen, Callaghan." [Calloway] "Calloway — I'm English, not Irish."' And again: [Martins] '"Tactful too, aren't we, Callaghan?" [Calloway] "Calloway."' The bad guys try to be nice with names. Kurtz asks 'I may call you Holly, mayn't I?' Martins repeatedly mispronounces

Dr Winkel's name (the name is *Winkler* in the novella, and Martins mispronounces that too): "'Dr Winkel?" [Winkel] "Vinkel.'" Anna gets his name wrong: "'We're both in it, Harry." [Martins] "Holly." [Anna] "I'm so sorry." [Martins] "It's all right. You might get the name right.'" The screenplay has him saying: 'I'm bad at names too'.[122] But later, in the film version, when Anna discovers Martins' intention to betray Harry, we see name insults flying: 'Honest, sensible, sober, harmless Holly Martins . . . Holly, what a silly name . . '. But Anna herself is not above criticism, according to Crabbin in the novella: 'You can't imagine a young English actress calling herself Schmidt, can you?'[123] It is all summed up in the film's final exchange between Calloway and Martins: "'Be sensible, Martins." "I haven't got a sensible name, Calloway.'" And the novella comments: 'There was always a conflict in Rollo Martins — between the absurd Christian name and the sturdy Dutch (four generations back) surname'.[124]

Virtually all the linguistic signals we have seen scattered throughout the other novels and short stories appear in a concentrated form in *The Third Man*. Nor is there any linguistic relief. This is, after all, a film, and people have to speak, so the features of accent, dialect, slang, and so on become foregrounded. On the whole, in Greene's novels, people do not talk to each other routinely in a nonstandard way. The only exceptions are motivated by the regional culture being described — or example, the African creole (*chop, humbug*, etc.) used in *The Heart of the Matter* and *Journey Without Maps*. Only Wordsworth in *Travels with my Aunt* is a character not in his normal linguistic milieu.

Let me paraphrase the story of *The Third Man* to reinforce my point. A professional language user (a novelist) arrives in a country where he is unable to speak the language, supposedly to write some special language material (propaganda) for a friend, encounters a situation where he has to rely on translation to find out anything at all, finds himself dealing with people who all have strange accents or names (that he sometimes gets wrong), cannot work out what is happening to him (in the taxi) or to others (with Anna, with the Porter) because he does not understand the language, ends up having to give a lecture on a subject he knows nothing about and loses his own language ability in the process: 'Well, yes. I suppose that is what I meant to say'. And at moments of possible revelation, language is of no help. In the film, there are no words, when the phone rings in Harry's apartment and Anna answers it: "'Hullo . . . hullo. Wer ist da? Hullo? Warum antworten sie nicht? Hullo?" [Martins] "Who was that?" [Anna] "I don't know. They didn't answer.'" Martins sees Harry in a doorway, but Harry doesn't reply to him. 'What kind of a spy do you think you are, satchel-foot?' In the novella, after talking to Harry on the Great Wheel, Rollo tries to warn him, but fails: 'Martins suddenly called after him, "Don't trust me, Harry," but there was too great a distance now between them for the words to carry'.[125] There are no words when Martins is taken round the children's hospital to see the damage caused by Lime's penicillin. There are no words between Martins and Lime in the sewer, when they meet for the last time.

In conclusion, we might ask why Greene had this myopic view of language. Are there clues in the biographical material? Well, linguistic confusion was certainly present in his early life. In *A Sort of Life*, he talks about visiting his uncle's family at Christmas: 'I used to be embarrassed by the carols in German round the tree because I was afraid I might be expected to sing too'.[126] Did it start there? Or here: 'The only children's party I can actually remember was up near Berkhamsted Common in a big strange house, where I never went again; a Chinese amah asked me if I wanted to make water and I did not understand her, so that always afterwards I thought of it as a Chinese expression'.[127] Who knows. Wherever or however it started, we know how it finished.

CHAPTER 9

Prophecy and Comedy in Havana: Graham Greene's Spy Fiction and Cold War Reality

Christopher Hull

INTRODUCTION

Renowned for his prescience of real events, Graham Greene surpassed himself with the 1958 'entertainment' *Our Man in Havana*. Published just weeks before the triumph of the Cuban Revolution on 1 January 1959, the main protagonist of this Cold War spy fiction satire is a British expatriate vacuum cleaner salesman recruited by MI6's (Secret Intelligence Service) Caribbean network. Jim Wormold invents subagents and intelligence in order to increase his remuneration and finance his daughter's expensive tastes. One such bogus subagent — pilot Montez of Cubana Airlines — flies over the 'snow-covered mountains of Cuba' in an attempt to obtain photographic evidence of 'concrete platforms and unidentifiable pieces of giant machinery'.[1] Wormold, agent 59200/5, bases diagrams of the fictitious military installations on the components of an Atomic Pile vacuum cleaner and sends them to his MI6 superiors in London.

In reality, just four years later, a US spy plane photographed Soviet medium-range ballistic missile sites in Cuba, and the world came closer than ever to nuclear annihilation as President Kennedy and Premier Khrushchev engaged in secretive diplomacy for the highest possible stakes. Greene had thus accomplished an impressive feat. His fictional account of invented intelligence and MI6 ingenuousness had not only encapsulated Cold War tension and East–West paranoia, but also presaged the initial phase of the Cuban Missile Crisis.

FICTION AND REALITY

Greene's novel was a product of its age and reflected tangible fear of a Third World War involving nuclear exchange. Eight years after the aggressive employment of atomic bombs against Japan at the end of the Second World War, the Soviet Union tested a hydrogen bomb in August 1953. In March 1954, its Cold War rival the United States detonated a hydrogen bomb in the Pacific archipelago of Bikini, followed three months later by the first production of atomic energy at a Soviet power station. Britain exploded its first H-bomb over Christmas Island in May 1957, and in October the Soviets stunned their US arms-race rivals with the launch of the sputnik satellite and its orbit of the earth. Public concern over such fast-paced technological developments and politicians' ability to resolve international tensions without recourse to a global war, led to the formation of the Campaign for Nuclear Disarmament (CND) and its inaugural march to the Atomic Weapons Research Establishment at Aldermaston in March 1958.

Within the narrative of *Our Man in Havana*, Wormold's German expatriate companion Dr Hasselbacher expresses such preoccupations in the novel's first pages. He points to reduced life expectancy in current times, adding: 'We live in an atomic age, Mr Wormold. Push a button — piff bang — where are we?'[2] A contemporary review of Greene's satirical spy fiction, meanwhile, highlighted the novel's 'unaccommodating realism'.[3] Within its storyline, Wormold's 'fictional' intelligence becomes real and tragic and the subagent for whom he invents military installations dies in a road accident. Hasselbacher tells the amateur spy he has invented his agents too well.[4] It is very evident that the distinction between fact and fiction — both within the novel's narrative and its depiction of Cuba and real events — is very blurred. As will be seen, in their respective attempts to depict reality on the ground and predict future events, there are notable parallels and differences between Greene's prose and despatches from British diplomats serving in the island. Likewise, and for very good reason, the links between the novelist's fictional account and the reality of intelligence gathering are also strong.[5]

There is little ostensible connection between diplomacy and intelligence in the narrative of Greene's spy novel. During a brief scene the British ambassador in Havana, expressing ignorance of his activities, informs Wormold of his recall to London following discovery of his deception.[6] But where the two worlds do converge — these most official and unofficial branches of overseas service — is in the person of Greene himself. He criticised Britain's 1958 arms sales to Cuba's dictator Fulgencio Batista in the press, and was in fact more directly involved in the decision to suspend the sales than is commonly known. And in the real world of British diplomacy, general intelligence gathering did become a function of Her Majesty's Government's embassy in Havana once Washington broke diplomatic relations with Fidel Castro's government in January 1961, shortly before the Bay of Pigs debacle.

While never 'snow-covered', the Sierra Maestra mountains in eastern Cuba were the refuge of Fidel Castro's bearded rebels from December 1956 to December 1958. After a two-year guerrilla campaign they ousted and sent into permanent exile Fulgencio Batista, then in his last incarnation as caudillo-style dictator of the Caribbean island. Greene's production of the novel paralleled the Castro-led guerrilla campaign; he commenced preparatory work in October 1956 (two months before the *Granma* landing of Castro's guerrillas in eastern Cuba) and began writing on 9 November 1957, finishing the script on 4 June 1958. The novel appeared simultaneously in British and US bookshops on 6 October 1958, just 12 weeks before the triumph of the Revolution.[7]

INTELLIGENCE AND GREENE

In the second of his autobiographies, *Ways of Escape*, the novelist tells us that the original germ of his spy story was plucked from reality during his MI6 service during the Second World War.[8] The main function of Greene's initial intelligence work in Sierra Leone was to report and prevent industrial diamond smuggling on Portuguese boats through the West African colony. By 1943, Germany had only eight months supply remaining of this essential commodity. One of his more outlandish plans was to establish a brothel for intelligence gathering. He found a suitable French *Madame* to run the establishment, but London vetoed his plan for its lack of 'cost-effectiveness'.[9]

From 1943, Greene worked on MI6's Portuguese desk in London under the supervision of Kim Philby, later unmasked as a Soviet double agent based at the British embassy in Washington. According to Greene's official biographer, he came across the reports of a Spaniard, an Abwehr (German Secret Service) agent based in Lisbon, who, given the opportunity to earn piece money for intelligence supplied, had sent fictitious reports via Madrid about Britain to his German handlers. The agent based his intelligence on a tourist's *Blue Guide* to Britain, Portuguese documents on the British fleet, and an Anglo-French vocabulary of military terms. Another charlatan spy was a Czech businessman, also based in Lisbon, who supplied the Germans with ostensibly 'valuable' intelligence from five subagents, all of them invented.[10]

In his autobiography, Greene describes the dilemma of where to locate his amateur spy fiction. His original film sketch, *Nobody to Blame*, had outlined Richard Tripp, an avid stamp collector and Singer Sewing Machines representative in a Baltic capital similar to Tallinn (Estonia) in 1938–39. Agent B.720 wants to give his much younger wife a better life in order not to lose her. To augment his income and achieve this aim he invents subagents throughout Germany, in addition to a factory near Leipzig that manufactures a secret explosive. But Greene later recalled that a pre-war tale about a British national betraying his country did not resonate well, and that he shelved his tentative film script. The idea germinated again after he visited Cuba in the early 1950s, where he discovered that among the 'absurdities of the Cold War' was 'a situation allowably comic'.[11]

In reality, Cuba was the only Latin American country to execute a spy during the Second World War. Heinz Lüning, a German with a Honduran passport residing close to Havana's harbour, allegedly transmitted details of allied merchant shipping movements to enemy U-boats in order to facilitate their sinking by torpedo.[12] The 'canary man' was so called because the din created by his caged birds masked Lüning's shortwave radio transmissions.[13] An in-depth study of the case disparages such claims, however, and also links this real spy case in Cuba with the conception of Greene's novel. Much like the fictional Wormold, the German national was an incompetent spy. His main motive for spying in Havana was to escape Nazi military service in Europe. But Lüning's radio never worked, and British intelligence services in Bermuda intercepted his secret ink letters. Following the sinking of several allied submarines in the Caribbean, Cuba and the United States craved a propaganda victory, and the 'canary man' became their sacrificial lamb. Even the German Abwehr exploited Lüning's value as a decoy, in order to distract attention from other spies operating in the region.[14]

Using circumstantial evidence, the same study asserts that Greene was aware of the Lüning case because of his own intelligence service during the war. Working on MI6's Portugal desk in London, he would have read the file on the executed German spy in Cuba. Indeed, Greene did recognise that his experience during this period was worthy of 'a Secret Service comedy', and furthermore a 'spectacular source of good, satiric material'.[15] But while the similarities between the real Lüning case and the fictitious Wormold are remarkable, there is unfortunately no substantive evidence to link the gestation of Greene's novel with the case of the German spy.[16]

Another real Cuban spy case involved two exotic dancers recruited by German agents in Belgium to extract 'information of naval, military and air force importance' from allied servicemen in the bars and nightclubs of Havana. The husband and wife spies were arrested in Trinidad returning from a European tour before carrying out their mission, and thence deported and interned in Britain until the end of the war. British intelligence officers who interrogated the vaudeville artistes considered them 'devoid of courage'. José Pacheco y Cuesta was a 'Cuban Romeo' who had given his wife syphilis. She was deemed physically broken with 'no dancing left in her', and received a more lenient sentence than her husband.[17]

GREENE'S FIRST VISIT

On visiting Havana for the first time in 1954, Greene described the island's capital as: 'a fascinating city, quite the most vicious I have ever been in. I had hardly left the hotel door before I was offered cocaine, marijuana and various varieties of two girls and a boy, two boys and a girl, etc'.[18] Much later he recalled 'the *louche* atmosphere of Batista's city', and a 'nude cabaret of extreme obscenity' in the Shanghai Theatre.[19] Greene's personal experience and tastes, his delectation of the exotic and risqué, made a direct transfer from the streets of Havana to the pages of his novel; the Shanghai, for example, remained unchanged as the workplace of Wormold's invented subagent, the dancer Teresa — 'mistress simultaneously of the Minister of Defence and the Director of Posts and Telegraphs'.[20]

Adrian Holman, British minister (1949–50) and then ambassador to Cuba (1950–54), served during the highly corrupt presidency of Carlos Prío and then witnessed Batista's return from exile and his virtually bloodless coup in 1952. He inherited from his predecessor a dilapidated residence, formerly used as a brothel, and situated opposite the Biltmore Yacht and Country Club. A decade later the Country Club was the film location for Jim Wormold's first drunken attempts (portrayed by Alec Guinness) to recruit subagents in *Our Man in*

Havana.[21] In the year that Greene first visited the island, Holman evidently felt more freedom in his valedictory letter to describe Cuba's 'setting of luxury and make-believe'. After 34 years as a diplomat, and on the point of sailing into retirement with his wife Betty and their beloved dachshund, he wrote of his five-year term as Britain's man in Havana:

> Much of what has been reported from this post may appear to have been exaggerated or verging on the ridiculous. It may have given rise to suspicious smiles and scepticism. But Cuba is indeed a country of a particular musical comedy variety, where frivolous intrigues and plots abound and so often change into ghastly tragedies over night.[22]

Cuba was not the only country in Latin America whose politics were ridiculed by the British. In a 1938 letter, Greene articulated the attractions of two Latin American nations he would like to explore: Paraguay, on account of its 'five revolutions or attempted revolutions since 1935'; and Ecuador, because of its 'opera bouffe politics'.[23] Political instability and tinpot dictators were both elements that inhabited what critics referred to — but not the novelist himself — as Greeneland. The novelist, like the many British diplomats who shared their public school and Oxbridge backgrounds, lampooned the chaos and turbulence of Latin American politics and the region's ruling class. Underlying such satire, if not outdated scorn for Johnny Foreigner, was an indirect absolving of British responsibility for this state of affairs.

In the case of Cuba, the British — both novelists and diplomats — could simultaneously denigrate the legacy of Spanish colonialism and what they viewed as the naive and counterproductive actions of successive US administrations and diplomats, who, in a paternalistic and overbearing manner, had tutored and ultimately failed to nurture a mature political tradition in their island neighbour. Cuba in particular, very much a field of experiment for Washington's hemispheric policy, also offered diplomats the opportunity to avenge frequent US criticism of British imperialism in other realms. Reciprocation for censure of British policy in Ireland was just one case in point.

Greene's novel and film, however, also satirise the British during an era of post-war and post-Suez decline. While the other (the Cuban) may be depicted as primitive, the self is incompetent and also the object of ridicule.[24] In a private letter to Greene, Noël Coward pointed to his own depiction of MI6 Caribbean station chief Henry Hawthorne, a caricature of all the 'hapless, bumbling bureaucrats' he had encountered during the war. Surely, he conjectured, the novelist had not needed to invent such comic figures.[25]

BRITISH DIPLOMACY AND THE CUBAN REVOLUTION

The ambassadorship of Stanley Fordham, who presented his cre-dentials in Havana just three weeks before the *Granma* landing in December 1956, led to abject embarrassment — for both the diplomat and the Foreign Office — when his assessment of events on the ground in the 1957–58 period proved wide of the mark. Fordham was an expe-rienced diplomat, previously minister to Argentina (by far and away Britain's largest commercial interest in Latin America) from 1954–56, when Juan Domingo Perón's regime collapsed. This gave him experi-ence of political tumult and the precipitous ending of dictatorship. In fact, apart from brief periods in London and San Francisco, Fordham had spent almost his entire foreign service in Latin America.[26]

Fordham was isolated from the civil conflict between the govern-ment's armed forces and Castro's rebels, not only because as an ambassador extraordinary and plenipotentiary he was accredited to Batista's foreign ministry, but because most guerrilla activity occurred in the east of the island. Despite the capital's distance from the seat of revolutionary activity in Oriente Province, however, the close proxim-ity of the British embassy to the Presidential Palace in Centro Habana meant that Fordham was a live witness in March 1957 to the attack and attempted assassination of Batista by the *Directorio Revolucionario*, urban guerrilla rivals to Castro's *26 de julio* movement.[27]

The Foreign Office relied almost solely on the analysis of its embassy in Havana when deciding to allow British arms sales in 1958, during the last months and weeks of Batista's rule. As a diplomat Fordham's contacts were limited, recognizing as early as February 1957 that his sources of information were poor. He relied on such people as the General Manager of the Royal Bank of Canada for reports on condi-tions in the provinces. To colleagues in London, reading such reports as those of *The New York Times* journalist Herbert Matthews, who had breached the Batista army's security cordon to interview Castro in the Sierra Maestra hills in February 1957, Fordham's view of the situation was 'more sanguine than many'. Normally, he would have expected to receive reports on conditions in Oriente province, the reb-els' stronghold, from the British vice-consul in the province's capital city, Santiago de Cuba. Unfortunately, again, not only was there no secure line of communication between Oriente and Havana, but Neil

Hone — an ex-sugar planter and long-term consular official — was convalescing at the US naval base at Guantanamo during a vital three-month period in 1958 when Batista's fortunes declined and the rebels came to ascendancy. Furthermore, Batista imposed press censorship within Cuba during the guerrilla insurgency.[28]

Fordham's confidence in the dictator's hold on power fluctuated during 1958, but actually strengthened as the year progressed. In April, he had been most noncommittal, writing: 'No one can guess as to what will happen in the next few days, let alone months. For what it is worth my guess is that that Batista will survive. But I shall not be much surprised if I am proved wrong'. In May, the department in London had placed more weight on the criticism it may incur rather than commercial considerations. But Fordham judged Batista's overthrow as unlikely, while admitting sales would be a gamble. His most important diplomatic contact, US Ambassador Earl T. Smith, was a Republican political appointee with no previous diplomatic experience. Late in 1958, he personally encouraged Britain, through Ambassador Fordham in Havana, to continue its arms supplies to the Cuban government. Even on New Year's Eve 1958, the night that Batista boarded a plane to Ciudad Trujillo and permanent exile, Fordham was still casting doubt on newspaper reports of the dictator's imminent demise.[29]

Reality preceded (or coincided with) fiction when Greene became directly involved in the guerrilla cause in the form of a personal visit to Santiago de Cuba, carrying warm winter clothing and meeting with urban representatives of the 26 de julio guerrilla movement in the capital of Oriente Province.[30] When the British government sold arms to Batista's government in 1958, replacing the US as Cuba's main arms supplier, Greene encouraged a Labour MP to ask questions in the House of Commons. So, while Greene's fiction would later demon-strate a remarkable prescience in anticipating a major world political event, in real life he condemned his government's lack of foresight in supplying heavy arms to Batista's regime just weeks before its precipi-tous demise. In this way fiction, reality, and the ability to predict (or not) and imitate actual events all came together in Greene's novel and the Cold War politics of this strategically important Caribbean island in the late 1950s and early 1960s.

Only when the Labour opposition, after encouragement from Greene, questioned the policy of Prime Minister Harold Macmillan's administration in the House of Commons, did the Conservative gov-ernment restrict arms sales to Cuba. Only two hours after returning from his latest trip to Cuba, Greene wrote to Hugh Delargy MP in late

October 1958: 'If only to prevent anti-British feeling on the part of the man who is likely to be the next ruler of Cuba, cannot you raise some opposition to the sale of these planes in the House of Commons?' This pronouncement is to be compared with that of the head of the Foreign Office's American Department 11 days later: 'There is very little reason to suppose that Fidel Castro will come to power in the foreseeable future'. Underlying the Foreign Office point of view was its confidence that when push came to shove, Washington would go to some lengths to avoid the suspected radical Castro from reaching power, and Britain's risky arms sales policy could shelter with confidence behind its ally's position.[31]

Batista's army subsequently imploded in sudden fashion and the dictator took advantage of New Year's Eve distractions to flee to the capital's military airport and thence to foreign soil in the first hours of January 1, 1959. Within a few days, *The Times* published letters from Greene strongly criticizing the Foreign Office's 'extraordinary ignorance' of events on the ground in Cuba. He wrote: 'Any visitor to Cuba could have given her [*sic*] Majesty's Government more information about conditions in the island than was apparently supplied by our official representatives'.[32]

In fact, the Labour opposition had saved Macmillan's Conservatives from even more embarrassment when Batista's regime did fall, as the government could claim that arms sales had indeed been restricted. An editorial in *The Guardian* highlighted this 'crowning piece of ironic Greenery'. With the arms sales, the editorial stated: 'fact has not merely imitated but outrun fiction'. The opposition had saved the face of the government, and the Foreign Office would have done better 'to sit at home reading the newspapers' rather than relying on the contacts and despatches of its chief envoy in Havana.[33] Unknown was the fact that the novelist himself had instigated the parliamentary process. While he had drawn attention to his government's misjudgement in the letter pages of *The Times*, he had also saved it and the Foreign Office from more embarrassment than it did in fact incur.

An internal inquiry in London provoked much navel gazing. The Foreign Office recognised that its decisions 'were not above criticism', that its information had been inadequate and it had drawn the wrong conclusions from what news it did receive. Greene's aforementioned criticism, intimating that the British government would have been better informed had it simply read the newspapers, touched a raw nerve, less than six months after the Foreign Office had been caught napping over a revolution in Iraq. Fordham pointed to the 'very unusual features' of the Cuban Revolution, extending an 'extraordinarily long time' compared to other revolutions in the region that had lasted just days or hours. He was defensive and evidently crestfallen by the turn of events, writing soon after the inquiry: 'Members of Her Majesty's Foreign Service are expected to be right when all around them are wrong. I have been greatly concerned that I have failed in this respect and that in consequence I led you and others astray'. He was perhaps suffering the 'existential despair' common to ambassadors from time to time. Fordham had found himself vulnerably exposed at the end of a long, sometimes delayed (and often encrypted) line of communication, when events conspired to overturn his considered predictions.[34]

In the post-mortem into the arms affair, Fordham cited the 'absence of any news from unbiased sources' that made it 'exceedingly difficult to appreciate what was going on'. Defending his reporting and that of the embassy's first secretary, he pointed out that diplomatic and commercial opinion in Cuba held the same sanguine view of Batista holding power until elections in February 1959. Fordham felt strongly enough to mention the arms embargo as a possible factor in Batista's sudden demise. This raises the intriguing possibility that Greene's intervention, his letters to a Labour opposition MP and subsequent questions in the House, contributed to Batista's isolation (months after the US ban on arms exports) and vulnerability in the face of a rebel advance.[35] Would Batista have fled into exile when he did had Britain continued its arms sales? Was the British arms embargo one of the straws that broke the back of his regime? Or was Fordham exaggerating the facts in order to save face?

THE CUBAN REVOLUTION

There were very definite comic possibilities when Castro's idealistic revolutionaries left the mountains and assumed political power — armed men in green fatigues, often hirsute and cigar smoking, few with administrative experience of government. After his first view in the flesh, Fordham likened them to 'Australian bushrangers or characters in a film of the Klondyke gold rush'. The Foreign Office and its diplomats, initially embarrassed by the arms sales and wary of the reaction and political orientation of the country's youthful leadership, patiently gauged the actions and reactions of the revolutionary government's new incumbents. Britain's trepidation was in the event unjustified, with *The Observer's* Havana correspondent soon noting: 'The Castro people have a sense of humour, and the embarrassment of the British Embassy has raised a smile'.[36]

Still unaccustomed to the orthodoxy of diplomatic protocol, the new regime demonstrated its ingenuousness when Castro called unannounced at the British ambassador's residence in early 1959, sending Fordham's butler into a panic. With the rebels installed in Havana, Fordham could at least travel freely around the island. On a visit to Oriente Province in August 1959, he reported the interest aroused in his official Austin Princess limousine, often surrounded by admiring crowds. He noted that many Cubans doffed their hats on seeing the car, under the mistaken impression they were viewing a hearse.[37] Generally, British diplomats trod carefully and patiently, negotiating with such newly founded government departments as the 'Ministry of Recovery of ill-Gotten Gains', formed to administer the confiscation and redistribution of private and foreign property.

In the wake of the arms embarrassment, it is not surprising that Fordham and his ambassadorial successors were guarded when predicting the course of events in Cuba in the tumultuous period covering Cuba's political and economic absorption into the Soviet bloc, the Bay of Pigs debacle, and the Cuban Missile Crisis. In the maelstrom of political events, and in the face of Castro's unpredictability, Fordham professed himself 'reluctant to crystal gaze', causing a senior Foreign Office official to remark: 'This man Fordham is too cautious'. Given his recent experience, he might be forgiven for his reluctance to offer little more than 'only very tentative and personal guesses'. He continued: 'The whole situation is still so confused and Castro himself so erratic an extrovert that anything like a rational forecast of what may happen in the next few months is completely impossible'.[38]

But in his role as ambassador it rested with Fordham to describe the Revolution's fluid events and offer predictions when he dare. Even for a diplomat as experienced as he in the unstable environs of Latin America, of alternating democracy and dictatorship, he reflected on his capacity to communicate his views on the written page. In August, following a series of inflammatorily anti-American speeches by Castro and increasing tensions with Rafael Trujillo's Dominican Republic, the events were such, he wrote, that 'to do them full justice calls for the fertile imagination and fluent pen of an Ian Fleming or an Eric Ambler (or even of a Graham Greene)'. Until the end of his posting in Havana, he was at least able to steer clear of controversy, dispelling rumours of an early recall to London. His frankest opinions were highlighted in his valedictory letter. Given free rein to express his true feelings, Fordham wrote: 'To have watched at close quarters the debauchment of a country one is fond of has been an interesting experience, but it has not been a pleasant one'.[39]

OUR INTELLIGENCE IN HAVANA

Fordham's successor, Bill Marchant, was not averse to the challenge of describing the tumultuous events unfolding before his eyes. He had an interest in amateur dramatics and had worked for the Government Code and Cypher School (later GCHQ) at Bletchley Park during the war. After the war he had served the Foreign Office in Bucharest, Zagreb, Dusseldorf, and the US (Colorado and San Francisco), mostly in consular roles. New to his post, he attempted to fathom, from the centre of the maelstrom, the direction of events and the true sympathies of the Cuban population at large: 'It is true that amongst the apparently faithful there may lurk a proportion of opportunists and waiverers, since no one can tell how may leaves still on a tree are ready to come fluttering to the ground until the cold winds blow'. And in hesitating to make any sort of prediction of longevity for Castro's regime, he wrote:

> It is particularly difficult for us here in Havana not to be influenced in our judgement by the hot-house atmosphere of feverish wishful thinking in which we live. Most of my colleagues and the few remaining Cubans who still associate with us confidently count the remaining months of Castroism on the fingers of one or at any rate, two hands. I am less convinced of the inevitably [*sic*] of the fall of this Revolutionary Government than they are.[40]

Following the break in US–Cuban diplomatic relations at the start of 1961, the Cuban authorities took very seriously the rumours about an imminent US invasion, borne out by the fiasco of the US-sponsored Bay of Pigs landing in April. British diplomats in Centro Habana again found themselves too close to the action in January when the military authorities mounted sandbagged machine-gun emplacements on the roof of the building of whose top three floors the embassy occupied.[41]

But when rumours of an imminent invasion reached a crescendo in early April 1961, just days before the actual Bay of Pigs debacle, Marchant was unequivocal in his assessment:

> Prospect of badly organized landings planned on the assumption that internal opposition is strong enough to give decisive support continues to cause considerable concern to me and to all my European colleagues. [I]f the American assessment is based exclusively on counter-revolutionary sources it is almost certainly wrong.[42]

The Bay of Pigs episode would highlight more than ever the dangers of misusing intelligence and bad planning. In this case the US executive, and particularly the Central Intelligence Agency (CIA) who advised President Kennedy, were responsible for a monumental error of judgement, wildly overestimating their chances of success. Here was a concrete case of an intelligence organisation if not fabricating, than at least wildly exaggerating its evidence. Soon afterward, Marchant proffered the view that neither potential counter-revolutionaries nor anyone else could now 'foresee what the future has in store for this country, now that is has been so helplessly caught up in the whirlwind of international politics'. Britain's man in Havana continued to be concerned that the distorted picture of Cuba reaching Washington's ears — from expelled journalists and embittered refugees — was forming 'a most dangerous intelligence basis on which to plan future policy'.[43]

Two months later, Marchant made a lengthy assessment of the Revolution's trajectory and his inclination to take more seriously the 'rumblings of discontent' within. But yet again, the reluctance to foretell the future in Cuba was evident in Marchant's despatch:

> The picture with which we find ourselves is not at all easy to assess [. . .] I must therefore once again admit that I do not yet have much confidence in my ability — and for that matter in anyone else's ability — to foresee how this country is going to react to the fate which is overtaking it. There are still too many unknowns.[44]

An insurmountable problem, exacerbated by Cuba's accommodation with Moscow, was that the circle of embassy contacts had decreased while the danger of informants had increased. This was particularly true in the case of diplomats' interactions with government officials. In the period leading up to the missile crisis, for example, Cuban officials abstained from all social contact with British officials. And at the most senior level, Marchant stated that Castro had absolutely nothing to do with Western diplomats during the first two years and 11 months of his ambassadorship (July 1960 to July 1963).[45] The difficulties of separating truth from fiction in the feverish atmosphere of revolutionary Havana, months after the Bay of Pigs invasion, were not to be underestimated. Cuba had become a locus of the world's superpower rivalries. How was a diplomat to distinguish rumour from fact when an embassy's contacts were reduced and both the intelligence gatherers and their reports were suspect?

Concerning the missile crisis of 1962, it is hard to think of a less comic scenario, with the death of millions of civilians just a button push away. The first intimations of the arrival of rocket tubes that went beyond the realm of conventional Soviet bloc arms contain elements very akin to Greene's novel. A source in a report from July 1961 described the arrival in port of tubes 10 meters long and 2 meters in diameter, eight with Russian characters in blue, the remainder in red. The embassy reported:

> Rumours and stories abound, but as you might imagine it is very difficult to obtain confirmation. Tales about the arrival of rockets have cropped up again, but these must be regarded with particular caution as they may well be spread by counter-revolutionaries under the impression that the establishment of rocket bases in Cuba would be a signal for American intervention.[46]

All of which led the head of the Foreign Office's American Department to annotate: 'Mr Graham Greene was prophetic'. A telegram from Marchant in January 1961 could almost have been lifted unedited from the pages of *Our Man in Havana*, relating the intelligence of a caller at the embassy, an 'independent source of unknown reliability', who reported seeing 'concrete rocket land sites' under construction in eastern Cuba. Foreign Secretary Lord Home valued Marchant's serene reports from Havana during the crisis, not so much from the eye of the storm, but from what the ambassador described as the 'edge of a cyclone', where 'an unnatural calm' prevailed.[47] After the political tempest had subsided, Britain's man on the spot offered the following post-mortem:

> Any record of the story of these first two weeks of the Cuban Crisis must necessarily read more like a wildly improbable sequel to 'Our Man in Havana' than a Foreign Office despatch. Indeed I doubt whether months ago any reputable publisher would have given a moment's consideration to a story in which Soviet Russia was to be credited with shipping some four dozen giant missiles, each one longer than a cricket pitch, across the Atlantic to Cuba, where, Russian military technicians disguised as agricultural advisers would set them up in secret on launching sites.[48]

Evidently, the diplomats of Her Majesty's Government, both in Havana and in London, saw a very tangible connection between Greene's satirical spy novel and the playing out of real-life Cold War events in Cuba.

In *Our Man in Havana*, Wormold leaves Havana in his 'ancient

Hillman' to investigate new recruitment possibilities in the provinces. Ostensibly, he is making his annual visit to vacuum cleaner retailers outside Havana, but his old Hillman breaks down in Santa Clara and he continues his journey to Santiago de Cuba by coach.[49] At the height of the Cuban Missile Crisis, all ranks of staff in the British embassy engaged in low-level intelligence gathering in order to monitor the movements of Cuban and Soviet military personnel and equipment. One member of staff reported leaving the embassy '"in the wee small hours" of the morning after late telegram duty'. At 00.25 on October 26, Mr Grace and Mr Capie spotted a large convoy of vehicles on 5th Avenue in Havana. They thought it prudent not to follow given its heavy guard, the quietness of the streets, and their 'rather conspicuous' white Ford Anglia. Even so, they were able to provide sketches and detail on the type and quantity of vehicles spotted.[50]

Staff in Havana and the vice-consul in Santiago de Cuba travelled the length and breadth of the island in a determined effort to provide intelligence on the Soviet military withdrawal. While US high-level air reconnaissance provided much direct intelligence, it could not, for example, distinguish particular types of tanks and Russian from Cuban operatives.[51] British Vice-Consul Stanley Stephenson made two trips traversing the island, travelling to Havana on November 4–5, 1962, and returning to Santiago by another route on November 8–9. Frustratingly, for staff on the ground, tarpaulins often covered equipment carried on trucks, and tentative identification was based on outline only.

There was minimal sophistication to British intelligence surveillance of the agreed Soviet military withdrawal following the crisis. Due to the unreliable reception in Key West of Cuban TV broadcasts, the British supplied Washington with photographs of military parades taken from television screens. The embassy's close proximity to Havana's harbour aided Marchant and his diplomatic colleagues when Washington requested reports on the movement and exact location of Soviet ships, their cargo and persons on board. Asked how he could be sure that the men embarking were Russians, the ambassador detailed their attire, pointing out that their check shirts and fair hair made them stand out from the average Cuban. He was even able to exchange a few words of Russian with them at the dockside.[52]

CONCLUSION

As the evidence shows, Greene intervened discretely in the British arms to Cuba controversy, making a modest contribution to Batista's downfall. Castro's rebels triumphed in adversity and the novelist ridiculed the Foreign Office for its lack of foresight. Two years later, one of the British fighter-bomber planes sold to Batista sunk the main supply ships of the CIA-sponsored invasion force at the Bay of Pigs, the day after Castro first proclaimed the 'socialist' nature of his Revolution. A further year and a half later, a US spy plane photographed the 'big military installations' of Wormold's (read Greene's) imagination.[53] There was little comedy to discern as millions of the world's population contemplated the very real prospect of thermo-nuclear annihilation.

The absurd was anything but implausible during the Cold War. Paranoia and efforts to outdo or preempt the enemy's actions led to bizarre plots and operations. For the CIA this led to outlandish schemes to kill Fidel Castro, such as its exploding cigar plan. To those looking from without, the humour is tragically palpable. But those directly involved, or to use Marchant's analogy, 'in the edge of a cyclone', can be forgiven for failing at times to perceive the comic absurdity of both their predicament and actions. The experience of British diplomats in Cuba's pre- and post-revolutionary periods highlights the difficulties of interpreting and predicting events in the island.

Was it Greene's prescience or 'a sheer fluke', as the author later stated, that led to his story of large concrete platforms and strange machinery in Cuba? According to Greene, his ability to discern a country's political trajectory was not a matter of 'foresight', but resulted from his essential 'ground reconnaissance'.[54] This gives further credence to the argument that ambassador Fordham, with limited contacts and freedom to travel, was at a distinct disadvantage vis-à-vis Greene — the travelling and investigative novelist — in knowing what was really happening on the ground in Cuba when it really mattered.

Was there any idea more outrageous in the context of Cold War superpower rivalry than the invented discovery of a military base in Cuba within close range of the United States? In fact what symbol was more potent and indeed more redolent of the Cold War than 'big military installations under construction'? Was there any imagined scenario that could make more of an impression on both Wormold's MI6 superiors and Greene's reading public? The invention of a military base in Cuba was audacious. But it was matched in reality just four years later by Khrushchev's audacious offer to locate Soviet nuclear missiles in the island, and Castro's risky acceptance of them.

Greene was not just being modest when he said later that his story 'was a sheer fluke'. He had simply reflected contemporary Cold War events and new technological developments. The genius of Greene was to locate the germ of his invented intelligence idea, informed by his own MI6 experience, in pre-revolutionary Cuba. His mastery was to recognise and fully realise the comic possibilities of his fiction in the satirical but very real backdrop of tropical vice, corruption, and repression on the cusp of major political upheaval. Was there another part of the world where his Cold War spy fiction satire would have resonated quite so magnificently?

CHAPTER 10

Graham Greene and
A Burnt-Out Case:
A Psychoanalytic Reading

Michael Brearley

INTRODUCTION

It is as a psychoanalyst that I am writing about Graham Greene. He himself describes the six-month treatment he had when aged 16, with Kenneth Richmond, as psychoanalysis.[1] To my mind, Richmond was neither a psychiatrist, nor in any real sense a psychoanalyst. Richmond (along with his wife, Zoe) provided a safe setting for him and for his thoughts. The troubled adolescent was offered the freedom to explore aspects of his inner world, especially his dreams, in the company of a non-judgemental and patient adult. He was introduced to a literary world; and he was encouraged to work things out for himself. He was also removed from the hated environment of boarding school, and from parents who were not able to understand him. He was placed in a setting that was, for this sensitive boy, agreeable, sensuous, literary, and spacious. However, there appears to have been little or no working in the transference, little or no recognition of the patient's negative feelings toward the therapist, little opportunity for free association, and not much attempt at neutrality from Richmond (or from his co-therapist, Zoe). Richmond seems not to have been alert to the possibility that, in response to the expectation that the main task was the reporting of his dreams, Greene might at times have complied by inventing them. The Richmonds may well have helped Greene in various ways, but not, or not primarily, through psychoanalysis.

Greene's second volume of autobiography is entitled *Ways of*

Escape.[2] What might this phrase mean? How does his novel writing fit into his various escapes? In this chapter, I will start by making use of a fundamental distinction of Sigmund Freud's between our inclination toward wishful evasion on the one hand, and the tendency to represent to ourselves things as they are, on the other. I suggest that this distinction throws light on different types of escape from emotional pain. I will then consider different forms of escape referred to in one novel, *A Burnt-Out Case*, which describes the visit of the distinguished ex-architect and ex-philanderer Querry to a leper colony on the Congo River. Finally, I will say something about the centrality in Greene's life of his fictional writing.

Greene uses the idea of escape for a wide range of instances. He writes of escaping to Russian roulette, to opium, to brothels, and to 'troubled places', like Malaya.[3] He also went to Mexico during the violent and doctrinaire repression of religion there, to Cuba, to Haiti, to Kenya at the time of Mau Mau, to the leper colony on the Congo — 'the furthest escape of all (I don't mean geographically)'.[4] He went to Vietnam during the French wars. But he also refers to less extreme escapes: writing for the theatre offered 'an escape from the everyday',[5] and films (he watched more than 400 of them during his four and a half years as a film critic) were an escape from the task of mastering the art and craft of narrative technique.

Much of what Greene says suggests a view of escape that is close to escapism. This version may be supported by some comments on his character, comments that imply that he was contemptuous of others in his search for various forms of escapist gratification. Some critics, like Michael Shelden, view Greene as cynical, caring only for sex and money.[6] His cousin Barbara, who accompanied him on his journey through Liberia, wrote in a rather different vein about his detachment and distance, saying that most 'of humanity was to him like a heap of insects that he liked to examine, as a scientist might examine his specimens, coldly and clearly'.[7] Greene himself also includes among his escapes writing itself. In *Ways of Escape* he says: 'I can see now that my travels, as much as the act of writing, were ways of escape'.[8] But he *also* says: 'Writing is a form of therapy; sometimes I wonder how all those who do not write, compose or paint can manage to escape the madness, the melancholia, the panic fear which is inherent in the human situation'.[9] He then quotes W. H. Auden: 'Man needs escape as he needs food and sleep'.[10] Therapy and escape — to my mind, these concepts are far apart, and this is what I wish to consider in this chapter. Therapy, or at least therapy as I understand it, that is, analytic therapy, is not an indulgence, and should not be thought of as escapist. It is difficult and painful to confront one's inner demons and despairs. The attempt at emotional truthfulness is not a retreat or an escape, even if it may successfully help us to move beyond our despair or terror.

ESCAPISM AND RETREAT

There are at least three questions that Greene's emphasis on escape suggests: What does Greene escape from? What does he escape to? And, third, what are the different qualities of the various escapes — does the escaper, 'distracted from distraction by distraction'[11] (in T. S. Eliot's memorable phrase), merely kill time, or does he or she come to terms with time and with problems, face up to them and emerge a stronger, fuller, and better person? Does the journey involve finding creative, transformative solutions or outcomes? Can we be cured, or, if this is the wrong, the too circumscribed, word, healed, of whatever it was that provoked our need to defend ourselves by means of escape?

Clearly, Greene wanted to get away from the ordinary frustrations of his life — like being stuck with some aspect of a novel, with the sheer hard work and difficulty of writing. But at a deeper level, he was often escaping from an inner emptiness. There is no doubting his ennui. 'I was in that mood for escape which comes, I suppose, to most men in middle life, though with me it arrived early, even in childhood — escape from boredom, escape from depression'.[12] As with his Russian roulette,[13] he gambled in order to bring himself from a dead state to excitement and life, a gamble that could not be lost: either he died, and thus put an end to the boredom, or he was revitalised with an erotic intensity of feeling — though I should add that the prospect of ordinary safety was not always irrelevant: writing about Saigon, Greene speaks of 'that feeling of exhilaration which a measure of danger brings to the visitor with a return ticket'.[14]

It is characteristic of such escapes that the value of that to which one goes is of little consequence. The main thing is to get away from something. This makes it a form of defence. Greene's escapist excitements could involve cruelty to others. Norman Sherry writes:

Greene's reactions (wishing a loved one dead; striking out in a letter in an intolerable fashion; dreaming of suicide *as a Catholic* deliberately to harm the person who discovers it) are to be seen now as methods of escaping from the grip of despair coupled with the feeling that unless something drastic is done madness might follow.[15]

In other words, escapism can veer over from defence toward a gratifying perversity. Even escapes in this sense — defensive with a perverse tinge, retreating as far as possible away from a devastated inner world, but devastating it further in the process — may bring with them a new lease of life, new values, a new sense of life worth living. In the first place, for some people, risk is an aphrodisiac. Without it they cannot find arousal or stimulation. But also, second and more significant, 'perhaps you do not find courage where there is no danger, and love too may be a product of active war' (Greene is describing the courage of two men in Malaya during the Emergency).[16] Greene is right about courage. 'Nothing in his life / Became him like the leaving it,' says Malcolm of Macbeth's predecessor as Thane of Cawdor.[17] In death's presence, in the felt presence of God, some display extraordinary courage. People came to public executions in eighteenth-century Britain to witness courage, or defiance, and sometimes repentance and remorse. Socrates was courageous both in war, saving Alcibiades' life when the latter was wounded, and also, in Plato's famous account, in facing the death penalty with extraordinary equanimity.[18]

There is too a third form of escape, where what is escaped from is a narrowly self-centred or obsessive mind-set, and what is escaped to enables a person to return to life, to realise that the world out there encourages a revival of real interest or passion. And actions and attitudes may, as Freud put it, be over-determined.[19] There may be more than one motive for an escape. Greene's nephew James Greene, in an unpublished article, suggests a possible psychological function of his uncle's fascination for brothels.[20] Was the unconscious or conscious purpose of his brothel visits, James Greene surmises, like that of his fictional novelist Jorge Julio Saavedra in *The Honorary Consul*, with his 'rule of self-imposed discipline' — that is, the weekly visit — to put himself into the shoes of the poor, the wounded and the vulnerable? Saavedra says: 'he learned a great deal about human nature. In the social life of the city there was no contact between the classes'.[21] I see no difficulty in imagining this as one strand in the novelist's motivation. And as James Greene suggests, the vector of solace for a child whose parents were not able to show physical affection may be another. People are complex, and the same activity may serve many different functions simultaneously.

ESCAPISM VERSUS WHAT?
FREUD'S DISTINCTION BETWEEN EVASION
OF REALITY AND ITS MODIFICATION

When we think of the defensive and perverse aspects of escape, aspects that readily link with escapism, what are we contrasting such behaviour and inner life with? What is the healthy, or healthier, or in some cases ideal, way of dealing with whatever it is that we need, or are tempted, to defend ourselves against? Writing in his 'Formulations on the Two Principles of Mental Functioning', Freud proposes that when something is unbearable to us, we characteristically rearrange our internal reality to deal with this disappointment or frustration.[22] He calls this mode of functioning 'acting according to the Pleasure principle', or 'perhaps more accurately', he says, the 'Unpleasure Principle'. If something is unpleasurable, our earliest resort, and a frequent later resort, is to create the desired outcome in our minds as if it were real. This is what we mean by wish-fulfilling hallucination. There are also, as Freud says in the first paragraph of the paper, less radical, less total, distortions, which may suffice to make reality bearable enough; these characterise less extreme — neurotic rather than psychotic — solutions. We all, he adds, to greater or lesser degrees, distort reality, some of us more than others, all of us more at some times than at others.

Freud points out that wish-fulfilling hallucination is bound to fail. Eventually we experience disappointment. We may, one may add, be reduced to screaming and kicking to force reality to change. To varying degrees we learn to abandon hallucination (and other major forms of distortion) and the demand for instant gratification. We learn this gradually, and over a certain range of activities. When a person functions more in accordance with the reality principle, he or she can begin to 'form a conception of the real circumstances in the external world, and to endeavour to make a real alteration in them . . . What was presented in the mind was no longer what was agreeable but what was real, even if it happened to be disagreeable'.[23] Such functioning involves the recognition of reality, and the willingness to enter into the struggle of moderating it by work or effort.

Here is an example of a patient who resorts to something close to wish-fulfilling hallucination as an escape from reality. A male patient is frightened of intimacy. One day he has a session in which there is closer contact with his therapist and recognition of his need for her and her help. Immediately after these moments, he has the shocking feeling that she and everything in his environment have gone distant.

He is shaken by this sudden change. Though he is not deluded (he does not literally believe that she and her chair have suddenly been transported away from him, or actually shrunk), his degree of consternation suggests that he has a visual experience of her as reduced in sise. I would say that she suddenly becomes small and distant in his psyche, and that this expresses a wish that was experienced as a reality: his making her small — an aspect of contempt — is a defence against (an escape from) something he finds terrifying: she had for a short while mattered greatly to him.

Note that, in the aforementioned paper, Freud makes an important connection between psychopathology and falsification, a link paralleled by that between the idea of the reality principle and mental health. We find a similar conviction in A *Burnt-Out Case* and in Greene's work in general.[24]

The story of the fox and the grapes provides a second example of defensive distortion of reality. The fox, you will recall, is hungry and thirsty, and sees appetizing grapes growing down from the other side of a wall. But he cannot quite reach them, however hard he tries. In order to evade disappointment and loss, he tells himself (and secondarily the world) that he never really wanted them in the first place: the grapes were no good; they were sour (though he has not tasted them, and though they did not strike him as sour when he was trying so hard to reach them). We might call the emotion the fox ends up with a *malformed emotion* — a term invented by Richard Wollheim.[25] The fox malforms his own psychic reality, and his perception of the world, to deal with unpleasure. We often find it easier to scorn what we cannot get, or what we fear not being able to get — thus operating according to sour grapes in advance, rather than acknowledging our needs and desires and thereby risking failure, disappointment, and sometimes a feeling of humiliation. In a sense we lie to ourselves. We may similarly deal with romantic or sexual disappointments by running down the person concerned. ('That slag! I would not be seen dead with her!') We thus cut ourselves off from life, and its risks, because our assumption so often is that the prospective humiliation will be unbearable. You remember the old saying 'it's better to have loved and lost than never to have loved at all'? We often work on the basis that this is *not* the case. We may even find a ready addictive alternative to these potential disappointments, like drugs or some other form of manic omnipotent flight, by which to escape or cover up the painful qualities of such situations. Hence the 'sour grapes' expression. Such mental moves can happen in the psychoanalytic process, where they may also be tracked, understood, and sometimes, over time, modified or reversed.

The result of these conflicts — between wishes and anxiety — is a defensive and often disturbing illusion that may have the force of a delusion. Such rearrangement of reality in the face of difficulty or conflict leads to our living compelled lives, imbued with neurotic and psychotic anxieties or emptiness.

My third example of rearranging reality comes from a paper by Neville Symington, where it takes the form of the patient's enlisting the analyst to play a complementary role to her (or his) own.[26] Symington describes how the analyst has to free himself from roles he is pushed into by the patient (and takes on himself). He argues that such freeing from compulsion and from lack of understanding can also help free the patient. Symington gives a brief example. He thought of one of his patients as 'Poor Miss M' Miss M 'paid me little more than half my regular fee'. To her analyst, her paying this low fee was 'an acknowledged fact . . . like the unreliability of the English weather . . . Until one day a startling thought occurred to me: "Why can't Miss M pay the same as all my other patients?"' Symington suddenly realised that there was no sound reason why she could not. His act of freedom was the realisation that she functioned with him as with others by getting him and them to treat her as ineffectual and immature. He came to see that he had been 'lassoed into this self-perception of his patient'. When he put it to her that there was no reason for her not to pay the fee, she was initially upset, but then resolved to meet the challenge. His raising the fee in the light of such understanding helped her to become more grown up. In place of being patronised by her boss (who always called her 'Little Mary'), she got a better job, more suited to her talent. And she got rid of her parasitic boyfriend.[27] Here the psychoanalyst's recovery of his freedom of thought helped the patient too to become able to recover or find independence of thought and action rather than escape from the burdens of maturity by arranging things so that she remained childlike in a dependent and inferior position.

As Symington's example suggests, we are not necessarily stuck with Freud's first principle of mental functioning. The second of his 'principles' he calls the reality principle: functioning in this mode, he says, is a matter of *modifying* reality rather than *evading or distorting* it. When he talks about the reality principle, Freud emphasises cases where external reality can be changed; I would like to emphasise that often in fact it cannot be changed, not, at least, directly. In all cases, what *can* (in principle at least) is our *attitude* to external reality, that is, our *internal* reality.

Thinking, Freud goes on to suggest, may be conceptualised as inhibited action; the reality principle means that we are able to put between stimulus and reaction something that delays or inhibits both the tendency to hallucination and the tendency to do something instantly.

Bearing the pain of reality, of both internal and external reality, is, then, central to the psychoanalytic conception of health, and to the psychoanalytic enterprise as a form of therapy. Psychoanalytic therapy differs from some other forms of treatment of psychopathology in its insistence on understanding the unconscious factors in action, in desire and in thinking, and second in the belief that only through facing reality can mental health be developed. Change of a healthy kind depends, therefore, on insight and the increasing ability to tolerate truth; and truth may be the mind's food.

We need defences to get by in the world, but we also use defences, including our hallucinating wish fulfilments, in pathological ways to protect ourselves against hated aspects of reality. Gaining insight includes, clearly, the growth of a space for thinking, a mental space rather than a stimulus–response system. It also allows for and is part of a richer inner world, a fuller self. As D. H. Lawrence puts it: our inner world is (or can be) 'a forest rather than a narrow enclosure'.[28]

A BURNT-OUT CASE

This 1960 novel shows us conflicting forms of escape in someone who has lost the capacity to love, hate, or suffer. And in the book's dedication, to Docteur Michel Lechat, Greene indicates that 'This Congo is a region of the mind'. Querry, the story's main character, makes a recovery as a result of his retreat to the leper colony on the banks of the River Congo. The extent of his recovery is uncertain. Greene, who clearly represents aspects of himself in Querry, found the task of writing unusually difficult: 'Never had a novel proved more recalcitrant or more depressing. The reader had only to endure a few hours of the company of the burnt-out character called Querry, but the author had to live with him and in him for eighteen months'.[29] What most appeals to Querry, when they stop off at a seminary on the banks of the river, is the fact that no one will ask him questions, no one will intrude.[30] His next thought hints at the extent and perhaps the nature of his sinfulness: 'If he had been a murderer escaping from justice, no one would have had the curiosity to probe his secret wound'.[31] Later Querry's loquacity is compared by Parkinson to a murderer's.[32]

Querry has lost his soul, one might say. Certainly he has lost his inner sense of value. He lacks all that makes life meaningful, including suffering. There is a hint of murder in this. He says 'I suffer from nothing. I no longer know what suffering is. I have come to an end of all that, too'.[33] He is in the doldrums; three times in the first 30-odd pages we hear that there is no fan, no breeze. On his journey upriver, on the first page of the novel, Greene writes 'if no change means peace, this certainly was peace'.[34] He lives in the peace of death, of deadliness. Like Albert Camus' characters, he is the victim of a plague that is both personal and cultural. The plague, the emptiness, the leprosy, are the result of his earlier narcissism, of his search for power, and of his presumption of a sort of knowingness, qualities most fully represented through the character of the factory manager, Rycker.

Querry is, as he himself avows, 'one of the mutilees'.[35] Like the leprosy victims who have literally lost parts of their bodies, he has lost parts of his psyche. Dr Colin tells him that 'mutilation is the alternative to pain'.[36] Like the lepers, he feels no pain (though we must not forget the 'panic of complete abandonment' referred to on the same page).[37] He has some insight into his predicament, but at the beginning of the novel, this does not appear to be enough to offer much hope of emotional change. After confessing how much his life has been predicated on the gratification of self (his buildings were to please himself alone, his women were used), Querry says to the doctor: 'Self-expression is a hard and selfish thing. It eats everything even the self. At the end you find that you haven't even got a self to express. I have no interest in anything any more, doctor. I don't want to sleep with a woman or design a building'.[38] He is like a patient I heard of who dreamed of working for the charity War on Want; she too had made war on wanting, and in this way deadened herself.

Soon after Querry's arrival he offers to help the doctor, with bandaging, say. He is willing to do anything except what he is actually skilled in, architecture. When the doctor tells him that the thing he has most need of is a designer for the new hospital, Querry declines. He writes a note, speaking of his having always built for himself, not for the glory of God or the pleasure of a purchaser: 'I will do anything for you in reason, but don't ask me to try to revive . . '.[39] Doctor Colin reacts with blunt commonsense: 'Scruples. Just scruples,' he says.[40] He is not concerned with Querry's complicated mental moves and hesitations. Like the Father Superior, he is suspicious of probing too deeply — the Father Superior has said, 'if I begin to probe into what lies behind that desire to be of use, oh well, I might find some terrible things, and we are all tempted to stop when we reach that point. Yet if we dug farther, who knows — the terrible too might be only a few skins deep'.[41] Colin cuts short Querry's 'I tried to explain' with 'Who cares?'[42]

As one learns in analysis, knowledge and reflection without commitment or feeling can be just another defence, another delaying tactic. Doubt, scruples, deep motives, can all be used in the service of stasis, of doing nothing, in the service even of pride. Ronald Fairbairn describes patients who adopt 'the technique of describing scenes enacted on the stage of inner reality without any significant participation on the part of the central ego either in these scenes or in an effective relationship with the analyst'. He goes on: 'One of my patients, who was a past master in this technique, said to me one day, after providing a comprehensive intellectual description of the state of impulse-tension in which he felt himself to be placed: "well what are you going to do about it?" By way of reply I explained that the real question was what he himself was going to do about it'.[43]

In *A Burnt-Out Case*, the Father Superior says of Rycker 'When a man has nothing else to be proud of, he is proud of his spiritual problems'.[44] One can be complacent about one's problems; indeed, one can appear to ask for help but secretly take pride in the display of apparent humility. Alternative currents of feeling and motive can interfere with our conscious plans. Here, George Eliot's narrator in *Middlemarch* alludes to one way in which we undermine our good intentions: 'A man vows, and yet will not cast away the means of breaking his vow. Is it that he distinctly means to break it? Not at all; but the desires which tend to break it are at work in him dimly, and make their way into his imagination, and relax his muscles in the very moments when he is telling himself over again the reasons for his vow'.[45] Glossing *Middlemarch*, F. R. Leavis notes that an intention can work through 'dark indirections and tormented inner casuistries'.[46]

To return to Querry. The night after the 'Who cares?' conversation with the doctor, he has a dream from which he wakes with a 'cry like an animal in pain'.[47] In the dream he is wearing ordinary clothes, but is in fact a priest, and is trying to get to another priest in order to confess. He fails in this, and feels 'he had had an appointment with hope at this turn of the road, and had arrived just too late'.[48] Sleepless, he reflects in anguish on the dream and on the doctor's 'Who cares?' When morning arrives, he seeks out the carpenter and arranges to have a desk and drawing board made. Thus Querry begins to revive or recreate his almost defunct drive for life. The dream speaks of his evasion (the ordinary clothes) of something sacred in him (he is a priest); it speaks of his wish, and need, for repentance. It speaks too of his not getting where he needs to be. He awakes. He is in anguish about this sense of not reaching. Instead of lamenting his failure to follow through, he makes a decision. He will, now, help with the design of the new hospital. He is less of a detective (Rycker-like) getting possession of knowledge rather as one gets possession of a woman or a building for one's own monstrous pride. He lets go this enthralment to the past and to indecision. The doctor says: 'I am glad for you. I know nothing about you but we are all made much the same way. You have been trying an impossible experiment. A man can't live with nothing but himself'.[49]

In the next chapter, Querry acts out of character, throwing off his old inertia by going to the rescue of his servant, the cured leper Deo Gratias, who has hobbled off into the forest at night, fallen, and broken his ankle. At risk to himself, Querry seeks him out, and stays with him till daylight. Querry has entered the forest, which is for Greene an image of his old hopelessness, described both as empty and as never silent, full of the chatter of insects — like a distracted and flailing mind. *This* forest *is* a narrow enclosure. Rather than sitting like Fairbairn's patient in the dress circle in a spirit of inert spectatorship, Querry has followed Joseph Conrad's prescription: 'in the destructive element immerse'.[50] Querry's motives may have been mixed — in setting off into the jungle at night alone, was he searching out an accident, in the form of either a disguised suicide, or of an exciting danger? Maybe, but he also recognised 'an odd feeling that he (the servant) needed me', and 'to be needed is a different sensation (from using people), a tranquilliser not an excitement'.[51]

In his conversation with the doctor, he even laughs (early in the novel we are told that he is 'taunted by the innocence of the laughter'): Querry is joining the human race.[52] In the course of his growing friendship (and, informally, therapy) with another person, the doctor (and, to a lesser extent, with the Father Superior), he has queried — this must, I imagine, be one source of the name Greene gives him — and interrogated his own ennui, and made a shift toward life.

One psychoanalytic account of the contrast is that he is torn between those forces within himself that are on the side of life and love, such forces encouraged and nurtured by the good figures (the doctor, with his values, the Father Superior) and on the other hand the forces on the side of death, forces expressed through the negative characters in the novel (Rycker, Parkinson, Father Thomas). At the beginning of the book, Querry is consumed by the latter forces. His hatred itself is disowned, and replaced by the deadly indifference that Greene describes so well, itself a form of evasion of the truth. As the novel progresses, and particularly in the course of Querry's therapeutic relationship with the doctor, he changes. The hospital begins to be constructed (he walks into 'rooms that are not yet built'[53] — another reference to his own growth in ways as yet unknowable). He has saved the life of Deo Gratias. He feels that some persistent poison had been drained from his system, and he experiences a different sort of peace from the deadly doldrums referred to in the early part of the novel.[54] Later he can offer something to Mrs Rycker without taking advantage of her. Meanwhile, others, who are in thrall to untruth, to perversions of the truth, misinterpret his actions in fateful ways.

There are many obstacles on the path to recovery or new life. We are reminded that cured lepers find it hard to adjust to the world: 'For burnt-out cases life outside isn't easy. They carry the stigma of leprosy. People are apt to think "once a leper always a leper"' (says the doctor), but this conversation moves on to the possibilities of the expansion of love: 'Suppose love were to evolve as rapidly in our brains as technical skill has done'.[55] Querry — and we — are now in a different psychological world, in which hope, love and life are possible, however difficult.

We know, too, the power of the destructive elements. When the journalist Parkinson, alerted by Rycker to the possibilities of a scoop in seeking out Querry, argues for the financial benefits to the leproserie of the publicity his sensational articles will create, the doctor says 'Where now will he [Querry] be able to find *his* therapy? Limelight is not very good for the mutilated'.[56] This is a reference to the dangers (and the appeal) of exaggeration and histrionics (the limelight of the stage and the flash photography of popular journalism), the exaggerations, exaltations and cynical disparagement coming from the corrupting negative characters as well as from inside Querry.

Before moving on to consider Greene's notion of escape in the light of the novel, I want to mention the central link between Greene and Freud. Like Freud, Greene emphasises truth and untruth, and makes it clear how much they have to do, respectively, with mental health and ill-health. A salient feature of both Rycker (the domineering busybody) and Parkinson (the representative of the yellow press, of whom it is said 'there is a strong allurement in corruption and there was no doubt of Parkinson's; he carried it on the surface of his skin like phosphorus, impossible to mistake') is their willingness to distort the truth.[57] Rycker exaggerates for effect in order to exalt himself and the person he is talking about, Parkinson to sell a story. 'They won't know the bloody difference,' he says, contemptuously.[58] Father Thomas (the doubter) also distorts the truth for his own purposes, though his lies are less conscious than those of the other two, especially Parkinson's. Like Rycker, he wants to make Querry into a saint.

It is a feature of Querry's change that he is able to recognise his own unconscious lies; the new understanding comes when he makes inner reparation to the figure of Marie (his ex-lover who killed herself — one source of the intimations that he is a murderer): 'I'm sorry. I really believed that I meant you no harm. I really thought in those days that I acted from love'. Greene's narrator adds: 'There is a time in life when a man with a little acting ability is able to deceive even himself'.[59] In contrast to the characters who tell or live lies, the doctor is blunt in his repudiation of all that Parkinson, Rycker and Father Thomas stand for. 'But these are lies,' he says.[60]

What is our assessment of Querry's 'cure'? How has his 'therapy' worked? I am inclined to agree both with the doctor, who says, 'It is more difficult to cure the mind than the body, and yet I think the cure is nearly complete,' and with Querry himself, who, despite his own tendency to diminish the changes he is achieving, admits, shortly before the final denouement with Rycker, 'I think I'm cured of pretty well everything, even disgust. I've been happy here'.[61]

GREENE AS A PERSON AND GREENE AS A WRITER

In *The Sunday Times* review of Jeremy Lewis's *Shades of Greene*, John Carey is critical of Lewis's assessment of Graham Greene, since it excludes Greene's writing. Carey writes: 'Greene did his feeling and thinking in his novels, and leaving them out means leaving out his heart and his brain'.[62] *Shades of Greene* catalogues Greene's sins and failings. So too does James Greene, Graham Greene's nephew, in the aforementioned unpublished article. James Greene describes his uncle as sometimes 'lonely, empty, depersonalised and wooden'. While giving space to the deficits in his uncle's upbringing (he refers to Graham Greene's emotionally inadequate, 'kind but cut-off' parents who could not understand the terrible impact of boarding school life on a sensitive boy who was cruelly bullied), James Greene is scathing about the solutions his uncle adopted. Graham Greene was 'loyal to disloyalty, serially polygamous and seriously sly where sex was concerned'. He was always 'heading for the other side of the border'. And 'no one', James Greene goes on, 'was exempt from his waspish petulance. This peevishness . . . allowed his intelligence to become bewitched by a pontifical and would-be crushing snappiness . . . Always easily offended and then on the offensive . . . Graham invariably knew best . . . there was always someone to get the better of, always something to prove, another summit to conquer or feel defeated by'.[63] Here, James Greene interprets, to my mind plausibly, Graham Greene's promiscuity and his dreams of treason as Oedipal revenge against his father.

All this may be true. But, when James Greene says, again correctly, that 'spiritual emptiness isn't so easy to abolish even if you devote a novel to it as he did in A Burnt-Out Case',[64] is the implication that the novel is thus something of a sideshow also correct?

I revert to my initial questions about escape. I would like to say that the writing of the novel, with its attendant depression and difficulty for the author, was his way of facing up to and working through his emptiness and the manic defences against it. He *is* Querry, not only in his deadly aridity but also in his struggle to move on, to acknowledge his sins without histrionics or pride (the sins also, to some extent, of Parkinson, Rycker, and Thomas). James Greene gives Graham Greene credit for the fact that he worked extremely hard. I think Graham Greene worked hard not only at the technical side of writing, but also emotionally. He struggled to get to the truth, to avow truths via these figures. He immersed himself in his own destructive element. He did not avoid it, nor did he use the writing of the novel as an escape (in the sense of 'escapism').

As we have seen, one form of distortion is histrionics, and the writer (Parkinson/Greene) is tempted by it. In his 'Introduction' to the 2004 reissue of A Burnt-Out Case, Giles Foden declares: 'Querry tells Rycker . . . that he dramatises too much. Can we interpret this as Greene's self-reproach about The Heart of the Matter and his still more reader-friendly "entertainments"'[65] — Greene's own term for his less serious novels? If so — and I have my questions about how far he was successful in this even in A Burnt-Out Case — Greene is fighting against what he calls 'the allurements of corruption' as represented in Parkinson.[66] It is not a mere exercise. It is emotional work. The novel evinces a genuine internal struggle.

Querry may have been, as Greene writes, 'a better man than I am'.[67] But Graham Greene the serious novelist is also Graham Greene living his life, even if the writer is often a better man than the person making relationships and moving around the world.

In The Analytic Attitude, Roy Schafer writes: 'The analyst makes use of and improvises on, their (sic) second selves, lived out with appropriate stamina'.[68] In our work we become different from, though of course related to, how we are at other times. As a result of our internal and external setting, we are no longer parent, child, lover, partner, businessman, friend, colleague, patient, though how we are in all these roles contributes to how we are as analysts. Like novelists, we may be capable of being better persons when working than when engaging in the rest of our lives. The novelist Greene was a central part of the person Greene, perhaps a better part. For the novelist as for the analyst there has to be first-hand knowledge of the range of human anxieties and their varied responses to them. For the analyst as for the novelist, there has to be acceptance of our shared humanity with our patients or subjects. Both aim to reach the point where (in the words of the Roman playwright Terence) 'I think of nothing human as alien to me'.[69] Both need to accept T. S. Eliot's 'The wounded surgeon plies the steel / That questions the distempered part'.[70] Of course it is true that words can be used in an empty fashion, without impact on our actual lives. And psychoanalysts, like novelists, are vulnerable to the accusation that with all this work on being open-minded, in attempting to understand our own and others' fallibilities, we ought to be better human beings than we are. Our narcissism can settle on, or float above, our oh-so-strenuous immersion 'in the destructive element'. But despite its flaws, A Burnt-Out Case is not, I think, such a book.

And despite it being true that Greene elides escapism with thera-peutic work, he is also aware of the distinction. I will end with his words, from Ways of Escape: 'What I was engaged in through those war years was not genuine action — it was an escape from reality and responsibility. To a novelist his novel is the only reality and his only responsibility. Like the man suffering from ju-ju I had to go back to my proper region to be cured'.[71] Put differently, 'genuine action' versus 'escape': 'responsibility' and 'proper region' versus 'ju-ju' and 'dirty work' as a police interrogator.

Narcissism can all too easily creep back in, of course, when the writer (or the psychoanalyst) forgets, denies, turns a blind eye to, escapes from all his other realities and responsibilities; from those to his wife, perhaps, or to his children. His 'second self' may be, as Greene said of Querry, a better person than himself. But he, too, is a self.

CHAPTER 11

A Touch of Evolutionary Religion

Darren J. N. Middleton

INTRODUCTION

Marked by the unblinking scrutiny of God, Graham Greene's life and literary art displays a touch of evolutionary religion, and this chapter considers how and why Christian process theology emerges in two Greene novels, *A Burnt-Out Case* and *The Honorary Consul*.[1] My starting point is Charles Darwin's theory of evolution, which holds that natural selection functions as evolutionary change's primary mechanism, an idea that when it first surfaced both challenged traditional Christian doctrine and questioned centuries-old ecclesiastical authority. The conventional view of the differences between species disappeared, for example, and this notion decentralised humankind; we lost our sense of privilege. Instead of occurring in the six days of Genesis, moreover, life unfurled over vast as well as complex stretches of time; and, for many religious, this model harmed scripture's reputation. Darwin's theory also altered life's overall significance. We are no longer God's special darlings, or so the understanding goes, and purpose is not guaranteed in evolution's seemingly blind, brutish, and random process. Very generally, traditional Christianity suffered a blow from Darwin's deliberations. And many recent thinkers consider this blow fatal — an assault from which Christianity has never recovered and will never recover.

Some Christians have tried to accommodate Christianity and evolution, using Darwin's insights to construct new theologies based either on a fresh sense of Christian doctrine's nature and function or else on innovative ways of picturing God's presence in an emerging world.

Regarding the former, consider John Henry Newman. He valued each believer's struggle to articulate the faith in light of their historical situatedness, for example, and he treasured belief's development across the centuries:

> In time [Christian doctrine] enters upon strange territory; points of controversy alter their bearing; parties rise and fall around it; dangers and hopes appear in new relations; and old principles reappear under new forms. It changes with them in order to remain the same. In a higher world it is otherwise, but here below to live is to change, and to be perfect is to have changed often.[2]

Greene admired Newman; and, although his appreciation 'was at times selective', as Mark Bosco notes, 'it nevertheless became the first formative lens in which his inchoate faith finds resonance in Catholicism'.[3]

Newman never stood alone in Greene's mind. A Jesuit palaeontologist whose writings were questioned by the Roman Curia, Pierre Teilhard de Chardin also endorsed the idea of faith still in the making. By all accounts, Teilhard found Greene's *The Heart of the Matter* so stirring that he appropriated and amended its title for his own book, *The Heart of Matter*, which makes explicit Teilhard's conviction that God employs evolution to create and stimulate life in the universe. Known as 'process theology', this worldview claims that the protracted yet dynamic advancement from simple life forms to more complex realities, such as humans, parallels the spiritual progress of women, children, and men toward a more Christ-like existence — the Omega Point.[4] In *A Sort of Life*, Greene endorses Teilhard's process theology.[5]

PROCESS THEOLOGY

Emerging in the last century in the writings of Henri Bergson, Alfred North Whitehead and Charles Hartshorne, process theology complains that traditional Christian theology remains yoked to the ancient Greek philosophical idea of the One and the Many, or permanence and change, and so presents God as the fixed and passionless Absolute. On this view whatever changes, decays, to state the issue briefly, and so the ancient Greeks not only equate change with imperfection, they think of the perfect God as changeless. Christian theology evolved beside Greek philosophy. And this development led numerous Christian thinkers, such as Thomas Aquinas, to hold to a static, unchanging universe — a view that Darwin rejected. Aquinas embraced Greek philosophy and described God as the Unmoved Mover — capable of initiating change in others but remaining unchanged in Godself. Such is Christian theology's presiding model of God, and I have heard it preached from the church and taught in the classroom, yet process theologians challenge it fiercely.[6] They point out that this Unmoved Mover remains essentially unrelatable; and I agree. For me, authentic Christian theology speaks of God's love for our hurting world, of faith as our response to the Divine Self-Offer, and it notes that both 'love' and 'faith' are relational, processive concepts. Let me explain.

We are not islands alone unto ourselves. Our actions matter or at least they ought to matter to every one of us. We are not inflexible entities that trek unchanged through time. Rather, we are the many experiences and changes we have had; therefore, we are relational and processive. The same is true of God. And to say anything less horrifies me religiously. If our tears twirl humanity's water mills, for example, but fail to move God, then I find myself forced to wonder whether this passionless Absolute is really, truly worthy of our worship. God is subject to change as we are subject to change. And so these days I think the divine is actually part of life's insubstantiality, intimately involved within our world, and sometimes to the point of being affected by what occurs within it. This position is sometimes called *process panentheism*, which should not be confused with *traditional theism* (as defined above) or *pantheism* (thinking of God *as* nature without remainder). Panentheism maintains that God includes all created life *within* God's life.[7] What happens to the world happens to God. In her reflection on Teilhard's work, Annie Dillard remarks: 'Not only is God immanent in everything, as plain pantheists hold, but more profoundly everything is simultaneously in God, within God the transcendent. There is a divine, not just bushes'.[8]

I commend process theology because it uses current understandings of the way the world goes — evolutionary theory — to form fresh, critically plausible, and theistically relevant God-talk. In process thought, that is, a dynamic conception of the divine, as opposed to a substantial model of God (i.e., the Eternal Absolute), more adequately grounds evolution, and may even inspire evolution's many world inhabitants both to proceed toward and adore Spirit. The valuational component in this theology — its existential fruitfulness, if you will — lies in the arresting notion that if the future is the future for God, not simply for us, then life itself is nothing less than an adventure of the spirit. Clark Williamson and Ronald Allen write:

A process spirituality will seek to encourage people to enhance their God-given creativity and capacity to envision the new way in which God now calls us to walk. It will help people with the difficult intellectual and moral reflection involved in figuring out in what ways faithful people should understand and act in the situation in which it is given us to live. It will recognize that not all new possibilities are from God (novelty is not to be deified), but that some are. The good role that conservatives play is that of forcing the rest of us to test the case that is made on behalf of any given possibility. An authentic spirituality will provide for us the strength and reassurance to take the heat that comes from being willing to leave Ur of the Chaldees and venture forward with the God of the ahead.[9]

Process theologians, like Teilhard, hold that being religious in a relational and processive world involves attending to the God who agitates, stimulates, and sways us in our restlessness by seeking creation's flourishing. Everything matters. And our sense that our struggle to seek transformation, higher goals, and ever new possibilities truly matters to God can serve to foster our commitment to a lifestyle that nurtures and sustains human togetherness and ecological sensitivity. Genuine faith and its practical embodiment — spirituality — thus flows out of a discernment of the part we play as co-creators with the divine in the evolutionary process. And so to Teilhard, whose Catholic version of process theology proved crucial to Greene's work.

TEILHARD'S PROCESS CATHOLICISM

A passionate reader of Bergson, Teilhard used his training in science and theology to marry basic Christian beliefs to central claims within evolutionary thought. For our purposes, his process Catholicism rests on four basic ideas. First, he views and describes life as a complex evolutionary process. Drawn by an enigmatic energy, a pulsating power that fructifies the heart of matter, life moves on. 'Those who look reality in the face,' he insists, 'cannot fail to perceive this progressive genesis of the Universe'.[10] Responding, as did Bergson, to ideas of progress prevalent in the last century, Teilhard asserts that *becoming*, not *being*, signifies the base of things. The world has been, always will be, malleable.[11]

A second Teilhardian idea focuses on guided evolution or, in longhand, the notion that God acts as the vivifying force at the heart of the ceaseless processes of cosmic and terrestrial becoming. 'It is in fact God, and God alone, who through his Spirit stirs up into ferment the mass of the universe,' Teilhard declares.[12] On this view, then, the unfolding cosmos is the field of divine activity; indeed, the universe is the total environment in which everything is grounded in an energetic God, and where God confers worth upon everything in the overall temporal development:

> God, at his most vitally active and most incarnate, is not remote from us, wholly apart from the sphere of the tangible; on the contrary, at every moment he awaits us in the activity, the work to be done, which every moment brings. He is, in a sense, at the point of my pen, my pick, my paint-brush, my needle — and my heart and my thought. It is by carrying to its natural completion the stroke, the line, the stitch I am working on that I shall lay hold on that ultimate end towards which my will at its deepest levels tends. Like those formidable physical forces which man has so disciplined that they can be made to carry out operations of amazing delicacy, so the enormous might of God's magnetism is brought to bear on our frail destines, our tiny objectives, without ever breaking their point.[13]

The third feature of Teilhard's vision follows from his belief in God's and life's dynamic as well as organic character. He holds that evil accompanies all changes and experiences, that our world-in-the-making is, by its nature, partially disorganised, replete with physical and ethical faults, and that such failures ensure that evolution proceeds. God both resides and proceeds out from the centre of this expanding cosmos, sharing in its pain and joy, inexhaustibly at work in a struggle against evil.[14] For his part, Greene shares this Teilhardian emphasis on the messy verities of becoming. 'I have always been preoccupied with the mystery of sin,' he once said, 'it is always the foundation of my books'.[15] A novelist who tried to illuminate divine mercy by using 'indirect lighting', Greene believes that God grants grace, and thus hope eternal, 'to the most degraded of human beings'.[16] Furthermore, Greene proclaims that life is a process, a vale of soul-making, and that personal development ought to continue after bodily death. 'I can't believe in a Heaven which is just passive bliss,' he ruminates, 'if there's such a thing as Heaven, it will contain movement and change'.[17]

A final aspect of Teilhard's theological imagination is his belief that the 'cosmic Christ' both complements and completes the 'historical Jesus'. Pictured as an intentional and energetic urge, which stimulates as well as cherishes the creative advance, the cosmic Christ beckons nature, history, and humanity into an open future. Christ the Evolver sanctifies every tiny droplet of experience that marks the processes of reality; and, as its culmination, its Omega Point, Christ ensures the final enrichment of the cosmic environment as a whole:

> Since Jesus was born, and grew to his full stature, and died, everything has
> continued to move forward because *Christ is not yet fully formed*: he has not
> yet gathered about him the last folds of his robe of flesh and of love which
> is made up of his faithful followers. The mystical Christ has not yet attained
> to his full growth; and therefore the same is true of the cosmic Christ. Both
> of these are simultaneously in the state of being and becoming; and it is
> from the prolongation of this process of becoming that all created activity
> ultimately springs. Christ is the end-point of evolution, even the *natural*
> evolution, of all beings; and therefore evolution is holy.[18]

The cosmic Christ is the basic source of unrest in a world still in the
making, the grammar and ground of the dissatisfaction that women
and men feel as they evaluate their previous accomplishments, become
aware of novel possibilities, and as they strive to actualise them:

> It is God himself who rises up in the heart of this simplified world. And the
> organic form of the universe thus divinized is Christ Jesus, who, through the
> magnetism of his love and the effective power of his Eucharist, gradually
> gathers into himself all the unitive energy scattered throughout his creation
> . . . Christ *binds* us and *reveals* us to one another.[19]

Such words shaped Vatican II's ecclesial documents. And these days
Catholic theologians, like Robert Kinast, link process theology to the
Council's arresting portrait of Jesus Christ mystically constituting
His Body out of those pilgrims called both onward and upward from
around the globe. 'The becoming of the church is the becoming of
its members, and part of the becoming of God,' Kinast declares, and
this notion 'translates into a sense of giving delight to God by shaping
the experience of the church as creatively and imaginatively as possible. For in the end whether viewed from the perspective of process
philosophy or process Catholicism, the aim of all creation is to serve
the becoming of God'.[20]

A BURNT-OUT CASE

Process theology surfaces in this novel's part 5, chapter 1, albeit briefly.
Here the famous builder of churches and a collector of women,
Querry, escapes the relentless attention of the European media and
flees to a leprosy clinic in a deserted African village. But even here he

seems hard pressed to avoid giving an account of himself. In one telling scene, Dr Colin tries to engage Querry on the subject of religion,
without much success, but it is Dr Colin's own beliefs, his 'very small
hope,' that represents one of Greene's earliest fictional allusions to
Teilhardian themes. Asked if he finds the Christian mythos existen-
tially sufficient, Dr Colin avoids the question, at least initially, and
upholds what appears at first blush to be another story entirely:

> 'I want to be on the side of change,' the doctor said. 'If I had been born an
> amoeba who could think, I would have dreamt of the day of the primates.
> I would have wanted anything I did to contribute to that day. Evolution, as
> far as we can tell, has lodged itself finally in the brains of man. The ant, the
> fish, even the ape has gone as far as it can go, but in our brain evolution
> is moving — my God — at what speed! I forgot how many hundreds of
> millions of years passed between the dinosaurs and the primates, but in our
> own lifetime we have seen the change from Diesel to jet, the splitting of the
> atom, the cure of leprosy'.[21]

Querry fails to thrum with this Victorian song of progress, as we
discover, and he derides the seemingly cheerful confidence that sup-
ports it. But Dr Colin remains resolute. He returns to Querry's initial
question, moreover, and he interpolates Christ into the evolutionary
process:

> 'The nineteenth century wasn't as far wrong as we like to believe. We have
> become cynical about progress because of the terrible things we have seen
> men do during the last forty years. All the same, through trial and error the
> amoeba did become the ape. There were blind starts and wrong turnings
> even then, I suppose. Evolution today can produce Hitlers as well as St. John
> of the Cross. I have a small hope, that's all, a very small hope, that someone
> they call Christ was the fertile element, looking for a crack in the wall to
> plant its seed. I think of Christ as an amoeba who took the right turning.
> I want to be on the side of the progress which survives. I am no friend of
> pterodactyls'.[22]

Dr Colin lives by this myth; it adds a string in the upper register of
the instrument within his soul that thrums. That the myth is Christian
becomes apparent as he speaks of love, whose movement and expression he serves as well as advances within the leprosy clinic's loveless
realm. And so to *The Honorary Consul*, where Greene develops this
hope that Christ will frustrate entropy's final victory.

THE HONORARY CONSUL

In part 5 of *The Honorary Consul* Dr Eduardo Plarr, the physician to the disease-ridden *barrio*, refuses to look at senseless suffering and think of God as anything other than 'the horror up there'.[23] Overwhelmed by the pain and sickness he finds in the slums, traumatised by the incurable conditions that his medical science cannot heal, and now puzzled by the revolutionary actions of his friend, the dissident priest Father León Rivas, Dr Plarr rejects a belief in a good God, and he questions the meaning and reason for human existence. As part of his initial response to Dr Plarr, Father Rivas declares: 'I am no theologian, I was bottom in most of my classes, but I have always wanted to understand what you [Dr Plarr] call the horror and why I cannot stop loving it'.[24] In my view, there are four points to Father Rivas's understanding.

First, Father Rivas appears to believe that some answers to the important questions about life and meaning and God are much too formulaic to be worthy of acceptance. Reflecting on his preparation for the ordained ministry, he announces:

> 'Not one of the Fathers was of any use to me. Because they never touched on the horror — you are quite right to call it that. They saw no problem. They sat comfortably down in the presence of the horror like the old Archbishop at the General's table and talked about man's responsibility and Free Will. Free Will was the excuse for everything. It was God's alibi. They had never read Freud. Evil was made by man or Satan. It was simple that way. But I could never believe in Satan. It was much easier to believe that God was evil'.[25]

Father Rivas's last remark would appear to place him *outside* the bounds of traditional Christian theological speculation. Very few Christians, Catholic or otherwise, would feel comfortable with this seemingly outlandish suggestion that evil lurks in God's heart. On their view, the New Testament witness does not support a knavish or sinister deity; rather, the Galilean origin of Christianity shows God to be tender and merciful. However, a close reading of the Bible reveals a scriptural precedent for Father Rivas's theology. For example, David Penchansky sees an insecure God in Genesis 3; an irrational God in 2 Samuel 6; a vindictive God in 2 Samuel 24; a dangerous God in Leviticus 10; a malevolent God in Exod. 4.24-26; and, finally, an abusive God in 2 Kgs 2.23-25. 'God in these passages is rough, violent, unpredictable, liable to break out against even his most faithful believers without warning,' he observes.[26] And these six passages are 'genuine expressions of an Israelite sensibility, an Israelite theology, and not primitive holdovers of an earlier, less monotheistic faith'.[27] Assuming that there is continuity between the God of the New Testament and the God of the Hebrew Bible, and assuming that God *evolves* within the pages of the Bible, and in the religious imagination of the writers responsible for composing and editing the Bible in different eras, Father Rivas's theological ruminations do not appear to be all that scandalous after all. They seem to be a part of a legitimate, if admittedly unsettling, biblical faith still in the making.[28]

Father Rivas's model of an evil or an ironic God scandalises Dr Plarr, at least initially, and so Father Rivas develops his idea by addressing the concept of divine goodness. In his view, and this is the second point to Father's Rivas's theological understanding, good and evil represent vital and necessary concomitants within the divine character. Put another way, at any one moment in the divine becoming, God coagulates numerous contradictions within Godself:

> 'I believe in the evil of God,' Father Rivas said, 'but I believe in His goodness too. He made us in His image — that is the old legend . . . He made us in His image — and so our evil is His evil too. How could I love God if He were not like me? Divided like me. Tempted like me. If I love a dog it is only because I can see something human in a dog'.[29]

While Father Rivas believes that God is holy, just, loving, and good, he also believes that God is volatile, sinister, prone to dark and inscrutable actions. Although it is fairly easy to see how this theology presents the conventional Christian with a real problem, Father Rivas insists that belief in an ironic God is the only way to explain the history of social distress in his seedy corner of Latin America.[30]

Even so, and this is the third point to his theological understanding, Father Rivas subscribes to theistic evolutionism; he believes an energetic God interacts with and grounds the complex process of the universe. The idea here is that God is not an eternal, unchanging, unmoved mover; according to Father Rivas, God is the circumambient matrix within which all created actualities live, move, and have their becoming. God is the dynamic mechanism that propels the creative advance. Because of this belief in theistic evolutionism, or guided evolution, Father Rivas entertains and articulates his version of Catholic process eschatology — a hope that God will one day evolve to the point where it is no longer necessary for God to embody *both* good *and* evil qualities. Confident that the divine is making *progress* in the midst of *process*, Father Rivas declares:

'The God I believe in must be responsible for all the evil as well as for all the saints. He has to be a God made in our image with a night-side as well as a day-side. When you speak of the horror, Eduardo, you are speaking of the night-side of God. I believe the time will come when the night-side will wither away . . . and we shall see only the simple daylight of the good God. You believe in evolution, Eduardo, even though sometimes whole generations of men slip backwards to the beasts. It is a long struggle and a long suffering, evolution, and I believe God is suffering the same evolution that we are, but perhaps with more pain'.[31]

Unconvinced by this seemingly audacious theology, Dr Plarr questions Father Rivas's belief that God proceeds toward perfection, and he ruminates that history itself provides the strongest support for his own supposition that the night-side of God has engulfed the day-side completely.

In response to such forthright scepticism, Father Rivas grounds his theistic evolutionism in a poetic vision of the Cosmic Christ evolving throughout history. This is the final point to his theological understanding. With each valiant act of women and men to mount a step higher in the evolutionary growth of the Spirit, history inches toward the Omega Point, which is the Christic consummation of life's creative advance:

'But I believe in Christ,' Father Rivas said, 'I believe in the Cross and the Redemption. The Redemption of God as well as Man. I believe that the day-side of God, in one moment of happy creation, produced perfect goodness, as a man might paint one perfect picture. God's good intention for once was completely fulfilled so that the night-side can never win more than a little victory here and there. With our help. Because the evolution of God depends on our evolution. Every evil act of ours strengthens His night-side, and every good one helps His day-side. We belong to Him and He belongs to us. But now at least we can be sure where evolution will end one day — it will end in a goodness like Christ's. It is a terrible process all the same and the God I believe in suffers as we suffer while he struggles against Himself — against His evil side'.[32]

Father Rivas does not accept entropy's final triumph. He remains optimistic. And the final aim of his Catholic process theology is human meaning and authenticity. We have a part to play in God's character development, a contribution to make to the enrichment and enhancement of the divine as well as temporal life. On this view evil actions — war, inequality and oppression — thwart the forward movement of

God and the world; by contrast, good actions — working for a higher standard of living, for a humane, free and equal society — accelerate the creative process. Hence, we face a challenge; for Father Rivas, we can live inauthentically, which involves becoming cut off from others, blind to the conditions of their existence, or we can live authentically, which involves working to make life better for the good of all, including God. Genuine Christian spirituality leads to the salvation of God as well as the transformation of women and men.

Having made his case for an evolving God, whose experience of the world is incremental, and who remains dependent upon us to assist the forward movement of the divine life, Father Rivas realises that one important question remains: How is his revolutionary behaviour, his willingness to murder Britain's honorary consul to Asunción, going to help the evolution of God and the world? His tentative answer makes use of the Apostle Paul's theological anthropology, especially Paul's belief that we display both good and evil traits (Rom. 7.18-19). While Father Rivas admits that carrying a gun impedes God's evolution, he insists that an evil God demands evil things. This shocking theodicy is an interim conviction, however, for Father Rivas believes God will emerge victorious, having sloughed off his evil side in favour of the good:

> 'But one day with our help He will be able to tear His evil mask off forever. How often the saints have worn an evil mask for a time, even Paul. God is joined to us in a sort of blood transfusion. His good blood is in our veins, and our tainted blood runs through His. Oh, I know I may be sick or mad. But it is the only way I can believe in the goodness of God'.[33]

Father Rivas believes the world will get better, not worse, but only through divine–human collaboration, and so he holds that we must work to reach the climax point that will be actualised in Christ.

CONCLUSION

My approach to Greene's life and literary art is not without critics. Greene experiments in one or two books with Teilhardian themes, some might say, but perhaps he simply conducts this experiment to find a way of putting evil into God's heart — something Teilhard never did — just as in all his other works he, Greene, situates evil deep in our hearts. Greene's enthrallment with evil appears un-Teilhardian, and, while Father Rivas seems Teilhardian, Greene himself is not,

Robert Doud holds.[34] I agree with Doud, at least for the most part, and I acknowledge that Greene and Teilhard display different emphases in their writing, emphases that stem from their work as novelist and priest respectively, but there is no mistaking Greene's Teilhardian confession in *A Sort of Life*.[35] Whatever else readers do, they should recognise and respect the way writers self-identify theologically.

More substantively, Cates Baldridge problematises Greene's 'furtive and enfeebled Deity'.[36] Greeneland's God lacks controlling power, for instance, and appears '*subject to entropy*, no less than the universe He presumably created'.[37] Greene's God is diminished, Baldridge asserts, and I agree, as long as it is understood that Greene is taking the Teilhardian and process view that God is not the all-powerful creator, responsible for everything.[38] Rather, God is a part — albeit a unique part — of an evolving universe, not unlimited in power but subject to the universe's own limitations. This God works persuasively, not coercively. Of course, some might say that process theology stands outside Christian orthodoxy. Perhaps. But doctrine's develop, they evolve over time, and one modern Christian approach to thinking about God in light of evolution questions, even abandons, the conventional belief that God uses controlling power in the universe. If faith's challenge is to present its truth afresh to each new generation, as some Christians believe, then Graham Greene, marked by more than a touch of evolutionary religion, is nothing if not a novel theologian.

CHAPTER 12

Inside and Outside: Graham Greene and Evelyn Waugh

Robert Murray Davis

The more closely one looks at the lives and letters of Graham Greene and Evelyn Waugh, the odder it seems that even critics anxious to discover a school of Leading Catholic Authors could find common ground between them besides the fact that both were converts. Temperamentally, the two could not have been more different. Waugh said that any internal changes brought about by the trip to British Guiana were private property, not literary material, and he maintained this attitude for most of his career.[1] Equally in character, Greene insisted that a major, if not the only, motive for his trip to Liberia was made at the urgings of his unconscious mind.[2] In other words, as an examination of their work and of their friendship will show, Greene projected his inner obsessions to create a world often called Greeneland, while Waugh's obsession with external speech and behaviour led him to recreate details and characters from the external world in a comic and satiric distortion of what most of us think of as reality. In other words, Greene's world is like an El Greco painting, distorted but compelling. Waugh's is like a caricature or a Hogarth print, exaggerated, monitory, and sometimes disturbingly accurate.

There are, of course, parallels in their biographies. Both men studied, or at least were nominally enrolled in, history at Oxford, though neither did much work except in undergraduate journalism. Both drank heavily. Both belonged to undergraduate clubs whose exploits were regarded as very different in the 1920s but in retrospect look fairly similar.

Both entertained thoughts of suicide — though, characteristically, Greene dealt with his playing Russian roulette in an essay as an intense experience that became boring, putting his inner life before the public, while Waugh transmuted his attempt to drown himself into the comic evasion of Captain Grimes in *Decline and Fall*, concealing the fact for almost 40 years before revealing it in his autobiography.

At Oxford, as later in their careers, the two budding writers followed parallel straight lines. Forty years later, Greene wrote to Waugh that their failure to meet at Oxford was the result of his belonging 'to a rather rigorously Balliol group of perhaps boisterous heterosexuals, while your path temporarily took you into the other camp'.[3]

Waugh's camp (the pun was probably intentional) was led by Harold Acton, who wrote a hostile review of Greene's undergraduate poems, *Babbling April*. Waugh published in Acton's magazine *The Broom*, for which he designed the cover, and, in a profile of Acton in the 'Isis Idol' series, concluded that 'Oxford has every reason to be proud of Mr Acton, both for his poetry and for himself'.[4] But Waugh never attained, and apparently did not seek, the kind of editorial position that Greene held on the *Oxford Outlook*.

In their youthful poetry, Waugh and Greene presented antithetical moods. Early in Waugh's Oxford career, he wrote to his friend Tom Driberg that 'One loses all ambition to be an intellectual. I am reduced to writing light verse for *The Isis* and taking politics seriously'.[5] The poem, 'History Previous', is a series of groans about books required for the examination, ending with: 'Would I were shipwrecked on some coral shore / Where print and paper never reached me more, / I'd gladly live a literary Crusoe, / Devoid of books, if so devoid of Rousseau'.[6] And in 'A University Sermon to Idealists Who are Serious Minded and Intelligent', he scorned the 'fierce young men! With flashing eyes, / ill tailored and unworldly wise' who were actually doing some work.[7]

Greene's 'The Gamble' looks inward rather than, as Waugh's poems do, outward — a symptom of their work and their personae for the rest of their lives. This poem is about playing Russian roulette: 'Will it be mist and death / At the bend of this sunset road, / Or life reinforced / By the propinquity of death? / Either is gain. / It is a gamble which I cannot lose'.[8]

Of course, the two did share a taste for film, and both were reviewers for the Oxford press. Waugh reviewed films for the Oxford magazine *Isis* with more interest in his cultivated persona than in cinematic technique. Of 'If Winter Comes', he concluded, 'I don't think I have ever been bored quite so much'. Of a circus film, in which 'the wicked nobleman' gets the girl, he says 'for so much injustice one was grateful'. He liked 'a noble public-house called the "Vomiting Dog", full of knives and wantons and drunkenness in "Pagliacci."' He does note bad scenery, bad acting, and bad captions (the shorter the better, he thought), but he made only a few comments on technique, and those are local rather than structural, as in 'the real charm of the cinema is in the momentary pictures and situations which appear'.[9]

Greene adopted a far more serious attitude at Oxford than Waugh, about film as about everything else. He read the periodical *Close Up*, a bound volume of which he kept in his flat in Antibes late in his life, Pudovkin on montage, and Eisenstein on everything, and he saw a great many films. According to David Parkinson, editor of *Mornings in the Dark / The Graham Greene Film Reader*, this is where 'he acquired the discerning appreciation of narrative structure, camera angle and cutting for effect that was to inform his earliest writings for *The Oxford Outlook* and *The Times*'.[10]

Greene edited the *Outlook* and appointed himself film critic. The review reprinted in *Mornings in the Dark* is far less frivolous and more technically sophisticated than Waugh's undergraduate efforts. Writing of *Warning Shadows*, Greene notes 'the use made of shadow and reflection to get its effect of illusion and terror' and comments upon the gulf between German impressionism [he means, I think, expressionism] and Hollywood naturalism and hopes for a synthesis because 'we cannot do without the clarity and agreeable definiteness that American studios have brought to perfection'. He thought film 'a popular and primitive form of art' at this stage, but he could see 'what unnumbered possibilities lie hidden in its technique — all this could some creative intelligence be found to direct it; and none has yet appeared'.[11]

As this shows, Greene adopted a far more serious and even scholarly attitude toward the world than Waugh, who, like Charles Ryder in *Brideshead Revisited*, regarded Oxford as a place to have a belated 'happy childhood'.[12] There is a similar contrast in the first European trips taken by the two men. At 19, Greene and Claud Cockburn (Waugh's 'communist cousin') went to Germany in 1924 as agents of, or in any case at the expense of, the German government with the promise to counteract Francophile sentiment at Oxford. Waugh's first trip was, post-Oxford, to Paris at the end of 1925, when he was 22, involved nothing more exotic than the usual tourist sights, a male brothel, and some excellent meals, including pressed duck, which nearly two decades later found its way into *Brideshead Revisited*.[13]

At Oxford, Greene had been the better bet to achieve literary fame, and after leaving Balliol he had taken sober jobs, first with a newspaper in Nottingham and then with *The Times* in order to marry Vivien Dayrell-Browning, whom he had assiduously courted — and who, at Basil Blackwell, published an early Waugh story. But by 1930, against considerable odds, Waugh had pulled ahead in the fame sweepstakes. Greene may have had, with *The Man Within*, success equal to Waugh's *Decline and Fall*, published a year earlier in 1928, but *Vile Bodies* had made Waugh famous not only for the novel but for the newspaper and magazine articles he secured as a result. One commission was a regular book page in the *Graphic*, for which he reviewed Greene's *The Name of Action* — which he called *The Name of Reason*. Waugh's review seems accurate, and years later Nancy Mitford wrote that she trusted his judgement because if he said a thing, it was so. Waugh praised Greene's 'sense of the importance of plot and the structure of narrative' and, perhaps a little condescend-ingly, predicted 'his early elevation to the position of a respectable, romantic best seller'. On the other hand, Waugh found 'many features of his style a little repugnant. It is all metaphor and simile, which often fails in its reason for existing by obscuring rather than illumi-nating the description' and wished 'he would write more freely and directly'.[14] No one who has read *The Name of Action* — not a large number — could argue with Waugh, and it is perhaps fortunate for their future relations that Waugh did not review *Rumour at Nightfall*. Five years later, Greene was more generous, calling Waugh's *Edmund Campion* 'a model of what a short biography should be. Sensitive and vivid, it catches the curious note of gaiety and gallantry . . . of an adventure which, in spite of the inevitable end at Tyburn, was never sombre'.[15]

By the time of the first recorded communication between the two, in 1936, both Waugh and Greene were firmly established as writers and travellers. Greene approached Waugh about 'a silly book', which an editor at Heinemann thought vulgar, based on their racing around the world.[16] Waugh had no objections to vulgarity if it involved money and travel and suggested an alternative based on economy rather than speed: 'Each competitor to start with no luggage and a limited sum — say £100 — and the one who arrives with most cash in hand to get a prize. And more competitors. Five at least . . . In fact it might be open to anyone who cares to put up his own stake — three or four professional tourists like ourselves to get paid for'.[17] Nothing came of that plan, but a year later Greene, now literary editor of the new weekly magazine *Night and Day*, approached Waugh about becoming drama critic. Waugh demurred because he could not promise to be in London every week. But after negotiations about fees and review books for sale, he became book critic for the magazine's six-month run, made twice what other contributors were paid, and at least once came too near libel for comfort.

During this period, Greene was as busy as Waugh in reviewing; on four occasions they reviewed the same books. Their responses exhibit not only similarities in religious and — oddly, in view of later perceptions of the two men — political perspectives but also striking and instructive differences in their judgements and, by extension, their critical principles. Three of the four reviews appeared in the second half of 1937 when Waugh and Greene were associates on *Night and Day*. Greene gave way to Waugh as book reviewer; three of Greene's reviews appeared in the *London Mercury*, founded by the eminently middlebrow J. C. Squire and at this time edited by R. A. Scott-James as a middle-of-the-road, rather staid journal that did not have the obligation to be amusing an obligation that was imposed on contributors to *Night and Day*.

Their reviews of G. M. Young's collection of essays, *Daylight and Champaign*, illustrate the different levels of seriousness with which each undertook the critical task — not least in Waugh's Freudian slip of 'champagne' the drink for 'champaign', the field. Greene obviously expects more scholarship and broader literary interests than he finds in Young.[18] And, while Greene finds Young's Victorian aesthetics tolerable, he rebuts the anti-Catholic sentiment of Young's remark that 'Jesuits and their Pope neither Elizabethan nor any other generation of Englishmen would endure' by citing recusants 'who sheltered Campion and the martyrs'. In contrast, although Waugh had been involved in controversy with Protestant supremacist critics of his biography of Campion, his review ignores Young's bias. Instead, Waugh concentrates on the essays as the product of a 'mellow and fastidious mind' and concludes — apparently with more irony for those who have or demand the attributes than for those who lack them — that Young 'seems to have avoided all the pitfalls of scholarship and good taste'. Waugh felt strongly about Elizabethan Catholicism, but here he is in search of amusement rather than controversy.[19]

The contrast between Waugh's casual appreciation and Greene's more formal and studied attitude is also evident in their comments on Robert Byron's *The Road to Oxiana*. Greene quotes extensively (43 lines out of 95) and carefully apportions praise and blame among what he calls three books forced into one. Waugh's comment on the work of an Oxford more-or-less friend is briefer and more suggestive. He quotes nothing but characterises features of style with phrases like 'discourteous take-it-or-leave-it, salt-on-the-tail, slap-dash jottings' in the fully justified view that paraphrase, or his paraphrase, is likely to be more interesting than Byron's prose.[20] Both reviewers note the ethnocentric bias and disjointed form of Byron's book. Greene called

Byron's rejection of alien sights and customs 'cheap, unsympathetic superiority'.[21]

Waugh, at this time more widely travelled than Greene, calls the habit of mind 'insularity run amok',[22] but finds stimulating, as one might expect from Waugh's travel books, 'the savage and pungent narrative of the actual events of his journey'. And while he notes the disjuncture in form, he does not seem to find it objectionable. Greene soberly judges the book both as a serious reportage and as a literary artifact. Waugh is content to point out the amusing features and a few lapses in style and method.

In reviewing Arthur Calder-Marshall's *A Date with a Duchess and Other Stories*, Greene out-Leavises *Scrutiny* in his demands for high seriousness and flattens Calder-Marshall under the combined weights of Conrad, Chekhov, and Joyce; with Maupassant, Bates, and some of Maugham added for good measure. He finds lacking 'the mood', by which he means the individual vision that, when rendered, gives us 'the sum added up: the mood released from the plot going out of the tale into life again'. Even 'A sympathy for the proletariat isn't really enough. That is the literature of escape: escape into battle: the urge to self-destruction'.[23] Except for a few quotations of particular awfulness, Greene presents little specific criticism and in fact mentions only two titles of stories in the collection.

Waugh had, only a week before his review of the same book, concluded that Calder-Marshall's *The Changing Scene* struck 'at the whole integrity and decency of art'. His review *of A Date with a Duchess* is therefore surprisingly generous and far more thorough than most of his reviews for *Night and Day*. While he notes, as Greene had done, echoes of other writers' styles and subjects, he devotes far more space to virtues he finds in stories or even parts of stories, such as 'the first seven pages [of "Pickle My Bones"] which give one the best drunk conversations I have ever read' — no mean praise from Waugh. Although himself far removed in sympathy from the proletariat, he praises the treatment of 'the mood of rebellion' in a story about miners clashing with police. After characterising Calder-Marshall as an anarchist rather than a Marxist and therefore subject to aesthetic and even theological redemption, he concludes that 'A robust discontent, whether it be with joint stock banking or the World, Flesh, and Devil, is good for a writer, and, if that is all that Mr Calder-Marshall meant by his 'Left' politics, I am sorry I grumbled about them'.[24]

Greene had the opposite problem in reviewing Somerset Maugham's *Christmas Holiday*. He admired much of Maugham's previous work but found this novel 'unconvincing and slackly written' and horribly sentimental. The story within a story he finds 'maladroitly handled' and full of 'clichés of extraordinary grotesqueness'. He particularly objects to a sequence in which the major characters go from a brothel to Midnight Mass as 'one example of the odd ignorance of human feeling'.[25] (In view of Greene's later confession, or boast, that he copulated behind many if not all the altars in Italy, the irony is almost too obvious to point out.)

Since Waugh was likely to make just this kind of transition in life as well as in his fiction, going from a prostitute one night to confession the next on one occasion and on another changing plans to go to a brothel in order to give money to some priests, Maugham's supposed lapse in taste did not bother him. Nor, since he judged the 'outrageous' and 'preposterous' characters to be 'absolutely convincing', did he object to them. Perhaps as a result, his plot summary is far more detailed and considerably more coherent than Greene's. The tale within the tale he thought brilliantly executed and worth study: 'The transitions from direct speech to stylised narrative, the change of narrator as Simon takes up part of the story, the suspense that is created even though the reader already knows what the climax will be, are models of technique'. He did criticise the ending as a 'prodigious piece of bathos', but he generously provided a more urbane and truer ending in which the central character 'will be just the same kind of fellow in future with a slightly wider and wiser outlook' — like Paul Pennyfeather at the end of *Decline and Fall*.[26] Greene has given up long before this point and in any case is not disposed to find good in any part when the whole is defective

On the whole, Greene was far more likely than Waugh at this point in their careers to obtrude social and religious convictions, and his aesthetic convictions, both modernist and highly serious, tend to come between the reviewer and the work. Waugh seems to approach books with fewer preconceptions, seems more willing to find what there is to praise, and offers a more thorough analysis of how and why the work affects him. As a result, he gives the somewhat surprising impression of being more tolerant and humane than Greene.

This is true to an extent of their books about Mexico, Greene's *The Lawless Roads* and Waugh's *Robbery under Law*. Waugh pointed out, in a very laudatory review of Greene, that while Greene's 'was an heroic journey, mine was definitely homely' and that Greene travelled 'as a poor man, I as a rich'. While Greene's method had some advantages, 'the chief disadvantage is that the physical exhaustion incurred in merely getting from place to place often makes one abnormally unresponsive to their interest. Mr Greene, particularly, suffers from this. He makes no disguise of the fact that Mexico disgusted him'. Of course, Waugh added, 'England disgusts him too', perhaps because he is 'an Augustinian Christian, a believer in the dark age of Mediterranean decadence . . . He abominates the picturesque and the eccentric; earth is for the growing of food, houses for the rectitude of family life. Contemplation of the horrible ways in which men exercise their right of choice leads him into something very near a hatred of free will'. And to forget that 'The Mexicans are not only the people who killed the martyrs; they are the people for whom the martyrs died. It is in that aspect alone that martyrdom is valuable'.[27]

As Waugh recognised, the book he was just finishing was very different from Greene's. The difficulties of Greene's journey were central features of *The Lawless Roads*, as if discomfort and authenticity were, as they often seem for Greene, indivisible. Engaged on a personal quest, Greene hopes to get to 'the centre of something — if it was only of darkness and abandonment'.[28] In contrast, Waugh travelled on commission from an oil company to write against Mexican expropriation of their interests, and he is writing polemical history — political, economic, religious — not so much to prove that the oil companies were right as to demonstrate that the Mexican government was high-handed and venal in expropriating them.

Of course, both men wrote as Catholic converts of some years' standing, but even here they illustrate the 'measureless diversity'[29] that, Waugh noted, the faith allows. As an apologist — in the strict sense of the term — for the persecuted Church in Mexico, Waugh emphasises the order, coherence, and unity of the faith, conceding and minimising abuses in its secular manifestation, emphasising again and again, directly and by implication, 'that it is only in material symbols that man is capable of recognizing the truth by which he lives'[30] and that, in effect, the Incarnation redeems not only individual humans but the world they inhabit. 'The world, the flesh, and the devil' did not trouble Waugh as they did Greene, whose appalled fascination with idiosyncratic definitions of all three is notorious and who, in this book as in *The Power and the Glory*, seems to believe that the only true church is, in an emphatic sense of the old term, the Church Suffering; the only true Catholic the fugitive; the only sincere Catholic in Mexico the Indian who has not been corrupted by the slackness and indifference of Spanish-Mexican society. The world of Waugh's faith in this book, as in *Remote People*, is spacious, open and logical. Greene's is claustrophobic, decaying, full of violence, giving an occasional glimpse of a goodness that is far more inexplicable and mysterious than the evil that surrounds it. Waugh speaks of the Faith with a capital letter, 'a habit of life and a social organisation',[31] Greene of faith with a small 'f', which came 'shapelessly, without dogma, a presence above a croquet lawn, something associated with violence, cruelty, evil across the way'.[32]

A different kind of contrast between the Puritanism of Greene, often called Jansenist, and Waugh's surprising tolerance can be seen in their attitudes of Anglo expatriates in Mexico. Greene condemned Taxco as 'a colony for escapists with their twisted sexuality and hopeless freedom',[33] while Waugh, taking a lighter view as social historian, terms the expatriates 'the last survivors of the international Bohemianism of the '20s — the army of semi-intellectual good-timers who once overran Europe . . . providing material for unnumbered light novels'.[34] Elsewhere he calls these people 'nostalgic for the Classical-Christian culture from which they remotely spring, which they can find transplanted, transformed in part but still recognisable, in Mexico'.[35] To an extent, Waugh shares this view, which accounts not only for his visual pleasure in Mexican landscape and architecture but for the concept of internationalism that underlies his support of the Church as social force and the idea of international law that forms the basic premise in his argument against expropriation. His real point, however, is that civilisation based on these premises is valuable and can, with effort, be preserved. For Greene, 'the world, one begins to feel, has been used up — we can only repeat our vices and our virtues'.[36] No wonder he has little hope and less interest in worldly processes and in fact, at the end of his book, comes very near to welcoming the apocalyptic violence of a bombing raid to cleanse England of its sterile lusts and empty greed.

Both books were soon obscured by the outbreak of World War II, and Greene and Waugh went separate ways. They did meet in May 1940 at the Ministry of Information, where, Waugh said, 'Graham Greene [who worked there] propounded a scheme for official writers to the Forces and himself wanted to become a Marine . . . I said the official writer racket might be convenient if we found ourselves permanently in a defensive role in the Far East, or if I were incapacitated and set to training'.[37] Ironically, though Waugh was officially a combatant, Greene was at this period probably in more danger from German air raids on London. This scheme, like the travel competition, came to nothing — probably just as well for the two writers' subsequent careers, but it was a rare point of contact for the two.

By 1942, it was clear that Waugh could admire Greene as an artist without agreeing with him. In reviewing *British Dramatists*, Waugh praised Greene as 'a writer of outstanding imaginative power' and a 'splendid novelist'. But he took issue with Greene's subscribing to 'the popular belief in "the People'" and the corollaries that 'only the poor are real and important and that the only live art is the art of the People'. This leads, Waugh thought, to two problems: Greene is forced to dismiss drama from Congreve to Maugham as 'unreal'; and he 'seems to ignore that a prime function of the theatre is to give pleasure'.[38] Here, as in the books on Mexico, Waugh gives greater weight to aesthetics than to politics or eschatology, whereas Greene was later to maintain overtly what he had long put into practice that 'one of the major objects of [the novelist's] craft . . . is the awakening of sympathy'.[39]

There is no record of contact between the two men for the rest of the war, but after both returned to England, their positions differed markedly. Waugh's *Brideshead Revisited* had not only made him famous on both sides of the Atlantic but had made him relatively, if temporarily, wealthy and disinclined to earn money that the Labour government's tax structure would make meaningless. Greene, on the other hand, was certainly respected as a novelist, but none of his books were highly profitable. Therefore, the offer of an editorship at Eyre & Spottiswoode was quite welcome. This position brought the two together once again. Apparently Greene asked Waugh to write the preface to Saki's *The Unbearable Bassington* for a series he was editing, and, agreeing to do so, Waugh refused payment 'because the state will snatch it' and suggested a trade: either free copies of novels in the series or 'some signed copies of your own work'.[40] (These duly arrived up through *A Burnt-Out Case*, received a few months before Waugh's death in 1966.)

Greene hit his own bonanza in 1948 with *The Heart of the Matter*, like *Brideshead Revisited* a Book of the Month selection in America, which, Waugh predicted, still smarting from American adulation of his own novel, 'will bring it to a much larger public than can profitably read it'. Waugh's long review, published both in England and America, began with high praise: Greene is 'alone among contemporary writers [of whom] one can say without affectation that his breaking silence with a new serious novel is a literary "event"' and goes on to maintain that Greene is in the vanguard because 'the artist's interest has moved from sociology to eschatology'. As a result, Greene is the kind of novelist (like Waugh, who had promised in 1946 to write only about his characters' relation to God in future) who implies that 'These characters are not my creation, but God's. They have an eternal destiny. They are not merely playing a part for the reader's amusement. They are souls whom Christ died to save. This, I think, explains his preoccupation with the charmless'.[41] (Waugh, of course, dealt, though not exclusively, with the charming — and in his last novel worked out the salvation of Virginia Troy, perhaps the most charming and among the least likely to be redeemed of all his characters.)

This enthusiasm did not extend to the theology of the novel as Waugh understood it. He thought that 'the idea of willing my own damnation for the love of God is either a very loose poetical expression or a mad blasphemy'.[42] (After receiving Greene's letter that Scobie was 'intended to show how muddled a man full of goodwill could become once "off the rails,"'[43] Waugh came to understand that Greene was showing Scobie's moral confusion — and, I suggest, an overriding desire for death that is subtly suggested very early in the novel — and made corrections for any future reprints of his review.)

More interesting to the student of fiction are Waugh's comments on Greene's technique. Waugh realised that Greene was a very different kind of writer than he was: 'The words are functional, devoid of sensuous attraction, of ancestry and of independent life. Literary stylists [very much including Waugh at this stage of his career] regard language as intrinsically precious and its proper use as a worthy and pleasant task. A polyglot could read Mr Greene, lay him aside, retain a sharp memory of all he said and yet, I think, entirely forget what tongue he was using'.[44] This comment is a description rather than a judgement, but had it been a judgement, Greene would probably not have been offended, for years earlier he had cited approvingly Ford Madox Ford's view that major contemporary novelists shared with great dramatic poets 'not the power melodiously to arrange words but the power to suggest human values'.[45]

Waugh put more value on the emphasis on arranging words, but he is clearly more sympathetic to Greene's objective, indeed filmic technique, which resembles, and, as I have argued elsewhere, accurately describes features of Waugh's pre-*Brideshead* method.[46]

Greene was delighted with the review, writing to Waugh that 'You've made me very conceited . . . There's no living writer whom I would rather receive praise and criticism) from'.[47] But in another mood, he wrote to Catherine Walston about the same time that 'life doesn't offer much. Perhaps if one was a failure, instead of a vulgar success, one would have success to look forward to'.[48]

Waugh had had his own problems with vulgar success, but he was less inclined to repine — a favourite word during this period. And he had practical advice about how to deal with American fame: have the earnings paid out gradually to minimise taxes and deal with 'the most ghastly post-bag for six weeks or so' by either reading no letters or by answering all with a scrawled postcard.[49] He predicted trouble with the American Catholic hierarchy who 'are waiting to jump on decadent European Catholicism . . . I just escaped delation by sending everyone to heaven', as Greene had not done in clearly unimpeachable fashion.[50]

There is no record of Waugh's response to Greene's review of *The Loved One*, also published in 1948. As Waugh did in reviewing *The Heart of the Matter*, Greene emphasises the theological implications (far less obvious in Waugh's novel): 'we cannot help noticing the genuine note of hate, the hate of a man who loves, of one who is aware that it was for this grotesque world a God died, who is bitterly ashamed of what we have made of ourselves'. Greene missed the 'good humour' and 'natural charity' of *Decline and Fall*, though he did not regret it, and he questioned the 'cruel ending' in which the character commits suicide and is incinerated in a pet cemetery because 'after all this is a redeemed world and a God died for Mr Joyboy too'.[51] Although one hesitates to say so, this may be the one instance in which Greene, perhaps misled by Waugh's essay on Forest Lawn Memorial Park, totally misread his friend by obtruding religion where it is not obviously relevant.

Oddly enough, though Waugh was far more orthodox than Greene, he did not always apply moral theology to personal behaviour, at least that of his friends. Waugh was as tolerant of Harold Acton's homosexuality as he was of Greene's affair with Catherine Walston. In fact, he was more likely to be amused than censorious, and he loved gossip. As he told Cyril Connolly, who had written reprovingly that he found nothing amusing in the misfortunes of his friends, 'I do not know how you can bear to go so much into society if you feel this'.[52] Thus, while he liked and admired Greene and welcomed him and Walston at his home in Piers Court, warning them of the privations they would experience, he wrote with relish to Nancy Mitford about the discharge of blood from Greene's penis. Doctors said that it could be caused by something fatal; later they said, '"Too much womanizing?" "No, not for weeks since I left my home in England." "Ah," they said. "That's it." "What a terrible warning. No wonder his books are sad."'[53] And, though he found Walston amusing and 'good at heart', he added that 'she lives in a terrible underworld of Jews and socialists and Americans and Cambridge dons and is not really house trained'. Greene, he added, 'thinks of nothing but money, in very small sums. It is odd. He must be about the richest man we know'.[54] But his letter to Walston in 1951 includes a warm invitation to accompany Greene to his country home, the visit in which Greene 'spent his days patrolling the built up areas round Dursley noting the numbers of motor cars. He takes omens from them'.[55]

This remark coincided with Waugh's review of *The End of the Affair*, based in part on Greene's situation with the Walstons, which is, of course, this being 1951, not mentioned. He noted the movement away from melodrama transfused with spiritual life, from 'tense, fast stories with the minimum of comment and the maximum of incident, his characters unreflective, unaesthetic, unintelligent, his villains have been vile and his heroines subhuman; all have inhabited a violent social no-man's-land. Every book has ended with death and a sense of finality'. The new book, however, is a transformation of 'domestic, romantic drama of the type of *Brief Encounter*'.[56] Waugh may not have remembered his prediction, two decades earlier, that Greene might become 'a respectable, romantic bestseller';[57] in any case, Greene has transcended the genre.

Waugh was particularly impressed by Greene's demonstration 'that in middle life his mind is suppler and his interest wider than in youth; that he is a writer of real stamina. He has triumphantly passed the dangerous climacteric where so many talents fail'.[58] This reaction may be due to Waugh's increasing fear that he might run out of material — since he was working on the first volume of what was to become his war trilogy, which he described as 'unreadable and endless'.[59]

Although Waugh wrote to Greene that he was 'the greatest novelist of the century'[60] he did not hesitate to criticise his grammar and his attitudes. Responding to Greene's gift of *The Lost Childhood and Other Essays*, Waugh agreed that the essays on James 'seem to me the best I ever read on the subject', but took issue with his disparagement of Eric Gill and added that 'Your praise of [D. H.] Lawrence sickens me. Do you sometimes confuse "genius" and "artist" as terms?'[61] Greene responded to this criticism by qualifying his use of 'genius' as 'not a term of praise but a psychologically descriptive one'.[62] A year later, thanking Greene for *The Little Horse Bus*, Waugh noted the agreement failure in the opening sentence 'Everybody . . . used to buy their groceries'.[63] In 1954, he praised some of the stories in *Twenty-One Stories* but 'wish[ed] you didn't think of "destruction as a sort of creation."'[64] And while he admired the skill of *Loser Takes All*, he found the characters so real that he could not believe the ending: 'that idiot girl . . . won't stay faithful to her ageing clerk for ten months'.[65]

Nevertheless, when *The Power and the Glory* was censured by the Holy Office on the grounds that 'it was "paradoxical"' and 'dealt with extraordinary circumstances',[66] Waugh called the condemnation 'as fatuous as unjust — a vile misreading of a noble book'[67] and offered to come to Greene's defence. This was not necessary, but throughout the late 1940s and early 1950s Waugh consistently defended Greene, and of course by extension himself, against 'loyal Catholics here and in America who think it the function of the Catholic writer to produce only advertising brochures setting out in attractive terms the advantages of Church membership'.[68]

When Greene moved toward more secular themes in the mid-1950s, Waugh began to question his attitudes though he continued to praise Greene's novels. Of course, he could not resist a joke, and, when Greene remarked one night in White's that he had an idea for 'a political novel. It will be fun to write about politics for a change, and not always about God', Waugh replied, 'I wouldn't give up writing about God at this stage if I was you. It would be like P. G. Wodehouse dropping Jeeves half-way through the Wooster series'.[69]

Greene's immediate impetus toward politics was the result of McCarthyism in the USA, which caused him to be branded as a Communist, but he had already been to Vietnam, and when he did write a political novel. *The Quiet American*, it was set there. Waugh thought it 'a masterly but base work',[70] but he told Greene of his 'deep admiration' for the book while admitting, 'I am afraid I let my dislike of Fowler run away with me. What a shit he is! But I hope I made it apparent that the book is first rate'.[71] Waugh's review argued that while *The Quiet American* was less ambitious than *The End of the Affair*, Greene had managed the 'masterly, original and vigorous' story with superb technique. He thinks Fowler, the narrator, so vile that 'it is a disagreeable experience to be forced into intimacy with him', and while 'This can hardly be called an artistic fault . . . I think it is a lapse in taste'. He points to Fowler's 'many solecisms of writing', his cultural ignorance, and his laziness as a journalist.[72] If Waugh overemphasised Fowler's baseness — Greene said that he was meant to balance Pyle's over-commitment with excessive detachment — there is no record that Greene took offence, and Waugh continued to thank him for presents of books and to praise his plays of the late 1950s.

Nor did Waugh resent Greene's review of his biography of Ronald Knox. Greene praised the whole but found the middle part unsympathetic: 'The Knox of Oxford, the Knox of the rather precious style and of the Latin verses, the chaplain and the translator, had his apostolate in a region which I have always found uninteresting and even at moments repellent', though he admitted that priests like Knox 'are as necessary to the Church as the apostles of the darker, poorer, more violent world'.[73] On a postcard, Waugh wrote 'I thought your review of Knox jolly decent. I knew you did not revere him. I wish you did'[74] — but, uncharacteristically, agreed to let Greene disagree.

The most intense discussion between the two men, at least the one that found its way into print, was occasioned by the publication of *A Burnt-Out Case* in 1961. Waugh received an advance copy for review but noted in his diary that 'There is nothing I could write about it without shame one way or the other' because he believed that the novel, in conjunction with the recent story 'A Visit to Morin', seemed to show that Greene 'has come out as specifically faithless'. He went on to say, 'What is more — no, less — Graham's skill is fading', especially in recording the hero's situation three times and in the badly handled episode of Deo Gratias's 'attempted escape and rescue', and concluded that 'His early books are full of self pity at poverty and obscurity; now self pity at his success. I am not guiltless as one of those who put him in the position of "Catholic artist."'[75] Waugh then wrote to Greene apologising for having 'behaved like Rycker', the journalist who stalks the central character.[76]

Greene tried to reassure his friend that he had not acted like Rycker, that he did not resent Waugh's criticisms, and that in the novel he was not saying that he had lost his faith. Waugh was unconvinced. 'I was not so dotty as to take Rycker as a portrait of myself. I saw him as the caricature of a number of your admirers (among whom I counted myself) who have tried to force on you a position which you found obnoxious'. They exchanged quotations from Browning, and the discussion ended happily.[77] It may be about this time that Greene gave Waugh the Classic Comic version of *The Brothers Karamazov* that now resides in the Waugh collection at the University of Texas — a gift calculated to delight and horrify both giver and recipient because it confirmed their mutual view of American culture.

However, Waugh had not stopped thinking about *A Burnt-Out Case*. A year later, in his article on 'Sloth', he pointed to the novel as 'the plainest representation' of the deadly sin. While he conceded that Querry's affection for Deo Gratias and his help in building sheds for the leper colony might be intended to imply contrition, he concluded that 'on the facts given us by Mr Greene, Querry was guilty and in hell'. Of course, he added, he was not imputing this sin to Greene, since 'It would be impossible for a man who was really guilty of Sloth to write about it, for he would be incapable of the intense work required to produce a novel like *A Burnt-Out Case*'.[78]

Waugh had made a kind of amends for not reviewing *A Burnt-Out Case* when he reviewed *In Search of a Character*, the notebook that Greene kept on his exploratory trip to the Congo. Waugh found it valuable 'not as a literary exercise, but as a study of the motions of a literary imagination'. He was particularly interested in discovering, since he knew the man and his work, something of 'the mechanics of his imagination', especially 'the pre-eminent importance he attaches to the opening sentences of a book' and 'recording dreams, which have always seemed one of the flaws in his almost flawless narratives'. The review ends with the hope that with the novel Greene had come 'to the end of his long exploration of the dark fever-country on the unmapped borders of superstition and apostasy. If that is so, we may look forward to a new creative period of serene maturity'.[79] The last communication now in print between the two friends came three months before Waugh's death in April, 1966, when he wrote to congratulate Greene on *The Comedians*. 'What staying power you have,' he wrote, conscious that his own powers had faded and that he was cancelling various contracts. 'It might have been written 30 years ago and could be by no one but you'. The letter ended, '1965 was a bad year for me in a number of ways — dentistry, deaths of friends, the "aggiornamento." I try to face the new wars with resignation. Of course don't answer'.[80]

There is no record that Greene did, unless one counts his brief eulogy when Waugh died. He praised Waugh's 'rare quality of criticizing a friend, harshly, wittily and openly to his face, and behind the friend's back of expressing only his kindness and charity'. (Clearly he had not seen Waugh's letters to Nancy Mitford.) Most important, 'Evelyn Waugh had an unshakable loyalty to his friends, even if he may have detested their opinions and sometimes their actions. One could never depend upon him for an easy approval or a warm weak complaisance, but when one felt the need of him he was always there'.[81]

Since Greene lived a quarter-century longer than Waugh, he had the privilege of summing up his friend's character as Waugh did not — and probably would have done in at most a pithy sentence had their positions been reversed. Greene pays tribute to *The Ordeal of Gilbert Pinfold*, not merely because it 'shows him technically almost at his most perfect' but almost certainly because it comes closest to Greene's method of examining the interior life. It is a pity that Waugh could not have read the comparison of his novel with 'Freud bravely doing his own self-analysis'.[82] The explosion would have been memorable.

Greene noted in his friend the 'conflict between the satirist and the romantic' and his 'too-great expectations of his fellow creatures, and too-great expectations even of his church'.[83] Of course, too-great expectations and a strong sense of the proper order of things are almost as essential to a satirist as are wit and style. Waugh was aware of 'the dangerous edge of things', the phrase from Browning that Greene might have used as epigraph for every book he wrote, but he really desired to stand on the still point at the centre of the great revolving wheel described in *Decline and Fall*, his first novel.

Until Greene's complete letters and diaries are made available, we cannot know what Greene thought of Waugh in private moments. And we may never know what Greene really needed. But the two men complemented and drew each other out in ways that perhaps no one else could have done for either. And at the very least we are privileged to see two of the major novelists of the twentieth century reacting to each other's work with a frankness and generosity as rare as it is heartening. Perhaps the greatest tribute to Greene can be found in Waugh's letter of 1955: 'I wish we met more often. I am deeply fond of you'.[84] Anyone immersed in the writings of Waugh will recognise that this is not only a touching but a uniquely direct expression of emotion.

CHAPTER 13

The Long Wait for Aunt Augusta: Reflections on Graham Greene's Fictional Women

Judith Adamson

In Gloria Emerson's 2000 novel *Loving Graham Greene*, Molly Benson is a wealthy, middle-aged American who has loved Greene since her teens and now travels in support of political causes she thinks he would have backed. Her somewhat less naïve sidekick is Bertie Einhorn, a woman whose enthusiasm for Greene's fiction is limited. Near the book's opening, Bertie is sitting in New York 'drinking carrot juice for breakfast and talking to her husband about Greene'.

> 'Of course he was a wonderful writer, but the women in his novels were so often prostitutes,' said Bertie. 'There was that idiot Phuong in *The Quiet American* and Clara in *The Honorary Consul*'.
>
> 'I think you slightly exaggerate,' said Arnold. 'I thought Aunt Augusta was hilarious — remember *Travels with my Aunt*? And for God's sake don't make that comment to Molly'.[1]

When I read this I quickly took Arnold's side; Aunt Augusta is wonderfully funny. But then I wondered if Bertie was not right too about Greene's women so often being prostitutes, being, we might say, disposable. While Aunt Augusta is secondary to no one — I have long considered her Greene's only fictional woman to approximate the narrative power of his men — she did put in 'a little part-time behind the *Messaggero*'.[2]

So I took up Bertie Einhorn's challenge and reread *The Quiet American*. Sure enough, there was Phuong still waiting for the dead Pyle to come home because, as Fowler tells the Sûreté, 'he was going to

210

marry her'.[3] The daughter of a mandarin, Fowler thinks Phuong 'wonderfully ignorant' politically, but her sister, who is not, has instilled in her the necessity for marriage. Phuong lives with Fowler, then attaches 'herself to youth and hope and seriousness' in Pyle, and when they fail 'her more than age and despair' she refocuses her sights and returns to Fowler. He says 'there was no scene, no tears, just thought — the long private thought of somebody who has to alter a whole course of life'. Her name means 'Phoenix' but, as Fowler tells us, 'nothing nowadays is fabulous and nothing rises from the ashes'.[4] Still, she is not just the prostitute Bertie Einhorn says she is; Phuong is an ordinary woman in difficult circumstances taking care of herself how she can. Even Fowler admits that she loved Pyle in her own way, and if women — or men for that matter — are to be condemned as prostitutes for mixing love with necessity we would have to redefine marriage.

What I had not remembered is that *The Quiet American* is as much about love as it is about politics. Pyle and Fowler are measured by how they behave toward Phuong as much as they are by their behaviour toward Vietnam. Pyle is the coloniser of Vietnam, and of Phuong; he wants to take her home to the statue of Liberty, to the land of the free, to his mother who will be needed to ease her way into the country of equal opportunity. But Fowler, who wants to leave the political problems of Vietnam to the Vietnamese, understands that away from her own country Phuong will wither. When he takes her to bed and feels her bones as small as a bird's his simile is less sexual than political; it is about Phuong's fragility and, by extension, the fragility of the Vietnamese faced with invasion by America. Pyle and Fowler both care about Phuong. They protect her from Granger and the other males who frequent the House of Five Hundred Girls, and they demand that the Sûreté call her *vous*. In fact, it is Pyle's respect for Phuong that makes Fowler like him. But Pyle is not changed by his love for her. His eye is always on America, while Fowler no longer cares what happens in London. He has seen that Phuong is 'indigenous like a herb' and he wants never to leave Vietnam. When he sides with the Viet Minh, in a way it is not a political act at all, and it is certainly not a jealous one against Pyle, although he does want Phuong back. In taking sides Fowler remains very human; he protects his fragile 'bird'[5] and her people in an immediate, practical way. So Phuong ends up with the wiser husband — even if after four opium pipes he does not know she is there: opium pipes, I should add, that she has obediently prepared.

Although it is serial, in Phuong's loyalty to her men she reminded me of Harry Lime's Anna, and I thought these women to be technically similar. As Fowler and Pyle are judged by their treatment of Phuong, in *The Third Man* Anna is the arbiter of our feelings about Harry and Holly Martins. It is her tough loyalty to Lime that gives him stature. She sticks with him: in the film, right to the end of that long walk past Holly, which Carol Reed insisted on, and about which Greene was so sceptical. Like Phuong, Anna is not sentimental. Holly needs to destroy the Harry who no longer matches his boyish memories. But Anna can just walk away. She is mature. She can disapprove of the penicillin racket while remaining loyal to the Harry who fixed her papers and made her laugh, the Harry she loves.

In *Brighton Rock*, Pinkie's much younger and less sophisticated Rose has this kind of courageous loyalty too — we might call it a loyalty that spans the border between faith and doubt. Said to be innocent, Rose knows everything Pinkie has done and, like Anna, she sticks to her man. Because the melodramatic stakes are raised in *Brighton Rock* with the introduction of Catholicism, Rose's technical position in the story is more complex than Anna's. Still, along with Ida, she is largely responsible for how we feel about Pinkie, and the priest suggests that she can save him even after he has damned himself, by making their child 'a saint — to pray for his father'.[6]

Betrayal has always been the worst sin in Greene's books, and none of these woman betray. They cross into that dangerous territory called love so wholeheartedly I am willing to bet that even if they found themselves forced to betray the person they love, they would not succumb. Rose, who is the hardest tested and the most betrayed, throws Pinkie's gun away only because she hears footsteps and 'it seemed to her that this must be news'[7] that will change the need for their suicides. After Pinkie's death she insists that she wants to be damned with him. This is far from betrayal.

But for all her loyalty, she is too emaciated for my liking. David Lodge has called Rose and Greene's other early heroines waif-like. Other critics have tagged them child-women. Then there is Ida. Greene does not like her. She is too deeply sunk into middle age, and there is her 'large friendly bosom' with the 'touch of the nursery' about it. Critics have taken his lead and not said many flattering things about Ida. In her humanism she is too cheerful, in her sense of fair play too tenacious, in her body too threateningly maternal. Yet try as he does to make her unlikable, in part by stressing Rose's devotion to Pinkie, Greene is too honest a novelist not to make Ida good hearted as she tracks down Fred Hale's killer. After all, she is right; Pinkie is a criminal. And Ida's loyalty extends beyond Fred to Rose. As Rose faces the 'worst horror of all' — the record on which Pinkie has recorded

'God damn you, you little bitch, why can't you go back home for ever and let me be'[8] — we have to be thankful that should she want to talk, Greene has left her someone more practical than the whistling priest. Unlike the child-woman Rose, Ida marches to her own drum.

So does Kate Farrant in *England Made Me*. The tall, elegant mistress of Swedish tycoon Eric Krough, Kate outstrips her twin brother Anthony 'in the pursuit of the more masculine virtues, reliability, efficiency'. If she lacks 'what would have served most women better, his charm', she is far more trustworthy than he is. After 30 years Kate and Anthony are 'like an old couple' but she has had the bad luck to be his sister. While this bad luck refers to their frustrated incestuous love, it also shows Kate disadvantaged simply because she is a woman. The 'two great standards, one for the men, another for the women', are clearly spelled out in *England Made Me*. They are 'the gate-posts' of Anthony's brain. He may be in love with his powerful sister but he does not 'believe in girls drinking'. He is 'full of the conventions of a generation older than himself', honouring 'other men's sisters' and believing, as his father did, that a brother is 'a sister's natural protector until she married'. In Sweden even the licensing law for schnaps decrees 'two for a man, one for a woman'.[9] But Kate survives. Here it is the men who are hollow; Krough lacks humanity, and Anthony hides his emptiness behind a spurious Harrow tie. Like Phuong, Kate may sleep her way to financial security, but like Anna and Ida she remains her own mistress. Still, I do not think Greene wants us to like her; her love for the jovial Anthony is raw and obsessive. She is domineering and she lacks Anthony's conscience. It is silly, helpless Loo Davidge, the waif-like child-woman Anthony picked up when he arrived in Stockholm, who might have saved him had been able to get back to England. Loo is safe as Kate is not.

Even beautiful, adulterous Sarah Miles has this childlike quality about her as *The End of the Affair* comes to a close. When sick and exhausted she flees into the church, she falls asleep like a child on Maurice's shoulder, then wakes and begins to cry, 'thrusting her fists into her eyes as a child does'[10] before she returns to the safety of her bed to die. She even crosses her fingers like a child as she tells a lie. But Sarah is not waif-like. She is a mature woman with a husband and a lover who makes her own decision when she bargains for Maurice's life. Yet while her struggle with the faith she never asked for is central in the novel, Maurice is our narrator. Sarah is only allowed to speak to us first hand in her diary, which is so personal it has a childish quality about it in its repetition; in any case, it has been clipped for us by Maurice. It leads him to pursue Sarah because he feels she needs taking care of. In fact, all the males in the novel pursue Sarah — Henry, who makes her feel guilty, Maurice, and God. Even as a child her mother thought she needed protection and had her baptised secretly as a talisman against the power of her father. For me, Sarah is like the character Maurice talks about who 'never began to live'[11] — or perhaps is not allowed to. Having made her quick bargain she has to be pushed along for the remainder of the book. In *The Quiet American* Helen's initial refusal to grant Fowler a divorce has substance: she is high church and does not believe in divorce. But Sarah's refusal to leave Henry has always seemed silly to me, and the secret baptism inserted only to give credence to her stubborn interpretation of Maurice's survival as the miracle that changes her life. Where the introduction of Roman Catholic symbols transformed melodramatic material in *Brighton Rock* by making sense of a corrupt world, here the argument for Sarah's faith seems rhetorically thin. It also reduces Sarah from the full woman she is at the beginning of the novel to a child-woman at the end where her children's books, in my opinion, turn 'the screw of absurdity too far'.[12] But most critics disagree, although Greene, who rarely asked the opinion of friends, was uneasy enough about *The End of the Affair* to send it to Edward Sackville-West, who did not think much of it. Edward Dmytryk thought the miracles silly and removed them in his 1955 film. And in 1974 Greene took his lead and changed them in his Collected Edition.

I much prefer *The Confidential Agent*'s Rose Cullen to the tormented Sarah Miles. She is a clear-headed, courageous young woman who is loyal to the point of being willing to marry Forbes if it will help D, the man she loves, to get out of England. She lives in the present, without regret about the past or sentimentality about the future. Rose Cullen is a whole, independent woman, although I must add that D loves her most at the novel's end when her hair is lank with spray and she looks plain; like Loo, or the shipwrecked Helen Rolt Scobie remembers fondly on her stretcher, Rose Cullen is safer when tired and helpless. I also prefer Doctor Fischer of Geneva's daughter to Sarah Miles. Anna-Luise stands up to her powerful father and marries a man she loves, a man who treats her as an equal. And I prefer the Captain's Liza who quietly makes her own life with Jim satisfactory while the Captain is off trying to compensate for what the enemy has done to her. And what about Mrs Smith in *The Comedians*? Here is an interesting and outspoken woman. And Greene's other Sarah, in *The Human Factor*. In love with another Maurice, Sarah Castle is beautiful, highly intelligent, and decisive. After Maurice has left, she stands up to Dr Percival brilliantly, frankly calling him the bastard he is, and walking out of the restaurant when there is nothing more she can say. At the end she faces the dead telephone line without sentimentality, knowing that if she is left alone to bring up Sam because her husband, even as a child, 'always gave away too much in a swap',[13] nothing can ever destroy the country she, Sam, and Maurice have made together. She, Rose Cullen, Anna-Luise, and Liza grow, as Sarah Miles does not.

The problem is that even Sarah Castle, a mature woman in a happy, credible marriage with a man who remains faithful to it no matter how conflicting and confusing his allegiances as a double agent, is not allowed to tell us her own remarkable story about South Africa. A woman of great courage and political sophistication, she could certainly have been our narrator. Instead, Sarah Castle is measured by how much she is loved by her husband. But then, like Greene's other novels, *The Human Factor* is not about a woman. It is about a man's world, about the firm and Maurice. However strong the women in it are, they are background wives, or secretaries, or prostitutes.

What, I wondered, would happen if Greene's heroines were released from their male narrators? What if they were standing on the platform at Euston waiting for the Berkhamsted train? They would not know one another although some of them would look, or at least behave, similarly. The train might be late, but they would not chat as women often do with strangers on the platform. Each would be too absorbed with her own inner story. Then a commotion might move down the platform. An older woman with red hair monumentally piled might turn up followed by two porters each bearing a suitcase, one of which would be red. Oddly, the train might arrive just as she reached the other women, and with a quick wave of her arm she might lead the way on board. 'Come ladies,' she might say with precise old-world diction. 'You have waited long enough. Come ladies. Tell me your stories'. She might even sit them in pairs — Ida with Rose, or perhaps Rose Wilson with Rose Cullen, Loo with Kate, Liza with Anna-Luise, Sarah Miles with Sarah Castle. What if Aunt Augusta were in charge?

But she has not come to help her sisters. She has come to claim Henry Pulling by telling him her story, and as Greene told us often enough, stories take on a life of their own. Perhaps Aunt Augusta should have heeded the warning; she captures Henry but I wonder if she imagined that he would become her narrator. Still, among Greene's other heroines she is unique because she is never controlled by Henry. Perhaps Greene thought her fairly harmless at 74 or 75.

The brilliance of his conception is that Henry, who as a child was greatly influenced by the Victorian books in his father's library, has

been trained at the bank 'neither to ask for nor to listen to any explanation'.[14] So static has he become that at the beginning of the novel
he can do no more than offer a childlike description of a story's bare
essentials. On his first trip with Aunt Augusta he cannot even read a
scene. When she tells him as they cross London by taxi that he is his
father's not his mother's child, he has no words at all; hiccups cover
his speechlessness. Then in her rooms above the Crown and Anchor,
he does not know what to say to her story about the premature crema-
tion and Wordsworth has to find the right words for him. But Henry
is not without a sense of irony. He finds himself agreeably excited by
his mother's funeral; in fact he has a weakness for funerals. When
he returns to Southwood with what he believes to be the ashes of his
mother who is not his mother, he is seriously tempted to wash them
down the kitchen sink and use the urn for damson jelly.

So magnetic is Aunt Augusta that from that day Henry wishes he
could 'reproduce more clearly the tones of her voice. She enjoyed
talking, she enjoyed telling a story. She formed her sentences carefully like a slow writer who foresees ahead of him the next sentence
and guides his pen towards it'.[15] How unregenerated Henry is when
he meets Aunt Augusta; he can not even write 'her' sentence and 'her'
pen. Still, her power is formidable and when soon she tells him about
Uncle Jo he tentatively begins to read life for himself. 'He died in the
passage?' he asks. 'He died on his travels,' Aunt Augusta says 'in a tone
of reproof'. A long pause follows in which Henry wonders if she is a
little imaginative, if perhaps the stories about Uncle Jo and his father
and mother might not be entirely true. Then something wonderful
happens. 'Without breaking the silence', Henry 'takes a reverent glass
of Chambertin to Uncle Jo's memory, whether he existed or not' and
asks, 'what did the truth matter? All characters once dead, if they
continue to exist in memory at all, tend to become fictions'.[16] This
revelation brings on another attack of hiccups.

Unfortunately, wine does not always sing irresponsibly in Henry's
head and he misinterprets Aunt Augusta's stories again and again
before he finally gets things right. Like every good mother she listens
to him not always patiently, and chastises him sometimes more gently
than others. When he misunderstands about M. Dambreuse she raises
her fists in exasperation and calls him a fool. When he condemns Mr
Visconti for taking her money she censures him as the little, provincial
banker he still is. 'Regret your own actions,' she shouts, 'if you like that
kind of wallowing in self-pity, but never, never despise. Never presume
yours is a better morality'.[17] Here at her maternal fiercest she is still
fully in charge of Henry and the narrative.

But in Boulogne where they meet Miss Paterson the tide begins to turn, for Henry is sympathetic to this woman who has loved his father and Aunt Augusta is jealous of Henry's misplaced sentiment. His insistence on the veracity of his own view draws 'calm and careful cruelty'[18] from her. She is in no hurry to turn her story over to him and begs a little time by offering that of Charles Pottifer, the income tax consultant who prolonged his life after death with a taped telephone message. But Henry refuses to hear it. Where in Brighton he could listen to several stories in an evening, here in Boulogne one story a day is enough. Shades of Greene have begun to deepen his view. Perhaps Aunt Augusta 'did have reason to despise Miss Paterson' he thought:

> Curran and Monsieur Dambreuse and Mr Visconti — they lived in my imagination as though she had actually created them: even poor Uncle Jo struggling towards the lavatory. She was one of the life-givers. Even Miss Paterson had come to life, stung by the cruelty of her question. Perhaps if she ever talked about me to another — I could well imagine what a story she could make out of my dahlias and my silly tenderness for Tooley and my stainless past — even I would come to some sort of life, and the character she drew, I felt sure, would be much more vivid than the real I.[19]

Finally, Henry has caught Greene's most brilliant metaphor, and I think his most brave. The author as aging mother — in a terrible hurry, shamelessly dragging, prodding, exaggerating, giving the performance of her life in order to convince her reluctant but most important reader. She moves fearlessly from the black square to the white; disloyalty is more than a virtue to Aunt Augusta; it is a duty she encourages in Henry, knowing it will allow him to roam through every human mind. But he still needs that extra dimension of understanding, and how terribly slow he is in picking it up.

Luck never enters Aunt Augusta's calculations; she is a pro and without scruples. She knows how to make her reader laugh, make him cry, make him wait. She does not return to England with Henry. She goes on to Paris alone, then vanishes. Perhaps even Greene did not know where she had gone; certainly when he started the book he had no idea what might happen the next day. But the pattern was in the carpet before she left Boulogne and when months later her letter 'written on stiff aristocratic notepaper' arrives, Henry is thirsty for adventure. He quickly packs the necessities — 'Palgrave's *Golden Treasury*, the collected poems of Tennyson and Browning, and at the last minute I had added *Rob Roy*, perhaps because it contained the only photograph I possessed'[20] of Aunt Augusta — and flies to Buenos Aires as directed.

If he cautiously buys a return economy ticket rather than the one-way first-class one she has suggested, he is nonetheless ready for his last lessons in narration. And when she welcomes him home in Paraguay she is almost ready to turn the story over to him.

Greene has given us other reflexive narrators: Bendrix, Fowler, Martins, Jim Baxter, and Brown (who, like Henry, has a mother with a younger black lover who dies for her). But only Henry has been prepared for the job by his mother, so that the retelling of her story is also his own. If this is as close as Greene could come to having a woman narrate, he more than made up for his timorousness with Aunt Augusta. Not only does her child-reader carry her story, he becomes the better narrator of it because he is the more honest. But then Henry can afford to be; he has not the necessity of an aging mother.

When he records his first story, about Wordsworth's death, he tells us he is manipulating the facts. Like a postmodern architect designing a building with all its mechanics hanging out, Henry explains that readers see things differently and that as narrator he chooses for us how we are to read Wordsworth. 'I closed the knife and put it in my pocket,' he writes:

> Had he drawn it when he first entered the grounds with the intention of attacking Visconti? I preferred to think otherwise — that he had come with the simple purpose of appealing to his love once more before abandoning hope and that when he heard someone move among the trees he had drawn the knife hurriedly in self-defence.[21]

Of course, this tells us as much about Henry — and Aunt Augusta — as it does about Wordsworth. It even tells us about that subversive romantic, Graham Greene. And it tells us about the process of reading and, therefore, about ourselves. We too prefer happy endings, however bittersweet. Like Henry, who by then has permanently crossed the border into Aunt Augusta's world, those of us who have to return to Southwood, and Berkhamsted, and even to Montreal, need to know there are people with Wordsworth's loyalty to the woman he loves: people worth their word.

Henry has learned Aunt Augusta's lessons well. He re-enters the *sala* and sees 'two old people bound in the deep incurable egotism of passion'. He sets the scene for us: no 'lights, and in the big room illumi-nated only from the terrace there rested pools of darkness between the windows'.[22] He watches, as Greene told me in 1988 that he watched his characters moving in front of him on his writing table. The old couple waltz in and out of the shadows. Henry loses their faces and finds them again. He says:

> At one moment the shadows gave my aunt a deceptive air of youth: she
> looked like the young woman in my father's photograph pregnant with
> happiness, and at another I recognized the old woman who had faced Miss
> Paterson with such merciless cruelty and jealousy. I called out to her as she
> went by, 'Aunt Augusta', but she didn't answer to the name; there was no
> sign that she even heard me . . . I took a few steps further into the room . . .
> calling to her a second time, 'Mother, Wordsworth's dead'. She only looked
> over her partner's shoulder and said, 'Yes, dear, all in good time, but can't
> you see that now I am dancing with Mr Visconti?'[23]

Greene told me he wanted the old couple to just dance away into the
shadows, to spend the rest of their lives in one another's arms. And they
do. But someone else has taken over his story; as they go a flashbulb
breaks up the shadows, and Henry's ironic pen petrifies them into a
family group. The viper is smiling toward him 'like an accomplice'.
Henry's hand is 'thrown out in a frozen appeal' while his mother —
perhaps still a little under Greene's control — quite rightly regards
her son 'with an expression of tenderness and reproof'. But Greene
need not have worried. Characters may have a will of their own, but
Henry was well trained by Aunt Augusta. He neatly cuts the other face
with the long moustaches out of the picture. Wordsworth's murder is
bloodlessly revenged, and a perfectly crafted ending supplied. In this
land where 'God's in his heaven' and Aunt Augusta's finest pupil is
holding the pen, 'all's right with the world'.[24]

Travels with my Aunt was conceived in Greene's euphoria at leaving England for France at the beginning of 1966. It is the only novel
he ever wrote for the fun of it and he rightly considered it one of his
best. His pleasure is everywhere in its pages — in its inventive stories,
its literary allusions, personal references and private jokes. It is in the
ease with which Henry, sunk deep in his middle age, lays his head
against Aunt Augusta's breast and feels like a boy who has run away
from school and will never have to return. And it is in Aunt Augusta's
tired confession to him that she has come to her journey's end, that
perhaps travel was for her always a substitute. Like all great comedians,
she has made us laugh without laughing much herself. Did she, like
Greene, who accused himself of having a splinter of ice in his heart
that enabled him to plunder other people's lives for material, feel a
sense of guilt for the 'awful selfishness'[25] Henry recognised in her as a
necessary part of an author's creative sensibility? If so, Henry lovingly
excused her. And perhaps as he released her to dance into the shadows

with Mr Visconti, Aunt Augusta took with her some of Greene's own sense of personal failure caused by the conflict of family — of all personal loyalties — and writing.

The last time I saw Greene in Antibes we spent the morning discussing his political ideas and journalism. At about 11.30, a little early for those dry martinis we were both thirsty for, the telephone rang. Greene went into the hall to answer it and what I overheard went something like this: 'No, I don't want to do that, thank you'. Silence. 'No, I don't want to do that'. Silence. 'I told you no in my letter, now please leave me alone'. Silence. 'I've said no. I'm busy now'. Silence. 'No, don't phone me back. Just leave me alone'. Silence. 'Why can't you leave me alone?' Bang. Greene returned to the living room shaking. It was a woman who wanted him to put some photos he had taken into an exhibition she was mounting, but that is unimportant. What is important is that he was inconsolable. Even the triple martini I made for him was powerless against his entangled anger, guilt, and resentment. The woman had got the better of him and he was deeply embarrassed. I was terrified by the strength of his feelings, and wondered what they would be like if he were crossed not by a stranger but by a woman he loved.[26]

The Human Factor is dedicated to his sister Elisabeth, *England Made Me* to his wife Vivien, *Doctor Fischer of Geneva* to his daughter Caroline, *The Confidential Agent* to Dorothy Craigie (Glover), *The End of the Affair* to Catherine Walston, *The Captain and the Enemy* and *Travels with my Aunt* to Yvonne Cloetta who, he wrote, 'helped me more than I can tell'.[27]

Greene may well have been, as he told Marie-Françoise Allain, 'a bad husband and a fickle lover'[28] — although he always remained on friendly terms with the women he loved. Were these dedications apologies to some of them? Do these books contain hidden explanations of what went wrong or, in the case of *Travels with my Aunt*, what went right? Or was Greene's apparent inability to create more independently spirited fictional women simply typical of the male writers of his generation rather than a reflection of the anguish and antagonism that seems to have characterised his relations with women?

If some of his novels are dated, it is in their depiction of women and the relations between the sexes. As Phuong prepares Fowler's opium pipe in *The Quiet American* he tells us she 'lay at my feet like a dog on a crusader's tomb'.[29] In *The Heart of the Matter* Louise will not let Scobie go because she has no way to survive on her own. In *Brighton Rock* Rose tells Pinkie 'I'll do anything for you. Tell me what to do'.[30] While we may empathise with these characters, they are not women most of us can identify with today. And many of the stronger female characters like Ida, and even Kate Farrant, draw misogynist flack, although I hate to use that word here because it does not apply in any simplistic way to Greene himself. He was a fine writer, and a self-reflexive writer, and when he learned to explore his art (which was to examine himself) through the use of writer-narrators, he seemed to free himself, and his women became strong, although not central. He was shy with women and perhaps that was part of the problem. Perhaps it is true, as he also told Allain, that with women he 'usually needed to be shown the green light'.[31]

But I am crossing the line into real life here, and I do not think anything will ever explain Greene better than his fiction; all we have to do is read it as acutely as Henry learned from Aunt Augusta to read life. So let us just say that in the act of creation experience and imagination merge, and if the resulting character happens to be a Greene woman she is likely to be young, and like Charley Fortnum's Clara, thin bodied with small breasts and immature thighs; helpless, or at least as Helen Rolt tells Scobie, not really good at anything; loyal; obliging, maybe even obedient; and certainly self-denying — except, of course, for Aunt Augusta. Something about Elisabeth Moor, the impossible Dottoressa of Capri, suggested Aunt Augusta to Greene, and something about his release from England and his relationship with Yvonne Cloetta allowed him to draw his own likeness fearlessly to Aunt Augusta. At 74 or 75 and, as Mr Visconti tells Henry, with the sexual urge behind her perhaps 'she presented no danger or infidelity or boredom'.[32] With Aunt Augusta Greene could safely take a rest from himself. She is the only woman he ever let come close to taking charge of his story.

And let me tell you something else about this. As Aunt Augusta stepped on to that train at Euston she looked over her shoulder at the taller of the two porters, the slightly stooped one, the one who had carried her red suitcase. They looked straight into one another's eyes — hers were 'sea-deep blue', his a lighter watery blue, with a magnetic transparency you never forget. He looked at her with amusement, and for a brief moment they were bound to one another in the deep incurable egotism of passion. Then, 'in very clear old accents'[33] she said: 'There now. Women aren't so painful, are they. You just had to learn not to be so hard on yourself. You've done very well — and you even had fun. Just keep watching. Life will provide the irony'.

CHAPTER 14

Graham Greene and Alfred Hitchcock

Mike Hill

In his paper on *The Comic Sense of Graham Greene*[1] Neil Sinyard makes, in passing, a comparison between Graham Greene and Alfred Hitchcock: they were both inveterate practical jokers. Sinyard's earlier book *Filming Literature: The Art of Screen Adaptation*[2] pursues this comparison much further, and should alert us to an area worth examining. The parallels between one of Britain's greatest twentieth-century novelists and one of her greatest film directors are indeed striking.

At first sight, the search for such parallels seems unpromising. Their backgrounds, for instance, were quite different. Greene was born into the 'intellectual' rather than the 'rich' branch of the family, but his background was nevertheless privileged: the comfortable middle-class surroundings of Berkhamsted, his father a public school headmaster and Greene himself able to attend the same school and, later, Oxford University. Hitchcock, by contrast, was born at Leytonstone in east London, the son of a greengrocer, and was obliged to leave school at 14 on the death of his father; his education was completed at night school, while earning a living.

Nor does there seem much comparison in terms of temperament and personality. Greene was notoriously restless and easily bored, someone with a liking for 'the dangerous edge of things'[3] — toying with Russian roulette as a youth, exploring the unknown interior of Liberia as a young man, and reporting from political hot-spots such as Vietnam and Kenya in the 1950s. At times, he seemed willing to provoke an argument just to stir things up a bit — what Shirley Hazzard calls 'the inclination or compulsion to foment trouble, to shake up tameness and disturb the peace'.[4] For Hitchcock, by contrast, happiness was 'a clear horizon'.[5] Happily married for over 50 years, Hitchcock was a creature of habit, routine, and the avoidance of 'scenes', a man who liked working in Hollywood, because, he told an interviewer, 'I can get home at six o' clock for dinner'.[6] The tall, angular Greene, happy to live in a small, simple flat in Antibes, contrasts with the overweight Hitchcock, connoisseur of good food, fine wines, and modern art.

The contrast apparently extends to their respective public personae. Greene shunned the publicity circuit, preserving his privacy in Antibes, inviting his public to judge him by his writings alone. Hitchcock became a master of self-publicity — with a famous cartoon outline, a personal signature tune, a 'personality' who made droll introductions to his own television dramas — and he became the only instantly recognisable film director in the world. Yet the contrast is reversed in relation to politics. Greene let his political opinions be known, and lent his name and support to groups such as the Sandinistas and the Panamanians in their struggles with the USA. Though some of his wartime films carried political messages, Hitchcock kept his opinions to himself, never endorsed a political party, and declared that 'Politics is none of my business'.[7] Greene became notoriously anti-American, criticising the imperialism and materialism of the USA; Hitchcock settled in the USA and became an American citizen.

Yet for all their differences, there are parallels. They did indeed, as Sinyard points out, share a penchant for hoaxes and practical jokes. It amused Greene to found and keep apparently alive the wholly fictitious Anglo-Texan Society, and to enter competitions with imitations of his own prose style. Likewise, Hitchcock found humour in paying a £3 loan in the form of 2,880 farthings, or in giving a dinner party at which, without explanation, everything to eat and drink was blue. Sometimes the joke had an edge of cruelty. Greene repeatedly telephoned a retired solicitor called Graham Greene, and berated him for writing such disgusting novels, until the exasperated victim went ex-directory. More cruelly still, Hitchcock once paid a studio props man to allow himself to remain handcuffed overnight — and then gave him a drink containing a strong laxative. (He tried to make amends the following morning with a 100 per cent bonus for the poor victim.)

Whether there is a psychological link between two men who enjoy such jokes is a moot point. There may be some truth in Vivien Greene's theory — quoted in Sinyard's paper on Greene and applied equally by him to Hitchcock — that 'people who are great on practical jokes are very unhappy'.[8] From the contrasts already drawn, this may seem more appropriate to Greene than to Hitchcock. Yet at least one biography of the director — Donald Spoto's *The Dark Side of Genius*[9] — suggests that the picture of Hitchcock as the stable, contented bourgeois is inadequate. Hitchcock, Spoto contends, was a man of obsession and of frustrated sexuality. He was an intensely private man who gave the world an official, anecdotal version of himself in order to protect his real, inner self. In this latter respect, Greene and Hitchcock were again alike. In interviews both men produced well-polished autobiographical anecdotes — Greene about his youthful dalliance with Russian roulette, Hitchcock about his early brief incarceration in a police station — which became part of the accepted versions of their early lives. And Greene's 'official' version of himself presented in *A Sort of Life* and *Ways of Escape* had arguably the same intention as Hitchcock's bluff self-publicity — the protection of privacy. Both men had essentially shy, introverted natures, and both protected themselves through control of publicity. The parallels are indeed worth pursuing.

What, then, are the parallels? The two were close contemporaries. Hitchcock lived from 1899 to 1980, Greene from 1904 to 1991. Both became celebrated British expatriates: Hitchcock in Hollywood from 1939; Greene in the south of France from the mid-1960s. The two enjoyed popular and critical acclaim. Greene's books were translated into many languages. Hitchcock's films were dubbed into almost as many, while both continue to be the subject of considerable critical attention. This attention included the publication of a book based on interviews with the artist about his work — *The Other Man*, with Greene in conversation with Marie-Françoise Allain, and *Hitchcock*, with François Truffaut the interviewer. The films of both men are the subjects of book-length studies by Gene D. Phillips, American academic and Jesuit priest, no less. The writer became a Companion of Honour in 1966, and was enrolled in the Order of Merit in 1986; the director was knighted in 1980. Yet neither, perversely, won the ultimate accolade in their respective spheres. Greene, famously and controversially, was never awarded the Nobel Prize for Literature, while Hitchcock never won an Oscar as Best Director. Perhaps in both cases the explanation for this lies in the unwillingness of some critics to forgive the two men for being so popular, for producing supposed 'entertainments' as well as 'serious' stuff. Perhaps, too, in both cases the distinction had a very limited validity anyway.

Nor are these parallels merely matters of biographical coincidence. Their work also yields obvious comparisons. Both Greene and Hitchcock had a range of work wider than is often acknowledged. Greene was not purely 'cops and robbers and Catholic angst',[10] nor did Hitchcock only direct chase thrillers. Just as Hitchcock could direct a screwball comedy, *Mr and Mrs Smith*, and a black comedy, *The Trouble With Harry*, so Greene could write an uncharacteristically light-hearted book in *Travels with my Aunt*. Both depicted a criminal milieu. 'Mr Hitchcock sometimes indulges in crime or "low life,"'[11] Greene wrote in a film review in 1935, three years before depicting Pinkie's criminal gang in *Brighton Rock*. Both artists, too, were concerned with the twentieth century; in their early careers, both had works based on a story of bygone smuggling — *The Man Within* by Greene, *Jamaica Inn* by Hitchcock — and neither work is convincing as the authentic voice of its author. Costume drama was the *métier* of neither; their strength lay in the examination of the twentieth-century world of guilt and doubt and moral ambiguity.

Both Greene and Hitchcock fashioned thrillers in the 1930s based on train journeys — *Stamboul Train* by Greene, *The Lady Vanishes* by Hitchcock; indeed, since the Greene novel produced a Hollywood film in 1933, *Orient Express*, it may be that Hitchcock's 1938 film was following a fashion partly begun by the novel. Both novel and film depicted with some humour various English types abroad. In particular, one might note the character of Mr Opie in the novel — a cricket-mad clergyman who talks of Hobbs and Sutcliffe just as earnestly as Charters and Caldicott talk of getting to the Old Trafford Test in the Hitchcock film.

Both Greene and Hitchcock drew inspiration and ideas from their own lives. The autobiographical elements of *The End of the Affair*, the parallels between Bendrix/Sarah Miles and Greene/Catherine Walston, are too well known to need rehearsing here. Less well known are the autobiographical elements of Hitchcock's film *Rich and Strange* about a bored suburban couple, Fred and Emily, who go on a cruise — as, recently, had Alfred and Alma, Mr and Mrs Hitchcock, who together developed the original idea for the film and wrote the screenplay. This use of autobiographical experience extended to small details. In 1942 in Sierra Leone Greene heard of his father's death through a mix-up of two telegrams — the first telling of his death, the second of his serious illness. Likewise in *The Heart of the Matter*, set in Sierra Leone, Scobie hears of the death of his daughter through two telegrams delivered in the wrong order. At the beginning of Hitchcock's film *Murder!*, an old woman dressing quickly in reaction to screams puts both feet down the same leg of her bloomers; Hitchcock had seen his own mother do just such a thing during a Zeppelin raid on London during the First World War. Both men were acutely observant, and willing to use their experience in their work.

Like many creative artists, the writer and the director were both willing to experiment in their respective spheres. Greene's tale *The Bear Fell Free* (1935), for instance, shuffles the time-sequence for ironic effect, while Hitchcock's film *Rope* (1948) experiments in the opposite direction, eschewing editing and telling a story in real time through 'long takes' of eight to ten minutes. Sometimes their experiments tended in the same direction. In his novels of the mid-1930s, *It's a Battlefield* and *England Made Me*, Greene tried out techniques of interior monologue and stream of consciousness. (In *The End of the Affair*, we are told that the novelist Bendrix had once used the stream of consciousness technique, but had now abandoned it.) Similarly, in Hitchcock's film *Murder!* (1930), we see a man looking into a mirror as he shaves, and we hear his thoughts, superimposed onto the soundtrack. It was the first use of such a technique in the still very young world of sound pictures, and it achieves what Charles Barr calls 'novelistic interiority'.[12] The parallels are clear. Indeed one wonders, given Greene's intense interest in the cinema at this stage of his life, whether he ever saw *Murder!*, and, if so, whether the film encouraged him to experiment in this way.

Just as in the 1930s, toward the end of their careers, Greene and Hitchcock showed similar tendencies. Both returned to their roots. In two of Greene's last few novels — *The Human Factor* (1978) and *The Captain and the Enemy* (1988) — Berkhamsted is a major setting, while for his penultimate film, *Frenzy* (1972), Hitchcock returned to the sights, sounds and smells of London. And, just as the Berkhamsted scenes in *The Captain and the Enemy* — scenes of the school, for instance — have the feeling of a much earlier period, so too does the Covent Garden Market of *Frenzy*. Both men seem to have been revisiting memories of long ago.

There are, too, parallels in their artistic preoccupations. As a young man, Greene was encouraged to recount and analyse his own dreams, and kept a dream diary, which was later published. As he said in *A Sort of Life*: 'Dreams have always had an importance for me . . . Two novels and several short stories have emerged from my dreams . . '.[13] Dreams therefore often feature prominently in his fiction, sometimes as prophecy, sometimes giving insights into the inner feelings and conflicts of his characters. Hitchcock, too, took a serious interest in dreams; various forms of trance and semi-consciousness appear frequently in his films, and in two — *Spellbound* and *Vertigo* — vivid dream sequences are included, in the former case in a sequence designed by Salvador Dalí. The two are not unique in this respect, but here again they are sons of the twentieth century, living in the shadows of Sigmund Freud and Carl Gustav Jung.

Greene and Hitchcock are also, of course, linked by the genre of the thriller, particularly of the spy thriller. For Greene, this may be particularly true of the 1930s, of the 'entertainments', novels with no particular claim to seriousness of message. But much later works such as *The Third Man* (1950), *Our Man in Havana* (1958) and *The Human Factor* (1978) should warn against any easy assumption that Greene outgrew an early interest in the thriller or in espionage; and these are matched by later Hitchcock spy films, *North by Northwest* (1959), *Torn Curtain* (1966), and *Topaz* (1968). Like Hitchcock, as a child Greene devoured the thrilling stories of writers such as John Buchan, and, while the director developed a lifelong interest in real-life murderers, the novelist built up a sizeable collection of Victorian detective fiction. Both carried their interest into their work. Nor was this simply an interest in thrills and spills. Both explored issues such as betrayal and loyalty in their work — betrayal of or loyalty to a cause, a country, a friend, a lover. Just as Rollo Martins has to choose between loyalty to his friend Harry Lime and to justice and decency in *The Third Man*, so Eve Kendall has to choose between her country and her lover Roger Thornhill, in *North by Northwest*, when she sends him to apparently certain death at Prairie Stop. And, just as Thornhill questions the methods America uses in its battle to win the Cold War, so we are left to consider the morality of Pyle in *The Quiet American*, a man who will sanction the bombing of innocent civilians for the good of the cause. Both could use melodrama to explore serious issues. Equally, both could combine the espionage thriller with comedy. *Our Man in Havana* was published just a year before the release of *North by Northwest*.

The joint interest in John Buchan is worth pursuing a bit further. 'An early hero of mine was John Buchan,'[14] Greene wrote in *Ways of Escape*, though he added that by the 1930s Buchan's brand of heroic patriotism was harder to derive pleasure from. When interviewed in 1950, Hitchcock said that as a filmmaker he was attracted to writers such as Buchan, because they 'use multiple chases and a lot of psychology'.[15] There was for both men a further attraction. Both realised, in the words of a character from Buchan's novel *Huntingtower*, that 'civilisation anywhere is a very thin crust'.[16] In 1941, in the depths of a world war, Greene concluded a review of a Buchan novel by quoting a character from *Greenmantle*, agreeing that 'certainly we can all see now "how thin is the protection of civilisation"'.[17] For his part, Hitchcock revealed this thinness during the same war by showing evil coming into small-time America in *Shadow of a Doubt* in the form of Uncle Charlie, a man who believes the world is a stinking mire. Hitchcock also provided audiences with what he called 'beneficial shocks'[18] — a phrase reminiscent of Buchan's description of his melodramatic novels as 'shockers'.[19] Such 'shocks' had a personal import for the director and the writer. With Hitchcock, the 'beneficial shock' was cathartic, a release from his lifelong fear of chaos; with Greene, the shock was another escape from boredom and a flirtation with 'the dangerous edge of things'.[20] But for both, and for Buchan, there was, more important, a realisation that beneath the thin veneer of civilised society was chaos and confusion. For Buchan, this meant exciting if implausible stories, in which the veneer was protected, but only just — by Richard Hannay. For Greene, it meant demonstrating the thinness of the veneer by describing white men going to pieces in the tropics or naive Americans preaching a 'Third Force' in Vietnam while providing plastic bombs to kill civilians. For Hitchcock, it meant secret agents planting bombs in Piccadilly Circus and the sudden eruption of danger into the lives of ordinary people. Volcanic, destabilizing forces lie just beneath the surface in a Greene novel or a Hitchcock film.

One of the most obvious parallels, of course, is religious. Hitchcock was a Roman Catholic by birth and upbringing; Greene by conversion. While Hitchcock never seems to have wavered from being an ortho-dox, believing Catholic, Greene said at various times in his later life that he had never believed in hell, that he was a 'Catholic agnostic'[21] and even a Catholic atheist. But Catholicism is there in both men's work. Greene famously declared that he was not a Catholic novelist but a novelist who happened to be a Catholic, but it is impossible to read some of his works without realising that a Catholic sensibility is at work; this includes much of his greatest work, from *Brighton Rock* and *The Power and the Glory* to *The Heart of the Matter* and *The End of the Affair*. For his part, Hitchcock implicitly acknowledged the impact of Catholicism on his work when he said, 'The only thing about my Jesuit education is that I was scared to hell the whole time I was there. Maybe that's how I learned fear'.[22] The first serious study of all of Hitchcock's works, by French film directors Rohmer and Chabrol in 1957, saw him specifically as a director with Catholic themes and preoccupations, particularly that of guilt. Neither Greene nor Hitchcock just happened to be a Catholic.

Catholicism is evident in both men's work even in surface detail. In the comic novel *Travels with my Aunt*, we are told in passing that Aunt Augusta is a Catholic — as a prelude to her tale about the doggies' church in Potters Bar. In Hitchcock's film, *Foreign Correspondent*, an assassination attempt takes the form of trying to push the victim off the tower of Westminster Cathedral, and in the comedy thriller, *Family Plot*, a bishop is kidnapped, while celebrating Mass in his cathedral. But the Catholic thread is stronger than this.

The impact that Catholicism had on the work of the two men was

too extensive and complex for a study of this scope, but two examples
will illustrate the parallels. One is a common interest in what one
might call the doctrinal technicalities of the Catholic religion. In
Brighton Rock Greene explores 'the . . . appalling . . . strangeness of
the mercy of God',[23] and suggests that, evil and vicious gangster though
he may be, Pinkie may yet be shown God's forgiveness and granted
eternal salvation; a Catholic at least believes in heaven and hell, the
technical apparatus of religion, whereas Ida only knows of right and
wrong with no spiritual dimension to her values. The same interest in
the strictly theological is present in *The Heart of the Matter* — sacrile-
gious communion and suicide, questions of salvation and damnation
— issues that greatly exercised Catholics and non-Catholics when
the novel first appeared, and that still do. Hitchcock showed a similar
interest in the technicalities of Catholicism in his film, *I Confess*, in
which a priest is accused of murdering a man. He knows the identity of
the real murderer, because he has heard the man's confession, and he
cannot therefore now clear himself without violating the confidentiality of the confessional; he becomes, potentially, a martyr to his beliefs.
Both writer and director were interested in the workings of Catholic
doctrine, and used them as mainsprings in their stories.

Both Greene and Hitchcock also made use of apparent miracles in
their work. In *The End of the Affair* Greene writes that Sarah makes
a pact with God through prayer. If God will allow Bendrix to survive
an apparently fatal V-1 explosion, she will believe in Him and give up
her adulterous relationship with Bendrix; and Bendrix immediately
appears, shaken but alive. Later in the same novel Sarah kisses the
cheek of the militant atheist Smythe, disfigured by a strawberry mark.
Smythe reveals, after her death, that his deformity has disappeared,
with Bendrix putting the phone down on him, just before Smythe has
the chance to call it a miracle. Apparently, supernatural intervention
is also present in Hitchcock's *The Wrong Man*, his film of a real-life
miscarriage of justice. Manny Balestrero has been wrongly arrested
for a robbery. Apparently without hope in the light of incriminating
circumstantial evidence Manny prays, staring at a picture of the
Sacred Heart. As he does so, the face of another man is gradually superimposed on his. The man is the real criminal, who is soon arrested for
committing another crime, and Manny is cleared. The implication
of divine intervention is clear, and the parallel with Greene's use of
apparent miracle is striking.

The essential difference between the two men would seem to be
the different nature of their two occupations — one a writer, the other
a film director. Yet here too the differences should not be overstated.

Both earned their living mainly by constructing fictional narratives, and both went beyond fiction at times — Greene in his essays and journalism, Hitchcock in *The Wrong Man* and two wartime propaganda films. Nor was the distinction between writer and director so clear-cut. Writing, it is said, is an essentially solitary activity; directing is a matter of being part of a large creative team. But it is worth remembering that Greene was himself often a member of cinematic teams in his role as screenplay writer; and even his most successful achievement in this area, the screenplay for *The Third Man*, was the product of artistic collaboration with the likes of Alexander Korda, Carol Reed, and Orson Welles. Equally, Hitchcock contributed a great deal to the stories he filmed, sometimes as screenplay writer himself, always as very close collaborator with other writers in preparing screenplays. Moreover, the term *auteur* — the idea of a director whose artistic vision and skills are so powerful that he is indeed the author of his films — was almost invented in the 1950s to apply to Hitchcock. We talk of a Hitchcock film just as readily as we refer to a Greene novel.

We are, now, right at the heart of the connections between the two men — the connection of the cinema. More than perhaps any other British novelist of critical acclaim, Greene was intimately connected with the cinema. In his early life he was an enthusiast of the developing medium; he was a prolific and perceptive film reviewer for a large part of the 1930s; he developed a 'filmic' style of writing, partly as a way of selling the rights to his stories to filmmakers, partly through recognising in films the value of attributes such as economy, concision, and the picking out of significant detail; he wrote film treatments of his own stories and those of others; and he lived to see a great many of his novels and stories made into films. With this in mind, it is scarcely surprising that the worlds of Greene and Hitchcock interlocked.

In the late 1920s, it seemed likely that Greene and Hitchcock would see eye to eye on the cinema. Greene attended shows at the Film Society, in which Hitchcock was a leading light and which encouraged a serious interest in film as an art form. In a letter to his future wife, Vivien Dayrell-Browning, in February 1927, Greene wrote of a film 'I very much want to see'[24] *The Lodger*, the film that made Hitchcock's name as a director of talent. When the talkies came, Greene was critical: 'If they succeed commercially the infant art of the screen may as well be abandoned,'[25] he wrote. In 1929 Hitchcock directed the first British talkie, *Blackmail*, but he shared Greene's concerns, believing that sound could mean the death of telling stories visually with films becoming merely static renderings of people talking. Greene and

Hitchcock clearly shared an early concern for the future of serious cinema.

The lives of the two men first became directly connected in the 1930s through Greene's film criticism. Greene was reviewing the work of a director rapidly coming to be regarded as the leader in his field in Britain, and one film, *Sabotage* (1936), Greene found to his taste. 'As a director,' he wrote, 'he has always known exactly the right place to put his camera . . . [and] he has been pleasantly inventive with his sound . . . In *Sabotage* for the first time he has really "come off."'[26] But the phrase 'for the first time' is the giveaway; in general, he was not impressed by Hitchcock's films. His strongest attack came in a review of *Secret Agent* in May 1936:

> His films consist of a series of small 'amusing' melodramatic situations: the murderer's buttons dropped on the baccarat board; the strangled organist's hands prolonging the notes in the empty church; the fugitives hiding in the bell-tower when the bell begins to swing. Very perfunctorily he builds up to these tricky situations (paying no attention on the way to inconsistencies, loose ends, psychological absurdities) and then drops them; they mean nothing: they lead to nothing.[27]

This may have been Greene's most thoroughgoing criticism of Hitchcock, but it was typical of his reactions in the decade. 'Mr Hitchcock's talent has always been for the surprise situation,'[28] Greene wrote; 'he has cared more for an ingenious melodramatic situation than for the construction and continuity of his story';[29] he was 'a specialist in sensation'[30] who directed 'polished fairy-tales'.[31] 'He amuses, but he does not excite,'[32] Greene wrote in an essay in 1936. Nor did Greene fundamentally change his views in hindsight. Speaking at the National Film Theatre in the 1970s, Greene said 'one has happy memories of his earlier English films'.[33] But in *Ways of Escape*, published in 1980, Greene repeats the review of *Secret Agent*, already quoted, adding, 'I still believe I was right . . . when I wrote [this]';[34] and, as a fan of John Buchan, Greene commented, 'how inexcusably [Hitchcock] spoilt *The Thirty-Nine Steps*'.[35]

Hitchcock was clearly not Greene's favourite film director. The two men met at least once in 1936, as Hitchcock was in the middle of turning Conrad's *The Secret Agent* into the film *Sabotage*. 'I shuddered at the things he told me he was doing' to the book, Greene wrote after the meeting; Hitchcock was 'A silly harmless clown'.[36] (Sadly, we have no record of Hitchcock's reaction to the meeting.) The antipathy carried through in later life. When, in 1952, Hitchcock was preparing *I*

Confess, a film with a strong Catholic theme, Greene was approached to write the screenplay. Greene refused on the grounds that he was interested in adapting for the screen only his own stories, but this did not prevent Greene from adapting Shaw's *Saint Joan* for Otto Preminger a few years later. Conversely, in the late 1950s Hitchcock was interested in filming Greene's *Our Man in Havana*, and submitted a pre-publication bid of £50,000 for it. Greene refused. At the National Film Theatre in 1980 Greene explained his refusal: 'I haven't got all that admiration for Hitchcock, that we'll say M. Truffaut has . . . and he was offering a rather derisory sum, and announced that he had bought it — so I said no'.[37] Instead, Carol Reed made the film in a version that disappointed Greene.

It is not intended to judge whether Greene was right in his criticisms of Hitchcock as film director. However, it might be asked whether Greene himself was innocent of the failings (if failings they are) that he saw in the director's work. Writing in *Ways of Escape*, Greene told the story of a meeting with film director and producer Alexander Korda, at which Korda asked Greene if he

> had any film story in mind. I had none, so I began to improvise a thriller — early morning on Platform 1 at Paddington, the platform empty, except for one man who is waiting for the last train from Wales. From below his raincoat a trickle of blood forms a pool on the platform.[38]

This may not have been Greene's customary way of developing a story, but it is a striking potential opening to a film, and rather a good example of the kind of 'ingenious melodramatic situation' Greene so criticised in Hitchcock. In his taped interviews with Truffaut, Hitchcock gave an example of how he developed such situations for his films. He told of a scene in a Detroit car factory, which he tried, unsuccessfully, to incorporate into *North by Northwest*:

> I wanted to have a long dialogue scene between Cary Grant and one of the factory workers as they walk along the assembly line. They might, for instance, be talking about one of the foremen. Behind them a car is being assembled, piece by piece. Finally, the car they've seen being put together from a simple nut and bolt is complete, with gas and oil, and is ready to drive off the line. The two men look at it and say, 'Isn't it wonderful!' Then they open the door to the car and out drops a corpse![39]

The comparison with Greene's impromptu film opening is interesting. Nor is the opening entirely untypical of Greene. In commenting on

Greene's opening, Grahame Smith says, 'The shock of the unexpected arises from the setting's banality, the keynote being the eruption of pain and terror in the everyday'. Smith adds that 'Such moments are to be found everywhere in Greene's earlier work, from the tiny detail to the large set piece'; he says that 'Both are present in the comic excitement of D's pursuit of K in *The Confidential Agent* when he persuades a policeman and a crowd of onlookers that K is drunk rather than in the abject terror of D from which he is attempting to escape by getting himself arrested'.[40] Whether Greene influenced Hitchcock in these 'ingenious melodramatic situations', or the reverse, the parallels are worthy of note.

In this context, it is worth pointing out two examples, where influence between the two men seems only too obvious. In Hitchcock's *The 39 Steps* (1935) the hero, Richard Hannay, is on the run from the police, and stumbles into a public meeting, where he is mistaken for an orator booked to speak in support of a parliamentary candidate. At first surprised and embarrassed, he starts to assume his character. Warming to his task, he delivers an empty but stirring set of platitudes, which has the crowd cheering. This became a standard Hitchcock situation — the man under pressure who finds himself in a public situation and has to do something striking to extricate himself. Fifteen years after *The 39 Steps*, Greene published *The Third Man*, the book of the film, in which Rollo Martins, the central character, becomes mistaken for a respected novelist, and finds himself answering questions from an earnest audience about James Joyce and the stream of consciousness. Overcoming his surprise and embarrassment, he stumbles through his answers, eventually — in the book, though not the film — assuming his new identity to the extent of signing the author's books. In both cases — Hitchcock's film and Greene's book and film — the plot does not require the scene; in both cases, the intention is a humourous diversion. Both are examples of the kind of irrelevant, but stylish, little vignette, for which the novelist criticised the director. And it is difficult not to see the Hitchcock scene as the inspiration for the Greene one.

It seems, however, that the process also worked the other way. In his 'entertainment' *The Confidential Agent* (1939) Greene has the character D on the run. He climbs into a basement room. A policeman knocks on the door. D answers, having first disguised himself by covering his face with shaving soap. The policeman asks a few questions, and then departs — though not before remarking how odd it is that the man is shaving with a small, ladies razor. Twenty years later cut to the Hitchcock film *North by Northwest*, in which Cary Grant escapes capture by covering his face with shaving foam, only to get puzzled looks from another man at the tiny lady's razor he is using. Another borrowing, it seems.

Given the extensive parallels between the two men and the apparent influence between them, the antipathy of the writer toward the director requires some explanation. If they were so similar in so many ways, why did Greene have so little regard for Hitchcock? Part of the explanation seems to be that in the 1930s Greene saw (and criticised) in Hitchcock's films some of the characteristics of his own fiction. This criticism reflects the distinction, adopted in the 1930s by Greene but dropped later, between the novelist's 'entertainments' and his more serious work. 'Entertainments' were popular, more commercial, not the stuff on which serious literary reputations were founded; one has the image of Greene earning a living in the mornings by dashing off *The Confidential Agent* in six weeks, while writing his masterpiece *The Power and the Glory* in the afternoons, using Benzedrine to sustain the effort. If he thought little of his own 'entertainments' (at least initially), then perhaps he saw in Hitchcock's successful films a reflection of his own commercial instincts. Here were tricky, merely popular thrillers that did not ennoble the art. Hence Greene jeered at Hitchcock's films, while the rest of the world applauded.

A further explanation turns on the question of influence. Greene was very aware of the influences that came to bear on his own writing. An example is Joseph Conrad, a writer about whose influence Greene eventually became very cautious. In *A Sort of Life* he describes his own novel *Rumour at Nightfall* (1931) as having 'no spark of life . . . because there was nothing of myself' in it; the book, he said, had only 'the distorted ghost of Conrad'.[41] Hence, Greene wrote: 'Never again, I swore, would I read a novel of Conrad's — a vow I kept for more than a quarter of a century'.[42] It is perhaps not too fanciful to suggest a similar reaction to Hitchcock's films in the 1930s. Greene would have seen the great majority of these films in that decade, first for pleasure and later as a job. As some of his written comments suggest, he saw talent in Hitchcock. But he also saw other traits — including a penchant for melodramatic situations — which were finding their way into Greene's own writing, and of which he was wary. Desperate as a young writer to find his own voice, he rejected the director's influence. Greene may have criticised Hitchcock's films precisely because they were all too influential.

As we have seen, Greene's criticisms of Hitchcock's films in the 1930s became a refusal to collaborate with him in the 1950s, and here there are further explanations of the hostility. The two men did have important differences of temperament, at least in public; the comic self-publicist — the 'silly harmless clown' of Greene's description — was doubtless not someone the reserved and intellectual novelist would care to work with. Moreover, one remembers Greene's comment in 1936 on how he 'shuddered' at what Hitchcock told him he was doing in adapting Conrad's *The Secret Agent* for the cinema. Greene may have had striking success with Carol Reed in making films of *The Fallen Idol* and *The Third Man*, but in general Greene was famously unhappy with most of the film adaptations of his work. He saw Hitchcock as a director capable of wrecking the novels of others. For Greene, he had 'inexcusably . . . spoilt *The Thirty-Nine Steps*'; what kind of mess might he make of Greene's work? 'I felt,' Greene told Quentin Falk of *Our Man in Havana*, 'the book just wouldn't survive his touch'.[43]

There is, too, in Greene's comments a whiff of someone whose views have not moved on. Much of Hitchcock's greatest critical acclaim came for the films he made in America, from 1940 to the 1970s. One wonders how many of these later films Greene actually saw. He told Quentin Falk that he liked some of Hitchcock's work in Hollywood, such as *Notorious*, made in 1946,[44] but by 1984 Greene was admitting that 'films are no longer part of my life'.[45] Greene's most intense period of cinema-going — as a reviewer, in the 1930s — was well in the past. It is not fanciful to suggest that Greene's negative views on Hitchcock were fixed firmly in the earlier decade, and subsequently little altered through viewing of later films. His refusal to collaborate with the director may thus simply reflect an inflexible, outdated attitude rooted in the 1930s.

Differences in temperament, a critical attitude stuck in the past and, above all, a recognition in the director's work of many of his own talents, concerns, and techniques — these may have been the bases of Greene's antipathy toward Hitchcock. And the result of this antipathy was that one of Britain's most accomplished twentieth-century novelists and her most successful filmmaker never worked together. The worlds these two created are distinctive — characters exist in 'Greeneland', and films are 'Hitchcockian' — but the worlds were never combined. For all the parallels in the lives and careers, their worlds never creatively intersected. We can only guess what Hitchcock's *I Confess* would have been like with a screenplay by Greene. And, when Hitchcock was denied the chance to film *Our Man in Havana*, he went on instead to make, in succession, three of his greatest films — *Vertigo, North by Northwest* and *Psycho*; we can only speculate what at the height of his powers Hitchcock might have made of Greene's witty spy story. Greene may have been right that the collaboration with Hitchcock would never have worked — but sadly, now we will never know.

CHAPTER 15

The Plays of Graham Greene

Michael Billington

It is startling how the plays of Graham Greene have fallen off the literary map. His full-length fiction, his short stories, his travel writing, his essays, his letters are all, it seems, avidly read, discussed, and critically examined. Yet, rifling through the several critical studies of Graham Greene to be found on the shelves of the London Library, I found nothing that offered more than a cursory mention of his plays. The theatre too seems to have totally forgotten Graham Greene. *The Living Room, The Potting Shed, The Complaisant Lover, Carving A Statue* go unrevived — in the last case, with some reason — even by those theatres, such as the Orange Tree in Richmond and the Finborough in Earl's Court, which show an interest in resurrecting works from the recent past.[1] And I suppose the first question I have to ask is why the work of Greene the dramatist is so totally forgotten. Is it just our ignorance: or is it because of some inherent problem in the works themselves?

Being a great novelist doesn't, of course, make you a great dramatist. Anton Chekhov was a notable exception in that his short stories reveal exactly the same mastery of mood and character as his plays. And, in the twentieth century, the plays of D. H. Lawrence have a Strindbergian potency, while Priestley and Maugham enjoyed equal success in fiction and drama. But it is worth recalling that one of the initial aims of George Devine, when he and Tony Richardson took over the Royal Court in 1956, was to entice novelists to write plays, but, although they presented work by Angus Wilson, Nigel Dennis, and Doris Lessing in their opening seasons, they soon gave up on the attempt. The history of modern drama is also filled with examples of writers who have signally failed to transfer their genius for fiction to the stage: Henry James, Thomas Hardy, William Golding, Saul

Bellow leap instantly to mind. I don't think we should necessarily be surprised by this. Obviously both fiction and drama depend upon an imaginative ability to enter into the consciousness of other people. But the techniques of the two forms are radically different. Fiction is an infinitely elastic affair in which descriptive detail and narrative tone are every bit as important as dialogue. Drama is a far more compressed business in which everything has to be conveyed through what is said. Confronted, as I often am, by stage adaptations of successful novels, I am also struck by the way time operates differently in the two forms. In fiction, the writer has the opportunity to show how character is modified and changed by time. Drama, however, is often at its best when time is artificially compressed and restricted: think of *Oedipus Rex*, *Phédre* or *A Doll's House*. All I am suggesting is that there is no golden rule that says a great writer has to be equipped to succeed in all genres: and that Greene, even if some of his plays are unjustly neglected, is in distinguished company.

I find Greene's case interesting for another reason, however, and that is that he was the victim of circumstance and history. He came to prominence as a dramatist in 1953 with *The Living Room*, a play that stands up to rereading and that merits revival. His next play, however, was *The Potting Shed*, which was produced exactly five years later in 1958. In that time, the English theatre underwent a series of profound changes. In my book *State of the Nation*, I question the use of the word 'revolution' to describe those changes because it implies a total overthrow of the existing order which did not happen. What you do see in the second half of the 1950s, however, is a different climate of opinion. In London the balance of theatrical power gradually began to shift away from the West End, ruled by the silken autocracy of Binkie Beaumont, toward the Royal Court in Sloane Square and the Theatre Royal in Stratford East. The actual nature of drama itself was also beginning to change. Samuel Beckett, with *Waiting For Godot*, had shown how it could dispense with such supposed essentials as plot, action, and elaborate scenery, and still survive. What Beckett grasped was that much of the human dilemma could be compressed into a single situation: that of two characters waiting for something that would give sense and purpose to their existence. Bertolt Brecht, through the visit of the Berliner Ensemble in 1956, had radically changed the whole aesthetic of theatre, breached the imaginary fourth wall and punctured the Stanislavskian notion of illusion. New dramatists had also emerged, most famously John Osborne, who regarded the authenticity of their own pain as more important than adherence to the strict rules of dramatic construction. All this was part of a wider shift in attitudes in the England of the late 1950s that showed itself in several ways: The 'angry young man' phenomenon, the political disillusion occasioned by the Suez fiasco, the growing contempt for established authority. With much of this, I suspect Greene would have been in sympathy. But one of the ironies of history is that the kind of traditional well-made play, in which Greene himself had been schooled and to which he was clearly attached, was being undermined by the shift in cultural values. In the five years between *The Living Room* and *The Potting Shed*, the world had changed, and, although Greene enjoyed commercial success with his later plays, he was never to experience the huge critical acclaim that greeted *The Living Room* in 1953.

It's worth examining this play in some detail and asking why it is so good, and what it tells us about Greene. Its heroine, Rose, is a 20-year-old Catholic orphan who comes to live with two old aunts in a house in Holland Park: a strange house in that every room in which anyone has died is sealed off. One of the aunts, Helen, is a monstrous bully. The other, Teresa, is her pathetic victim. They also have a brother, James, confined to a wheelchair, who is that not unfamiliar Greene figure: the priest whose faith in the rituals and orthodoxies of the Roman Catholic Church is robbed of any real potency. The dramatic crisis, however, is triggered by the fact that Rose has fallen violently in love with a married psychology lecturer, Michael, who hesitates to leave his wife. And the action consists of the insidious pressure on Rose as she conducts a clandestine affair with her lover: from Aunt Helen, who seems as afraid of life as of death, from Father James who seeks to intensify Rose's feeling of Catholic guilt and from Michael's wife who threatens to kill herself if Rose doesn't call off the affair. In the end, it is Rose who commits suicide. But the play ends on a defiant note of hope as the previously bullied Aunt Teresa determines to sleep in the room where Rose has died thus liberating the house from its antique superstitions.

I've noted elsewhere the fascinating parallels between *The Living Room* and Terence Rattigan's *The Deep Blue Sea*, which had appeared a year earlier.[2] Both show a heroine whose ardour is far stronger than that of her vacillating lover and who is driven by despair toward suicide: the difference is that Greene's Rose succeeds where Rattigan's Hester chooses life. Both plays also show a rejected partner turning up to try to reason with the heroine: in Greene's case it's Michael's neurotic wife; in Rattigan's it's Hester's outwardly calm husband. Both plays also tell us a lot about England in the 1950s. Where Greene attacks the doctrinal severity of a Catholic Church that narrows the possibilities of life, Rattigan attacks a puritanical repressiveness that cannot accommodate intense sexual desire. I'm not suggesting for a moment that Greene was, either consciously or unconsciously, imitating Rattigan with whom, of course, he had co-written the movie script for *Brighton Rock*. What is important is that two major writers, at a time when drama was supposedly dominated by gilt-edged escapism, used the stage to anatomise England.

What also strikes me is Greene's technical adroitness as a debutant playwright. He understands a basic fact of drama: that, at its best, it acts as a metaphor. Even in the stage-directions, he points out that there is something odd about the living room in which the action takes place: the furniture doesn't quite fit, one door opens directly onto a lavatory and slowly we come to realise that the room's elderly occupants are only there because they have partitioned off the rest of the house. As Kenneth Tynan accurately noted in his original 1953 review, 'this sepulchral mansion symbolises the obscurantist aspects of the Roman faith'.[3] Greene uses the setting as a dramatic weapon. He also, as you would expect, writes very well about the pathos of those who adhere to the externals of a Catholic faith without embracing its essence. There's a very good scene between Father James and his sister Teresa where he is reading to her from St. John of the Cross and talking about the dark night of the soul. 'It's a bit difficult to understand', he says, 'for me and you who've not got that far. You see, it's nearness to God that withers a man up. We are all such a comfortable long distance away. He is trying to describe the black night he found himself in — a night that seemed to be without love or even the power to pray'.[4] As James explains, he will never reach the kind of black despair that is a concomitant of true faith. He exists simply in a world of settled comfort and, as he tells Teresa, 'I can read you what the saints say from books, even though I can't feel with them', which is why, of course, he fails Rose in her hour of need.[5]

Greene is constantly attacked by rationalist critics for his religious preoccupations. Yet it seems to me he writes in this play, with compassion and understanding, both about the deficiencies of faith and about the conflict between sensuality and religion in a way that everyone can understand. It also doesn't seem to me impertinent to suggest that the play is informed by Greene's own personal experience. *The Living Room* is dedicated 'to Catherine with love', Catherine being, of course, Catherine Walston with whom Greene conducted a passionate affair that began in 1946 and that continued for over a decade. The circumstances in the play are different from those in real life; yet you only have to read some of his letters to realise how much Greene and Catherine agonised over the conflict between sex and religion. At one point, for instance, Catherine had clearly suggested the relationship would continue on a non-physical level. 'I think,' wrote Greene in 1951, 'the only way to stay together for life is to go back and back to Confession and Communion after every time or period but I *don't* believe — even Thomas doesn't believe in the possibility, I think — of suddenly switching a relation onto the unphysical level'. He also quotes Robert Browning's line (from his poem 'Before') 'Better sin the whole sin, sure that God observes'[6] and suggests that his and Catherine's fidelity to each other, over the past four and a half years, has been better than the life they lived before. This is Greene writing from the heart, and part of the strength of *The Living Room* stems from his own resentment of a Catholic orthodoxy that would regard his relationship with Catherine as a mortal sin.

I am not claiming that *The Living Room* is a perfect play. The scene where Rose is confronted by Michael's wife lapses into melodrama. And Eric Bentley, in a very wise review of the play's American production, suggested that Greene lacked Shaw's ability to give the best arguments to the opposition: in this case the academic psychologist, Michael, who, says Bentley, spouts what Mr Greene evidently believes to be modern ideas. Bentley goes on: 'When the priest says "I thought Freud said there was no such thing as guilt" there is no-one on stage to retort "Then you thought wrong." If Mr Greene wants to do public battle with modern ideas, he should at least find out what they are'. But Bentley also said how good it was to see religion shown on stage as a substantial part of people's lives. 'How pleasant,' he added, 'to encounter a religious playwright who is not naive or inhibited about sexual passion!'[7] Although the play in fact failed in New York, it was a great success in London and Paris and stands out as Greene's best work for the theatre: a serious and intelligent study of the conflict between sex and religion that can be discussed in the same terms as a novel such as *The End of the Affair,* which preceded it by a couple of years.

The End of the Affair, as you will remember, contains an episode in which the heroine, Sarah, promises to renounce her adulterous affair with the writer, Maurice Bendrix, if God will restore him to life after his apparent death in an air raid. Clearly that idea of a bargain with the divinity haunted Greene, for it lies at the core of his next play for the theatre, *The Potting Shed,* which was staged at the Globe Theatre in 1958. It was put on by the leading management of the day, H. M. Tennent. It had a star cast including John Gielgud, Irene Worth, and Gwen Ffrangcon-Davies. And it enjoyed a respectable run, despite a devastatingly rude notice from Tynan in *The Observer.*[8] Yet, looking at it now, it seems to me a problematic play: one in which there is a clash between the form and content. Greene, it seems to me, was trying to write a traditional West End play filled with narrative suspense. Yet the issues with which he is dealing in the play — such as the conflict between reason and faith, the danger of dogmatism in either area and the possibility of miracles — cry out for something less restricted. You want the play to open out into a full-blown dialectical debate, but Greene seems tied, as T. S. Eliot was to some extent in his later plays, by the conventions of Shaftesbury Avenue theatre.

I come back to my earlier point: that by 1958 these conventions were themselves increasingly under attack. In fact, the whole context in which *The Potting Shed* appeared was very different from that in which *The Living Room* had flourished in 1953. If you look at the month in which *The Potting Shed* opened — February 1958 — what else do you discover going on in London? Well, the Royal Court was putting on John Osborne's first co-written and heavily autobiographical play, *Epitaph for George Dillon*. Even more significant, it went on to stage Ann Jellicoe's *The Sport of My Mad Mother*, which is an astonishing, mind-blowing piece about urban violence and female fertility that employs everything from jazz rhythms to parodic advertising jingles. Clearly the female principle was much in evidence that month, since out at Stratford East Joan Littlewood was staging Fernando de Rojas's great story about a Spanish bawd, *La Celestina*. Alongside this, more conventional fare still flourished with N. C. Hunter's *A Touch of the Sun* opening at the Saville, with both Michael and Vanessa Redgrave, and Norman Wisdom starring in an amiable musical based on *Charley's Aunt* at the Palace. Greene's play, in short, would have been seen by young radicals at the time as part of a West End theatre that was looking increasingly out of touch, and this, in many ways, sums up the irony of Greene's relative short career as a playwright. Politically, not least in his habitual anti-Americanism, in his exposure of corrupt dictatorships and in his espousal of freedom, he had much in common with the Young Turks who were taking over British theatre. Yet, aesthetically, Greene was wedded to a form of drama that they increasingly rejected. Rattigan suffered something of the same dilemma. The second half of *Separate Tables* is a great and daring plea for sexual tolerance, yet was seen in the mid-1950s as pandering to Rattigan's mythical Aunt Edna because of its conventional form. The difference is that Rattigan's work has endured, whereas Greene's plays have, mysteriously, been erased from our collective memory.

Admittedly, *The Potting Shed* is, in many ways, a difficult and problematic piece. Its hero, James Callifer, is facing a crisis. He works, as Greene himself once did, as a journalist in Nottingham but his life seems barren and empty. His marriage is dead. He is in the hands of a shrink. And, when his father — a once famous rationalist — dies, the family attempts to exclude him from the funeral. James returns nevertheless and discovers the family is haunted by a dark secret: something occurred in the potting shed when James was a boy, and it has been hushed up. Greene keeps us in suspense about what that might be for half the play. It transpires that, as a boy, James had hanged himself in the potting shed and was assumed to be dead, but he was discovered by his uncle, a practising priest, who offered God his faith in exchange for the boy's life. So James lived but at some cost. The possibility of a miracle destroyed his father's inflexible rationalism. And his uncle, having sacrificed his faith, became one of Greene's whisky priests, though not, like the character in *The Power and the Glory*, one living in the heat of Latin America but in the slightly less exotic circumstances of a presbytery just outside Wisbech. In the end, however, Greene strikes a positive note. James is liberated from his lifelong nightmare. His mother admits to the joys of doubt, and his shrink reveals the courage of his lack of convictions.

So what's the problem? Simply this. If you want to write a play about the conflict between reason and faith or about the nature of miracles I think you need to give the subject more air time: this is exactly what George Bernard Shaw does in *Saint Joan* where the heart of the drama lies not in physical action but in dialectical discussion. I also find what Henry James called the 'donner' — the premise on which the whole play depends — somewhat tenuous and implausible. It makes sense for Sarah in *The End of the Affair* to promise to sacrifice a guilt-ridden, adulterous relationship to save her lover's life. But I don't fully understand the logic of a priest's saying: 'Take away my faith but let him live'.[9] In *The Potting Shed* Father William Callifer justifies the bargain by saying that he was a poor man with nothing to offer except the thing he loved most: his Catholic faith. But what kind of God is it that would engage in such a bargain? What use to God, in fact, is a priest without faith? And why, if Father William was such a model priest, did he not rely on the efficacy of prayer?

As in *The Living Room*, Greene writes well about the after effects of loss of faith. The sight of Father William in his dingy lodgings, pulling out a bottle of whisky from behind the second volume of the *Catholic Encyclopedia*, is both funny and sad. And his nephew James has a very eloquent speech about the emotional impact of his meeting with the old priest: 'I've seen that room. I've seen my uncle. I don't need any other proof of God than the lack of Him there. I've seen the mark of His footsteps going away'.[10] A friend of mine, who saw the play in 1958, still remembers that line 50 years on. Greene, intuitively foreseeing the emergence of a proselytising atheist such as Richard Dawkins, also suggests that rationalists can be as doctrinaire as true believers. James's mother has a touching speech toward the end when she talks about the way that doubts engendered by the Darwinian revolution hardened into certainties. 'Doubt — that was human liberty. But my generation, we didn't doubt, we *knew*. I don't believe in this miracle — but I'm not sure any longer. We are none of us sure. When you aren't sure, you are alive'.[11] But, although *The Potting Shed* has many flashes of Greene at his best, it also shows him relying too much on the tricks of the typical West End play of the period: the carefully withheld information, the belated revelation, the touch of symbolic uplift at the climax. *The Potting Shed* is not a bad play. But it's one that suggests Greene, although a rebel in many ways, was the prisoner of the dramatic conventions of his time. In fiction, he was prepared to experiment with form. In drama, he too-readily accepted the rules of the game.

Sometimes, I will admit, those rules can still work to good effect, and Greene's next play, *The Complaisant Lover*, strikes me, along with *The Living Room*, as his best work for the theatre. Once again, it got the full West End treatment. It starred Ralph Richardson, Paul Scofield, and Phyllis Calvert. It was directed by John Gielgud. And, opening at the Globe Theatre in June 1959, it enjoyed a long and successful run. I would say deservedly so, since it plays intelligent variations on the eternal triangle and, under the guise of comedy, confronts certain truths. Again, like Rattigan's *The Deep Blue Sea*, it acknowledges that a well-bred, middle-class woman may have a strong sex-drive that bourgeois marriage cannot satisfy. Like a lot of sophisticated French plays, it suggests that a *ménage à trois* may be the most rational way of accommodating human desire. It also, in a very Greene-like way, implies that the third party in such a relationship, the lover, is locked into an assigned role as much as the husband whom he cuckolds. Boulevard plays, such as André Roussin's *The Little Hut*, had toyed with such themes before: if memory serves, that play concluded that adultery loses its spice, once the husband becomes a consenting party. But Greene gives the subject his own peculiar ironic twist, and he does that partly through characterisation and partly though social observation.

The real success of the play lies in Greene's portrait of the husband, Victor Rhodes: a dentist with a compulsive love of practical jokes. Outside Shaw's *You Never Can Tell* and a Tom Stoppard play called *Teeth*, dentistry doesn't figure much in world drama. But it was an inspired choice of profession for Greene's hero. It was partly because dentists then, if not now, seemed in some way outsiders: as someone says in the play, you invite your doctor to dinner more readily than your dentist. But Greene also suggests that dentists are, by nature, obsessives. In the middle of the play Victor's wife, Mary, goes off to Amsterdam for a secret liaison with her lover, Clive Root. Victor, meant to arrive later, turns up prematurely, but he is blinded to the reality of the situation by the excitement of being given a tour of an Amsterdam dental factory and encountering new surgical instruments. Even after Victor has woken up to the truth about his wife's affair, he cannot overcome his professional preoccupations. When he finally confronts Clive, an antiquarian bookseller, to decide how they are going to resolve the situation, his first instinct is to get him to open his mouth. 'I'm afraid,' he says, 'you don't have a very good dentist. That filling in the upper canine — it shows too much. Like an old sardine tin. I would say it's a very old-fashioned amalgam'.[12] As Clive nervously fingers his tooth, Victor suggests that he rings his secretary to make an appointment.

This seems to me vintage Greene. It's absurdly comic. It also suggests that Victor, a good man who resists violent emotional engagement, is delaying things: the inspection of tooth postpones the moment of truth. But, more cunningly still, it shows Victor using his professional expertise to put the lover, Clive, at a disadvantage: even the image of the cuckolded husband having his wife's lover in the dentist's chair is rich with possibilities. But this opening to the scene prepares the ground for what is to come. In the end it is Victor who dictates terms and enjoys a kind of rueful triumph. Earlier Greene has suggested that Victor, with his love of joke cigar butts and whoopee cushions, his endlessly repeated anecdotes and his dental obsessiveness, is a likeable bore. He is even so emotionally myopic that he expresses no surprise at discovering Clive in his wife's Amsterdam hotel room. Yet this same Victor is the man who, out of love for his wife and children, finally proposes that Mary should not be forced into making a choice between himself and Clive: that she should be allowed to have her cake and eat it. 'A child's cake,' he says, 'with silver balls and mauve icing and a layer of marzipan'. 'Bad for the teeth, my nurse used to say,' counters Clive. 'Not for children's teeth,' replies Victor once again having the last word.[13]

Victor is one of Greene's best creations, and, even though Tynan carped that Ralph Richardson performed in a vein of fantasy that seemed incompatible with dentistry, it's a role that seems perfectly suited to Richardson's gift for being airy and earthbound at the same time.[14] Like all good comedy, Greene's play is also rooted in observable reality. The lovers' desire for a foreign fling, for instance, comes up against a series of practical obstacles: a Dental Association dinner, a daughter's half term, a son's medical appointment, even the exigencies of the £100 travel allowance. Adultery, as Greene clearly knew, is conditioned as much by synchronised diaries as by intemperate lust. Clive, who makes a habit of having affairs with married women and deceiving complaisant husbands, also offers shrewd advice to an innocent young girl who has fallen for him: 'Don't,' he counsels, 'marry an Englishman. Englishmen prefer their friends and their clubs to their wives, but they have great staying power and a great sense of duty. The lover relieves them of their duty'.[15] This is another of Greene's variations on a constant Rattigan theme: the homosocial nature of English life, the inequality of passion in any relationship and the idea that sexual and emotional ardour is to be found more among women than men. In the end, most male British dramatists in mid-life feel compelled to write about marriage and infidelity. In later years Harold Pinter was to do it in *Betrayal*, Peter Nichols in *Passion Play*, and Stoppard in *The Real Thing*. And, even if Greene's play is more formally conventional than any of those works, it is imbued with its own brand of worldly wisdom and quiet irony: no more so than in its suggestion that there is no more neutered figure than a lover who is tolerated by the husband he is deceiving.

Up to this point, Greene's plays had all enjoyed commercial success in not unalloyed critical acclaim. They had contained good parts for actors, presumably made Greene a fair amount of money and at least tried to inject ideas into standard West End forms. As I've said repeatedly, I think Greene was sometimes imprisoned by those forms. You don't find in the plays the same risk-taking or self-reflexive quality you get in the fiction. As Peter Conrad has pointed out, in *The Power and the Glory* and *The Heart of the Matter*, the detective story is raised to the status of a metaphysical fable.[16] And *The End of the Affair* is, among other things, an exploration of the relation of fiction to reality. But Greene's first three plays were all popular successes.

It was only with *Carving a Statue*, seen at the Haymarket in 1964, that Greene came a cropper, and the play's failure is one that left a bitter after-taste. The published edition contains an Epigram in which Greene admits the play was no fun to do and in which he says it has faults different from those detected by the critics. Greene reveals that the play's sculptor-hero was partly inspired by the figure of Benjamin Robert Haydon, who was obsessed by the desire to do great biblical subjects but whose daemonic dream was not accompanied by any talent. Greene goes on to suggest that the play was not a symbolic drama. It was meant to move from farce to tragedy, but it never worked that way in performance. Privately, Greene put the blame for this on his star, Ralph Richardson, who played the lead role of an artist — called simply The Father — who concentrates all his energies on a massive sculpture of God and who treats with casual cruelty a teenage son, whom he uses as a handyman. Greene saw the Father as a farcical figure, who comes to a tragic end: Richardson, according to one critic, played him like Michelangelo.[17] Three days before the play's West End opening Greene wrote a devastating letter to Richardson, in which he accused him of a total failure of comprehension. 'Alas,' wrote Greene, 'you fancy yourself as a literary man and I have as little faith in your literary ability as in your capacity to judge a play. I have found you — not for the first time — incapable of understanding even your own part'. Greene went on to accuse Richardson of mangling and rewriting the text. 'The vanity of an ageing star,' he concluded, 'can do far more damage to the living theatre than any censorship exercised by the Lord Chamberlain'.[18]

Not having seen the production, I have no idea if there was any justice in Greene's claim. But, having read the play, I can only say that it fails on just about every level. Since the characters are called The Father, His Son, First Girl, Second Girl — with only a doctor who appears in the third act given a name — it seems *faux-naïf* of Greene to disclaim any symbolic intent. Since it also deals with a Father who sacrifices his Son to his own gigantic creative ends, it is difficult not to see the play in theological terms. Even the sculptor's ability to depict God's vengeful anger, but not his counterbalancing love, implies that the Old Testament God has somehow prevailed over the New. There is, of course, absolutely nothing wrong with writing a symbolic play with a sculptor as the hero: Henrik Ibsen did it in his final play, *When We Dead Awaken*, which has certain similarities with Greene's work in that both are about creators who make the fatal mistake of sacrificing life to art. But Ibsen, at this best, realised that in drama an upper-story of symbolism always depends on a ground floor of realism, and that is a lesson that Greene neglects to learn.

There is no real action to drive the story forwards, and, when action does occur, its implausibility takes one's breath away. First, The Father seduces the girl friend that the virginal Son has brought home. And, when a second girl friend appears, she is a deaf mute, who is driven to her death in a road accident, when running away from the clamorous attentions of the Father's doctor. Having accused Greene of sticking rigidly to existing West End forms in his earlier work, it may seem harsh to attack him for launching what was obviously an experiment. And somewhere inside the play's inert mass I suspect there is an interesting piece of self-accusation about the artist's subordination of other people to his own overriding obsession. As The Father says toward the end, 'As long as I work, I can hold the pain of the world away from me. That's the only subject I've got — my indifference and the world's pain'.[19] But, while that may be a valid subject for drama, I feel Greene deluded himself in believing he had written a farcical tragedy, or that the reason for the play's failure lay exclusively at Richardson's door.

It's not a great surprise that, after the failure of *Carving a Statue*, which ran for only a month, Greene stayed away from the theatre for a decade: in fact, he never returned to the commercial theatre at all. But in 1975 the RSC presented, over the Christmas season at the Aldwych and later in Stratford, *The Return of A. J. Raffles*. This was obviously one of Greene's entertainments based on his childhood love of E. W. Hornung's gentleman burglar and cricketer. Interestingly, in a letter to George Orwell, dating to 1945, Greene says that Hornungs's books, other than *Raffles*, generally struck him as too 'homosexually sentimental'.[20] That's interesting because, in his own nostalgic pastiche, Greene leaves us in no doubt that Raffles and his companion, Bunny, are lovers. The plot also revolves around a break-in at the house of the Marquess of Queensberry organised at the behest of Lord Alfred Douglas. Back in 1975 there was what Martin Esslin called a good deal of humourless carping by the daily critics — of whom I was one — at the play's resurrection of a somewhat antiquated hero.[21] But read today, the play stands up well, is elegantly written and suggests that Greene got fun out of the whole enterprise.

Greene's final theatrical venture was a slightly more curious enterprise: a double bill presented at the Leicester Haymarket Studio in 1980. Once again I felt that Greene, freed from the tyranny of commercial imperatives, was simply enjoying himself. The first play, *Yes and No*, was a two-hander in which a director agonises with a young actor over the motivations behind the simple monosyllables he has to speak in a contemporary play: clearly it is meant as an affectionate swipe at the kind of cryptic Pinter play in which Sir Ralph and Sir John, both mentioned by name, had recently appeared. Yet, despite the mild satire on Pinter, what strikes me is how close Greene and Pinter were in their political attitudes: indeed, on Greene's death in 1991, Pinter praised his fellow writer for his ability to look beyond political rhetoric at the reality of 'a tortured, naked body'.[22] The other play, *For Whom the Bell Chimes*, is more substantial. It's an intricately plotted black comedy about a dead body stashed away in a hidden bed. Since the play involves a transsexual police inspector, a bogus charity worker, a demented colonel and is much obsessed with death, it's not hard to see it as a perverse tribute to Leicester's most famous literary son, Joe Orton. It's odd, in one way, to see Greene in his seventies essaying this kind of macabre comedy: you feel he's jumping on a bandwagon that, given the fact that Orton had died in 1967, was already rolling over the hill. But the piece has a certain dramatic energy and leaves one wondering what might have happened if Greene had allied himself, earlier in his career, with the new subsidised theatre.

This, I suppose, would be my final thought about Greene the dramatist. Born in 1904, he was inescapably a product of a time, when theatre was primarily a commercial entertainment and when the 'well-made' play imposed certain rules and obligations. For most of his life, Greene worked within those rules, and in *The Living Room* and *The Complaisant Lover*, he exploited them with great skill and wrote plays that deserve revival. You could, of course, say that in his fiction Greene also acknowledged the existence of rules. But, in his novels, he brilliantly extends the accepted conventions. He widened the map of modern British fiction and took it away from parochial concerns. He dealt with Conradian heroes who, confronted by modern history, face some form of metaphysical trial and who discover a sense of sin without setting their feet on the way to salvation. Greene also experimented with the form of fiction and raised fascinating questions about the novel's inherent mendacity and the unreliability of the narrator. What he brought to drama was his inbuilt sense of guilt, his technical accomplishment, and an awareness of the governing conditions of the West End drama of his time. I can't help feeling that inside Greene there was a more challenging dramatist struggling to get out. But his intermittent career in the theatre, spread over a period of nearly 30 years, is a reminder that even the greatest writers are a product of their time and that, while it is possible to break the rules in one genre, it is very difficult to do it in two.

CHAPTER 16

Graham Greene and Charlie Chaplin

Neil Sinyard

It is a curious fact that two of the most universal and cosmopolitan artists of the twentieth century, Graham Greene and Charlie Chaplin, should die in the same region and be buried not far from each other in Switzerland — the land of 'the cuckoo clock', as Harry Lime impudently (and erroneously) described it in *The Third Man* (1949). Their closeness was felt in other ways too: for example, in their political views; in their depiction of the impact of a traumatic childhood; and in their complex and ambivalent attitude to America. It was also felt on a personal level and in the influence each occasionally had on the other, be it artistic or professional. In discussing, then, the 'relationship' between Greene and Chaplin, I wish to cover various and varied aspects of their complex and fascinating interaction.

In his very first piece of published writing on the cinema entitled 'The Province of the Film', published in *The Times* (April 9, 1928), Greene makes particular reference to a sequence from Chaplin's *A Woman of Paris* (1923), a serious drama that Chaplin directed but in which he did not appear. The article is an early example of film aesthetics, in which Greene muses on the differences between film and prose and what images can do that words cannot. 'Words are a clumsy unmalleable material,' he writes. 'The thought, which takes pages to express, arises from one sharply focused picture in the mind. The object of the film should be the translation of the thought back into images'.[1] He goes on:

> For an image of despair and fatalism, let us go to one adventurous film produced in America, Mr Chaplin's *A Woman of Paris*. A girl, deserted by her lover, stands on a village platform at midnight waiting in vain. The Paris express, in which they were to have gone together, draws into the station, but

we do not see the train. Only across her still face the shadows of the windows pass and then stay still. There are no tears, no subtitles, and no movement save of shadows.[2]

For Greene the drama and psychological intensity of the situation is suggested through visual means and the expressiveness of Chaplin's deployment of imagery and symbolism. Twenty years or so later, in *The Third Man*, it seems to me that Greene and his director Carol Reed will pay homage to that Chaplin moment in a scene where Anna (Alida Valli) is due to catch a train that leaves Vienna but does not do so when she realises that the price for her freedom is the betrayal of her lover, Harry Lime. As in the Chaplin sequence, we do not see the train: the dramatic situation and psychological mood are conveyed entirely through light and shadow.

Greene's appreciation of the Chaplin sequence also provides a key to his future literary style. It is an example of what he learnt from the cinema to the benefit of his fiction, and what led to his style being called 'cinematic' and his novels being referred to as 'verbal movies', to borrow a phrase from James Agee's review of the 1945 film adaptation of *The Confidential Agent*.[3] The lesson of that sequence for him as a novelist was that to convey thought and psychological intensity on the page, you do not verbalise in the hope that a picture will come; you visualise the scene and then describe and evoke as sharply as you can what you have seen in your mind's eye. As an example of that, I would cite the opening paragraph of *The Power and the Glory*, with its sweeping aerial view of its Mexican setting as a few vultures look down disdainfully at Tench before one of them flies off across the town toward the sea. Another vivid example would be that scene in chapter 1, part 5, of *Brighton Rock* where Spicer's girlfriend takes Pinkie to have sex in a car park: the indication of montage, point of view and even lighting in the writing has the precision of a screen storyboard.

During his film criticism days in the 1930s for *The Spectator*, Greene had occasion to review Chaplin's new film, *Modern Times* (February 14, 1936) and again the review is as revealing about Greene as it is about Chaplin. The famous scene with the automatic feeding machine, created in order to limit the lunch hour and that goes out of control when demonstrated on Chaplin's hapless worker, was described by Greene as the best scene Chaplin had ever invented and 'horrifyingly funny'. Given Greene's avowed distaste for adverbs in his work, his use of the word 'horrifyingly' in that context is very noticeable. He recognises the human horror behind the comic conceit. The scene is about the depersonalisation of the individual and, although the breakdown of the machine is comical, the kind of managerial treatment it exemplifies is not and could lead to human breakdown. Greene concludes his review as follows: 'Mr Chaplin, like Conrad, has "a few simple ideas"; they could be expressed in much the same phrases: courage, loyalty, labour, against the same nihilistic background of purposeless suffering. "Mistah Kurtz — he dead." These ideas are not enough for a reformer, but they have proved amply sufficient for an artist'.[4] The comparison with Joseph Conrad and indeed the conscious imitation of his style are intriguing; and the quotation from *Heart of Darkness* (and it is interesting to ponder how many of his readers at that time would have picked up that reference) gives a new dimension to 'horrifyingly funny', with its recollection of Kurtz's last words in the novella, 'The horror, the horror'. (Greene will allude to this even more starkly in the cruelly unforgettable last sentence of *Brighton Rock* when Rose will return 'to the worst horror of all'.) When one recalls Greene's adulation of Conrad, his talking about Chaplin in the same artistic breath could be seen as the highest compliment of them all.

Greene's artistic admiration of Chaplin was to extend into a close personal friendship, particularly after Chaplin's exile in Switzerland, when Greene would visit him quite frequently and they would dine together. It was during these visits that Greene first encouraged Chaplin to write his autobiography; and when Greene moved to the Bodley Head publishers in 1960, he took this commission with him and, with the support of Max Reinhardt, helped accomplish one of the great publishing coups of the decade. Chaplin's *My Autobiography* was published to great acclaim in 1964, and its success might well have encouraged Greene to think about writing his own autobiography, something he had always previously resisted. He would have been particularly encouraged by the way Chaplin accomplished it: very evocative and poignant but also very selective, shrewd in what it wants to include and exclude, and the impression of himself he wants to give before future biographers come in and complicate the picture. Greene's first autobiography, *A Sort of Life* — and the title itself is suggestive of selection and partiality — was published in 1971.

Most critics agreed that the most memorable part of Chaplin's autobiography was the account of his Dickensian childhood, which was to be at the root of his creativity and his creation of the figure of the Tramp. As François Truffaut summarised it:

Charlie, abandoned by his alcoholic father, lived his first years in the fear of seeing his mother dragged to the asylum and then, after she was taken away, in the terror of being carried off by the police. He was a nine-year-old vagrant hugging the walls of Kensington Road . . . When Chaplin will enter the Keystone world to make chase films, he will run faster and further than his colleagues because, if he is not the only film-maker to have described hunger, he is the first to have lived it, and this is what the spectators of the entire world will feel when the reels begin to circulate in 1914.[5]

As Truffaut suggested, audiences sensed something authentic as well as artistic in the creation of the Tramp. Even when Chaplin was rich and famous, his friend Francis Wyndham could claim convincingly that he would 'still consider himself maimed for life by that early catastrophic shock'.[6] Greene also experienced severe anxieties in childhood that would colour his development and perhaps suggest one of the reasons that he felt such empathy with Chaplin. In the last year of his life, Chaplin would read and reread his favourite novel, *Oliver Twist*, which undoubtedly reminded him in a fundamental way of his childhood in the workhouse; and it is striking that when Greene wrote about that novel, he was less concerned than, say, George Orwell with the novel's social anger and more impressed by Charles Dickens's specific dramatisation of one boy's nightmarish introduction to the world. 'Oliver's predicament,' Greene wrote, 'the nightmare fight between the darkness, where the demons walk, and the sunlight, where ineffective goodness makes its last stand in a condemned world, will remain part of our imagination forever'.[7]

Although nowhere near as dreadful as Chaplin's childhood, it is still a fact that the unhappiness and bullying Greene endured at the school where his father was headmaster took him to the point of near-suicide and, as in Chaplin, the childhood experience had a profound effect on his life and work. As his authorised biographer Norman Sherry said of him: 'In school was born Greene's deep concern for the underdog (for so he felt himself to be), the hunted man and the downtrodden everywhere'.[8] Chaplin felt exactly the same way. 'I've known humiliation,' he said. 'And humiliation is a thing you never forget. Poverty — the degradation and helplessness of it! I can't feel myself any different at heart from the unhappy and defeated men, the failures'.[9] In a 1950 essay entitled 'The Burden of Childhood' Greene writes feelingly about writers such as Dickens and Rudyard Kipling who have been emotionally scarred by their upbringing, and his fiction is full of characters (the boy in 'The Basement Room', Raven in *A Gun for Sale*, Pinkie in *Brighton Rock*, to name but a few) traumatised by what they saw and endured in childhood and unable to shake off that trauma when they attain maturity. Similarly, one of Chaplin's most famous and successful films, *The Kid* (1921) consciously draws on his childhood memories, the Tramp's squalid living quarters being carefully modelled after the attic where he lived as a child and that was so small he would always hit his head on the ceiling when he woke up. The central situations of that film — the agony of separation from parent figures, the fear of welfare workers and the police who represent the unfeeling authority of society — were drawn directly from personal experience. One thing both men shared and understood about each other and their work was a feeling about the impact their childhood had on their sensibility: the desire to escape it but never to forget it, to draw from it artistically, to get their own back in their art on a world that had wounded them. One of Greene's favourite aphorisms was Paul Gauguin's 'Life being what it is, one dreams of revenge'; and his principal tormentor at school, a boy named Carter, will appear in various unattractive guises in his fiction and come to a nasty end.[10] (It is the name of the villain in *Our Man in Havana*, for example, whom the hero will be compelled to kill.) In Chaplin also, one feels that the pathos bordering on sentimentality in his work — undoubtedly the most controversial aspect of his artistry — is motivated principally by vengeance, a desire to wring the world's heart for making him weep so bitterly as a child.

One physical characteristic that they shared and that might seem trivial, except that it has been much remarked on, was their striking blue eyes. In her memoir on Greene, Yvonne Cloetta remarked on Chaplin's 'extraordinary blue eyes'.[11] In a meeting between Igor Stravinsky and Greene, Stravinsky's biographer Robert Craft mentioned Greene's 'implacable blue eyes' that, he said, focused on you but seemed to be seeing something else as well;[12] and Paul Theroux described them as 'pale blue and depthless, with a curious icy light that made me think of a creature who can see in the dark'.[13] Sherry confessed that Greene's eyes frightened him. Those pairs of blue eyes saw with extraordinary intensity. Greene had astonishing perceptiveness about places and people, while Chaplin was the most accomplished mime artist and mimic that the screen has ever seen. To prolong this imagery of sight, it would also be true to say that they had a similar vision of life, particularly in terms of their social and political views, which they expressed with absolute fearlessness and which in both cases made them at times objects of scorn and even hatred, most especially in America.

Like Greene, Chaplin was suspicious of nationalism and felt

himself to be a citizen of the world. Consequently, although he lived in America for 40 years, he never took out American citizenship, a decision that was to be held against him during the McCarthyist years in America when overtly patriotic values were being demanded of all its citizens, and artists with socialist and even liberal sympathies could find themselves blacklisted and unable to find work. One might say that England made both Greene and Chaplin in the sense that their English backgrounds, character, and experience were deeply embedded in their work, however little time they spent in the country. Yet both over a period of time developed a profound ambivalence about America that had consequences for their careers. In Greene's case, this ambivalence reaches its highest expression in *The Quiet American* (1955), his prophetic critique of American involvement in Vietnam that Kim Philby (admittedly not the most objective of commentators) declared on Moscow television to be the closest of all Greene's books to perfection. 'It is a perfect criticism of the CIA,' he said. 'I am not going to state that he doesn't like Americans, but . . . the American chauvinism, their principle that they can teach people how to live — this Graham hates'.[14] In Chaplin's case this ambivalence culminates in his comic satire *A King in New York* (1957), whose release was suppressed in America for 16 years.

In 1938 20th Century Fox had brought a libel action against the magazine *Night and Day* over what they called the 'gross outrage' of Greene's review of the film *Wee Willie Winkie* (October 28, 1937) in which his references to the 'dimpled depravity' and 'dubious coquetry', among other things, of the nine-year-old Hollywood child star Shirley Temple had caused considerable offence.[15] (The only wonder is that they had not reacted to Greene's earlier review in *The Spectator* of August 7, 1936, of Temple's previous film, *Captain January*, with its reference to her 'oddly precocious body as voluptuous in grey flannel trousers as Miss Dietrich's').[16] Such comments would not have endeared him either to Hollywood moguls or to the moral guardians of America, any more than did Chaplin's amorous relationships with and marriages to women who were young enough to be his daughter. Greene went even further in his disdain for things American in his *Night and Day* review (October 7, 1937) of James Whale's film *The Road Back*, based on a novel by Erich Maria Remarque about postwar reconstruction in Germany, but which, in Greene's view, had been horribly Americanised. After condemning what he called 'the unformed unlined faces and the well-fed bodies of American youth, clean limbed prize-cattle mooing into the microphone', he goes on:

It might be funny if it wasn't horrifying. This is America seeing itself in its own image . . . What use in pretending that with these allies it was ever possible to fight for civilisation? For Mother's Day, yes, for anti-vivisection and humanitarianism, the pet dog and the home fire, for the co-ed college and the campus. Civilisation would shock them.[17]

His phrase about 'America seeing itself in its own image' is at the core of what he distrusted about America and central to his critique of American diplomatic adventurism in *The Quiet American*.

However, there is no doubt that what particularly concerned the American authorities about Greene and Chaplin were their similar, left-leaning political views. In his definitive biography of Chaplin, David Robinson has noted that the FBI file on Chaplin was begun in 1922 and totalled no fewer than 1900 pages. 'What is alarming in the files,' he concluded, 'is not any investigative skill or deviousness in the methods of the Bureau but rather the degree of sloppiness and stupidity that many of the reports reveal'.[18] As he noted, the files tell you much more about the FBI than they do about Chaplin and not a hint of subversion is uncovered over a 50-year surveillance. 'What did the FBI finally turn up on Chaplin?' asked Aldous Huxley. 'That he had once attended a Shostakovich concert, that he'd seen some Soviet films, and that he'd praised President Roosevelt's stand against racial discrimination'.[19] In the case of Greene, the FBI had a secret file stretching over 40 years and generally detailing the 'undesirable' people Greene was seen to encounter, who included such unlikely bedfellows as Fidel Castro, Mikhail Gorbachev, Yoko Ono, Gregory Peck and Kris Kristofferson. Things came to a head inevitably in the immediate postwar period of the Cold War, the House of Un-American Activities Committee and McCarthyism.

In 1947, Chaplin had made *Monsieur Verdoux*, a black comedy about a serial killer that brazenly conflicted with the mood of an America engaged in Cold War and insisting on patriotism and positive messages from its filmmakers. Chaplin's personal life had often attracted adverse publicity in America: there had been a scandalous paternity case in which he had been unjustly accused of violating the Mann Act (transporting a minor across state lines for immoral purposes); and there had been widespread disapproval of his marriage, at the age of 54, to the 18-year-old daughter of the playwright Eugene O'Neill, Oona (in the event, a happy marriage that lasted until Chaplin's death in 1977). So *Monsieur Verdoux* was immediately greeted as a morally suspect film from a director whom many considered also morally corrupt. Even worse in American eyes, though, the film seemed to be an attack on capitalism. Verdoux is a French bank clerk who has lost his savings in the Depression, which has imperilled his support of his invalid wife and son. His solution is a scheme whereby he courts and marries rich women and then murders them for their money. In other words, he speculates; and then makes a killing. To him, murder seems a logical extension of big business. 'Wars, conflict, it's all business,' he will tell a journalist toward the end while in his death cell awaiting execution. 'One murder makes a villain; millions a hero. Numbers sanctify'. There is a chilling postwar logic to this, as Chaplin the humanist surveys a world that has gone mad and committed horrors on an unprecedented scale. His 1940 film, *The Great Dictator* had tried — and failed — to reverse the tide of history through ridiculing a leader bent on world domination. *Monsieur Verdoux* looks this brave new world in the eye and does not like what it sees. Chaplin contemplates the proposition that the insanity and injustice of the world might finally overwhelm even a decent family man like Verdoux and turn him into a monster. Verdoux is, in a way, the shadow side of the Tramp, the little man who now strikes back at society rather than turns the other cheek; who is permanently embittered not permanently hopeful; misogynistic not romantic; murderous not compassionate.

The contemporary cinematic villain who most resembles Verdoux is surely Harry Lime, another charming amoral killer who, like Verdoux, believes in God but who, as we see in his great confrontation with Holly Martins on the Great Wheel in Vienna, has become a monster of materialism, cynicism, and self-interest. When Holly asks him if he has ever seen any of the victims of his diluted penicillin racket (and Holly is shortly to encounter some in a children's hospital), Harry replies, 'Victims? Don't be melodramatic,' before inviting Holly to look down at the mass of people below:

'Look down there. Would you really feel pity if one of those dots stopped moving for ever? If I said you can have twenty thousand pounds for every dot that stopped, would you really, old man, tell me to keep my money — or would you calculate how many dots you could afford to spare? Free of income tax, old man. Free of income tax . . . In these days, nobody thinks in terms of human beings. Governments don't, so why should we? They talk about the people and the proletariat and I talk about the suckers and the mugs. It's the same thing. They have their five-year plans; so have I'.[20]

If there are two works of art of the late 1940s that catch better than any other the moral malaise of the immediate postwar period — its lingering trauma as the full horror of what has occurred dawns on human consciousness — then *Monsieur Verdoux* and *The Third Man* would have a strong claim.

Chaplin's strained relations with American officialdom came to a head in 1952. While in England for the premiere of his new film *Limelight*, he was informed by the US Attorney General, James McGranery that his re-entry permit would not be honoured without Chaplin answering charges against his character of 'moral turpitude' and 'Communist affiliation'. He was essentially being treated as a suspicious immigrant by the Immigration and Naturalisation Service of the country in which he had been living for 40 years. One wonders if, at that moment, his mind flipped back to one of the most extraordinary images in his entire work — that moment in his short film *The Immigrant* (1917) when the Tramp and the other immigrants excitedly crowd on deck to get their first sight of the Statue of Liberty, only to be immediately roped off like cattle by the crew. Not much of a welcome from the land of opportunity. In the event Chaplin decided not to return to America rather than face inquisition as an undesirable alien and chose exile in Switzerland, a decision some critics have interpreted as cowardice. For example, when reviewing Chaplin's autobiography in the Fall 1966 edition of *Film Comment*, Harry Feldman wrote:

> Chaplin left this country voluntarily. He was not an American citizen because, for reasons of his own, he chose to remain a British subject. Subsequently he was informed that his right to re-enter the United States would be challenged because of a morals charge. Chaplin, again for reasons of his own, chose not to contest the charge. Martyrs should be made of sterner stuff.[21]

This seems to me at best ingenuous and at worst calculatedly insulting. Certainly Chaplin had his own reasons for remaining a British citizen: he was loyal to his roots, a character trait that Greene much admired in him. 'Graham thought highly of Charlie,' wrote Cloetta, 'particularly because Charlie, who was born in the gutter, went back, despite his success, to South London every time he visited England, so that he could re-discover the atmosphere of his childhood'.[22] His refusal to answer a morals charge was not cowardice but commonsense, since he would be dealing with people whose objectivity was dubious, to say the least; who had their own political agenda; and whose own moral probity might be best described as questionable. It is well known — indeed, legendary — that when the Hollywood Ten were sent to prison for contempt for refusing to answer the question of whether or not they had been members of the Communist Party, they were soon to be joined in confinement by the Chairman of the very Committee that had tried them, Parnell Thomas. He was being imprisoned not because of a contested point of constitutional principle, like the Ten, but for the rather baser crimes of fraud and corruption.

It was at this time that Greene wrote his famous Open Letter to the *New Statesman* (September 27, 1952) in defence of Chaplin and addressed to him as 'the screen's finest artist' and as 'one of the greatest liberals of our day'. He went on:

> Your films have always been compassionate towards the weak and the under-privileged; they have always punctured the bully. To our pain and astonishment you paid the United States the highest compliment in your power by settling within her borders, and now we feel pain but not astonish-ment at the response — not from the American people in general, one is sure, but from those authorities who seem to take orders from such men as McCarthy.[23]

Having thus demolished the argument about Chaplin's not taking out American citizenship (the fact that an artist of his greatness resided there was honour enough) and later wondering mischievously where McCarthy was on the occasion when Chaplin, at the request of President Roosevelt, had spoken out in support of the Russian people at the time of the Nazi invasion of the Soviet Union, Greene con-cluded by suggesting that English writers and actors should consider boycotting any organisation that is in league with McCarthy and the witch-hunters and against Chaplin. To those who would say it is none of our business Greene counters that 'the disgrace of an ally is our disgrace, and in attacking you the witch-hunters have emphasised that this is no national matter. Intolerance in any country wounds freedom throughout the world'.[24] It says much about the atmosphere of the time that the letter generated some hate mail against Greene, but he would have regarded that as a compliment and proof that he had 'drawn blood', as he liked to put it. It is surely no coincidence that Greene at this time was beginning to work on *The Quiet American*, his most critical work about what he saw as America's misguided ideological zeal.

In the middle of his Open Letter, Greene mentions that, when the two met shortly after Chaplin's arrival, he had suggested that he revive the character of the Tramp for an encounter with House Un-American Activities Committee (HUAC). 'Suddenly he is summoned from obscurity,' Greene suggests, 'to answer for his past before the Un-American Activities Committee at Washington — for that dubious occasion in a boxing ring, on the ice-skating ring, for mistaking that Senator's bald head for an ice pudding, for all the hidden significance of the dance with the bread rolls. Solemnly the members of the Committee watch Chaplin's early pictures and take away their damaging notes'.[25] Greene wrote that Chaplin laughed away the suggestion, but the idea seems to have stayed with him, because it reappears in a modified form in Chaplin's next film, A King in New York (1957), about a deposed King who has been forced to flee from his country and is now living in exile in a strange land. The autobiographical allusions are transparent and it is a nicely ironical touch that the welcoming country for the deposed monarch is America. The first half of the film is often very funny, as Chaplin pokes fun at television commercials, facelifts and even himself, but the second half takes a more serious turn when the King meets a disturbed schoolboy (movingly played by Chaplin's son, Michael) and learns that the boy's parents are facing prison sentences because they were once members of the Communist Party but are refusing to disclose the name of their associates to the HUAC. In befriending the boy, the King himself falls under suspicion of being a communist sympathiser and being guilty by association (a common enough peril at that time in America). He is summoned to appear before the committee, which is a fearful prospect: What will he do? Suddenly Greene's idea for a new Chaplin film becomes very real. Through a complicated sequence of comical events, the confrontation with HUAC will conclude with the King inadvertently reducing the occasion to farce by dousing the entire committee with cold water from a fire hose. It is a sweet slapstick revenge by Chaplin on the authorities that had tormented him, and a revenge courtesy of an idea planted in him by Greene.

With a pathos worthy of Dickens himself, Chaplin died on Christmas Day in 1977. In a macabre footnote to his death that might have been inspired by The Third Man, his body was stolen from the grave for ransom, but was later recovered and he was buried for a second time — almost, one might say, like Harry Lime. In her memoir, Cloetta drew a comparison between Greene and Chaplin, noting that, if they were spotted dining together and journalists swarmed round their table, Chaplin would perform and be photographed, whereas Greene would stay in the background. 'Why is it, Graham,' Chaplin would ask, 'that they all want to photograph me, but not you?' 'But it's quite normal, Charlie,' Greene replied. 'You're a public personality. I'm not one and I don't ever want to be'.[26] Until late in his life, Greene was reluctant to be interviewed on television, partly through natural reticence, partly because he thought you became an actor when appearing on screen (he had seen it happen to his friend Malcolm Muggeridge and he did not approve), but also because he thought it might inhibit his movement and freedom as an observer if he became a public figure and widely recognised. Even so dedicated a bibliophile as Truffaut initially failed to identify him when he cast him under the pseudonym of Henry Graham in the small part of the insurance man in his film, *Day for Night* (1973). Yet, although very different personalities, Greene and Chaplin shared a deep mutual respect and admiration. They also probably shared a rueful curiosity about whether their work would be given its proper critical due after their deaths.

There is a certain similarity in the course of their artistic reputations, and particularly in the way their immense popularity and accessibility have at times worked against them. In the years immediately before and after his death, Chaplin's reputation sank like a stone; and a man who in his heyday was regarded as the foremost artist of the screen was widely derided as old-fashioned, his sentiment Victorian, his technique unadventurous, and both technically and as a performer, considered much inferior to, say, Buster Keaton. Similarly, Greene, although widely read, was rarely considered as being of sufficient stature to figure on the syllabus of a university English department. He had never embraced the joys (and agonies) of modernism, or the avant-garde or the nouveau roman. To paraphrase E. M. Forster: Oh dear, yes — his novels told a story. Cloetta mentioned how 'wounded' he was by John le Carré's comment on Greene that he was a 1930s writer. 'He was suddenly terribly hurt,' she said, 'and it remained with him'.[27] Whether or not it was a hurtful remark, it was certainly an inaccurate one: Greene cannot as a writer be defined by the style and sensibilities of a single decade. On the contrary, it is hard to think of any artists in their comparable fields who can rival Greene and Chaplin in the range and comprehensiveness of their commentary on the twentieth-century experience.

When Chaplin was making his early comedies, he was doing more than simply helping people forget their troubles in times of hardship: in Truffaut's phrase, 'without willing it or knowing it, he helped men live'.[28] He was the cinema's first Everyman, a tramp victimised by society who refused to submit to his fate. His popular impact was unprecedented. When he made his famous European tour in 1921, he received 73,000 fan letters in London alone. His anti-Fascist film, *The Great Dictator* was made defiantly at a time when America was still isolationist in its foreign policy and even impressed George Orwell, who was normally disdainful of the cinema but who admired the film's courageous attack on the allure of power politics. When people in Eastern Europe were allowed to see the film for the first time after the war, they were spellbound. As the distinguished Czech director Miloš Forman said on the DVD release of the film: 'It seemed to liberate us *spiritually* [his emphasis] from the spectre of Nazism'. 'When I hear a critic describe Chaplin as over-rated,' the critic Sean French reflected, 'I feel as if a molehill has said that Mount Everest's reputation for height was undeserved'.[29]

Bryan Forbes felt the same about Greene. When he heard Malcolm Bradbury assert that he thought Greene was the best of the second-rank novelists, he could barely contain his rage.[30] Like Chaplin, Greene had the gift of being able to universalise his vision, so that audiences internationally across a wide range of cultural and intellectual back-grounds could recognise something fundamental about the human condition. In the same way that Chaplin's films were funny and popu-lar but at the same time survey and anatomise poverty, the immigrant experience, the Great War, the Depression, modern industrial society, Fascism, and McCarthyism, so too are Greene's novels readable and entertaining, but also expose individual and political evil, religious persecution, intolerance, the heartlessness of the State, and the brutal-ity of dictatorships across decades and continents. In a ceremony of celebration in 2004 at his birthplace of Berkhamsted, Greene's niece, Louise Dennys, toasted a writer whose centenary, she said, would be celebrated not only in the UK but in Vietnam, Cuba, Haiti, Mexico, Central America, and in all those parts of the world about which he had written and where the oppressed knew that, in Greene, they had a champion and a voice. Both Greene and Chaplin might be thought flawed individuals in their private lives (what great artists are not?), but their work not only gave solace to the insulted and injured in society but could inspire fear and apprehension in political bullies and dictators. After seeing Chaplin's *A King in New York*, the great Italian director, Roberto Rossellini declared: 'It is the film of a free man'. It is hard to imagine a higher tribute and the sentiment could be applied equally to Greene as a writer. One recognises in both Greene and Chaplin — as they recognised and respected in each other — that sense of individuality and fearlessness that required them to speak out against a perceived outrage or injustice whatever opprobrium or hatred it might attract to them personally. Conscience made heroes of them both, as did courage, compassion, commitment — and a unique talent.[31]

CHAPTER 17

The Later Greene:
From Modernist to Moralist

Frances McCormack

Since the eighteenth century artists, writers, architects, and musicians have consistently turned to the Middle Ages for creative inspiration. The historio-cultural reasons for this are manifold. The increased focus on empire and the resultant growth of nationalism found justification in the Arthurian cycle of legends, and can be most clearly seen in the paintings of the Pre-Raphaelites and the poems of Alfred Lord Tennyson. The renewal of Anglo-Catholicism led to a Gothic Revival in architecture (growing partly out of a reaction against the neoclassical alternative, and partly from the hierarchy and order to be found in medieval culture), which provided a relief from the religious nonconformism of the age. Scientific advancement and an increasingly rationalistic worldview caused a search for solace in the focus on the supernatural, the superstitious, and the sublime that is seen in Gothic fiction.

The interest in the medieval world continued unabated into the twentieth century. Ezra Pound's translation of the Old English poem 'The Seafarer' reflected modernist concerns, particularly with its emphasis on detachment and desolation, and with the foregrounding of a psychological response to the collapse of a golden age. J. R. R. Tolkien and C. S. Lewis both turned to medieval folklore to provide a fantastical retort to the harsh realities of modern society. Neither was Graham Greene immune to the revival of medieval studies. Perhaps as a convert to Catholicism he found nourishment in the works of the Church Fathers and later scholastic theologians; he certainly would have found it impossible to escape their influence. Brennan, for example, signals Greene's debt to Augustine on a number of occasions.[1] Perhaps most interesting:

He proposed to his agent an anthology illustrative of historical and contemporary Catholic concerns with, for example, one of Crashaw's verses followed by a murderer's statement (similar to that included in *The Lawless Roads*) and a passage from St Augustine's City of God (recalling its relevance to *The Confidential Agent*) alongside a coroner's report on a suicide case. He hoped thereby to depict the modern world as 'full of horror, grotesqueness, courage, meanness, spirituality', with the 'shadow of the City of God' falling across the whole selection.[2]

Augustine's *De Civitate Dei contra Paganos* could, indeed, be part of the key to deciphering Greeneland. It is possible to read Greene's landscape in terms of the City of Men — sullied by earthly gratification and futile in its search for sovereign happiness in this life — and overseen by a City of God, which is everpresent and which causes a moral lesion in the spirit of the individual who is both drawn to sin and called by divine grace. Space does not permit analysis here. It is, however, one particular aspect of Greene's connection with medieval thought that I wish to examine in this chapter: namely, the influence of the moral fable.

In his 1942 critical work entitled *British Dramatists* Greene describes the medieval morality play as

> a vehicle to illustrate the beauty of virtue and the ugliness of vice. [. . .] It is the bones without the flesh, just as so often in twentieth century drama we have the flesh without the bones — characters who act a plot before us and have no significance at all outside the theatre, who are born when the curtain rises and die when it falls.[3]

Medieval morality drama, so heavily influenced by the contemporary moral fable favoured in the *ars praedicandi* (the art of preaching), depicts the life of an individual as a battleground between vice and virtue, and it cautions spectators that salvation may only be found in divine love. In this chapter, I shall demonstrate how Greene, in his later novels, employs fabulist discourse in order to create his own version of the morality drama for modern times. Here, I shall examine some of the tropes shared between Greene's novels of the 1980s and what is arguably the most popular mode of storytelling in the Middle Ages.

Medieval literature had two main functions — namely those of entertainment and instruction ('sentence and solaas' was the collocation that was often used in Middle English during the period; 'utile e diletto' in Italian).[4] In an age in which illiteracy was the norm rather than the exception, and in which textual reception was often a communal activity, the recreational function of literature was frequently accompanied by material for debate, and for intellectual and moral stimulation.

Medieval popular preaching frequently took on the same functions desired from literature. Jacques de Vitry, arguably the most celebrated French preacher of the Middle Ages, was conscious of the need to create a diversionary, as well as moral, level to sermons. Craun writes:

> According to the great preacher of the early thirteenth century Jacques de Vitry, even when clerics wrangled over the use of *exempla* to provide recreation and so arouse a sleepy audience unreceptive to 'serious and useful words,' they all agreed that *exempla* incite auditors for sorrow to sin. [5]

The best-known of the materials employed to make the sermons more lively was the fable. Generally, these fables had as their subject matter animals and birds that personified human turpitude. Schlauch, however, describes some more of the techniques of the *ars praedicandi* employed throughout the period:

> The friars welcomed the most heterogeneous and seemingly inappropriate anecdotes, provided only they were entertaining and could be given a perfunctory moral twist at the end, after they had aroused the listeners' attention. Not only the more lively episodes from the Bible and saints' lives, from classical and medieval history were exploited to this end, but also fiction, fairy tales, jokes, bits of gossip, folklore and real events in the district which preachers mention as 'seen and heard by myself' (*visa et audita*).
>
> Since the aim was mass appeal, and to an exceptional degree the friars identified themselves with the masses, many of the anecdotes are laden with bitter satire against the vices inherent in rich people [. . .].[6]

Medieval preaching was therefore often concerned with imparting a moral and/or spiritual lesson by providing brief narratives that could be read figuratively. These narratives would often decry covetousness, pride, and worldliness, and would frequently employ personifications or even mere *exempla* of virtues and vices against which the listeners could model themselves.

In fact, the protagonist in the morality play frequently offers himself as an *exemplum* to the audience. Everyman, for instance, cautions the audience thus: 'Take example, all ye that this do here or se,'[7] and, in fact, many of the plots of these plays are indebted to sermon exempla.[8] Speirs describes the morality play thus:

Such a play is a theatrical projection of the moral consciousness, the knowledge of good and evil. A man — any or each and every man — is imagined as faced with two alternative sets of choices, sharply distinguished as good and evil, right and wrong. These are visualised as two sets of persons and, indeed (when the moral allegory is made into a Morality Play), impersonated by actors together with Everyman himself. The idea of two sets of alternatives gives rise to the idea of a conflict between them for possession of the soul of each man. Where there is conflict there is certainly the potentiality of drama.[9]

The reader may already be able to detect resonances here with Greene's literary oeuvre: the moral dilemma, the leading of a double life, divided loyalties, high soteriological stakes. One only has to think of Rose in *Brighton Rock*, for example, Scobie in *The Heart of the Matter*, or the whisky priest in *The Power and the Glory* (these characters, though, are too vividly drawn to be indebted to the morality tradition). Greeneland itself, with its modernist psychological landscape of regret, of isolation, of shame, is a manifestation of this double life, and characters are often torn between their worldly impulses and a despair in the damnation that will be likely to result from their earthly lives. It is the very doubleness of man's existence that creates this desolation, bringing with it a sense of hopelessness in the face of a power one cannot comprehend; alienation juxtaposed with the bonds of earthly fellowship; a contempt for the body and its attraction to sin; an urgent desire for the release that comes in death.

The morality play is frequently marked by the protagonist's struggle against the inevitable sense of despair evoked by the spiritual emptiness of the earthly life. In this genre of drama the protagonist (representing all human kind and going by such names as 'Everyman', 'Humanum Genus' or 'Mankind') undertakes a spiritual quest through which his faith is tested and his soul becomes a moral battleground. Here, I shall briefly summarise three of the best-known English morality plays in order to give the reader some insight into their common narrative techniques and themes.

The most famous of all of the morality plays, *The Somonyng of Everyman*, is a late fifteenth-century work. Testifying to the era's preoccupation with *memento mori* (reminders of death) designed to lead to a contemplation of one's moral and spiritual endeavours, *Everyman* is a play about death and reconciliation, and about the transitory nature of earthly life. Opening with a reminder to the audience that all people will be called before God to give reckoning after their deaths, the play tells of a character who is summoned to justify his time on earth. Everyman seeks support from former friends and acquaintances, but all of these personifications of earthly comforts — Fellowship, Goods, Discretion, Strength, Beauty, and so on — forsake him, either upon his request that they accompany him, or later when they discover how arduous the journey will be. The only one of his companions who remains constant is Good Deeds, who initially feared herself too weak to travel with Everyman.

Another morality play survives at under 3,700 lines, with an elaborate plot and an extensive *dramatis personae*. Dating from the early fifteenth century, it is unique in its inclusion of a staging plan. *The Castle of Perserverance* is a lengthy and intricate allegorical drama, treating the entire life of the individual from cradle to grave. The World, the Flesh and the Devil are antagonists of God and will send their servants — the Vices — to compete against the forces of good for victory over man's soul. The protagonist, *Humanum Genus*, elects to ignore his Good Angel, and follows his Evil Angel, who leads him into the company of Covetousness, a servant of the World, under whose influence he accepts the fellowship of the seven deadly sins. Pricked in the heart by Penance, *Humanum Genus* confesses his sins and is absolved. He enters the Castle of Perseverance, which is then sieged by the Vices. The Virtues, armed with roses — symbols of the Passion of Christ — defeat the Vices, but *Humanum Genus* is tempted again to return to Covetousness. A dart fired by Death reminds *Humanum Genus* of the transience of life, and as he dies he prays for the salvation of his soul.

The last of the three morality plays to be discussed here differs in style from those two discussed above. It is often farcical and earthy in its humour, yet entirely pious, with a profound moral resolution. *Mankind* is, perhaps, the most accessible of these three morality plays. Mercy, a rather punctilious cleric, is preaching about the importance of resisting temptation and of good moral behaviour when he is joined and parodied by Mischief. Mischief and his minions (the three Vices called Newguise, Nowadays and Naught) are determined to lead Mankind (a labourer) astray, and Mercy cautions Mankind about the destruction that they are likely to cause. Mankind's resistance is, at first, firm, but the Worldlings recruit a devil, Titivillus, who repeatedly impedes Mankind's labour and who eventually converts him, through despair, to reject Mercy and to join the Worldlings in their depravity and crimes. Led further into despair, Mankind is coaxed toward suicide by the Worldlings, but Mercy appears and drives the Vices away. Mercy informs Mankind that his salvation is in his own hands, and that he only has to ask to be forgiven. As with the other moralities, this play ends with the defeat of the Vices and with reconciliation of the protagonist to the side of good.

The experience of despair facilitates a pivotal point in the narrative for each of these texts. Potter, writing on the influence of the morality play on Marlowe's *Dr Faustus*, writes that the play focuses on

> probing the mind of a believer whose God is terrible, just, and unforgiving to the unsatisfied. Despair, the unenacted threat in a Morality Play, becomes the impulse for Faustus' every tragic action, from his rejection of humane and divine studies to his obliterating unforgiven death. Repentance, the easy remedy for despair in a Morality Play, becomes the unattainable tragic ideal.[10]

Despair serves several functions in these morality plays: it may be, as in *Everyman*, the source from which resignation to the transience of life may grow; its rejection may be the salvation of the protagonist, as it is in *The Castle of Perseverance* when *Humanum Genus* makes a deathbed prayer and trusts in God's grace; it may also be the sign of faith in crisis, as it is in *Mankind*. Mankind's despair, according to Bevington, is more detrimental to his soul than his sinful acts:

> When the day of reckoning inevitably arrives, Mankind is so overwhelmed by self-reproach that he falls into yet another psychological trap, that of believing he is beyond saving. His evil companions goad him toward this state of despair, just as they earlier enticed him into debauchery and crime. Mankind's spiritual fall, then, is ultimately his own responsibility, even though he is sorely tempted. Like all humanity, Mankind cannot maintain a steadfast faith in the vision of goodness that has been offered him by Mercy. Confounding illusion with reality, he allows the devil's insinuations to overwhelm his weak senses and his fallible will. From such a dismaying fall he can be reclaimed only by a power greater than himself.[11]

Despair becomes a prominent theme in the writings of the later Greene. Already in *The Heart of the Matter* he has dealt explicitly with the paradoxical nature of despair:

> Despair is the price one pays for setting oneself an impossible aim. It is, one is told, the unforgivable sin, but it is a sin the corrupt or evil man never practises. He always has hope. He never reaches the freezing-point of knowing absolute failure. Only the man of goodwill carries always in his heart this capacity for damnation.[12]

Both Scobie and the whisky priest of *The Power and the Glory* perceive their despair to result from a loss of faith, while Rose, in *Brighton Rock*, actively seeks out despair in order to bring her closer to Pinkie — 'sitting there in the smell of petrol she tried to realize despair, the mortal sin, but she didn't; it didn't feel like despair'.[13] In the later novels, however, despair becomes something more human, more inevitable, more comprehensible.

Greene's later novels, while also examining the nature of despair, have more in common with the medieval typological writings — namely with fables, morality tales, and parables. As Bosco writes, these later works

> showed Greene's surprising turn to fablelike compositions: the stark realism of narrative style was fused with romantic idioms that heightened the symbolic weight of his characters.[14]

Here, we encounter generally unremarkable protagonists who find themselves in circumstances that challenge their moral identity. The texts themselves frequently contain didactic interpolations, and question the role of God in the life of humankind.

In *Doctor Fischer of Geneva*, a novel that most closely resembles the medieval morality play in both theme and tone, Jones is repeatedly tempted to despair by the eponymous doctor. The novel examines the nature and problem of evil by positing Fischer as the personification of pride, and the Toads as personifications of avarice, tempting an already-fragile Jones to despair and, ultimately, to collusion in their vices. Homage to the medieval morality fable may be detected in the characterisation of the novel. Alfred Jones, in his unremarkable life and entirely ordinary name, is a type of Everyman; in fact, the only detail about him that warrants any attention is his missing left hand (perhaps the absence of the *sinistra* is a hint toward Jones' predisposition toward the good). The Toads are surrogates for the Vices who attempt to draw the protagonist of the morality into fellowship; two-dimensional and generally indistinguishable from each other, they operate according only to impulse and conditioning like Pavlov's dogs.[15] Only the character of Fischer is fully realised. In a similar manner to the figure of the Devil in the morality play, he is grotesque and darkly comic. Through his invention of Dentophil Bouquet, he profits from a decay that is symbolic of the putrefaction of the human spirit that so amuses him. Fischer's name carries with it, furthermore, both the sense of the Latin *fissura*, *findere* (to split) and the paradoxically symbolic resonances of fish and fishermen that appear throughout the

Bible: Christ's disciples as fishers of men; the feeding of the multitude, and the parable of drawing in the net.

Throughout the novel, the demonic Fischer is likened to a deity. Of him, Jones says:

> 'I'm not Christ, and he's not Satan, and I thought we'd agreed he was God Almighty, although I suppose to the damned God Almighty looks very like Satan'.[16]

Fischer, too, compares himself to God, and in so doing damns God with the comparison. When Jones interrogates him as to the limits of his greed, Fischer tells him that his 'greed is a little more like God's'.[17] Elaborating, he continues:

> 'Well, the believers and the sentimentalists say that he is greedy for our love. I prefer to think that, judging from the world he is supposed to have made, he can only be greedy for our humiliation [. . .]. The world grows more and more miserable while he twists the endless screw, though he gives us presents — for a universal suicide would defeat his purpose — to alleviate the humiliations we suffer'.[18]

Fischer's attempts at humiliation (of the Toads, of Steiner, and of Jones) function like those of Titivillus in *Mankind*, and, like Mankind, Jones is eventually led to attempt suicide. Fischer's efforts to bring Jones to despair are not fully realised until the death of Anna-Luise. Apart from giving in to his own humiliation by overdosing on whisky and aspirin, Jones also becomes culpable in the humiliation of others, throwing a 50-centime piece onto the floor and watching the waiter pick it up.[19]

Jones becomes, paradoxically, further mired in sin as his contempt for Fischer increases. At the Bomb Party, he arouses the interest of the doctor when he is tempted to keep the check for 2 million francs, but again incurs Fischer's wrath when he trades the check for another chance at death — death that will reunite him with Anna-Luise:

> Unlike the boy with a cap pistol I felt no excitement — only a quiet sense when I touched the cracker that I was closer to Anna-Luise than I had been since I waited in the hospital room and the young doctor came to tell me she was dead.[20]

In expressing this sentiment of hope (which he paradoxically considers to be despair),[21] Jones rejects the hopelessness of humankind for which Fischer stands, and both affirms and confirms his faith in God. His 'greed' for death is ultimately what drives Fischer himself to the brink of despair — he is driven by facilitating and witnessing greed — not for human love, but for material goods — and, arguably, to his suicide:

> 'You've irritated me all evening by your mere presence. You aren't like the others. You aren't in the picture. You haven't helped. You prove nothing. It isn't money you want. You are just greedy for death. I'm not interested in that sort of greed'.[22]

The effects of this suicide are paradoxical. As witness to the collapse of what he perceives to be a human manifestation of evil, Jones loses his faith, asking why goodness should have any more immortality than evil.[23] His hope is restored upon the death of Fischer — paradoxically, by the collapse of his faith in the existence of goodness. The death of Fischer eliminates his focus on the value of divine love, and instead reaffirms his faith in the power of human love:

> I had felt Anna-Luise close to me when I held the whisky in my hand and again when I pulled the cracker with my teeth, but now I had lost all hope of ever seeing her in any future. Only if I had believed in a God could I have dreamt that the two of us would ever have that *jour le plus long*. [. . .] There was no longer any reason to follow Anna-Luise if it was only into nothingness. As long as I lived I could at least remember her. [. . .] Death was no longer an answer — it was an irrelevance.[24]

The Tenth Man presents the despair of Chavel as both wholly natural and entirely condemnable. It is despair that leads him into the bargain with Janvier, and despair that causes him to return to St. Jean de Brinac. On returning to his old family home and assuming the identity of Charlot, however, the nature of the despair changes. This is no longer despair at the prospect of death, but despair created by and founded in lies and deception. The empathy of Thérèse, who is also sullied by the contagion of hopelessness — contracted from Chavel's bargain with her brother — only serves to exacerbate Chavel's condition:

> She had told him all about her hate and now she wanted to indicate by a small gesture of service that she had other capacities. She could be a friend, she seemed to indicate, and she could be gentle. That night, lying in bed, he felt a different quality in his despair. He no longer despaired of a livelihood: he despaired of life.[25]

Despair, however, turns to hope when Chavel falls in love with Thérèse, only for this hope to be again threatened by the appearance of Carosse. The novel therefore becomes about more than the battle for life (Chavel finds this to no longer be of any value), or even for identity (his love for Thérèse causes him to adopt that of Charlot with little discomfort) — it becomes about Chavel's battle for his soul.

Chavel is not surrounded by external personifications of vice throughout the text: the threat to his soul comes from within. Thérèse, too, looks to Chavel for salvation — not the Chavel who presents himself under the assumed name of Charlot, but the Chavel she longs to return to present himself so that she may spit in his face. When Carosse arrives at the house, he reminds Chavel of the devil:

> God came into the house in an attaché case, and when God came the Enemy was always present. He was God's shadow: he was the bitter proof of God. The actor's silly laugh tinkled again, but he heard the ideal laughter swinging behind, a proud and comradely sound, welcoming him to the company of the Devil.[26]

Carosse is an externalised manifestation of Chavel's own sin. As a surrogate for Chavel, he echoes Chavel's trade with Janvier, and signifies to him the horror in which he has implicated himself.

The Tenth Man is very much the morality tale: Chavel has the opportunity to purchase his salvation on earth, but possibly buys into his eternal damnation with the same action. The lack of resolution in the plot means that reader becomes culpable in the imaginative determining of Chavel's fate. Furthermore, the intentional lack of depth in the depiction of the characters means that they function better on a figurative, rather than literal, level.

The themes of salvation and damnation take a central role in the novel. Salvation takes the form of a temporary and superficial release from the terror of death, which morphs into a damnation that haunts the protagonist throughout the novel. Thérèse imagines that the man who bought her brother's life will die 'in a state of grace with the sacrament in his mouth, forgiving all his enemies. He won't die before he can cheat the devil'.[27] In fact, throughout all three of the novels discussed here the motif of a Faustian bargain is reflected in the emphasis on gambling and probability. Chavel, who posits the method of drawing marked papers from a shoe in response to the mayor's suggestion that the prisoners draw lots for their lives, calculates the probability of his salvation with increasing despair. Jones and the Toads participate in the game that promises their humiliation and perhaps their death with a keen eye to the odds — the Toads hoping the odds will be with them, and Jones hoping they will be against him. Both of these novels carry echoes of *The Pardoner's Tale* by Geoffrey Chaucer — a medieval moral *exemplum* on avarice in which gamblers set out to kill death and are drawn into a lethal game in which they draw lots for their lives, and in which material wealth and death are ultimately equated.

The most interesting use of the motif of gambling occurs in *The Captain and the Enemy*. Victor Baxter is offered as a gambling stake by his father, and is lost to the Captain in a game of chess or backgammon — the competitors cannot agree as to the nature of the contest. The motif may remind readers of the folktale of the sixteenth-century Paulo Boi who allegedly played chess against the devil and won; it also carries echoes of the fifteenth-century Church painting by Albertus Pictor in Täby Kyrka, Stockholm, in which a man plays chess against the skeletal figure of Death. Throughout medieval fables, *exempla*, moralities and folklore, human life is a commodity that can be easily traded or exchanged, won or lost. The downgrading of human life to a bargaining tool is intended to emphasise its transience and relative worthlessness in the soteriological scheme. Here in *The Captain and the Enemy*, however, it serves as merely one more device in a text that, in its depreciation of the value of human life, is entirely optimistic about the salvific power of human love.

The fabulist elements in *The Captain and the Enemy* are certainly present, although they do not dominate. It is in the metaphorically named Alma Terrace that Baxter learns something about the amorphous and ambivalent nature of human love. The typological title of the book suggests an epic soteriological battle between God (as *capitaneus*, from Latin *caput* [head]) and the Devil (frequently figured in exegetical literature as the enemy of mankind; the identity of 'the Enemy' in the novel remains tantalizingly open to speculation). Furthermore, although the text is generally unmarked by religious doctrine, the Devil's malevolent shadow (or that of Jim's father) is cast over the text proclaiming his absence (and, by corollary, that of God) from the lives of the characters.

While Jones is confronted with a demonic and self-proclaimed surrogate deity in Fischer, and Chavel sees a demonic image of himself in Carosse, the protagonist of *The Captain and the Enemy* is born of the Devil. Speaking of his aunt, he recalls how

> She too referred to my father as the Devil on the few occasions when she
> spoke of him, and I began to feel a distinct respect for him even though I
> feared him, for to have a devil in the family was after all a kind of distinction.

An angel one had to take on trust but the Devil in the words of my prayer book 'roamed the world like a raging lion'.[28]

Once again, Greene returns to the Manichaeistic treatment of material creation, which Brennan describes thus:

> [Manichaeism] envisaged a materialistic duality and primordial conflict between two eternal principles of good (or spirit and light) and evil (or matter and darkness). It supported the efficacy of pure reason as opposed to a Christian emphasis upon virtuous credulity and trusting faith. In the Manichaean view of the world, the forces of evil were ever-present. [. . .] Only the soul of man possessed inherent virtue and was seen as an elemental particle of light tragically entangled in darkness.[29]

Similarly, the vices and virtues coexist in the morality play as earthly manifestations of soteriological forces competing for the soul of Everyman.

Jim, though, is a different sort of Everyman from Jones; he is a *tabula rasa* who may appear disaffected but who is actually without innate ideas, preconceptions or aims. He is, therefore, the ideal candidate over whom competing forces may battle for ultimate influence. His abandonment and eventual reclamation echo the human's relinquishment by God, abandoned into the mortal world and left to find love for himself. This, in fact, is Jim's quest: he comes to question the nature of love, and if, in fact, it exists at all; whether he has been loved, and whether he, in turn, can love. His only experience of love is vicarious — through that of the Captain and Liza, and the metaphor for this love that echoes through the novel in the grotesquely poignant affection of the monster King Kong for Fay Wray. When Jim, watching the movie with the Captain, asks why the ape does not drop his kicking prey, the Captain 'replied harshly, "He loves her, boy. Can't you understand that — he loves her?"'[30]

Jim remains a disinterested observer, though, immune to and unaffected by human love. When Liza falls ill, his attitude is entirely pragmatic:

> I had heard of Liza's grave state in hospital from the police and so I came to what I still reluctantly called my home to do all the tiresome things which are required when one prepares for the death of a parent. There was no real next of kin to whom I could pass this disagreeable task.[31]

Jim's spiritual failure is not down to any concupiscence. As a moral *tabula rasa* he is not predisposed to sin. Quigly notes, of his uncertain heritage, 'At least with an adopted father like that you won't have to worry about the very unjust statement in what I like to call the Unholy Bible — "The sins of the fathers are visited on the children."'[32]

Jim's flaw is his blindness to, and disinterest in, the virtues that surround him; he refuses to believe in the Captain's love for Liza — a love that is poignantly proven in the final line of the novel. As he remains blind to the Captain's virtue — especially his capacity for love — he spins for himself an intricate web of deceit from which he can only escape by attempting to determine where he stands in the Captain's affections. The second part of the novel — the part that echoes the tone and techniques of Greene's earlier entertainments — functions for the reader as a deliberate obfuscation of the theme of the redemptive power of human love that permeates it.

In fact, all of these later works refigure the medieval opposition of *caritas* and *cupiditas* around which the fables, moralities and *exempla* often revolve. The opposition between charity (the outpouring of love for God) and cupidity (the inordinate love of anything else). Augustine, who frequently wrote about the opposition, describes the two types of love as follows:

> *caritas* is the motion of the soul toward the enjoyment of God for His own sake, and the enjoyment of one's self and of one's neighbour for the sake of God; but *cupiditas* is a motion of the soul toward the enjoyment of one's self, one's neighbour, or any corporeal thing for the sake of something other than God.[33]

Greene opens the definition of *caritas* to include Augustine's emphasis on the motivation from which the type of love springs. Just as Augustine asserts that there is an inversely functional relationship between charity and cupidity — that the more one increases the more the other declines[34] — Greene too posits that the growth of *caritas* may purge the contagion of *cupiditas*. Jones' love for Anna-Luise protects him from the avarice that infects the Toads, and it ultimately results in the destruction of Fischer himself. Chavel's cupidity, which causes him to value inordinately his own life, is defeated by his experience of human love and the self-sacrifice it engenders. Jim remains ultimately untouched by both cupidity and charity, but the latter redeems the Captain in the eyes of the reader.

The medieval morality play questions which of the results of earthly endeavour are of value to the individual spirit. Greene's moral fables examine the parameters of earthly endeavour itself — of how best to survive on the dangerous edges of a Manichaeistic wasteland when competing forces are vying for control over, or destruction of, the spirit. Greene's later works, though, differ from the morality play in one significant way. Rather than attempting to portray a vision of hope by reiterating the promise of the eternal happiness that is to be found in divine love, these novels instead paint a rather bleaker picture by focusing instead on the redemptive power, and yet the transience, of human love.

Reading Graham Greene in the Twenty-First Century

Monica Ali

Earlier this year, while teaching on the MFA course at Columbia University, I had a lively discussion with a group of students about *The Quiet American*. For some of the students, mainly in their mid-twenties, it was their first (print) encounter with Graham Greene. Most had seen the movie — the remake version, starring Brendan Fraser. Everyone had plenty to say, particularly about the character of Alden Pyle and what he signified about American society, culture, and politics, and the role of the United States in international affairs. What was remarkable about the discussion was that if someone had walked into the seminar halfway through they would have had little idea that the book being discussed was written and published over half a century ago, such was the contemporary heat of the debate.

Of course my students were hardly the first to notice the relevance of Greene's fictional construct to the real-world politics of the twenty-first century. Phillip Noyce, the director of the 2002 film version, drew this comparison in an interview with *Salon* magazine, prior to the invasion of Iraq: 'George Bush is the ultimate Alden Pyle! He's hardly been out of the country, he's steeped in good intentions, believes he has the answer, is very naïve, ultimately not that bright, and extremely dangerous'. In a November 2005 article in *Newsweek*, journalist Christopher Dickey, had this to say: 'Once again, President Bush's lethally misguided good intentions are reminiscent of Alden Pyle in Graham Greene's novel *The Quiet American*, about the early days of the US involvement in Vietnam'. He goes on to quote a key passage from the book. 'He was absorbed already in the dilemmas of Democracy and the responsibilities of the West; he was determined — I learnt that very soon — to do good, not to any individual person but to a country, a continent, a world . . . When he saw a dead body he couldn't even see the wounds. A Red menace, a soldier of democracy'. Replace the word 'Red' with 'Islamic', and fast forward 50 years.

President Bush himself, in a speech to the Veterans of Foreign Wars convention in 2007, referred to the novel. 'In 1955, long before the United States had entered the war, Graham Greene wrote a novel called *The Quiet American*. It was set in Saigon and the main character was a young government agent called Alden Pyle. He was a symbol of American purpose and patriotism and dangerous naïvety'. Bush's, surely misguided, intention was to turn around Greene's idea of American naïvety in entering the war and apply it to those now calling for troop withdrawal from Iraq. That Greene should have written a novel that remains so alive today, called upon by both sides of a contemporary political divide, is testament to his brilliance not only as a chronicler of the trouble spots of the twentieth century, but also as a writer who cuts to the quick of the ideas, attitudes, and human foibles that continue to fuel conflicts in this new millennium.

It is perhaps somewhat ironic that Pyle, a character who has frequently been decried as mere caricature, retains the power to stir controversy so long after his inception. Characterisation, however, is one of Greene's great strengths. He can draw in a line or two a clearer portrait than many writers produce over several pages. Consider this description of the soldier briefing journalists visiting the field of combat. 'A young and too beautiful French colonel presided'. Or this, of the American Economic Attaché. 'He was a man one always forgot'. An indelible way of describing an unmemorable average Joe. Fowler, the apparently cynical British reporter, who is Greene's narrator, wants nothing more than not to be involved. 'It had been an article of my creed'. But, as with all of Greene's major characters, his desires are deeply conflicted and complex. Fowler has an opium habit, a Vietnamese girlfriend, and a wife back at home in London. He is a classic Greene creation — a mixture of seedy habits and tortured conscience. Why continue to read Greene in the twenty-first century? The reasons are legion, but one is simply as an antidote to what the critic James Wood has referred to as a 'contagion of moralising niceness', in contemporary literary fiction, in which the reader is invited to empathise entirely with the protagonist. From the cynical Fowler to the world-weary Querry of *A Burnt-Out Case* via the Catholic murderer of *Brighton Rock* and the obsessive adulterer Bendrix in *The End of the Affair*, Greene's protagonists are sharply drawn and deeply flawed.

Greene's major methods of characterisation are dialogue and action. Above all (a lesson to us all, this) he never stops the story in order to characterise. In his obituary of Greene, published in *The Guardian*, Ian McEwan wrote of the experience of reading Greene's novels as a child, 'One of the first lessons I took from them was that a serious novel could be an exciting novel — that the novel of adventure could also be a novel of ideas'. This powerful combination certainly provides a large part of the explanation of Greene's popularity and one of the reasons why his work endures so well. At the same time, it perhaps underlies why he has been ranked lower in the canon than the great modernists of the twentieth century, such as James Joyce and Virginia Woolf. Greene is committed to telling a story, and described himself as a storyteller. In a biting exchange in *The End of the Affair*, Bendrix, a novelist and the book's narrator, is asked by a literary critic, 'You used the stream of consciousness in one of your books . . . Why did you abandon the method?' Greene himself had indeed experimented with the method in an early novel, *England Made Me*, and never turned back to it again. 'Oh, I don't know,' Bendrix replies to the critic, 'Why does one change a flat?'

The literary snob, typified by the critic in *The End of the Affair*, has tended to look down somewhat on the conventional narrative techniques at which Greene excels. E. M. Forster in *Aspects of the Novel* refers to story as 'this low atavistic form' and laments that a 'gaping audience of cave men . . . can only be kept awake by "and then . . . and then . . ."' Forster was onto something there. For it does indeed seem that our lust for story is primal and innate. Story is something we cannot do without. We need it in our lives, in order to make sense of the world around us and our place within it. It is as essential as food and drink. With human biologists such as Lewis Wolpert now theorizing that the compulsion to create story is biological and represents a 'cognitive imperative', it seems clear that we will be reading Greene, the master storyteller long into this century, sitting on the edge of our seats, eagerly awaiting the next 'and then . . '.

Notes

Notes to Foreword

1 Stade, G., (ed.) (1976), *Six Contemporary British Novelists*. New York: Columbia University Press, 56.
2 Butcher, T. (2010), *Chasing the Devil: The Search for Africa's Fighting Spirit*. London: Chatto and Windus.

Notes to Introduction

1 Greene, G. (1971), *A Sort of Life*. New York: Simon & Schuster, 13.
2 Ibid., 17.
3 Ibid., 74.
4 Greene, G. (1951), *'The Lost Childhood' and Other Essays*. New York: Viking, 15.
5 Ibid., 16.
6 Greene, *A Sort of Life*, 166.
7 Greene cites the poem in *'The Lost Childhood' and Other Essays*, 17.
8 Cassis, A. F. (ed.) (1994), *Graham Greene: Man of Paradox*. Chicago: Loyola University Press, 277.
9 Greene, G. (1982), *The Lawless Roads*. New York: Penguin, 139.
10 Greene, G. (1980), *Ways of Escape*. New York: Simon & Schuster, 99.
11 Sherry, N. (1994), *The Life of Graham Greene: Volume II: 1939–1945*. New York: Viking, 257.
12 Greene, *Ways of Escape*, 145.
13 Ibid., 297.
14 Malamet, E. (1998), *The World Remade: Graham Greene and the Art of Detection*. New York: Peter Lang, 114.
15 Greene, *Ways of Escape*, 310.
16 http://www.grahamgreenebt.org/
17 http://www.grahamgreenefestival.org/
18 *Graham Greene at Random* is a posthumous publication, available via the website of the Graham Greene Birthplace Trust: http://www.grahamgreenebt.org/PDFs/quotations.pdf
19 http://www.facebook.com/home.php?#!/pages/Graham-Greene-International-Festival/55327438605
20 http://twitter.com/GreeneFestival

21 http://grahamgreenefestival.blogspot.com/

Notes to Chapter 1: Stamboul Train: *The Timetable for 1932*

1 Sherry, N. (1989), *The Life of Graham Greene: Volume I: 1904–1939.* London: Jonathan Cape, 260.
2 Greene, G. (1980), *Ways of Escape.* London: Bodley Head, 31.
3 Greene, *Ways of Escape*, 31; Sherry, *The Life of Graham Greene: Volume I*, 434.
4 Greene, G. (2004), *Stamboul Train.* London: Vintage, 16.
5 Greene, V. (1999), Personal interview.
6 Sherry, *The Life of Graham Greene: Volume I*, 389.
7 Etherege, G. (1973), *The Man of Mode*, edited by J. Conaghan. Edinburgh: Oliver & Boyd. See Act 2, Scene 2. Also see Greene, G (1976), *Lord Rochester's Monkey*. London: Futura, 164.
8 Greene, *Lord Rochester's Monkey*, 213.
9 Ibid., 74.
10 Sherry, *The Life of Graham Greene: Volume I*, 442.
11 Greene, *Stamboul Train*, 88.
12 Ibid., 89.
13 Ibid., 186.
14 Ibid., 52.
15 Greene, *Ways of Escape*, 27.
16 Ibid., 27.
17 Sherry, *The Life of Graham Greene: Volume I*, 409.
18 Greene, *Stamboul Train*, 9, 32, 92.
19 Ibid., 19.
20 Ibid., 181.
21 Ibid., 149.
22 Ibid., 43.
23 Ibid., 3.
24 Ibid., 183.
25 Shelden, M. (1994), *Graham Greene: The Man Within.* London: Heinemann, 167.
26 Greene, *Stamboul Train*, 47.
27 Couto, M. (2008), Personal correspondence.
28 Greene, G. (1971), *A Sort of Life.* Harmondsworth: Penguin, 34.
29 Greene, *Stamboul Train*, 194.
30 Ibid., 76, 82.
31 Ibid., 79.
32 Ibid., 4, 17, 20, *passim.*
33 Ibid., 188.
34 Ibid., 4, 32, *passim.*
35 Ibid., 42.
36 Ibid., 42.

Notes to Chapter 2: 'Ghost on the Rooftops': How Joseph Conrad Haunted Graham Greene

1 Greene, G. (1971), *A Sort of Life*. Harmondsworth: Penguin, 139.
2 Conrad, J. (1996), *An Outcast of the Islands*, edited by C. Watts. London: Everyman Dent Orion, 219.
3 An agnostic claims not to know whether God exists; an atheist alleges that God does not exist; and an antitheist alleges that God exists but is hostile to human beings.
4 Conrad, J. (1988), *The Collected Letters of Joseph Conrad*, volume 3, edited by F. R. Karl and L. Davies. Cambridge: Cambridge University Press, 112.
5 Quoted in Watts, C. (1993), *A Preface to Conrad*. Harlow: Longman, 38. Greene, in contrast, appeared as an insurance agent in F. Truffaut's *La Nuit Américaine (Day for Night)*, 1973. See Falk, Q. (1984), *Travels in Greeneland: The Cinema of Graham Greene*. London: Quartet Books, 214.
6 Conrad, J. (1988), 'Preface' to *The Nigger of the 'Narcissus'*, edited by C. Watts. London: Penguin, xlix.
7 Conrad, J. (1946), *A Personal Record*. London: Dent, xi.
8 Greene, G. (1990), *Reflections*. London: Reinhardt, 67.
9 Conrad, J. (1955), *Last Essays*. London: Dent, 17.
10 Greene, G. (1970), *Collected Essays*. Harmondsworth: Penguin, 241.
11 Sherry, N. (1989), *The Life of Graham Greene: Volume I: 1904–1939*. London: Jonathan Cape, 421. Also see Greene, G. (1961), *In Search of a Character: Two African Journals*. London: Bodley Head, 48 and 51.
12 Jones is reported as explaining his career thus: 'Having been ejected [. . .] from his proper social sphere because he had refused to conform to certain usual conventions, he was a rebel now, and was coming and going up and down the earth'. The phrasing deliberately recalls Satan's rebellion and fall, and Job (1.7 and 2.2) tells us that Satan is 'going to and fro in the earth, and [. . .] walking up and down in it'. See Conrad, J. (1994), *Victory*, edited by C. Watts. London: Everyman Dent Orion, 250, 340. 'Davy Jones' is seamen's slang for 'the Devil'.
13 Greene, *Collected Essays*, 138. In *Travels in Greeneland*, 154, Q. Falk says: '*The Comedians* is Greene's most political novel [. . .]. Positively Conradian, we follow the descent of a handful of hearts in darkness into a kind of living hell'.
14 Quoted in Watts, C. (1997), *A Preface to Greene*. Harlow: Longman, 86.
15 Greene, *A Sort of Life*, 145.
16 Greene, G. (1980), *Ways of Escape*. London: Bodley Head, 15.
17 Greene, *In Search of a Character*, 48. Also see Greene, *A Sort of Life*, 208.
18 Greene, G. (1936), *Journey Without Maps*. London: Heinemann, 312.
19 Ibid., 8 and 9.
20 Ibid., 310–11.
21 Conrad, J. (2002), *'Heart of Darkness' and Other Tales*, edited by C. Watts. Oxford: Oxford University Press, 106.

22 Greene, G. (1971), *'The Third Man' and 'The Fallen Idol'*. Harmondsworth: Penguin, 89.
23 Conrad, *Victory*, 160.
24 Greene, *In Search of a Character*, 51.
25 For this cluster of quotes, see Conrad, *Heart of Darkness*, 125 and 152. In addition, see Greene, G. (1968), *Brighton Rock*. Harmondsworth: Penguin, 109 and 132. (In the latter case, the Penguin text erroneously inserts 'with' before 'the stain', making the setting sun bizarrely soar; but I have corrected this error.) Also see Greene, G. (1970), *The Power and the Glory*. Harmondsworth: Penguin, 53. Finally, see Greene, *Brighton Rock*, 118.
26 Greene, *Ways of Escape*, 18.
27 Conrad, *Heart of Darkness*, 66.
28 Conrad, J. (1950), *'The Shadow Line' and 'Within the Tides'*. London: Dent, 112.
29 See Watts, C. (1984), *The Deceptive Text: An Introduction to Covert Plots*. Brighton: Harvester.
30 Guerard, A. (1958), *Conrad the Novelist*. Cambridge, MA: Harvard University Press, 177.

Notes to Chapter 3: The Making of the Outsider in the Short Stories of the 1930s

1 Greene, G. (2005), *Complete Short Stories*. London: Penguin, 168.
2 Ibid., 163.
3 Ibid., 163.
4 Ibid., 164.
5 Ibid., 166.
6 Ibid., 165.
7 Ibid., 166.
8 Ibid., 166.
9 Ibid., 151.
10 Ibid., 150.
11 Ibid., 152.
12 Ibid., 152.
13 Ibid., 114.
14 Ibid., 108.
15 Ibid., 110.
16 Ibid., 112.
17 Ibid., 113.
18 Ibid., 113.
19 Ibid., 120.
20 Ibid., 117.
21 Ibid., 119.
22 Ibid., 122.
23 Ibid., 125.
24 Ibid., 130.
25 Auden, W. H. (1977), *The English Auden: Poems, Essays and Dramatic*

Writings, 1927–1939, edited by E. Mendelson. London: Faber, 25.

26 Greene, *Complete Short Stories*, 161.

27 Ibid., 156.

28 Ibid., 157.

29 Ibid., 137.

30 Ibid., 138.

31 Sherry, N. (1989). *The Life of Graham Greene: Volume I: 1904–1939*. London: Jonathan Cape, 457.

32 Greene, *Complete Short Stories*, 567.

33 Ibid., 568.

34 Ibid., 574.

35 Ibid., 574.

36 Ibid., 589.

37 Ibid., 103.

38 Ibid., 101.

39 Ibid., 105.

40 Ibid., 88.

41 Ibid., 87.

42 Ibid., 93.

43 Ibid., 90.

44 Ibid., 94.

45 Ibid., 89.

46 Ibid., 97.

47 Ibid., 92.

48 Ibid., 93.

Notes to Chapter 4: The Riddles of Graham Greene: Brighton Rock Revisited

1 The HRC houses numerous materials related to Graham Greene — 96 boxes of documents, 40 linear feet, seven galley folders, and three oversize folders — and, in 2010 as well as 2007, I was fortunate to visit and study there. Some of the citations that appear in this chapter originate with the HRC. For details, see: http://www.hrc.utexas.edu/

2 Graham Greene Collection, HRC, Austin, Texas.

3 Durán, L. (1994), *Graham Greene: Friend and Brother*, translated by Euan Cameron. London: HarperCollins.

4 Greene, G. (1980), *Ways of Escape*. London: Bodley Head.

5 Shelden, M. (1994), *The Man Within*. London: Heinemann.

6 http://greeneland.tripod.com/bio.htm

7 Graham Greene Collection, HRC, Austin, Texas.

8 Greene, R. (ed.) (2007), *Graham Greene: A Life in Letters*. London: Little, Brown, 411.

9 Forster, E. M. (1965), *Two Cheers for Democracy*. London: Hodder Arnold, 1.

10 Graham Greene Collection, HRC, Austin, Texas.

11 Ellmann, R. (1959), *James Joyce*. Oxford: Oxford University Press, 1.

12 From an audio interview with Lodge, D. (2006), 'The Voice of Graham Greene', Graham Greene Birthplace Trust.

13 Greene, *Ways of Escape*, 62.
14 Greene, G. (1951), *The Lost Childhood and Other Essays*. Harmondsworth: Penguin, 1964.
15 Greene, G. (1971), *A Sort of Life*. Harmondsworth: Penguin, 1971, 13.
16 Graham Greene Collection, HRC, Austin, Texas.
17 Ibid.
18 Greene, G. (2004), *Brighton Rock*. London: Penguin, 216.
19 Greene, R., ed. *Graham Greene: A Life in Letters*, 137.
20 Lodge, D. (2006), Personal correspondence.
21 Greene, G. (2001), *A Gun for Sale*. London: Vintage, 123–4.
22 Greene, *Ways of Escape*, 56.
23 Graham Greene Collection, HRC, Austin, Texas.
24 Knox, R. A. (1958), *Literary Distractions*. New York: Sheed & Ward, 180–98.
25 Auden, W. H. (1948), 'The Guilty Vicarage', *Harper's Magazine*, 196 (1176), 406.
26 Sayers, D. L. (2003), *Les Origines du Roman Policier: A Wartime Wireless Talk to the French: The Original French Text with an English Translation*, edited and translated by S. Bray. Hurstpierpoint, West Sussex: Dorothy L. Sayers Society, 11.
27 Bergonzi, B (2006), *A Study in Greene*. Oxford: Oxford University Press, 82–3.
28 Ibid., 83.
29 Greene, *Brighton Rock*, 178.
30 Lodge, D. (2005), Personal correspondence.
31 Greene, *Brighton Rock*, 4.
32 Ibid., 90.
33 Ibid., 178.
34 Ibid., 178.
35 Ibid., 178–9, 195.
36 Greene, *Ways of Escape*, 58, 60.
37 From 'The Voice of Graham Greene'.
38 In France, *The Power and the Glory* was recently a set text for the *agrégation*, the National Examination for aspiring university teachers.
39 Greene, *Brighton Rock*, 268.
40 Greene, *Ways of Escape*, 62.

Notes to Chapter 5: Innocence and Experience: The Condition of Childhood in Graham Greene's Fiction

1 James, H. (1926), *The Turn of the Screw*. London: Martin Secker, 152.
2 James, H. (1966), *What Maisie Knew*. Harmondsworth: Penguin, 18.
3 Ibid., 17.
4 Ibid., 18.
5 Mudford, P. (1996), *Graham Greene*. Plymouth: Northcote House, 40.
6 Greene, G. (2001), *The Quiet American*. London: Vintage, 37.
7 Greene, G. (1975), *Brighton Rock*. Harmondsworth: Penguin, 51.

8 See: http://www.ewtn.com/library/papaldoc/jp2tb15.htm

9 Greene, *Brighton Rock*, 239.

10 Ibid., 133.

11 Ibid., 141.

12 Ibid., 181.

13 Ibid., 185.

14 Ibid., 239.

15 Ibid., 240.

16 Ibid., 242.

17 Ibid., 242.

18 Ibid., 243.

19 Wordsworth, W. (1984), *William Wordsworth: The Oxford Authors*, edited by S. Gill. Oxford and New York: Oxford University Press, 299.

20 Greene, G. (2002), *The Lawless Roads*. London: Vintage, 14.

21 Greene, *Brighton Rock*, 68.

22 Greene, G. (2001), *The Ministry of Fear*. London: Vintage, 11.

23 Ibid., 12.

24 Ibid., 13.

25 Ibid., 13.

26 Greene, *The Ministry of Fear*, 18.

27 Ibid., 65.

28 Ibid., 128.

29 Ibid., 137.

30 Ibid., 187.

31 Shakespeare, W. (1911), *The Complete Works of William Shakespeare*, edited by W. G. Clark and W. A. Wright, with complete notes of the temple Shakespeare by I. Gollancz. New York: Grosset and Dunlap, 992 [Act III, Sc. II, 45–6.]

32 Greene, G. (1972), *Collected Stories*. London: Bodley Head, 187–8.

33 Ibid., 236.

34 Keats, J. (1973), *John Keats: The Complete Poems*, edited by J. Barnard. Harmondsworth: Penguin, 348.

35 Greene, *Collected Stories*, 236–37.

36 Ibid., 452.

37 Ibid., 455.

38 Ibid., 456.

39 Ibid., 456.

40 Greene, G. (1991), *The Power and the Glory*. Harmondsworth: Penguin, 63.

41 Ibid., 81.

42 Ibid., 81.

43 Ibid., 54.

44 Ibid., 54.

45 Ibid., 54.

46 Ibid., 39.

47 Greene, G. (1989), *The Captain and the Enemy*. Harmondsworth: Penguin,

50.
48 Greene, *Collected Stories*, 480.
49 *Ibid.*, 471.
50 *Ibid.*, 479.
51 *Ibid.*, 475.
52 *Ibid.*, 465.
53 *Ibid.*, 470.
54 *Ibid.*, 478.
55 *Ibid.*, 337.
56 *Ibid.*, 338.
57 Auden, W. H. (1964), *Selected Essays*. London: Faber & Faber, 103.
58 Greene, *Collected Stories*, 339.
59 Greene, G. (1971), *The Confidential Agent*. Harmondsworth: Penguin, 39–40.
60 *Ibid.*, 49.
61 *Ibid.*, 51.
62 Greene, *The Quiet American*, 176.

Notes to Chapter 6: Janiform Greene: The Paradoxes and Pleasures of The Power and the Glory

1 This essay sometimes draws on parts of Watts, C. (1997), *A Preface to Greene*. Harlow: Pearson Education, but revises and augments the material.
2 Lodge, D. (1966), *Graham Greene*. New York: Columbia University Press, 27.
3 Greene, G. (1970), *The Power and the Glory*. Harmondsworth: Penguin, 28.
4 Ibid., 196.
5 Ibid., 196.
6 Ibid., 210.
7 Ibid., 207.
8 Eliot, T. S. (1963), *Selected Essays*. London: Faber, 429. Greene quotes this passage with approval in Greene, G. (1970), *Collected Essays*. Harmondsworth: Penguin, 41.
9 Watt, I. (1980), *Conrad in the Nineteenth Century*. London: Chatto & Windus, 175–9, 270–71.
10 Watts, C. (1984), *The Deceptive Text: An Introduction to Covert Plots*. Brighton: Harvester.
11 Greene, G. *The Power and the Glory*, 221.
12 J. W. Dunne's *An Experiment with Time* (1927) and *The Serial Universe* (1934) influenced various writers, including J. B. Priestley, John Buchan, and T. S. Eliot. 'I am convinced that Dunne was right,' remarked Greene. See Watts, *A Preface to Greene*, 128–36.
13 The gangster's surname brings to mind 'Calvary', and there is a hint of 'carver' (given that he bears a knife). Sir Arthur Conan Doyle's *The Lost World* mentions 'an American named James Colver': see Doyle, A. C. (1995), *The Lost World and Other Stories*. Ware: Wordsworth, 82.

14 Greene, *The Power and the Glory*, 189.

15 All references are Ibid., 213.

16 Conrad, J. (1969), *Joseph Conrad's Letters to R. B. Cunninghame Graham*, edited by C. T. Watts. London: Cambridge University Press, 46.

17 For the *Olney Hymns* online, see http://www.ccel.org/ccel/newton/olney hymns.toc.html

18 Greene, *The Power and the Glory*, 41.

19 Ibid., 214.

20 Ibid., 209.

21 See (1996) *The New International Webster's Comprehensive Dictionary of the English Language*. Naples, FL: Trident Press International, 828. In some versions of the code, the sign represents ö, the German o surmounted by an umlaut.

22 Greene, *The Power and the Glory*, 209.

23 Greene, G. (1991), *The Last Word and Other Stories*. London: Penguin, 18.

24 Greene, *The Power and the Glory*, 24–5.

25 Ibid., 140, 201.

26 The links between the priest and the lieutenant are emphasised when both are curiously likened to question marks. See Greene, *The Power and the Glory*, 15 and 35. Furthermore, as Dermot Gilvary has pointed out to me, the linkage is lethally sealed when (in a sequence of delayed decoding) we realise that it was the lieutenant who, with a bullet from his revolver, administered the *coup de grâce* to the priest: for thereafter the officer has 'a brisk and stubborn' manner of walking, 'as if he were saying at every step. "I have done what I have done."' Ibid., 220.

27 Ibid., 184.

28 Ibid., 216.

29 Greene, G. (1939), *The Lawless Roads*. London: Longmans, 121.

30 Greene, *The Power and the Glory*, 18, 19, and 28.

31 Greene cites Newman's *Apologia pro Vita Sua* as an epigraph to *The Lawless Roads*.

32 Greene, *The Power and the Glory*, 131.

33 Ibid., 100.

34 Ibid., 55.

35 Ibid., 216.

36 Greene, G. (1970). *A Sort of Life*. Harmondsworth: Penguin, 138.

37 Greene, *The Power and the Glory*, 169; 53.

38 Ibid., 32.

39 Ibid., 89.

40 Ibid., 96–7.

41 Ibid., 97, 109.

42 Ibid., 100.

43 Eliot, *Selected Essays*, 287.

44 Greene, *The Power and the Glory*, 152.

45 Ibid., 45.

46 Woolf, V. (1964), *To the Lighthouse*. Harmondsworth: Penguin, 183.
47 Greene, *The Power and the Glory*, 45.
48 Plato (1952), *The Symposium*, translated by W. Hamilton. Harmondsworth: Penguin, 113–14.
49 Conrad, J. (1957), *Under Western Eyes*. Harmondsworth: Penguin, 175.

Notes to Chapter 7: Sigmund Freud and Graham Greene in Vienna

 1 Greene, G. and Reed C. (1968), *The Third Man*. London: Lorrimer, 12.
 2 Spiel, H. (1987), *Vienna's Golden Autumn*. London: Grove Press.
 3 A small town with a large Jewish population in the kingdom of Galicia, the easternmost territory of the Austro-Hungarian Empire.
 4 Freud, S. (1994), *Sigmund Freud Museum*, edited by H. Leupold-Löwenthal et al. Vienna: Verlag Christian Brandstaetter, 73. This is part of a letter of Freud to A. Schnitzler, May 14, 1922.
 5 A popular saying.
 6 Greene, G. (1986), *A Sort of Life*. Harmondsworth: Penguin, 72.
 7 Ibid., 73.
 8 Ibid., 74.
 9 Ibid., 77.
10 Greene, G. (1977), *The Third Man and the Fallen Idol*. London: Penguin, 14.
11 Ibid., 14.
12 Ibid., 14.
13 Greene and Reed, *The Third Man*, 14.
14 Ibid., 82.
15 Many expatriates who worked on the film had fled from Austria to England in the years between 1933 and 1939.
16 Greene and Reed, *The Third Man*, 111. Also see Timmermann, B. (2005), *The Third Man's Vienna*. Vienna: Shippen Rock Publishing.
17 http://www.bfi.org.uk/features/bfi100/1-10.html

Notes to Chapter 8: Going Especially Careful: Language Reference in Graham Greene

 1 Greene, G. (2001), *The Ministry of Fear*. London: Vintage, 43.
 2 Greene, G. (2004), *The Comedians*. London: Vintage, 4.
 3 Greene, G. (2006), *The Confidential Agent*. London: Vintage, 3.
 4 Ibid., 22.
 5 Greene, G. (1943), *England Made Me*. London: Penguin, 29.
 6 Greene, G. (1940), *It's a Battlefield*. London: Penguin, 7.
 7 Greene, G. (2004), *Stamboul Train*. London: Vintage, 3.
 8 Ibid., 5.
 9 Ibid., 8.
10 Ibid., 16–17.
11 Ibid., 19.
12 Ibid., 21.
13 Ibid., 7.

14 Ibid., 126.
15 Greene, G. (1999), *Doctor Fischer of Geneva, or The Bomb Party*. London: Vintage, 48.
16 Ibid., 48.
17 Ibid., 86.
18 Greene, G. (2004), *The Honorary Consul*. London: Vintage, 25.
19 Greene, *England Made Me*, 68.
20 Greene, G. (1999), *Travels with my Aunt*. London: Vintage, 15.
21 Ibid., 71.
22 Greene, G. (1955), *The Quiet American*. London: Heinemann, 40.
23 Greene, *The Comedians*, 141.
24 Greene, G. (2005), *Complete Short Stories*. London: Penguin, 33.
25 Ibid., 494.
26 Ibid., 501.
27 Greene, G. (2004), *Our Man in Havana*. London: Vintage, 7.
28 Ibid., 73.
29 Greene, *Complete Short Stories*, 370.
30 Ibid., 374.
31 Greene, G. (1999), *The Captain and the Enemy*. London: Penguin, 141.
32 Ibid., 139.
33 Greene, *The Quiet American*, 241.
34 Greene, G. (1978), *The Human Factor*. London: Bodley Head, 252.
35 Greene, *Travels with my Aunt*, 51.
36 Greene, *Complete Short Stories*, 443.
37 Greene, *The Quiet American*, 30.
38 Greene, *Complete Short Stories*, 492.
39 Ibid., 77.
40 Greene, G. (1955), *The Lawless Roads*. London: Heinemann, 30.
41 Greene, *Complete Short Stories*, 534.
42 Ibid., 497.
43 Greene, G. (2004), *A Burnt-Out Case*. London: Vintage, 1.
44 Ibid., 3.
45 Greene, *Travels with my Aunt*, 91:
46 Ibid., 187.
47 Greene, *It's a Battlefield*, 37.
48 Ibid., 139.
49 Greene, *The Confidential Agent*, 44.
50 Ibid., 74.
51 Greene, *England Made Me*, 96.
52 Greene, *Complete Short Stories*, 216.
53 Ibid., 216.
54 Greene, *Our Man in Havana*, 127.
55 Greene, *The Captain and the Enemy*, 60.
56 Ibid., 90.
57 Greene, *Complete Short Stories*, 551.
58 Ibid., 552.

59 Greene, *A Burnt-Out Case*, 49.
60 Ibid., 129.
61 Greene, *Stamboul Train*, 123.
62 Greene, *The Human Factor*, 340.
63 Greene, *Complete Short Stories*, 437.
64 Greene, *The Honorary Consul*, 7.
65 Greene, *The Human Factor*, 219.
66 Greene, G. (2006), *Monsignor Quixote*. London: Vintage, 158.
67 Ibid., 159.
68 Ibid., 158.
69 Greene, *Complete Short Stories*, 537.
70 Ibid., 345.
71 Ibid., 454.
72 Greene, *Monsignor Quixote*, 205.
73 Greene, *The Comedians*, 227.
74 Greene, *Complete Short Stories*, 474.
75 Greene, *A Burnt-Out Case*, 96.
76 Greene, *The Human Factor*, 168, 270.
77 Greene, *The Honorary Consul*, 135.
78 Greene, *Complete Short Stories*, 476.
79 Ibid., 478.
80 Ibid., 309.
81 Ibid., 309.
82 Ibid., 421.
83 Ibid., 421.
84 Ibid., 421.
85 Greene, *The Comedians*, 11.
86 Ibid., 188.
87 Greene, *Complete Short Stories*, 397.
88 Ibid., 397.
89 Greene, *The Confidential Agent*, 176.
90 Greene, *Complete Short Stories*, 163.
91 Ibid., 163.
92 Greene, *The Human Factor*, 241.
93 Greene, *The Honorary Consul*, 12.
94 Greene, *The Quiet American*, 94.
95 Greene, *Complete Short Stories*, 391.
96 Ibid., 391.
97 Ibid., 548.
98 Ibid., 363.
99 Ibid., 228.
100 Greene, *The Comedians*, 3.
101 Greene, *Monsignor Quixote*, 97.
102 Greene, *Doctor Fischer of Geneva, or The Bomb Party*, 12.
103 Greene, *It's a Battlefield*, 122.
104 Greene, *Complete Short Stories*, 301.

105 Greene, *England Made Me*, 171.
106 Greene, G. (2004), *The End of the Affair*. London: Vintage, 3.
107 Greene, *Our Man in Havana*, 55.
108 Greene, *The Honorary Consul*, 65.
109 Greene, R. (ed.) (2007), *Graham Greene: A Life in Letters*. London: Little, Brown, 350.
110 Greene, G. (2004), *The Power and the Glory*. London: Vintage, 11.
111 Greene, G. (1999), *A Sort of Life*. London: Vintage, 140.
112 Scholars recognise the challenge of discussing *The Third Man*, which exists as a film, as a screenplay and as a novella. See Greene, G. (2007), *The Third Man*. London: Vintage [novella]; Greene, G. and Reed, C. (1984), *The Third Man*: London: Faber & Faber [screenplay]. The published screenplay is not an accurate text, but an early iteration, which was later revised. Most of the quotations in this chapter are transcribed from the film, unless otherwise stated, and it has not been possible to provide page references in such instances. A new text of the screenplay, made directly from the film, has been produced by Dermot Gilvary, and will be made available to scholars in due course.
113 Greene, *The Third Man*, 74.
114 Ibid., 75.
115 Greene and Reed, *The Third Man*, 70.
116 Greene, *The Third Man*, 48.
117 Ibid., 51.
118 Greene and Reed, *The Third Man*, 33.
119 Greene, *The Third Man*, 35.
120 Ibid., 51.
121 Greene and Reed, *The Third Man*, 79.
122 Ibid., 65.
123 Greene, *The Third Man*, 23.
124 Ibid., 10.
125 Ibid., 88.
126 Greene, *A Sort of Life*, 16.
127 Ibid., 25.

Notes to Chapter 9: Prophecy and Comedy in Havana: Graham Greene's Spy Fiction and Cold War Reality

1 Quotes taken from the film version of *Our Man in Havana* (directed by Carol Reed; screenplay by Graham Greene: Columbia Pictures, 1959). The name Montez plays on the Spanish word *montes* (mountains). The pilot is named Raul Dominguez in the novel.
2 Greene, G. (1958), *Our Man in Havana*. London: Heinemann, 5–6.
3 See *The Times Literary Supplement*, 10 October 1958, 573.
4 Greene, *Our Man in Havana*, 175.
5 Smyth, D. (1991), 'Our Man in Havana, Their Man in Madrid: Literary Invention in Espionage Fact and Fiction', in Wesley K. Wark (ed.), *Spy Fiction, Spy Films and Real Intelligence*. London: Frank Cass, 117–35.

6 Greene, *Our Man in Havana*, 255–7.
7 Sherry, N. (2004), *The Life of Graham Greene: Volume III: 1955–1991*. London: Jonathan Cape, 94, 102–3.
8 Greene, G. (1980), *Ways of Escape*. London: Bodley Head, 238–9.
9 This last observation was provided later by Kim Philby. See Sherry, N. (1994), *The Life of Graham Greene: Volume II: 1939–1955*. London: Jonathan Cape, 119–20.
10 Ibid., 172–3.
11 Greene, G. (1985), *The Tenth Man*. London: Bodley Head, 17–19. Also see Greene, *Ways of Escape*, 238–41.
12 *New York Times*, 'Cuban Police Seize Key German Spy', 6 September 1942, 19.
13 Thomas, H. (1971), *Cuba: Or the Pursuit of Freedom*. London: Eyre & Spottiswoode, 457.
14 Schoonover, T. D. (2008), *Hitler's Man in Havana: Heinz Lüning and Nazi Espionage in Latin America*. Lexington, KY: The University Press of Kentucky, 89; 120–2; 139–40.
15 Ibid., 147.
16 Ibid., 141–9.
17 'Exotic dancers enlisted to trap soldiers', *The Guardian*, 10 Nov. 2000; 'Liquidation Report on the case of José Pacheco y Cuesta, alias S. Moreno', September 1943, The National Archives of the United Kingdom, Kew Gardens, London (henceforward TNA): KV2/296 and KV2/297 (Records of the Security Service).
18 Greene, R. (ed.) (2007). *Graham Greene: A Life in Letters*. London: Little, Brown, 211.
19 Greene, *Ways of Escape*, 40.
20 Greene, *Our Man in Havana*, 113–14.
21 Holman, B. (1988), *Memoirs of a Diplomat's Wife*. York: Wilton 65, 145–6; 'His Men in Havana', *Time*, 27 April 1959.
22 Holman to Eden, 1 April 1954, TNA: Foreign Office papers (henceforward FO) 371/108991 AK1016/1.
23 Greene, R. (ed.) *Graham Greene: A Life in Letters*, 85–6.
24 On what the film version says about Britain's decline as a world power and 'Englishness' of the period, see Evans, P (2005), *Carol Reed*. Manchester: Manchester University Press, 106.
25 Day, B. (ed.) (2007). *The Letters of Noël Coward*. London: Methuen, 659–60.
26 *The Times*, 7 July 1960, 10.
27 Fordham to FO (Foreign Office), 13 March 1957, TNA: FO371/126467 AK1015/11.
28 Fordham to Hankey, 22 February 1957, TNA: FO371/126467 AK1015/8; 'Cuban Rebel is Visited in Hideout', *New York Times*, 24 February 1957, 1; Minute by Pease, 12 July 1957, TNA: FO371/126467 AK1015/28; Hone (Santiago de Cuba) to Fordham, 6 May 1958, TNA: FO371/132164 AK1015/28.

29 Fordham to Hankey, 2 April 1958, TNA: FO371/132164 AK1015/20; FO to Havana, 23 May 1958, TNA: FO371/132174 AK1191/9; Fordham to FO, 23 May 1958, TNA: FO371/132174 AK1191/10; Fordham to Lloyd, 18 November 1958, TNA: FO371/132165 AK1015/62; Fordham to Hankey, 31 December 1958, TNA: FO371/139398 AK1015/14.

30 Greene, *Ways of Escape*, 244–9.

31 Greene, R. (ed.) *Graham Greene: A Life in Letters*, 232–3; Memorandum by Hankey 'Anglo-Cuban Relations', TNA: FO371/132168 AK1051/14, 4 November 1958; See Oliver to Hankey, 24 September 1958, TNA: FO371/132168 AK1051/1.

32 Graham Greene to the Editor, 'Cuba's Civil War', *The Times*, 3 January 1959, 7.

33 'Our Men in Havana', *The Guardian*, 8 January 1959, 8.

34 Hankey to Fordham, 12 June 1959, TNA: FO371/138897 AK10113/1; Fordham to Lloyd, 5 March 1959, TNA: FO371/139400 AK1015/77; Fordham to Lloyd, 3 July 1959, TNA: FO371/138897 AK10113/3; See Sharp, P. (2004), 'For Diplomacy: Representation and the Study of International Relations', in Christer Jönsson and Richard Langhorne (eds.), *Diplomacy, Volume 1: Theory of Diplomacy*. London: Sage, 208–30.

35 Fordham to Lloyd, 9 January 1959, TNA: FO371/139398 AK1015/20; Fordham to FO, 19 January 1959, TNA: FO371/139399 AK1015/27; Fordham later described the US ban on arms sales as 'a severe moral blow to Batista and also a considerable physical handicap' with Castro's rebels 'correspondingly encouraged'. Fordham to Lloyd, 'Annual Review for Cuba 1958', 3 February 1959, TNA: FO371/139396 AK1011/1.

36 Fordham to Lloyd, 9 January 1959, TNA: FO371/139398 AK1015/20; 'Arms finds tell Cuba secrets', *The Observer*, 11 January 1959, 13.

37 The ambassador was not at home on either occasion. Fordham to Hildyard, 17 February 1959, TNA: FO371/139400 AK1015/67; Fordham to Lloyd, 28 August 1959, TNA: FO371/139405 AK1017/2.

38 Fordham to FO, 24 February 1959, TNA: FO371/139400 AK1015/68; Phleps to Symon, 27 February 1959, AK1015/71; Fordham to Lloyd, 5 March 1959, TNA: FO371/139400 AK1015/77.

39 Fordham to Lloyd, 21 August 1959, TNA: FO371/139402 AK1015/139; There had been speculation in the British press in early 1959 that Fordham would be replaced. See memorandum by Campbell, 12 January 1959, TNA: FO371/139517 AK1891/1; Fordham to Lloyd, 17 June 1960, TNA: FO371/148190 AK10111/1.

40 Obituary: Sir Herbert Marchant, *The Independent*, 15 August 1990, 11; Marchant to Home 'Annual Review 1960', 17 January 1961, TNA: FO371/156137 AK1011/1.

41 *The Guardian*, 23 January 1961, 9; Sutherland to FO, 19 January 1961, TNA: FO371/156138 AK1015/6.

42 Marchant to FO, 6 April 1961, TNA: FO371/156140 AK1015/41.

43 Marchant to Home, 10 May 1961, TNA: FO371/156147 AK1015/184; Marchant to Brain, 24 May 1961, TNA: FO371/156149 AK1015/207.

44 Marchant to Home, 31 July 1961, TNA: FO371/156151 AK1015/252.
45 Marchant to Home, 7 Dec. 1961, TNA: FO371/156153 AK1015/282; Watson to Slater, 8 December 1964, enclosing memorandum by Hitch 'Cuba 1962–1964: A Personal Account', 3 December 1964, TNA: FCO7/528; Marchant (Tunis) to Slater, 8 October 1963, TNA: FO371/168136 AK1012/2.
46 Sutherland to Edmonds, 6 July 1961, TNA: FO371/156219 AK1195/5/G.
47 Minute by Hankey, 17 July 1961, TNA: FO371/156219 AK1195/5/G; Marchant to FO, 18 January 1961, TNA: FO371/156218 AK1192/8/G; Thorpe, D. R. (1997) *Alec Douglas-Home*. London: Sinclair-Stevenson, 236–7; Thorpe says the Foreign Secretary regarded Marchant 'as one of the unsung heroes of the Cuban crisis' (517, n. 7); Marchant to Home, 24 October 1962, TNA: FO371/162377.
48 Marchant to Home, 10 November 1962, TNA: FO371/162408 AK1261/667.
49 Greene, *Our Man in Havana*, 74–82.
50 Byatt (Havana) to Parsons, 10 November 1962, enclosing minute and drawings by Capie (26 October 1962), TNA FO371/162374 AK1201/26.
51 Sutherland (Washington) to Scott (Havana), 27 December 1962, TNA FO371/162435 AK1962/20(E).
52 Marchant to FO, 14 December 1962; Greenhill (Washington Embassy) to FO, 19 December 1962: TNA: FO371/162373 AK1193/33(A)&(B); Ormsby Gore (Washington Embassy) to FO, 2 March 1963; Marchant to FO, 4 March 1963: TNA: FO371/168202 AK1193/10/G(F)&(H).
53 Greene, *Our Man in Havana*, 89.
54 M.-F. Allain (ed.) (1983), *The Other Man: Conversations with Graham Greene*. London: Bodley Head, 100.

Notes to Chapter 10: Graham Greene and A Burnt-Out Case: A Psychoanalytic Reading

1 Greene, G. (1971), *A Sort of Life*. London: Bodley Head, 72–6. In addition, see Sherry, N. (1989), *The Life of Graham Greene: Volume I: 1904–1939*. London: Jonathan Cape, 92–108.
2 Greene, G. (1980), *Ways of Escape*. New York: Simon & Schuster.
3 Ibid., 146.
4 Ibid., 147.
5 Ibid., 237.
6 This is the thesis of Shelden, M. (1994), *Graham Greene: The Enemy Within*. New York: Random House.
7 Sherry, N. (1989), *The Life of Graham Greene: Volume I: 1904–1939*. London: Jonathan Cape, 517.
8 Greene, *Ways of Escape*, 9–10.
9 Ibid., 10.
10 Ibid., 10.
11 Eliot, T. S. (1943), *Four Quartets*. New York: Harcourt, Brace & Company, 6.
12 Greene, *Ways of Escape*, 145.

13 Greene, *A Sort of Life*, 92–6.

14 Greene, *Ways of Escape*, 161.

15 Sherry, *The Life of Graham Greene: Volume I*, 277.

16 Greene, *Ways of Escape*, 152.

17 Shakespeare, W. (1911), *The Complete Works of William Shakespeare*, edited by W. G. Clark and W. A. Wright, with complete notes of the temple Shakespeare by I. Gollancz. New York: Grosset & Dunlap, 982. [Act I, Sc. IV, 7–8.]

18 Plato, *The Last Days of Socrates*, translated and with an Introduction by H. Tredennick. Harmondsworth: Penguin, 45–76.

19 Strachey, J. (1953), *The Standard Edition of the Complete Psychological Works of Sigmund Freud*, vol. 9 (1900). London: The Hogarth Press and the Institute of Psycho-analysis, 627.

20 Greene, J. (2010), 'Graham Greene and his Dreams of Treason'. Unpublished essay, 2.

21 Greene, G. (1973), *The Honorary Consul*. London: Bodley Head, 54.

22 Strachey, J. (1953), *The Standard Edition of the Complete Psychological Works of Sigmund Freud*, vol. 12 (1911). London: The Hogarth Press and the Institute of Psycho-analysis, 213–26.

23 Ibid., 219.

24 Greene, G. (2004), *A Burnt-Out Case*. London: Vintage. On reading Greene's literary art through a psychoanalytic lens, see Pierloot, R. A. (1994), *Psychoanalytic Patterns in the Work of Graham Greene*. Amsterdam and Atlanta, GA: Rodopi.

25 See Wollheim, R. (1999), 'Emotion and the Malformation of Emotion', in D. Bell (ed.), *Psychoanalysis and Culture: A Kleinian Perspective*. London: Duckworth, 122–35. Also see Wollheim, R. (1999), *On the Emotions*. New Haven, CT: Yale University Press.

26 Symington, N. (1983), 'The Analyst's Act of Freedom as Agent of Therapeutic Change'. *International Review of Psychoanalysis*, 10, 283–91.

27 Ibid., 283.

28 Lawrence, D. H. (1971), *Studies in Classic American Literature*. London: Penguin, 17.

29 Greene, *Ways of Escape*, 259.

30 Greene, *A Burnt-Out Case*, 6.

31 Ibid., 6.

32 Ibid., 107.

33 Ibid., 8.

34 Ibid., 1.

35 Ibid., 37.

36 Ibid., 16.

37 Ibid., 16.

38 Ibid., 37.

39 Ibid., 42.

40 Ibid., 42.

41 Ibid., 15.

42 Ibid., 42.
43 Fairbairn, R. (1952), *Psychoanalytic Studies of the Personality*. London: Tavistock, 87.
44 Greene, *A Burnt-Out Case*, 13.
45 Eliot, G. (1994), *Middlemarch*, complete and unabridged and with an introduction by A. S. Byatt. New York: The Modern Library, 675–6.
46 Leavis, F. R. (1948), *The Great Tradition*. London: Chatto & Windus, 72.
47 Greene, *A Burnt-Out Case*, 43.
48 Ibid., 43.
49 Ibid., 44.
50 Conrad, J. (1986), *Lord Jim*, edited by C. Watts and R. Hampson. London: Penguin, 200.
51 Greene, *A Burnt-Out Case*, 50.
52 Ibid., 7; also see 168.
53 Ibid., 118.
54 Ibid., 115.
55 Ibid., 116.
56 Ibid., 100.
57 Ibid., 101.
58 Ibid., 89.
59 Ibid., 110.
60 Ibid., 97.
61 Ibid., 170; 185.
62 Carey's review is available online: http://www.johncarey.org/reviews.html
63 These are scattered remarks within the James Greene paper that I have collated, hence Greene, J. 'Graham Greene and his Dreams of Treason', 6–17.
64 Ibid., 17.
65 Foden, G. (2004), 'Introduction', in G. Greene, *A Burnt-Out Case*. London: Vintage, vi.
66 Greene, cited in Foden, 'Introduction', vi.
67 Greene, *Ways of Escape*, 263.
68 Schafer, R. (1983), *The Analytic Attitude*. London: Karnac, 291.
69 Terence's famous inscription — *Homo sum: humani nihil a me alienum puto* — is from his *Heautontimorumenos*, and, among other things, was on a roof-beam of Michel de Montaigne's tower.
70 Eliot, *Four Quartets*, 15.
71 Greene, *Ways of Escape*, 123–4.

Notes to Chapter 11: A Touch of Evolutionary Religion

1 Greene describes 'a touch of religion' in one of his posthumous publications. See Greene, G. (1994), *A World of My Own: A Dream Diary*, New York: Viking, 53–65. Concerning dreams and Greene's evolutionary theism, see 59–60.
2 Newman, J. H. (1963), 'An Essay on the Development of Christian Doctrine', in V. F. Blehl (ed.), *The Essential Newman*. New York: Mentor-Omega, 123.

3 Bosco, M. (2005), *Graham Greene's Catholic Imagination*. Oxford and New York: Oxford University Press, 39.

4 Regarding Teilhard's theology, see King, U. (1998), *Spirit of Fire: The Life and Vision of Teilhard de Chardin*. Maryknoll, NY: Orbis.

5 Greene, G. (1971), *A Sort of Life*. Harmondsworth: Penguin, 120–1.

6 Overviews of process theology include: Bracken, J. (2006), *Christianity and Process Thought: Spirituality for a Changing World*. Philadelphia and London: Templeton Foundation Press; Bowman, D. and McDaniel, J. (eds.) (2006), *A Handbook of Process Theology*. St. Louis: Chalice; Faber, R. (2008), *God as Poet of the World: Exploring Process Theologies*. Louisville, KY: Westminster John Knox Press; and, Suchocki, M. H. (1992; 1986), *God-Christ-Church: A Practical Guide to Process Theology* (2nd edn). New York: Crossroads.

7 On this idea, see Cooper, J. W. (2006), *Panentheism: The Other God of the Philosophers*. Grand Rapids, MI: Baker Academic.

8 Dillard, A. (1999), *For the Time Being*. New York: Alfred A. Knopf, 176–7.

9 Williamson. C. and Allen, R. J. (1997), *Adventures of the Spirit: A Guide to Worship from the Perspective of Process Theology*. Lanham, MD: University Press of America, 60.

10 de Chardin, P. T. (1964), *The Future of Man*. New York: Collins, 13.

11 Ibid., 12–13.

12 de Chardin, P. T. (1965), *Hymn of the Universe*. New York: Harper, 79.

13 Ibid., 84.

14 de Chardin, P. T. (1960), *Le Milieu Divin: An Essay on the Interior Life*. London: Collins, 86. On Teilhard's process spirituality, see King, U. (1997), *Christ in All Things: Exploring Spirituality with Teilhard de Chardin*. Maryknoll, NY: Orbis.

15 H. J. Donaghy (ed.) (1992), *Conversations with Graham Greene*. Jackson, MS: University of Mississippi Press, 17.

16 Ibid., 18.

17 Ibid., 62.

18 de Chardin, *Hymn of the Universe*, 133.

19 Ibid., 119.

20 Kinast, R. L. (1999), *Process Catholicism: An Exercise in Ecclesial Imagination*. Lanham, MD: University Press of America, 125.

21 Greene, G. (1962), *A Burnt-Out Case*. New York: Bantam, 122.

22 Ibid.,122. On Greene's fictional approach to Africa, see the essays in Hill, Wm. T. (2001), *Perceptions of Religious Faith in the Work of Graham Greene*. Bern and New York: Peter Lang.

23 Greene, G. (1973), *The Honorary Consul*. Beccles: Book Club Associates, 283.

24 Ibid., 283. The Harry Ransom Humanities Research Center (HRC), The University of Texas at Austin, Texas, USA, houses many drafts of this novel, beginning with handwritten notes and an autograph manuscript (1970). They also have the first to fifth typescripts (1970–72), the final typescript (1972), and galley as well as page proofs (1973). The proofs and drafts

contain autograph corrections. For details on the HRC, see: http://www.hrc.
utexas.edu/

25 Greene, *The Honorary Consul*, 284. An earlier typescript of this novel has
    Father Rivas complain that his seminary professors talked of the 'Beatific
    vision' only. On page 274 of the novel's third typescript, Greene instructs
    his secretary to omit this reference.

26 Penchansky, D. (1999), *What Rough Beast?: Images of God in the Hebrew
    Bible*. Louisville, KY: Westminster John Knox Press, 1–2.

27 Ibid., 1.

28 Interestingly, in the briefest of references, Penchansky connects Greene's *The
    Honorary Consul* to the Yahwist's 'seditious formulation of deity' in Genesis
    3. See *What Rough Beast*, 19. Greene's characterisation of an ironic God
    appears throughout his cycle of so-called Catholic novels.

29 Greene, *The Honorary Consul*, 284. The phrases 'divided like me' and
    'tempted like me' do not appear in early drafts of the novel; Greene inserts
    them in the third typescript. Assuredly, such sentences point up Greene's
    awareness of the anthropological conditioning of theological understanding.
    For their part, process theologians would struggle to admit what Father Rivas
    admits, at least at this point in his theologising, but they concede that God
    'must be partly responsible for natural evil in this world as well as for moral
    evil because God is the source of the power of creativity which can be used
    for evil as well as good decisions by nonhuman creatures'. See Bracken,
    Christianity and Process Thought, 25.

30 Greene, *The Honorary Consul*, 285. On Greene's own approach to this part
    of the world, see Benz, S. (2003), 'Graham Greene and Latin America'.
    Journal of Modern Literature, 26, (2), 113–28. Also see Ramirez, L. E. (2007),
    British Representations of Latin America. Gainesville, FL: University Press
    of Florida.

31 Greene, *The Honorary Consul*, 285. Compare with the following exchange
    in *A Burnt-Out Case*:

    'Your god must feel a bit disappointed,' Doctor Colin said, 'when he looks at
    this world of his'.

    'When you were a boy they can't have taught you theology very well. God
    cannot feel disappointment or pain'.

    'Perhaps that's why I don't care to believe in him'.

    See Greene, *A Burnt-Out Case*, 196. Most process theologians claim that
    classical or traditional theology, with its notion of God as a passionless
    Absolute, is precisely the reason why women and men, like Dr Colin, aban-
    don belief. The classical God does not suffer and, as a result, seems beyond
    accessibility or approachability; God appears unlike us. By contrast, process
    theology accentuates the suffering God, who groans with God's creation, and
    who experiences sorrow as well as joy. See Bracken, *Christianity and Process
    Thought*, 14–27.

32 Ibid., 286. The arresting phrase 'the redemption of God' is not added until
    the second typescript. In addition, I view the early drafts of *The Honorary
    Consul* as decidedly more Christological than the final version. On page 271

of the second typescript, for example, Father Rivas declares that Christ is 'someone of perfect goodness', and that Christ's Incarnation, the point at which eternity touched time, caused the day-side of God to become 'invulnerable'. On page 276 of the third typescript, Greene instructs his secretary to remove these remarks. Returning to the second typescript, page 271, Father Rivas says that 'the degree of Christ's goodness was so great, his intention was so perfect, that the night-side now can never win more than a temporary victory here and there'. Finally, Father Rivas declares that 'at least we can be sure now where evolution ends — it ends in Christ'. In the fourth typescript, page 276, Greene alters the last sentence to read '. . . it will end in a goodness like Christ's'. This is a small but not insignificant difference.

33 Greene, *The Honorary Consul*, 286–7.
34 See Doud, R. (2003), review of Middleton, D. J. N. (ed.) (2003) *God, Literature and Process Thought*, in *Process Studies*, 32, (2), 313–15.
35 Greene, *A Sort of Life*, 120–1.
36 Baldridge, C. (2000), *Graham Greene's Fictions: The Virtues of Extremity*. Columbia and London: University of Missouri Press, 88.
37 Ibid., 65.
38 Ibid., 60, 70–1, 76–7, 85, 89. Baldridge uses 'diminished' several times.

Notes to Chapter 12: Inside and Outside: Graham Greene and Evelyn Waugh

1 Waugh, E. (2003), *Waugh Abroad: Collected Travel Writing*. New York: Knopf Everyman's Library, 543.
2 Greene, G. (1983), *Journey Without Maps*. New York: Viking, 10.
3 Greene, R. (ed.) (2007), *Graham Greene: A Life in Letters*. London: Little, Brown, 270.
4 Waugh, E. (1984), *The Essays, Articles and Reviews of Evelyn Waugh*, edited by D. Gallagher. Boston: Little, Brown, 18.
5 Waugh, E. (1980), *The Letters of Evelyn Waugh*, edited by M. Amory. New Haven, CT: Ticknor & Fields, 10.
6 Waugh, E. (1985), *Evelyn Waugh, Apprentice: The Early Writings, 1910–1927*, edited by R. M. Davis. Norman, OK: Pilgrim Books, 122.
7 Ibid, 123.
8 Sherry, N. (1989), *The Life of Graham Greene. Volume I: 1904–1939*. New York: Viking, 157.
9 Waugh, E. (1924), 'Seen in the Dark', *Isis* 23 January 1924, 5.
10 Greene, G. (1995), *Mornings in the Dark: The Graham Greene Film Reader: Reviews, Essays, Interviews, and Film Stories*, edited by D. Parkinson. New York: Applause Books, xiii. The subtitle is used for the American edition.
11 Ibid., 3.
12 Waugh, E. (1945), *Brideshead Revisited*. London: Chapman & Hall, 41.
13 Waugh, E. (1976), *The Diaries of Evelyn Waugh*, edited by M. Davie. Boston: Little, Brown, 239–41.
14 Waugh, *Essays*, 101.
15 Stannard, J. (ed.) (1984), *Evelyn Waugh: The Critical Heritage*. London: Routledge & Kegan Paul, 165.

16 Sherry, *The Life of Graham Greene: Volume I*, 606.
17 Waugh, *Letters*, 108–9.
18 Greene, G. (1937), "Daylight and Champaign", *The London Mercury*, 36, November, 195–6.
19 Waugh, E. (1937), 'Saint's-Eye View', *Night and Day*, 28 October, 24.
20 Waugh, *Essays*, 198.
21 Greene, 'Daylight and Champaign', *The London Mercury*, 195–6.
22 Waugh, E. (1937), 'Civilization and Culture', *The Spectator*, 159, 2 July 1937, 27–8.
23 Greene, G. (1937), 'A Novelist's Notebook', *The Spectator*, 159, 1 October 1937, 557.
24 Waugh, *Essays*, 204–6.
25 Greene, G. (1939), 'Underworld', *The London Mercury*, 39, March, 550–1.
26 Waugh, *Essays*, 247–8.
27 Ibid., 249–50.
28 Greene, G. (1968), *Another Mexico*. New York: Viking, 132.
29 Waugh, E. (1939), *Mexico: An Object Lesson*. Boston: Little, Brown, 250.
30 Ibid, 268.
31 Ibid., 293.
32 Greene, *Another Mexico*, 3.
33 Ibid., 258.
34 Waugh, *Mexico*, 51.
35 Ibid., 13.
36 Greene, *Another Mexico*, 41.
37 Waugh, *Diaries*, 471.
38 Waugh, *Essays*, 272, 273.
39 Bowen, E., Greene, G. and Pritchett, V. S. (1948), *Why Do I Write?: An Exchange of Views between Elizabeth Bowen, Graham Greene and V. S. Pritchett*. London: Marshall, 47.
40 Sherry, N. (1994), *The Life of Graham Greene: Volume II: 1939–1955*. New York: Viking, 190.
41 Waugh, *Essays*, 361.
42 Ibid., 365.
43 Greene, R., *Graham Greene: A Life in Letters*, 160.
44 Waugh, *Essays*, 361–2.
45 Greene, G. (1990), *Reflections*. London: Reinhardt, 61.
46 Davis, R. (1965), 'Evelyn Waugh's Early Work: The Formation of a Method', *Texas Studies in Literature and Language*, 7, (Spring), 97–108.
47 Greene, R., *Graham Greene: A Life in Letters*, 160.
48 Sherry, N. (2004), *The Life of Graham Greene: Volume III: 1955–1991*. New York: Viking, 301.
49 Waugh, *Letters*, 278–9.
50 Ibid., 280.
51 Greene, G. (1973), *The Portable Graham Greene*, edited by P. Stratford. New York: Viking, 557–60.
52 Waugh, *Letters*, 265.

53 Waugh, E. (1996), *The Letters of Nancy Mitford and Evelyn Waugh*, edited by C. Mosley. Boston: Houghton Mifflin, 106.
54 Ibid., 179.
55 Waugh, *Letters*, 356.
56 Waugh, *Essays*, 404.
57 Ibid., 101.
58 Ibid, 406.
59 Waugh, *Letters*, 354.
60 Ibid., 338.
61 Ibid., 346.
62 Greene, R., *Graham Greene: A Life in Letters*, 186.
63 Waugh, *Letters*, 386.
64 Ibid., 433.
65 Ibid., 439.
66 Greene, G. (1980), *Ways of Escape*. New York: Simon & Schuster, 90.
67 Waugh, *Letters*, 422.
68 Waugh, *Essays*, 361.
69 Sykes, C. (1975), *Evelyn Waugh: A Biography*. Boston: Little, Brown, 357.
70 Waugh, *Diaries*, 747.
71 Waugh, *Letters*, 455.
72 Waugh, E. (1955), 'Quixote Goes East', *Sunday Times*, 4 December, 4.
73 Stannard, *Evelyn Waugh: The Critical Heritage*, 400, 401.
74 Waugh, *Letters*, 529.
75 Waugh, *Diaries*, 775.
76 Waugh, *Letters*, 557.
77 Greene, *Ways of Escape*, 264–5; see also Greene, R., *Graham Greene: A Life in Letters*, 251–4.
78 Waugh, *Essays*, 574.
79 Waugh, E. (1961), 'Last Steps in Africa', *Spectator*, 207, 27 October, 594–5.
80 Waugh, *Letters*, 635.
81 Greene, G. (1966), "Mr. Evelyn Waugh", *The Times*, 15 April, 15.
82 Greene, *Ways of Escape*, 270.
83 Ibid., 267.
84 Waugh, *Letters*, 456.

Notes to Chapter 13: The Long Wait for Aunt Augusta: Reflections on Graham Greene's Fictional Women

1 Emerson, G. (2000), *Loving Graham Greene*. New York: Random House, 7–8.
2 Greene, G. (1969), *Travels with my Aunt*. London: Bodley Head, 130.
3 Greene, G. (1996), *The Quiet American*. New York: Viking Critical Library, 19.
4 Ibid., 12, 19, 19, 22, 11.
5 Ibid., 14, 12.

NOTES

6 Greene, G. (1965), *Brighton Rock*. Harmondsworth: Penguin, 249.
7 Ibid., 244.
8 Ibid., 162, 17, 250, 179.
9 Greene, G. (1935), *England Made Me*. London: Heinemann, 3,8,24,74,26,31.
10 Greene, G. (1978), *The End of the Affair*. Harmondsworth: Penguin, 131.
11 Ibid., 19.
12 Ibid., 143.
13 Greene, G. (1978), *The Human Factor*. London: Bodley Head, 236.
14 Greene, *Travels with my Aunt*, 18.
15 Ibid., 66.
16 Ibid., 73, 74.
17 Ibid., 131.
18 Ibid., 191.
19 Ibid., 191.
20 Ibid., 225, 226.
21 Ibid., 317.
22 Ibid., 317.
23 Ibid., 318.
24 Ibid., 318, 319.
25 Ibid., 191.
26 Adamson, J. (1988). Antibes: Author's interview with Graham Greene.
27 Greene, *Travels with my Aunt*, Dedication.
28 Allain, M.-F. (1983). *The Other Man*. London: Bodley Head, 142.
29 Greene, *The Quiet American*, 120.
30 Greene, *Brighton Rock*, 128.
31 Allain, *The Other Man*, 180.
32 Greene, *Travels with my Aunt*, 298.
33 Ibid., 10.

Notes to Chapter 14: Graham Greene and Alfred Hitchcock

1 Sinyard, N. (1999), *The Comic Sense of Graham Greene*. Berkhamsted: Graham Greene Birthplace Trust.
2 Sinyard, N. (1986), *Filming Literature: The Art of Screen Adaptation*. London: Croom Helm.
3 Browning, R. (1972), 'Bishop Blougram's Apology', l. 395, in *Men and Women 1855*, edited by P. Turner. Oxford: Oxford University Press, 141.
4 Hazzard, S. (2000), *Greene on Capri: A Memoir*. London: Virago, 71.
5 Bouzereau, L. (1993), *The Alfred Hitchcock Quote Book*. New York: Citadel Press, 88.
6 Ibid., 153.
7 Ibid., 153.
8 Sinyard, *The Comic Sense of Graham Greene*, 7.
9 Spoto, D. (1983), *The Dark Side of Genius: The Life of Alfred Hitchcock*. London: Plexus.
10 A phrase used by a former teaching colleague of mine to summarise Greene's novels.

11 Parkinson, D. (ed.) (1993), *The Graham Greene Film Reader: Mornings in the Dark*. Manchester: Carcanet Press, 52.

12 Barr, C. (1999), *English Hitchcock*. Moffat: Cameron & Hollis, 111.

13 Greene, G. (1971), *A Sort of Life*. London: Penguin, 24.

14 Greene, G. (1982), *Ways of Escape*. London: Penguin, 54.

15 Bouzereau, *The Alfred Hitchcock Quote Book*, 155.

16 Buchan, J. (1998), *Huntingtower*. Oxford: Oxford University Press, 116.

17 Greene, G. (1988), *Collected Essays*. London: Penguin, 169.

18 Said by Hitchcock at a news conference in 1947. Quoted in Wolf, W., 'The Thrill is Gone', *New York Magazine*, 26 May 1980, 70.

19 Buchan, J. (1994), *The Thirty-Nine Steps*. London: Penguin, dedicatory epistle, 3.vvvv

20 *Men and Women 1855*, 141.

21 Ian Thomson (ed.) (2006), *Articles of Faith: The Collected Tablet Journalism of Graham Greene*. Oxford: Signal Books, 25. The quotation is from an interview that Greene gave in 1989.

22 Bouzereau, *The Alfred Hitchcock Quote Book*, 151.

23 Greene, G. (1981), *Brighton Rock*. Geneva: Heron Books, 310.

24 Parkinson, *The Graham Greene Film Reader: Mornings in the Dark*, xvi.

25 Ibid., xvii.

26 Ibid., 163.

27 Ibid., 102.

28 Ibid., 293.

29 Ibid., 163.

30 Ibid., 52.

31 Ibid., 92.

32 Ibid., 399.

33 Ibid., p. 537.

34 Greene, *Ways of Escape*, 47.

35 Ibid., p. 47.

36 Both statements are quoted in Sherry, N. (1989), *The Life of Graham Greene: Volume I: 1904–1939*. London: Jonathan Cape, 607.

37 Parkinson, *The Graham Greene Film Reader: Mornings in the Dark*, 559.

38 Greene, *Ways of Escape*, 50.

39 Truffaut, F. (revised edition, 1986), *Hitchcock*. London: Paladin, 392–3.

40 Smith, G. (1986), *The Achievement of Graham Greene*. Brighton: Harvester Press, 211–12.

41 Greene, *A Sort of Life*, 147.

42 Ibid., 151.

43 Falk, Q. (revised edition, 2000), *Travels in Greeneland*. Richmond: Reynolds and Hearn, 101.

44 Ibid., 101.

45 Parkinson, *The Graham Greene Film Reader: Mornings in the Dark*, 559.

Notes to Chapter 15: The Plays of Graham Greene

1 *The Potting Shed* was briefly revived in a production directed by Svetlana Dimčović at the Finborough Theatre, London, in 2010 and given an extended run in January 2011.
2 Billington, M. (2007), *State of the Nation*. London: Faber, 65–7.
3 Tynan, K. (1964), *Tynan on Theatre*. Harmondsworth: Penguin, 22.
4 Greene, G. (1954), *The Living Room*. New York: Viking Press, 80.
5 Ibid., 81.
6 Greene, R. (ed.) (2007), *Graham Greene: A Life in Letters*. London: Little, Brown, 189.
7 Bentley, E. (1969), *What is Theatre?* London: Methuen, 202.
8 Tynan, *Tynan on Theatre*, 67–9.
9 Greene, G. (1957), *The Potting Shed*. New York: Viking Press, 94.
10 Greene, G. (1985), *The Collected Plays of Graham Greene*. London: Penguin, 135.
11 Greene, *The Potting Shed*, 120.
12 Greene, G. (1959), *The Complaisant Lover*. New York: Viking Press, 81.
13 Ibid., 85.
14 Tynan, *Tynan on Theatre*, 85.
15 Greene, *The Complaisant Lover*, 16.
16 Conrad, P. (1985), *Cassell's History of English Literature*. London: Cassell, 670.
17 See O'Connor, G. (1982), *Ralph Richardson*. London: Hodder & Stoughton, 194. The critic is J. W. Lambert.
18 Greene, R. *Graham Greene: A Life in Letters*, 271–2.
19 Greene, *The Collected Plays of Graham Greene*, 261.
20 Greene, R. *Graham Greene: A Life in Letters*, 134.
21 Esslin, M. (1976), 'The Return of A. J. Raffles', *Poets and Players*, 23, (February), 30.
22 Billington, M. (2006), *Harold Pinter*. London: Faber, 329.

Notes to Chapter 16: Graham Greene and Charlie Chaplin

1 Parkinson, D. (ed.) (1995), *Mornings in the Dark: A Graham Greene Film Reader*. Manchester: Manchester University Press, 395.
2 Ibid., 395.
3 Agee, J. (1963), *Agee on Film*. London: Peter Owen, 179.
4 Parkinson, *Mornings in the Dark: A Graham Greene Film Reader*, 75.
5 Truffaut, F. (1982), *The Films in My Life*. London: Penguin, 61.
6 Robinson, D. (1985), *Chaplin: His Life and Art*. New York: McGraw-Hill, 606.
7 Greene, G. (1969), *Collected Essays*. London: Bodley Head, 86.
8 Sherry, N. (2002), 'Graham Greene', *A Sort of Newsletter*, Spring, 3.
9 Giannetti, L. (1981), *Masters of the American Cinema*. New Jersey: Prentice-Hall, 80.
10 Greene, *Collected Essays*, 104.

11 Cloetta, Y. (2004), *In Search of a Beginning: My Life with Graham Greene*, translated by E. Cameron. London: Bloomsbury, 153.

12 Craft, R. (1972), *Stravinsky: Chronicles of a Friendship 1948–1971*. London: Victor Gollancz, 72.

13 Theroux, P. (1978), *Picture Palace*. London: Hamish Hamilton, 18–19.

14 Sinyard, N. (2003), *Graham Greene: A Literary Life*. London: Palgrave Macmillan, 7.

15 Parkinson, *Mornings in the Dark: A Graham Greene Film Reader*, 234.

16 Ibid., 128.

17 Ibid., 226.

18 Robinson, *Chaplin: His Life and Art*, 750.

19 Dunaway, D. (1989), *Huxley in Hollywood*. London: Bloomsbury, 249.

20 Taken from the screenplay of *The Third Man*. See Greene, G. and Reed, C. (1973), *The Third Man*: London: Faber & Faber, 97–8.

21 Lynn, K. (1997), *Charlie Chaplin and His Times*. London: Aurum Press, 514.

22 Cloetta, *In Search of a Beginning*, 152.

23 Greene, G. (1980), *Yours Etc: Letters to the Press 1945–89*, selected and introduced by C. Hawtree. London: Reinhardt, 25.

24 Ibid., 26.

25 Ibid., 26.

26 Cloetta, *In Search of a Beginning*, 49.

27 Ibid., 157.

28 Truffaut, *The Films in My Life*, 55.

29 Sinyard, N. (1992), *Classic Movie Comedians*. London: Bison Books, 17.

30 Forbes, B. (1992), *A Divided Life*. London: Heinemann, 217.

31 Milne, T. (ed.) (1972), *Godard on Godard*. London: Secker & Warburg, 29.

Notes to Chapter 17: The Later Greene: From Modernist to Moralist

1 Brennan, M. G. (2010), *Graham Greene: Fictions, Faith and Authorship*. London and New York: Continuum.

2 Ibid., 68.

3 Greene, G. (1942), *British Dramatists*. London: Collins. Reprinted in W. J. Turner (ed.) (1944), *Impressions of English Literature*. London: Collins, 102.

4 See, for example, Gaylord, A. T. (1967), 'Sentence and Solaas in Fragment VII of the *Canterbury Tales*: Harry Bailly as Horseback Editor', *PMLA*, 82, 226–35; Leitch, L. M. (1982), 'Sentence and Solaas: The Functions of the Hosts in the *Canterbury Tales*', *Chaucer Review*, 17, (1), 5–20; Luxon, T. H. (1987), '"Sentence" and "Solaas": Proverbs and Consolation in the *Knight's Tale*', *Chaucer Review*, 22, (2), 94–111; Hollander, R. (1985–86), '*Utilità* in Boccaccio's *Decameron*', *Studi sul Boccaccio*, (15), 215–33.

5 Craun, E. D. (1997), *Lies, Slander, and Obscenity in Medieval English Literature: Pastoral Rhetoric and the Deviant Speaker*. Cambridge: Cambridge University Press, citing Jacques de Vitry, *Exempla*, xliii.

6 Schlauch, M. (1956), *English Medieval Literature and its Social Foundations*. Warsaw: Państwowe Wydawnictwo Naukowe, 163.

7 *Everyman*, in D. Bevington (ed.), *Medieval Drama*. Boston: Houghton Mifflin, l. 867.

8 Lester, G. A. (1981), 'Introduction', to G. A. Lester (ed.) *Three Late Medieval Morality Plays*. New York: Norton, xvi.

9 Speirs, J. (1990; 1982), 'A Survey of Medieval Verse and Drama', in Boris Ford (ed.), *Medieval Literature* (reprint). Harmondsworth: Penguin, 89–90.

10 Potter, R. A. (1975), *The English Morality Play: Origins, History, and Influence of a Dramatic Tradition*. New York and London: Routledge, 129.

11 Bevington, D. (1975), *Mankind*, in D. Bevington (ed.), *Medieval Drama*. Boston: Houghton Mifflin, 901–2.

12 Greene, G. (1962), *The Heart of the Matter*. Harmondsworth: Penguin, 58–9.

13 Greene, G. (1977), *Brighton Rock*. Harmondsworth: Penguin, 228.

14 Bosco, M., SJ (2005), *Graham Greene's Catholic Imagination*. Oxford: Oxford University Press, 130.

15 Greene, G. (1980), *Doctor Fischer of Geneva or The Bomb Party*. Harmondsworth: Penguin, 115.

16 *Ibid.*, 33.

17 *Ibid.*, 61.

18 *Ibid.*, 61–2.

19 *Ibid.*, 91.

20 *Ibid.*, 130.

21 *Ibid.*, 142.

22 *Ibid.*, 133.

23 *Ibid.*, 142.

24 *Ibid.*, 142–3.

25 Greene, G. (1985), *The Tenth Man*. Harmondsworth: Penguin, 89.

26 *Ibid.*, 130–1.

27 *Ibid.*, 79.

28 Greene, G. (1989), *The Captain and the Enemy*. Harmondsworth: Penguin, 12.

29 Brennan, *Fictions, Faith and Authorship*, 2.

30 Greene, *The Captain and the Enemy*, 44.

31 *Ibid.*, 83.

32 *Ibid.*, 123.

33 St. Augustine (1958), *On Christian Doctrine*, translated by D. W. Robertson, Jr. New Jersey: Prentice Hall, 3.10.

34 *Ibid.*

Further Reading

The following lists have no pretensions of comprehensiveness; they simply showcase those materials in Graham Greene Studies all or part of which many have found instructive.

BIBLIOGRAPHICAL AND ARCHIVAL RESOURCES

Cassis, A. F. (1981), *Graham Greene: An Annotated Bibliography of Criticism*. Metuchen, NJ and London: Scarecrow Press.

Costa, R. H. (1985), 'Graham Greene: A Checklist'. *College Literature*, 12, (1), 85–94.

Gale, R. L. (2006), *Characters and Plots in the Fiction of Graham Greene*. Jefferson, NC: McFarland.

Miller, R. H. (1979), *Graham Greene: A Descriptive Catalog*. Lexington, KY: University of Kentucky Press.

Vann, J. Don (1970), *Graham Greene: A Checklist of Criticism*. Kent, OH: Kent State University Press.

Wobbe, R. A. (1981), *Graham Greene: A Bibliography and Guide to Research*. New York and London: Garland.

The Graham Greene Collection, Graham Greene Birthplace Trust, Berkhamsted, England, UK.

The Graham Greene Collection, The John J. Burns Library, Boston College, Boston, MA.

The Graham Greene Collection, The Joseph Mark Lauinger Memorial Library, Georgetown University, Washington DC.

The Graham Greene Collection, The Harry Ransom Humanities Research Center, The University of Texas at Austin, Austin, TX.

FIRST EDITIONS OF GRAHAM GREENE'S WORKS (BRITISH AND AMERICAN)

In the following list, Greene's works are listed chronologically, beginning with 1925. A single date of publication (e.g. 1929) indicates that the British and American first editions were published in the same year and, unless where stated, two separate dates of publication (e.g. 1930; 1931) signify the year of publication for the British and the American first editions respectively. Title changes for the American edition are noted in parentheses.

Greene, G. (1925), *Babbling April*. Oxford: Blackwell.

—.(1929), *The Man Within*. London: Heinemann; New York: Doubleday.

—.(1930; 1931), *The Name of Action*. London: Heinemann; New York: Doubleday.

—.(1931; 1932), *Rumour at Nightfall*. London: Heinemann; New York: Doubleday.

—.(1932; 1933), *Stamboul Train* (US title: *Orient Express*). London: Heinemann; New York: Doubleday.

—.(1934), *It's a Battlefield*. London: Heinemann; New York: Doubleday.

—.(1935), *England Made Me*. London: Heinemann; New York: Doubleday.

—.(1935), *The Bear Fell Free*. London: Grayson & Grayson.

—.(1935), *The Basement Room and Other Stories*. London: Cresset Press.

—.(1936), *Journey Without Maps*. London: Heinemann; New York: Doubleday.

—.(1936), *A Gun for Sale* (US title: *This Gun for Hire*). London: Heinemann; New York: Doubleday.

—.(1938), *Brighton Rock: A Novel*. London: Heinemann; New York: Viking Press.

—.(1939), *The Lawless Roads* (US title: *Another Mexico*). London: Longmans; New York: Viking Press.

—.(1939), *The Confidential Agent: An Entertainment*. London: Heinemann; New York: Viking Press.

—.(1940), *The Power and the Glory* (US title: *The Labyrinthine Ways*). London: Heinemann; New York: Viking Press.

—.(1942), *British Dramatists*. London: Collins.

—.(1943), *The Ministry of Fear: An Entertainment*. London: Heinemann; New York: Viking Press.

—.(1946; 1958), *The Little Train*. London: Eyre & Spottiswoode; New York: Lothrop, Lee, & Shepard.

—.(1947; 1949), *Nineteen Stories*. London: Heinemann; New York: Viking Press.

—.(1948), *The Heart of the Matter*. London: Heinemann; New York: Viking Press.

—.(1950), *The Third Man and the Fallen Idol* (US title: *The Third Man*). London: Heinemann; New York: Viking Press.

—.(1950; 1953), *The Little Fire Engine* (US title: *The Little Red Fire Engine*). London: Eyre & Spottiswoode; New York: Lothrop, Lee, & Shepard.

—.(1951; 1952), *The Lost Childhood and Other Essays*. London: Eyre & Spottiswoode; New York: Viking Press.

—.(1951), *The End of the Affair*. London: Heinemann; New York: Viking Press.

—.(1952; 1954), *The Little Horse Bus*. London: Max Parish; New York: Lothrop, Lee, & Shepard.

—.(1953; 1954), *The Living Room*. London: Heinemann; New York: Viking Press.

—.(1953; 1955), *The Little Steamroller* (US title: *The Little Steamroller: A Story of Adventure, Mystery, and Detection*). London: Max Parish; New York: Lothrop, Lee, & Shepard.

—.(1954; 1962), *Twenty-One Stories*. London: Heinemann; New York: Viking Press.

—.(1955; 1957), *Loser Takes All*. London: Heinemann; New York: Viking Press.

—.(1955; 1956), *The Quiet American*. London: Heinemann; New York: Viking Press.

—.(1957; 1958), *The Potting Shed*. New York: Viking Press; London: Heinemann.

—.(1958), *Our Man in Havana*. London: Heinemann; New York: Viking Press.

—.(1959; 1961), *The Complaisant Lover*. London: Heinemann; New York: Viking Press.

—.(1960), *A Visit to Morin*. London: Heinemann.

—.(1961), *A Burnt-Out Case*. London: Heinemann; New York: Viking Press.

—.(1961), *In Search of a Character: Two African Journals*. London: Bodley Head; New York: Viking Press.

—.(1963), *A Sense of Reality*. London: Bodley Head; New York: Viking Press.

—.(1964), *Carving a Statue*. London: Bodley Head.

—.(1966), *The Comedians*. London: Bodley Head; New York: Viking Press.

—.(1967), *'May We Borrow Your Husband?' and Other Comedies of the Sexual Life*. London: Bodley Head; New York: Viking Press.

—.(1969), *The Third Man: A Film by Graham Greene and Carol Reed*. London: Lorrimer.

—.(1969), *Collected Essays*. London: Bodley Head; New York: Viking Press.

—.(1969), *Travels with my Aunt*. London: Bodley Head; New York: Viking Press.

—.(1971), *A Sort of Life*. London: Bodley Head; New York: Viking Press.

—.(1972; 1973), *Collected Stories*. London: Bodley Head and Heinemann; New York: Viking Press.

—.(1972), *The Pleasure Dome: The Collected Film Criticism 1935–1940* (US title: *Graham Greene on Film*), edited by John Russell Taylor. London: Secker & Warburg; New York: Simon & Schuster.

—.(1973), *The Honorary Consul*. London: Bodley Head; New York: Viking Press.

—.(1974), *Lord Rochester's Monkey*. London: Bodley Head; New York: Viking Press.

—.(1975; 1976), *The Return of A. J. Raffles*. London: Bodley Head; New York: Simon & Schuster.

—.(1978), *The Human Factor*. London: Bodley Head; New York: Simon & Schuster.

—.(1980), *Doctor Fischer of Geneva or The Bomb Party*. London: Bodley Head; New York: Simon & Schuster.

—.(1980), *Ways of Escape*. London: Bodley Head; New York: Simon & Schuster.

—.(1981), *The Great Jowett*. London: Bodley Head.

—.(1982), *Monsignor Quixote*. London: Bodley Head; New York: Simon & Schuster.

—.(1982), *J'Accuse: The Dark Side of Nice*. London: Bodley Head.

—.(1983), *'Yes and No' and 'For Whom the Bell Chimes'*. London: Bodley Head.

—.(1984), *Getting to Know the General: The Story of an Involvement*. London: Bodley Head; New York: Simon & Schuster.

—.(1985), *The Tenth Man*. London: Bodley Head and Anthony Blond; New York: Simon & Schuster.

—.(1988), *Collected Plays*. Harmondsworth: Penguin.

—.(1988), *The Captain and the Enemy*. London: Bodley Head; New York: Viking Press.

—.(1989), *Yours, Etc.: Letters to the Press 1945–89*, edited by Christopher Hawtree. London: Reinhardt.

—.(1990), *The Last Word and Other Stories*. London: Reinhardt; New York: Viking Press.

—.(1990), *Reflections*, selected and introduced by Judith Adamson. London: Reinhardt.

—.(1992), *A World of My Own: A Dream Diary*, edited by Yvonne Cloetta. London: Reinhardt.
—.(1993), *The Graham Greene Film Reader: Mornings in the Dark*, edited by David Parkinson. Manchester: Carcanet Press.
—.(1995), *Under the Garden*. London: Penguin.
—.(1999), *Dr Fischer*. London: Hesperus Press Limited.
—.(2005), *No Man's Land*. London: Hesperus Press Limited.

MISCELLANEOUS OTHER WORKS

Greene, G. (ed.) (1934), *The Old School: Essays by Divers Hands*. London: Jonathan Cape.
Greene, G. (1948), *Why Do I Write? An Exchange of Views Between Elizabeth Bowen, Graham Greene and V. S. Pritchett*. London: Percival Marshall.
Greene, G. (ed.) (1950), *The Best of Saki*. London: British Publishers' Guild.
Greene, G. (1953), *Essais Catholiques*, translated by Marcelle Sibon. Paris: Editions du Seuil.
Greene, G. (ed.) (with Hugh Greene) (1957), *The Spy's Bedside Book*. London: Hart-Davis.
Greene, G. (1962), *Introductions to Three Novels*. Stockholm: Norstadt & Söners.
—.(1966), *Victorian Detective Fiction*, edited by Eric Osborne. London: Bodley Head.
Greene, G. (ed.) (1975), *An Impossible Woman: The Memories of Dottoressa Moor of Capri*. London: Bodley Head; New York: Viking Press.
Greene, G. (1983), *The Other Man: Conversations with Graham Greene*, edited by Marie-Françoise Allain. London: Bodley Head; New York: Simon & Schuster.
Greene, G. (ed.) (with Hugh Greene) (1984), *Victorian Villainies*. Harmondsworth: Viking.
Greene, G. (1992), *Conversations with Graham Greene*, edited by Henry J. Donaghy. Jackson, MI and London: University Press of Mississippi.
—.(1994), *Graham Greene: Man of Paradox*, edited by A. F. Cassis and with a foreword by Peter Wolfe. Chicago: Loyola University Press.
—.(2006), *Articles of Faith: The Collected Tablet Journalism of Graham Greene*, edited and with an introduction by Ian Thomson. Oxford: Oxford University Press.
—.(2007), *Graham Greene: A Life in Letters*, edited by Richard Greene. London: Little, Brown.
Hogarth, P. (1986), *Graham Greene Country*, with a foreword and commentary by Graham Greene. London: Pavilion Books, 1986.

SELECTED CRITICISM

Adamson, J. (1984), *Graham Greene and Cinema*. Norman, OK: Pilgrim Books.
—.(1990), *Graham Greene, The Dangerous Edge: Where Art and Politics Meet*. New York: St. Martin's Press.

Allit, P. (1997), *Catholic Converts: British and American Intellectuals Turn to Rome.* Ithaca, NY: Cornell University Press.

Allott, K. and M. Farris (1983), *The Art of Graham Greene.* New York: Russell & Russell.

Atkins, J. (1966), *Graham Greene.* London: Calder & Boyars.

Baldridge, C. (2000), *Graham Greene's Fictions: The Virtues of Extremity.* Columbia, MO and London: University of Missouri Press.

Benz, S. (2003), 'Taking Sides: Graham Greene and Latin America'. *Journal of Modern Literature,* 26, (2), 113–28.

Bergonzi, B. (2006), *A Study in Greene: Graham Greene and the Art of the Novel.* Oxford and New York: Oxford University Press.

Bhavani, D. (1999), *Graham Greene: A Study in His Language and Style.* New Delhi: Prestige.

Bloom, H., editor (1987), *Graham Greene: Modern Critical Views.* New York: Chelsea House.

Boardman, G. R. (1971), *Graham Greene: The Aesthetics of Exploration.* Gainesville, FL: University of Florida Press.

Bosco, M. (2005), *Graham Greene's Catholic Imagination.* Oxford and New York: Oxford University Press.

Breitwieser, M. R. (2008), 'Materializing Calloway: The Sorrows of Occupation in *The Third Man'. Hopkins Review,* 1, (3), 437–68.

Brennan, M. G. (2006), 'Graham Greene's Catholic Conversion: The Early Writings (1923–29) and *The Man Within'. Logos,* 9, (3), 134–57.

—.(2010), *Graham Greene: Fictions, Faith and Authorship.* London and New York: Continuum.

Brindley, D. (1983), 'Orthodoxy and Orthopraxis in the Novels of Graham Greene'. *Theology,* 86, 29–36.

Bryden, R. (1970), 'Graham Greene Discusses the Collected Edition of his Novels'. *Listener,* 23 April, 544–5.

Bushnell, W. S. (2008), '*The Quiet American*: Graham Greene's Vietnam Novel through the Lenses of Two Eras,' in P. C. Rollins and J. E. O'Connor (eds.), *Why We Fought: America's Wars in Film and History.* Lexington, KY: University Press of Kentucky, pp. 404–27.

Cargas, H. (ed.) (1969), *Graham Greene.* St. Louis, MO: Herder.

Carlsten, J. (2006), '"Somehow the Hate Has Got Mislaid": Adaptation & *The End of the Affair'. UBCinephile,* 2, 3–7.

Cash, W. (2000), *The Third Woman: The Secret Passion That Inspired The End of the Affair.* New York: Carroll & Graf.

Cassis, A. F. (1994), *Graham Greene: Life, Work and Criticism.* Fredericton, New Brunswick: York Press.

Choi, J. S. (1990), *Greene and Unamuno: Two Pilgrims to La Mancha.* New York: Peter Lang.

Couto, M. (1988), *Graham Greene: On the Frontier: Politics and Religion in the Novels.* New York: St. Martin's Press.

Cummings, O. F. (2003), 'The Grace of Graham Greene (1904–1991): A Centenary Reflection'. *Literature and Belief,* 23, (2), 111–21.

Dalm, R. E., van (1999), *A Structural Analysis of The Honorary Consul by Graham Greene*. Amsterdam: Rodopi.

Davis, E. (1984), *Graham Greene: The Artist as Critic*. Fredericton, New Brunswick: York Press.

Dern, J. A. (2005), 'The Revenant of Vienna: A Critical Comparison of Carol Reed's Film *The Third Man* and Bram Stoker's Novel *Dracula*'. *Literature Film Quarterly*, 33, (1), 4–11.

Devereux, J. A. (1987), 'Catholic Matters in the Correspondence of Evelyn Waugh and Graham Greene'. *Journal of Modern Literature*, 14, 111–26.

De Vitis, A. A. (1986), *Graham Greene* (revised edition). New York: Twayne Publishers; London: Prentice Hall International.

Diemert, B. (1996), *Graham Greene's Thrillers and the 1930s*. Montreal and Kingston; London; Buffalo, NY: McGill-Queen's University Press.

Donaghy, H. J. (1983), *Graham Greene: An Introduction to His Writings*. Amsterdam: Rodopi.

Drazin, C. (2000), *In Search of The Third Man*. London: Methuen.

Durán, L. (1995), *Graham Greene: Friend and Brother*, translated by Euan Cameron. London: HarperCollins.

Erdinast-Vulcan, D. (1988), *Graham Greene's Childless Fathers*. New York: St. Martin's Press.

Erlebach, P. and Stein, T. M. (eds.) (1991), *Graham Greene in Perspective: A Critical Symposium*. Frankfurt am Main and New York: Peter Lang.

Evans, R. O. and Webster, H. C. (eds.) (1963), *Graham Greene: Some Critical Considerations*. Lexington, KY: University of Kentucky Press.

Falk, Q. (2000), *Travels in Greeneland: The Cinema of Graham Greene* (revised and updated third edition). London: Reynolds & Hearn.

Fiengo-Varn, A. (2009), '*The Captain and the Enemy*: Graham Greene's Central American Experiences'. *Valley Voices*, 9, (2), 56–64.

Franklin, R. (2004), 'God in the Details: Graham Greene's Religious Realism'. *New Yorker*, October 4, 80, (29), 100–104.

Fraser, T. P. (1994), *The Modern Catholic Novel in Europe*. New York: Macmillan.

Friedman, M. J. (1970), *The Vision Obscured: Perceptions of Some Twentieth-Century Catholic Novelists*. New York: Fordham University Press.

Gallix, F. and V. Guignery (eds.) (2007), *Plus sur Greene: The Power and the Glory: The Sorbonne Conference*. Neuilly: Atlande.

Gasiorek, A. (2007), 'Rendering Justice to the Visible World: History, Politics and National Identity in the Novels of Graham Greene,' in M. MacKay and L. Stonebridge (eds.), *British Fiction after Modernism: The Novel at Mid-Century*. New York: Palgrave Macmillan, pp. 17–32.

Gaston, G. (1984), *The Pursuit of Salvation: A Critical Guide to the Novels of Graham Greene*. Troy, NY: Whitston.

Gilvary, D. (ed.) (unpublished screenplay, 2011), *The Third Man: A Film by Graham Greene and Carol Reed*.

Godman, P. (2001), 'Graham Greene's Vatican Dossier'. *The Atlantic Monthly*, July/ August, 84–8.

Gordon, H. (1997), *Fighting Evil: Unsung Heroes in the Novels of Graham Greene*. Westport, CT: Greenwood Press.

Gotia, A. (2007), 'God's Image: The Betrayer and the Betrayed in Graham Greene's *The Power and the Glory*'. *Logos*, 10, (1), 106–15.

Greeley, A. (2000), *The Catholic Imagination*. Berkeley: University of California Press.

Greene, B. (1938), *Land Benighted*. London: Geoffrey Bles.

Greene, H. (1984), 'Childhood with Graham' *Adam International Review*, 46, (446–8), 8–14.

Gribble, J. (1998), '*The Third Man*: Graham Greene and Carol Reed'. *Literature Film Quarterly*, 26, (3), 235–9.

Hand, R. J. (2011), *Adapting Graham Greene: Cinema, Television, Radio*. New York: Palgrave Macmillan.

Hazzard, S. (2000), *Greene on Capri*. New York: Farrar, Straus & Giroux.

Henry, P. (2002), 'Dostoevskian Echoes in the Novels of Graham Greene'. *Dostoevsky Studies: Journal of the International Dostoevsky Society*, 6, 119–33.

Hestenes, M. (1999), 'To See the Kingdom: A Study of Graham Greene and Alan Paton'. *Literature and Theology*, 13, (4), 311–22.

Hill, W. T. (1999), *Graham Greene's Wanderers: The Search for Dwelling: Journeying and Wandering in the Novels of Graham Greene*. San Francisco: International Scholars Publications.

Hill, W. T. (ed.) (2002), *Perceptions of Religious Faith in the Works of Graham Greene*. Bern and New York: Peter Lang.

—.(2008), *Lonely Without God: Graham Greene's Quixotic Journey of Faith*. Bethesda: Academica Press.

Hodgkins, H. H. (2006), 'The Apophatic Heart: Graham Greene's Negative Rhetoric'. *Renascence*, 59, (1), 53–75.

Hoskins, R. (1998), *Graham Greene: An Approach to the Novels*. New York: Garland.

Hynes, S. L. (ed.) (1973), *Graham Greene: A Collection of Critical Essays*. Englewood Cliffs, NJ: Prentice-Hall.

Islam, N. (1987), *Graham Greene: An Inverted Humanist*. Dhaka, Bangladesh: Jahangirnagar University.

Johnstone, R. (1982), *The Will to Believe: Novelists of the Nineteen-Thirties*. Oxford: Oxford University Press.

Kaur, S. (1988), *Graham Greene: An Existentialist Investigation*. Amritsar, India: Guru Nanek Dev University Press.

Kellogg, G. (1970), *The Vital Tradition: The Catholic Novel in a Period of Convergence*. Chicago: Loyola University Press.

Kelly, R. M. (1992), *Graham Greene: A Study of the Short Fiction*. New York: Twayne; Toronto: Maxwell Macmillan Canada; New York: Maxwell Macmillan International.

Ker, I. (2003), *The Catholic Revival in English Literature, 1845–1961*. Notre Dame, IN: University of Notre Dame Press.

Kulshrestha, J. P. (1977), *Graham Greene: The Novelist*. Delhi: Macmillan.

Kunkel, F. L. (1959), *The Labyrinthine Ways of Graham Greene*. New York: Sheed & Ward.

Kurismmootil, K. C. J. (1982), *Heaven and Hell on Earth: An Appreciation of Five Novels of Graham Greene*. Chicago: Loyola University Press.

Lamba, B. P. (1987), *Graham Greene: His Mind and Art*. New York: Apt Books.

Land, S. K. (2008), *The Human Imperative: A Study of the Novels of Graham Greene*. New York: AMS Press.

Lewis, J. (2010), *Shades of Greene: One Generation of an English Family*. London: Jonathan Cape.

Lewis, K. (1998), 'The Third Force: Graham Greene and Joseph L. Mankiewicz's *The Quiet American*'. *Film History*, 10, (4), 477–91

Lodge, D. (1966), *Graham Greene*. New York and London: Columbia University Press.

—.(1991), 'Graham Greene: A Personal View. Encounters between Two Catholic Novelists'. *Times Literary Supplement*, 12 April, 9–10.

Malamet, E. (1998), *The World Remade: Graham Greene and the Art of Detection*. New York: Peter Lang.

Maamri, M. R. (2008), 'Cosmic Chaos in *The Secret Agent* and Graham Greene's *It's a Battlefield*'. *Conradiana: A Journal of Joseph Conrad Studies*, 40, (2), 179–92.

Maurois, A. (1968), *Points of View: From Kipling to Graham Greene*. New York: Fredrick Ungar.

McEwan, N. (1988), *Graham Greene*. Houndmills and New York: St. Martin's Press.

Mesnet, M. B. (1954), *Graham Greene and The Heart of the Matter: An Essay*. London: The Cresset Press.

Middleton, D. J. N. (1999), 'Graham Greene's *The End of the Affair*: Toward an Ironic God'. *Notes on Contemporary Literature*, 29, (3), 8–10.

—.(2008), *Theology after Reading: Christian Imagination and the Power of Fiction*. Waco, TX: Baylor University Press.

Miller, R. H. (1990), *Understanding Graham Greene*. Columbia, SC: University of South Carolina Press.

Miyano, S. (2006), *Innocence in Graham Greene's Novels*. New York: Peter Lang.

Mockler, A. (1994), *Graham Greene: Three Lives 1904–1945*. Arbroath: Hunter Mackay.

Mudford, P. (1996), *Graham Greene*. Plymouth, England: Northcote House in association with the British Council.

Meyers, J. (ed.) (1990), *Graham Greene: A Revaluation: New Essays*. New York: St. Martin's Press.

Miyano, S. (2006), *Innocence in Graham Greene's Novels*. New York: Peter Lang.

Newman, J. H. (1963), *The Essential Newman*, edited by Vincent Ferrer Blehl. New York: Mentor-Omega Books.

Norman, E. R. (1985), *Roman Catholicism in England: From the Elizabethan Settlement to the Second Vatican Council*. Oxford: Oxford University Press.

O'Prey, P. (1988), *A Reader's Guide to Graham Greene*. New York: Thames & Hudson.

Osborne, K. (1988), *Sacramental Theology: A General Introduction*. New York: Paulist Press.

Pandit, P. N. (1989), *The Novels of Graham Greene: A Thematic Study in the Impact of Childhood on Adult Life*. New Delhi: Prestige Books in association with the Indian Society for Commonwealth Studies.

Pearce, J. (2000), *Literary Converts*. San Francisco: Ignatius Press.

Peat, H. W. (1986), '*Beyond the Limit*: Familiar Shadows from the World of Graham Greene'. *Literature Film Quarterly*, 14, (2), 133–6.

Pendleton, R. (1996), *Graham Greene's Conradian Masterplot*. New York: St. Martin's Press.

Petersen, G. W. (1971), *Graham Greene: The Aesthetics of Exploration*. Gainesville, FL: University of Florida Press.

Phillips, G. D. (1974), *Graham Greene: The Films of His Fiction*. New York and London: Teacher's College Press.

Pierloot, R. A. (1994), *Psychoanalytic Patterns in the Work of Graham Greene*. Amsterdam and Atlanta: Rodopi.

Prasad, K. (1982) *Graham Greene, the Novelist*. New Delhi: Classical Publishing Company.

Price, M. (2004), 'Sinner Take All: Graham Greene's Damned Redemption'. *BookForum*, 11, (4), 8–11.

Priest, K. (2010), 'The Overlooked Oxymoron in Graham Greene's *Brighton Rock*'. *Explicator*, 68, (2), 122–6.

Pryce-Jones, D. (1963), *Graham Greene*. Edinburgh and London: Oliver & Boyd.

Radal, K. M. (1987), *Affirmation in a Moral Wasteland: A Comparison of Ford Madox Ford and Graham Greene*. New York: Peter Lang.

Rai, G. (1983), *Graham Greene: An Existential Approach*. Atlantic Highlands, NJ: Humanities Press; New Delhi: Associated Publishing House.

Rama Rao, V. V. B. (1996), *Graham Greene's Comic Vision*. New Delhi: Reliance Publishing.

Rawa, J. M. (2005), *The Imperial Quest and Modern Memory from Conrad to Greene*. New York: Routledge.

Reinhardt, M. (1984), 'Publishing Graham Greene'. *Adam International Review*, 46, (446–8), 25–6.

Restuccia, F. L. (2003), 'Graham Greene's Lacanian Encore: *The End of the Affair*'. *Religion and the Arts*, 7, (4), 369–87.

Roston, M. (2006), *Graham Greene's Narrative Strategies: A Study of the Major Novels*. Basingstoke and New York: Palgrave Macmillan.

Ryan, J. S. (1972), *Gleanings from Greeneland*. Armidale, NSW, Australia: University of New England Press.

Salvatore, A. T. (1988), *Greene and Kierkegaard: The Discourse of Belief*. Tuscaloosa: University of Alabama Press.

Schwartz, A. (2005), *The Third Spring: G. K Chesterton, Graham Greene, Christopher Dawson, and David Jones*. Washington, DC: Catholic University Press of America.

Schwerdt, L. M. (2005), 'Graham Greene's Search for Faithfulness'. *EAPSU Online*, Fall, (2), 150–76.

Sharma, S. K. (1990), *Graham Greene: The Search for Belief*. New Delhi: Harman Publishing House.

Sharrock, R. (1984), *Saints, Sinners, and Comedians: The Novels of Graham Greene*. Tunbridge Wells: Burns & Oates; Notre Dame, IN: University of Notre Dame Press.

Sherry, N. (1989), *The Life of Graham Greene: Volume I: 1904–1939*. London: Jonathan Cape; New York: Viking.

—.(1994; 1995), *The Life of Graham Greene: Volume II: 1939–1955*. London: Jonathan Cape; New York: Viking.

—.(2004), *The Life of Graham Greene: Volume III: 1955–1991*. London: Jonathan Cape; New York: Viking.

Shelden, M. (1994), *Graham Greene: The Man Within*. London: Heinemann.

Sinha, S. (2007), *Graham Greene: A Study of His Major Novels*. New Delhi: Atlantic Publishers and Distributors.

Sinowitz, M. (2007), 'Graham Greene's and Carol Reed's *The Third Man*: When a Cowboy Comes to Town'. *Modern Fiction Studies*, 53, (3), 405–33.

Smith, G. (1986), *The Achievement of Graham Greene*. Brighton: The Harvester Press; •Totowa, NJ: Barnes & Noble.

Smith, J. L. (2000), *Traveling on the Edge: Journeys in the Footsteps of Graham Greene*. New York: St. Martin's Press.

Sonnenfeld, A. (1982), *Crossroads: Essays on the Catholic Novelists*. York, SC: French Literature Publications.

Spurling, J. (1983), *Graham Greene*. London and New York: Methuen.

Sternlicht, S. (1971), 'Prologue to the Sad Comedies: Graham Greene's Major Early Novels'. *Midwest Quarterly*, 12, 427–35.

Stratford, P. (1964), *Faith and Fiction: Creative Process in Greene and Mauriac*. South Bend, IN: University of Notre Dame Press.

Swift, B. C. (1992), '"The Dangerous Edge of Things": Mauriac, Greene and the Idea of the Catholic Novel'. *Journal of European Studies*, 22, (2), 111–26.

Sykes, C. (1975), *Evelyn Waugh: A Biography*. London: William Collins & Sons.

Thomas, B. (1988), *An Underground Fate: The Idiom of Romance in the Later Novels of Graham Greene*. Athens, GA: University of Georgia Press.

Thomson, B. L. (2009), *Graham Greene and the Politics of Popular Fiction and Film*. Basingstoke and New York: Palgrave.

Timmermann, B. (2005), *The Third Man's Vienna*. Vienna: Shippen Rock Publishing.

Turnell, M. (1967), *Graham Greene: A Critical Essay*. Grand Rapids, MI: Eerdmans.

Watts, C. (2000; 1997), *A Preface to Greene* (2nd edn). Harlow: Pearson Education.

—.(2005), '*The Heart of the Matter* and the Later Novels of Graham Greene,' in B. W. Shaffer (ed.), *A Companion to the British and Irish Novel, 1945–2000*. Malden, MA: Blackwell, pp. 278–88.

Wendorf, T. A. (2001), 'Allegory in Postmodernity: Graham Greene's *The Captain and the Enemy*'. *Christianity and Literature*, 50, (4), 657–77.

Weselinski, A. (1983), *Graham Greene, the Novelist: A Study of the Cinematic Imagination*. Warszawa: Uniwersytetu Warszawskiego.

West, W. J. (1997), *The Quest for Graham Greene*. London: Weidenfeld & Nicolson.

Whitehouse, J. C. (1990), *Vertical Man: The Human Being in the Catholic Novels of Graham Greene, Sigrid Undset, and Georges Bernanos*. New York: Garland Publishing.

Wilson, R. G. (1983), *Greene King: A Business and Family History*. London: Bodley Head and Jonathan Cape.

Wise, J. and M. Hill (2012), *The Works of Graham Greene: A Reader's Bibliography and Guide*. London; New York: Continuum.

Wolfe, P. (1972), *Graham Greene: The Entertainer*. Carbondale, IL: Southern Illinois University Press.

Woodman, T. (1991), *Faithful Fictions: The Catholic Novel in British Literature.* Milton Keynes: Open University Press.

Wootton, A. (2011), *Screening Graham Greene.* Harpenden: Pocket Essentials.

ADAPTATIONS FOR FILM AND TELEVISION

The following list, arranged chronologically and beginning with the most recent attempt 'to screen Greene', is taken from the Internet Movie Database (IMDb), which may be found at: http://www.imdb.com/name/nm0001294/. Titles within parentheses give either the title of the book or story from which a film is derived, or a translation of a film's non-English title.

Brighton Rock (UK, 2010)
The End of the Party (UK, 2006)
The Quiet American (UK, 2002)
Double Take (Across the Bridge) (USA, 2001)
The End of the Affair (UK, 1999)
This Gun for Hire (A Gun for Sale) (USA, 1991)
Strike It Rich (Loser Takes All) (UK, 1990)
El amante complaciente (The Complaisant Lover) (Spain, 1989)
The Tenth Man (USA, 1988)
Monsignor Quixote (USA, 1987)
May We Borrow Your Husband? (UK, 1986)
Doctor Fischer of Geneva (Doctor Fischer of Geneva or The Bomb Party) (UK, 1985)
The Honorary Consul (UK, 1983)
The Heart of the Matter (1983)
A Shocking Accident (UK, 1982)
El amante complaciente (The Complaisant Lover) (Spain, 1982)
L'amant complaisant (The Complaisant Lover) (France, 1980)
Il Treno per Istambul or The Istambul Train (Stamboul Train) (Hungary/Italy, 1980)
The Human Factor (UK, 1979)
Shades of Greene (UK, 1975–76. Television series: 18 episodes)
  1 'When Greek Meets Greek and Dean' (1975)
  2 'Cheap in August' (1975)
  3 'Special Duties' (1975)
  4 'The Invisible Japanese Gentlemen' (1975)
  5 'Two Gentle People' (1975)
  6 'The Root of All Evil' (1975)
  7 'A Little Place Off the Edgware Road' (1975)
  8 'The Blue Film' (1975)
  9 'The Destructors' (1975)
10 'Chagrin in Three Parts' (1976)
11 'The Case for the Defence' (1976)
12 'A Chance for Mr Lever' (1976)

13 'Alas! Poor Maling' (1976)
14 'Mortmain' (1976)
15 'A Drive in the Country' (1976)
16 'Under the Garden' (1976)
17 'Dream of a Strange Land' (1976)
18 'The Overnight Bag' (1976)

El poder y la gloria (*The Power and the Glory*) (Spain, 1974)
England Made Me (Yugoslavia/UK, 1973)
Travels with my Aunt (USA, 1972)
The Wounded Wolf (*A Gun for Sale*) (Turkey, 1972)
Das Herz aller Dinge (*The Heart of the Matter*) (West Germany, 1971)
Una pistola in vendita (*A Gun for Sale*) (Italy, 1970)
La fine dell'avventura (*The End of the Affair*) (Italy, 1969)
The Comedians (USA/France, 1967)
Pelon talo (*The Living Room*) (Finland, 1966)
Quinta colonna (*The Ministry of Fear*) (Italy, 1966)
Der letzte Raum (*The Living Room*) (West Germany, 1966)
The Third Man (UK, 1959–65. Television series: 77 episodes)
1 'Confessions of an Honest Man' (1959)
2 'A Question of Price' (1959)
3 'The Hollywood Incident' (1959)
4 'Death of an Overlord' (1959)
5 'Sparks from a Dead Fire' (1959)
6 'The Trouble at Drill Hill' (1959)
7 'The Man Who Died Twice' (1959)
8 'The Angry Young Man' (1959)
9 'Dark Island' (1959)
10 'The Girl Who Didn't Know' (1959)
11 'The Third Medallion' (1959)
12 'Castle in Spain' (1959)
13 'The Indispensible Man' (1959)
14 'Listen for the Sound of a Witch' (1959)
15 'A Man Takes a Trip' (1959)
16 'A Pocketful of Sin' (1959)
17 'How to Buy a Country' (1959)
18 'As the Twig Is Bent' (1959)
19 'Broken Strings' (1959)
20 'Five Hours to Kill' (1959)
21 'The Best Policy' (1959)
22 'One Kind Word' (1959)
23 'Three Dancing Turtles' (1959)
24 'An Offering of Pearls' (1959)
25 'The Importance of Being Harry Lime' (1959)
26 'Barcelona Passage' (1959)
27 'A Collector's Item' (1959)

28 'Dinner in Paris' (1959)
29 'High Finance' (1959)
30 'Toys of the Dead' (1959)
31 'The Man with Two Left Hands' (1959)
32 'The Man Who Wouldn't Talk' (1959)
33 'A Deal in Oils' (1959)
34 'The Tenth Symphony' (1959)
35 'An Experiment with Money' (1959)
36 'A Box of Eyes' (1959)
37 'The Widow Who Wasn't' (1959)
38 'Death in Small Instalments' (1959)
39 'Harry Lime and the King' (1960)
40 'A Question of Libel' (1962)
41 'Mischka' (1962)
42 'The Cross of Candos' (1962)
43 'Happy Birthday' (1962)
44 'Queen of the Nile' (1962)
45 'The Unexpected Mr Lime' (1962)
46 'A Calculated Risk' (1963)
47 'No Word for Danger' (1963)
48 'Lord Bradford' (1963)
49 'A King's Ransom' (1963)
50 'Hamburg Shakedown' (1963)
51 'A Diamond in the Rough' (1963)
52 'Portrait of Harry' (1963)
53 'The Man in Power' (1963)
54 'Meeting of the Board' (1963)
55 'Hansel and Son' (1963)
56 'An Act of Atonement' (1963)
57 'Ghost Town' (1963)
58 'Gold Napoleons' (1963)
59 'Bradford's Dream' (1963)
60 'The Way of McEagle' (1963)
61 'Who Killed Harry Lime?' (1963)
62 'A Question in Ice' (1964)
63 'I.O.U.' (1964)
64 'A Crisis in Crocodiles' (1964)
65 'Judas Coat' (1964)
66 'A Little Knowledge' (1964)
67 'The Day of the Bullfighter' (1964)
68 'Mars in Conjunction' (1964)
69 'The Big Kill' (1964)
70 'Frame Up' (1964)
71 'Proxy Fight' (1965)
72 'Members Only: Part 2' (1965)
73 'Members Only: Part 1' (1965)

74 'The Trial of Harry Lime' (1965)
75 'The House of Bon Bons' (1965)
76 'Man at the Top' (1965)
77 'The Luck of Harry Lime' (1965)

The Living Room (UK, 1965)
Stamboul Train (UK, 1962)
The Power and the Glory (USA, 1961)
The Potting Shed (USA, 1961)
The Power and the Glory (USA, 1959)
Günes dogmasin (*A Gun for Sale*) (Turkey, 1961)
When Greek Meets Greek (Canada, 1960)
Our Man in Havana (UK, 1959)
The Fallen Idol (*The Basement Room*) (USA, 1959)
Verschlossene Räume (*The Living Room*) (Switzerland, 1958)
The Quiet American (USA, 1958)
Short Cut to Hell (*A Gun for Sale*) (USA, 1957)
Across the Bridge (UK, 1957)
Saint Joan (UK/USA, 1957)
Die Kraft und die Herrlichkeit (*The Power and the Glory*) (West Germany, 1957)
Loser Takes All (UK, 1956)
The End of the Affair (UK, 1955)
The Stranger's Hand (Italy/UK, 1954)
The Heart of the Matter (UK, 1953)
I Spy! (USA, 1951)
England Made Me (USA, 1951)
The Third Man (UK, 1949)
The Fallen Idol (*The Basement Room*) (UK, 1948)
Brighton Rock (UK, 1947)
The Fugitive (*The Power and the Glory*) (Mexico/USA, 1947)
The Man Within (UK, 1947)
Confidential Agent (USA, 1945)
Ministry of Fear (*The Ministry of Fear*) (USA, 1944)
Went the Day Well? (*The Lieutenant Died Last*) (UK, 1942)
This Gun for Hire (*A Gun for Sale*) (USA, 1942)
21 Days (based on *The First and The Last*, John Galsworthy) (UK, 1940)
The New Britain (UK, 1940)
The Green Cockatoo (UK, 1937)
The Future's in the Air (UK, 1937)
Orient Express (*Stamboul Train*) (USA, 1934)

OPERAS

Griffiths, W. E. (1998), *The Quiet American: An Opera in Two Acts*. Ann Arbor, MI: UMI Dissertation.

Heggie, J. et al. (2005), *The End of the Affair: An Opera in Two Acts*. San Francisco: Bent Pen Music.

Williamson, M. et al. (1964), *Our Man in Havana: An Opera in Three Acts*. London: J. Weinberger.

WEBSITES RELATING TO GRAHAM GREENE

The John J. Burns Library, Boston College
http://www.bc.edu/libraries/collections/burns.html

The Graham Greene Birthplace Trust
http://www.grahamgreenebt.org/

Graham Greene: Filmography
http://www.imdb.com/name/nm0001294/

Graham Greene: National Public Radio Centenary Profile
http://www.npr.org/templates/story/story.php?storyId=4057711

Graham Greene: Quotations (compiled by Rudolf van Dalm)
http://www.grahamgreenebt.org/Pages/quotations.php

Graham Greene: ScreenOnline
http://www.screenonline.org.uk/people/id/451551/

Graham Greene: Works and Criticism
http://worldcat.org/identities/lccn-n79-21903

Greeneland: Fan Site
http://greeneland.tripod.com/

The Joseph Mark Lauinger Memorial Library, Georgetown University
http://www.library.georgetown.edu/dept/speccoll/index.htm

The Harry Ransom Humanities Research Center, University of Texas at Austin
http://www.hrc.utexas.edu/

Contributors

Judith Adamson is the author of many books, including *Graham Greene and Cinema* (1984), *The Dangerous Edge* (1990), a political biography of Graham Greene, *Charlotte Haldane: Woman Writer in a Man's World* (1998), a biography of J. B. S. Haldane's first wife, and *Max Reinhardt: A Life in Publishing* (2009). She selected and introduced the essays in Graham Greene's much acclaimed last book *Reflections* (1990), and edited and introduced *Love Letters* (2001), the 30-year correspondence between Trekkie Ritchie Parsons and Leonard Woolf. She is Professor of English at Dawson College (Montreal, Canada).

Monica Ali is the author of *In the Kitchen* (2009), *Alentejo Blue* (2006), and *Brick Lane* (2003), which was shortlisted for the Man Booker Prize for Fiction, and adapted for film (directed by Sarah Gavron, UK, 2007). She wrote the introduction to the centenary edition of Greene's *The End of the Affair* (Vintage, 2004), and she lectures at Columbia University (New York, USA).

Michael Billington is the theatre critic for *The Guardian* daily newspaper (London, UK). He has published several biographical and critical studies of subjects relating to British theatre and the arts, including *State of the Nation: British Theatre since 1945* (2007), *Harold Pinter* (2007), *One Night Stands: A Critic's View of Modern British Theatre* (2001), *Stoppard the Playwright* (1987), and *Alan Ayckbourn* (1983). He is the authorised biographer of the playwright Harold Pinter, who won the Nobel Prize for Literature in 2005.

Mark Bosco, SJ, is associate professor of English and Theology at Loyola University (Chicago, USA). Widely published, he is the author of *Graham Greene's Catholic Imagination* (2005) and the introduction to Greene's *The Honorary Consul* (Penguin Classics, 2008). He is the joint editor of *Academic Novels as Satire: Critical Studies of an Emerging Genre* (2007).

Michael Brearley is a psychoanalyst, and a former president of the Institute of Psychoanalysis (London, UK). He once taught philosophy at the University of Newcastle-upon-Tyne (Newcastle, England, UK). He was a professional cricketer, captaining Middlesex and England, and was president of the Marylebone Cricket Club. He is the author of *The Art of Captaincy* (1985). Recently he was a guest on BBC Radio 4's literary program 'A Good Read,' when his chosen book was Graham Greene's *A Burnt-Out Case*.

David Crystal is Honorary Professor in the Department of Linguistics, University of Bangor (Bangor, Wales, UK). He is the author of over a hundred books, including *The Cambridge Encyclopedia of the English Language* (2nd edn, 2003), *The Stories of English* (2005), *How Language Works* (2007), *Evolving English* (2010), and *Internet Linguistics* (2011). He was awarded the Order of the British Empire (OBE) in 1995, and became a Fellow of the British Academy in 2000.

Robert Murray Davis is Emeritus Professor of English at the University of Oklahoma (Oklahoma, USA). His many publications include *Evelyn Waugh, Writer* (1981), *Playing Cowboys: Low Culture and High Art in the Western* (1992), *The Ornamental Hermit: People and Places of the New West* (2004), and *The Literature of Post-Communist Slovenia, Slovakia, Hungary and Romania* (2008).

François Gallix is Emeritus Professor of Contemporary Literature in English at the University of the Sorbonne (Paris, France). He is the author of books and articles on twentieth-century British authors, including Graham Greene, and he has edited and translated into French two volumes of Greene's short stories. He is the manager of conferences on *The Power and the Glory* at the Sorbonne, and he is the editor of Greene's early, unfinished and previously unpublished story *The Empty Chair*. Following his research at the University of Texas at Austin, Texas, USA, in 2010 he was awarded a research grant by the Harry Ransom Humanities Research Center at that university.

Dermot Gilvary was the director of the Graham Greene International Festival (Berkhamsted, England, UK), 2008–2010. He teaches English language and literature at Oakham School (Oakham, Rutland, England, UK). He is a playwright and the editor of Brigitte Timmermann's *The Third Man's Vienna* (2005).

Mike Hill was the director of the Graham Greene Festival (Berkhamsted, England, UK), 2005–2007. With Jon Wise, he is the co-author of a bibliographical and contextual reference book, *The Works of Graham Greene: A Reader's Bibliography and Guide*. He was deputy headteacher of the North Halifax Grammar School (Halifax, West Yorkshire, UK).

Peter Hollindale was a Reader in English and Educational Studies,

University of York (York, England, UK). He is the editor of many published volumes including Shakespeare's *As You Like It* (Macmillan,
1974) and *Henry IV, Part 1* (Macmillan, 1975), J. M. Barrie's *Peter
Pan and Other Plays* (Oxford, 1995) and *Peter Pan in Kensington
Gardens and Peter and Wendy* (Oxford, 1991) as well as studies such as
Shakespeare: A Midsummer Night's Dream (Penguin, 1992) and *Signs
of Childness in Children's Books* (Thimble Press, 1997).

Christopher Hull has taught in the Department of Spanish,
Portuguese and Latin American Studies at the University of Nottingham
(Nottingham, England, UK), since 2004. He obtained his doctorate
at Nottingham in 2009, investigating the history of Anglo-Cuban relations from 1898 to 1964. He is currently researching the four Graham
Greene books set in Cold War Latin America, and recently won a
research grant from the Harry Ransom Humanities Research Center
at the University of Texas at Austin (Texas, USA), to study its collection
of Greene's personal papers.

David Lodge is Honorary Professor of Modern English Literature
at the University of Birmingham (Birmingham, England, UK). His
extensive critical work includes *Graham Greene* (1966). His many fiction titles include *Small World* (1984) and *Nice Work* (1988), for each
of which he was shortlisted for the Booker Prize. He was awarded the
Hawthornden Prize and the Yorkshire Post Fiction Prize for *Changing
Places: A Tale of Two Campuses* (1975). He was made a Chevalier dans
l'Ordre des Arts et Lettres by the French Ministry of Culture in 1997,
and in 1998 he was appointed Commander of the Order of the British
Empire (CBE) for his services to literature.

Frances McCormack is Lecturer in English, National University
of Ireland, Galway (Galway, Republic of Ireland). She is the author
of *Chaucer and the Culture of Dissent* (2007), and she was the
lexicographical consultant for Terence Patrick Dolan's *Dictionary of
Hiberno-English* (2nd edn). Her research interests also include Old
and Middle English literature, political, religious, and devotional
literature of those eras, mystical writing, anticlericalism, penitential
writings, and heresy.

Rod Mengham is Fellow, Director of Studies in English, and
Curator of the Works of Art at Jesus College, University of Cambridge
(Cambridge, England, UK). He is the author of *The Descent of
Language* (1993) and studies on Emily Brontë, Dickens, Hardy, and
Henry Green. He is the editor of collections of essays on contemporary
fiction, violence and avant-garde art, and 1940s fiction, and he is the
author on art and editor of the *Equipage* series of poetry pamphlets.
His own poems have been published under the title *Unsung: New and*

Selected Poems (1996). He is co-editor and co-translator of the new anthology of contemporary Polish poetry, *Altered State* (2003).

Darren J. N. Middleton is Professor of Literature and Theology at Texas Christian University (Fort Worth, Texas, USA). He has published seven books including, most recently, *Theology after Reading: Christian Imagination and the Power of Fiction* (2008). Currently, he is researching the work of Shusaku Endo, whom Greene introduced to the West.

David R. A. Pearce is a founder of the Graham Greene Birthplace Trust (Berkhamsted, England, UK), and between 2000 and 2004 he was director of the Graham Greene Festival, at which he has spoken every year. For many years he was Head of English at Berkhamsted School (Berkhamsted, England, UK).

Neil Sinyard is Emeritus Professor of Film Studies, University of Hull (Hull, England, UK). He has published numerous monographs devoted to films, actors, and directors, including *Richard Lester* (2010), *Fred Zinnemann: Films of Character and Conscience* (2003), *Jack Clayton* (2000), *Clint Eastwood* (1995), *Silent Movies* (1995), *Children in the Movies* (1992), *Marilyn Monroe* (1989), *The Films of Mel Brooks* (1988), *Directors: The All Time Greats* (1986), *Filming Literature: The Art of Screen Adaptation* (1986), and *Journey Down Sunset Boulevard: Films of Billy Wilder* (1979). In addition, he is the author of *Graham Greene: A Literary Life* (2004).

Brigitte Timmermann is an historian and film historian. She is the author of *The Third Man's Vienna* (2005), and she has delivered various papers on Graham Greene and *The Third Man* at the Graham Greene International Festival. She was awarded a doctorate by the University of Vienna (Austria) for her research on British colonial history.

Cedric Watts is Research Professor of English at the University of Sussex (Brighton, England, UK). He is the author of various books on Shakespeare, Keats, Hardy, Conrad, Graham Greene, and others, and he is the editor of numerous works by Shakespeare, Hardy, Conrad, and Cunninghame Graham. Among his many publications are *A Preface to Greene* (1997), *Literature and Money* (1990), *A Preface to Keats* (1985), *Joseph Conrad: A Literary Life* (1989), *Hamlet* (1988), *The Deceptive Text: An Introduction to Covert Plots* (1984), and *A Preface to Conrad* (1982). He is the co-author of *'Henry V, War Criminal?' And Other Shakespeare Puzzles* (2000) and *Cunninghame Graham: A Critical Biography* (1979).

Index